Politics and Statesmanship

Politics and Statesmanship

Essays on
the American Whig Party

THOMAS BROWN

New York   Columbia University Press   *1985*

Library of Congress Cataloging in Publication Data

Brown, Thomas, 1954-
Politics and statesmanship.

Bibliography: p.
Includes index.
1. Whig Party (U.S.)–History.   I. Title.
JK2331.B76   1985   324.2732'3'09   84-15601
ISBN 0-231-05602-8 (alk. paper)

As a dissertation this book was awarded the Bancroft Dissertation Award
by a committee of the faculty of the Graduate School of Arts and Sciences
of Columbia University

Columbia University Press
New York   Guildford, Surrey
Copyright © 1985 Columbia University Press
All rights reserved

Printed in the United States of America

*Clothbound editions of Columbia University Press Books are
Smyth-sewn and printed on permanent and durable acid-free paper*

ACKNOWLEDGMENTS

VARIOUS VERSIONS OF THIS WORK have benefited from the perceptive criticisms of Professors Eric McKitrick and James Shenton of Columbia University. Portions of Chapter 6 originally appeared in "Southern Whigs and the Politics of Statesmanship, 1833–1841," *Journal of Southern History* (August 1980), 46:361–80, Copyright [1980] by the Southern Historical Association. Reprinted by permission of the Managing Editor. Portions of Chapter 7 originally appeared in "The Southern Whigs and Economic Development," *Southern Studies: An Interdisciplinary Journal of the South* (Spring 1981), 20:20–38, and are reprinted here by permission of the Southern Studies Institute. Quotations from the William Seward and Thurlow Weed Papers are by permission of the Manuscripts Librarian of the University of Rochester Library.

CONTENTS

Politics and Statesmanship

CHAPTER 1

Introduction

W HAT THE Whig party has lacked in interpreters, it has more than made up for in detractors. Henry Adams set the tone for modern evaluations of Whiggery when he wrote: "Of all the parties that have existed in the United States, the famous Whig party was the most feeble in ideas."[1] Similarly, Henry Wilson, the radical Republican senator from Massachusetts, declared in 1865 that "the old Whig Party . . . never professed to have an idea on earth, [it was] a party that simply advocated tariffs and banks and moneyed measures."[2] Neither of these men, it might be pointed out, was an unprejudiced commentator. Adams was a compulsive fault-finder, while Wilson was a former Whig, who denounced his old party with the relentless ferocity of the politically twice-born. Yet long before the Whigs could compile a record deserving of either praise or censure, one of their number complained: "Our Whig Party is made up of such a 'mixed multitude of discordant materials' that it is enough to sicken anyone of having aught to do with it."[3]

American political parties have rarely won praise for doctrinal purity or ideological consistency, but the Whig party seems especially vulnerable to such aspersions as those quoted. Its history appears to have been a dismal tale of evasions piled on equivocations. United by their hostility to the actions of Andrew Jackson rather than adherence to clearly defined principles, the Whigs were able to win presidential elections only in 1840 and 1848, when they did not encumber themselves with a party platform and ran military heroes of few known political convictions. On both occasions, the Whigs' General-President died in office, only to be succeeded by a man of far different views. The one time a Whig presidential candidate—Henry Clay—did frankly avow his political principles, he lost. Thus, the precipitate collapse of the Whig party in the 1850s seems more like the last scene of a farce than a tragedy—something to be applauded rather than deplored.

Perhaps because of their reputation for intellectual and political bankruptcy, the Whigs have received less attention from historians than their Democratic opponents. Nevertheless, there are several clearly distinguishable interpretations of Whiggery in studies of antebellum American politics. In one view, the Whigs were nothing more than quondam Federalists who tried to disguise their aristocratic pretensions with insincere professions of love for the people.[4] According to another line of thought, they were enlightened conservatives who sincerely believed that the public promotion of economic development would contribute to equality of opportunity and social progress.[5] In yet another conception, the Whigs were political elitists who were repelled by the Democrats' mastery of the organization and techniques of mass party politics.[6] A far different notion has been suggested by several students of popular voting behavior in the Jacksonian era. They assert that the Whigs—at least the northern Whigs—were militant evangelical Prot-estants who sought to promulgate their social ideals through political action.[7] In the most recent (and ambitious) study of the Whigs, they have been depicted as the bearers of a "political culture" which placed a premium on the bourgeois values of economic modernization and personal self-control.[8]

To various degrees, all these views have contributed something to our understanding of the Whigs, and short summaries cannot do them full justice. Yet they are all flawed by a tendency toward reductionism; they assume that the key to a comprehension of the Whigs is the discovery of some model constituency for the party, whose outlook it "expressed" or "reflected." None can account for the remarkable scope and diversity of the Whig party's popular appeal.[9] What is more, the analysis of a political party solely by reference to its popular base of support confuses correlations with causes. The members of certain groups may indeed have tended to vote Whig, but this does not mean that they supported the Whigs because of their membership in such groups. Instead, they may have seen the Whig party as a vehicle for the realization of ideas, beliefs, and values they held in common. Students of Jacksonian-era politics have noted that both the Democratic and the Whig party commanded the support of large and intensely loyal followings, whose partisanship manifestly had little to do with the expression of group interests. As Richard P. McCormick has written, "those who identified strongly with the party were influenced in their behavior by virtue of having assumed such an identity. They were no longer free to calculate objectively their own course of political action; as identifiers they reacted as partisans."[10]

In the case of the Whigs, a group interest explanation of party loyalty would seem particularly inappropriate. The Whigs were drawn together by an issue—opposition to Andrew Jackson's enlargement of presidential power—which was patently unrelated to matters of economic well-being or cultural identity. Rather, it would seem that the Whigs' appeal "reached beyond interest to the realm of public value."[11] The Whigs demonstrate Wilson Carey McWilliams' observation that the political party in the United States must make an attempt at inculcating

> a generalized loyalty, at creating a bond of identification between rulers and ruled, private man and public values. Its success depends on how well it forms a civic identity in its members, a coherent picture of the self in relation to the political community over and above the divisive effects of private roles and life. It lays claim, in other words, to the whole individual, and the partisan act requires a consolidation of reference groups, a decision as to which loyalties the individual values most.[12]

The civic ideals of the Whigs were derived from *republicanism*. This was the ideology nineteenth-century Americans inherited from their revolutionary forbears. The Whigs believed that the Jacksonian Democrats endangered the maintenance of the conditions for fulfilling republican ideals in the United States, while they claimed their own allegiance to those ideals. Superficially, republicanism required nothing more than devotion to the idea of elective government, deriving its authority from the consent of the governed. But in the peculiar formulation it was given by Americans, republicanism embraced a broad variety of cultural, political, and social concerns; indeed, it recognized no clear barriers between the private and public spheres of human experience.

The central problem in any polity, according to republicanism, was the maintenance of a balance between power and liberty. Power, as it was defined in republicanism, was the ability to control the persons and possessions of individuals; liberty, the inherent right men had to their lives and property. Power was insatiably aggressive, constantly threatening to encroach upon liberty. Yet republican thinkers conceded that it was a necessary attribute of authority, which had to restrain liberty so it did not degenerate into anarchy. In a monarchy, liberty was sacrificed to power; order was obtained through coercion, obedience, and fear. But in a republic, where authority sprang from the people, order had to come from below. It was vital, then, that good citizens be willing to subordinate their private interests to the welfare of the community—that they be capable of "public virtue" (or "patriotism"). If they lost the capacity for such self-restraint, they would confuse liberty with license, and a despot would eventually have to be called upon to impose authority.[13]

Republicanism was predicated upon the assumption that public virtue flowed from private virtues, so Americans were much concerned with the state of social morality. Republicanism, they believed, thrived in a society whose inhabitants were simple, industrious, frugal, and socially conscious. These virtues kept men vigilant in defense of their freedom. By contrast, public virtue declined wherever selfishness, idleness, luxury, and licentiousness became prevalent. These vices led men to lose all sense of connectedness with the interests of others, and to pursue their personal well-being without concern for the public good.[14] Also essential to the preservation of public virtue was the existence of an independent, self-sufficient citizenry. When men were reliant upon others for their livelihood, they lost the capacity for free political judgment, unconstrained by obligations to another. They therefore could not make a disinterested decision as to what was in the best interest of the entire community.[15]

Although no government by itself could guarantee the survival of republican society, the state was nevertheless an important institution in republicanism. Deriving its authority from the consent of the citizenry, its function was to secure the interest of the entire community—the *res publica* or common weal. Republican thinkers conceived of this public interest as something different from the mere sum total of the constituent interests of society. As Gordon Wood has written, it was thought of as an entity "unto itself, prior to, and distinct from, the various concerns of groups."[16] However, republicans saw no inherent conflict between the good of the community and the good of the individual. Since they conceived of the people as a single body, linked organically in a harmony of interests, they believed that what was good for the collectivity was good for its parts.[17]

The republican notion of the public interest shaped a distinctive notion of politics: ideally, it was an activity in which different interests were not simply reconciled but transcended in pursuit of the single, common good. For this reason, it was considered vitally important that republican rulers be especially virtuous and high-minded. There was always the danger, however, that elected officials might become corrupt—that they might use their authority for selfish, private ends rather than for the public good. Equally dangerous was the possibility that the state might fall captive to special interest groups—"factions"— which conspired to fulfill their own objectives at the expense of the common weal. If either of these developments occured, or the people lost their "virtue," the state would enter a cycle of degeneracy, from which it could only be rescued by a moral purgation or reform—a "return to first principles."[18]

Republicanism also connoted a devotion to *equality*. This was the most ambiguous of republican ideals. On the one hand, Americans feared that the accumulation of great wealth was a temptation to corruption and luxury, so they saw great benefits in a general equality of condition. On the other, they were attracted to an ideal of equal opportunity, with its stress on social distinctions. Restraints on the acquisition of fortunes might, after all, require limitations on individual liberty, a cherished republican value. Thus, most republicans did not propose to eliminate social and political preeminence, only change its origins. They believed that merit, talent, and virtue, rather than privilege, should be the sources of individual distinction; accordingly, they placed great importance on the elimination of monopolies and of legally sanctioned favoritism, save in forms that served the public good. American republicans also believed that equal opportunity would provide a foundation for the social harmony essential to the survival of republics. If each man's status was dependent on his own efforts and abilities, there would be no legitimate reason for contention.[19]

In the Revolutionary era, Americans began to see their country as a special preserve of republicanism. With its large population of independent, liberty-loving freeholders, the United States seemed especially immune to the corruptions of the decadent Old World.[20] This idealized self-image continued to dominate the American political consciousness in the Jacksonian era, but economic change was rendering it increasingly anachronistic. The factory system was creating a working class without landed property—the optimum basis of civic attachment and personal independence. Modern systems of banking and credit were forging new bonds of dependency between men. Most important, interregional methods of transportation—canals, railroads, and steamboats—were creating a national marketplace economy. The results of this last development were many and various. Much of the country was affected by periodic booms and busts, with even modest citizens being caught up in periodic speculative fevers. Subsistence farmers converted to growing cash crops for the market. Once-isolated communities found themselves affected by remote and impersonal forces beyond their control. Marginal farmers in the East were undercut financially by competition from cheap western produce, and many began to leave the countryside for the city. To Americans, accustomed to thinking in traditional republican categories, these changes were full of portent. Even the prosperity generated by economic and technological change gave them cause for worry, as it might make their fellow citizens materialistic and selfish, thereby subverting public virtue.[21]

There were also changes in the political system that might threaten the ideals of republicanism. Although by the Jacksonian period Americans had considerable experience of party strife, they had, with few exceptions, considered it at best a necessary evil. Parties stirred up conflict within the republic and might easily degenerate into factions which selfishly aimed at their own aggrandizement. Understandably, the collapse of the Federalist party after the War of 1812 had been welcomed by many Americans, who hoped that a new era of harmony, unity, and consensus was in the offing. President Monroe quite deliberately presented himself as a symbol of a unified people, whose ideals were presumably embodied in a virtually all-embracing Republican party. But republican unity was shattered in the four-cornered presidential election of 1824, and partisan acrimony reached unprecedented heights in the election four years later. Slowly but inexorably, the nation began to develop a new party system.[22]

The parties that emerged in the Jacksonian era were more broadly based than those of the first party system. This was in part because of changes in political institutions that undermined the power of established elites. The choosing of presidential electors by popular vote, which only two states permitted in 1800, spread to all but six states by 1824, and all but one (South Carolina) by 1836. This change deprived state legislative caucuses of the ability to choose the electors, and necessitated the creation of state party organizations which appealed directly to the electorate. Similarly, the abandonment after 1824 of the congressional caucus as a device for nominating presidential candidates led to the creation of national party conventions. By 1824, virtually universal white male suffrage had been established in all the states save three, increasing the potential voting public that could be mobilized. There was also a tendency in the states during the 1820s to make more offices elective, creating new incentives for politicians to appeal for popular support. All these changes in the structure of politics placed a premium on the talents of emerging professionals who were willing to devote considerable time and energy to managing party affairs, and who could approach the common man on his own terms. Conversely, they created a very uncongenial climate for political notables who lacked the common touch and expected leadership to fall to them as a prerogative of birth, wealth, or social connections.[23]

Despite their role in broadening popular participation in politics, the new parties aroused misgivings in many Americans. For one thing, they were ongoing organizations with special interests of their own. Men worked for the parties not out of selfless devotion but for the spoils of office. In addition, party leaders imposed strict discipline upon their underlings when partisan interests were at stake; those who refused to toe the party line were cast into the political wilderness. Could the men who were attracted into such institutions be independent and principled public servants? Would they not more likely be irresponsible spoilsmen and demagogues who were willing to go to any length to ensure the party (and themselves) success? Without stature or intrinsic importance, and thus unable to win votes on their own merits, they would persuade the people to vote blindly for the party. They would thereby subvert public virtue, for fealty to party deprived the citizen of the ability to make a calm and disinterested judgment of what (and whom) would serve the public good.[24]

In short, material change and party organization in the Jacksonian era introduced Americans to new and disturbing forms of institutions and social relations. Both the modern economy and the mass political party placed a premium on self-interested behavior incompatible with republicanism's prescriptions for desirable personal morality.[25] At the same time, most Americans welcomed the transformations of their age, considering them signs of "progress." Few proposed a literal return to agrarian simplicity and spartan frugality. Neither did many propose to abandon or destroy the parties; all things considered, they were too useful. Jacksonian Americans were hence pulled between received ideals and immediate practicalities. And characteristically, men proclaimed their adherence to cherished verities the more their behavior deviated from them.

How did the parties respond to the perplexities of their times? Marvin Meyers has suggested that the Whigs spoke to Americans' hopes, the Democrats, to their fears. The Jacksonians, according to Meyers, looked backward, longing (though not realistically hoping) to restore a golden age of agrarian republicanism, while the Whigs "affirmed the material promise of American life as it was going," and "promised to make it go faster."[26] Meyers' argument is persuasive, but the distinction he draws between the two parties is largely limited to the field of economic policy. The roles Meyers assigns the Democrats and Whigs seem to have been reversed when it came to attitudes toward party organization. It was the Democrats who first perfected the arts of party discipline, and who developed the most cogent arguments for the benefits of partisanship and the two-party system. They were quite optimistic that the collective organization of politics would not subvert public virtue.[27] The Whigs, by contrast, were slow to organize, and never wholeheartedly embraced the idea of party government. They condemned the Democrats for spreading the blight of "party spirit" and for instituting a system of partisan regimentation which reduced public officials to the "slaves" of a political "machine."[28]

To the Whigs, the worst features of Jacksonian party politics were personified in the figure of the politician. Often an obscure nobody, he attained power and prominence through party discipline and organization. Only a strictly regimented and unquestioning partisan following would vote for such a man. Pliant, manipulative, and devious, he had no concern for the public good. The party was everything to him, for it was only through it that he had his being. Hence, he was willing to do or advocate anything, no matter how irresponsible, if it promoted the welfare of the party.[29]

The best elements of the Whigs' self-conception were personified in the statesman. The statesman was an enlightened public servant whose only concern was the public good. He possessed exceptional knowledge and breadth of vision, which were the products of deep learning and broad experience. Since he was entrusted with the welfare of all, he had to "know *what are* the rules of right reason and how to *apply* them rightly; to know the various constituents of general and individual happiness, and how both may be combined in the highest possible proportions." And since power was always a temptation to its abuse, the statesman possessed a special strength of character—"without this, without principle, without morality, the man of large information is apt to be an arsenal for faction, and genius itself but a splendid mischief."[30]

Whigs often feared that the statesman's devotion to principle placed him at a disadvantage in competition with the politician. The statesman, unlike the politician, would not pander to the whims and fancies of the electorate. No demagogue, he risked unpopularity because of his devotion to the common, long-range interests of the entire polity:

> He must legislate for the future, when it is, as yet, but dimly seen; and he must put aside much, which might now win popular favor, in order to found systems of solid utility, whose results will require ages to develop; but still, whose results are indispensable for the safety, the glory, and the happiness of the country.[31]

The statesman's principles also prevented him from employing the electioneering tricks of the politician. He was "willing to win favor only by fair means; by high character, inflexible virtue, and a liberal and enlightened policy." This was because he was "conscious of his own humiliation and dishonor, when he rises by subterfuges and intrigues." However, the demagogue, who had no such reservations, would "unscrupulously employ all means, which subserve his main purpose."[32] But the most serious political problem for the statesman was his independence of judgment. Because of this trait, he would not submit to "the overwhelming spirit of party, which substitutes devotion to the party for the good of the country; and neither acknowledges, nor respects, any candidates, but those, who are found close wedged in its own ranks."[33]

For some Whigs, particularly those of the patrician class, the statesman was a nostalgic ideal through which they could express anger and dismay at the advance of majoritarian democracy. The politician, to these men, was the end product of a political system in which the *demos* ran wild. The people, trusting solely to their own judgment, no longer deferred to the "natural leaders of society," but instead preferred men who would grovel before them. As the self-appointed historian of the Whig party complained: "Let no man who desires to rise to high office in a popular government ever dare to express sentiments distasteful to popular prejudice." "The theory of Democratic governments," he lamented, "is that the people are always right, and that the statesman who shall advocate measures not in accordance with the popular opinion, must not be trusted or honored."[34]

Yet it would be a mistake to think that the appeal of the statesman ideal was confined to a small elite. To Americans of the Jacksonian era—and ever since—the politician was at best an ambivalent symbol. Although perhaps necessary in a mass democracy, in which millions had to be mobilized at election time, he aroused deep misgivings because of his very responsiveness to the popular will. His apparent willingness to please often seemed a contemptuous disregard for principle, or a cynical pose through which he manipulated others for his own ends. The statesman, by contrast, personified some of the highest ideals in the republican canon: independence, selflessness, and virtue. Moreover, the distinctive style of leadership the Whigs ascribed to the statesman placed a high valuation upon the public intelligence. In the terminology of nineteenth-century faculty psychology, the Whig statesman appealed to men's "rational" attributes of prudence and conscience: he believed men were capable of reason, moderation, and self-control. In contrast, the politician appealed to the lower, "animal" faculties: he pandered to men's appetites and instincts. The Whigs argued that by supporting statesmen and rejecting politicians, Americans could affirm the dominion in themselves of reason over passion. The good Whig, it followed, was not a slavish partisan, held captive by his emotions, but a free republican citizen, rationally and selflessly devoted to the pursuit of principle. The Whigs' national periodical made this point by implication in an article contrasting different styles of oratory:

> Put the case that the same multitude were addressed by two orators, and on the same question and occasion; that the first of these orators considered in his mind that the people he addressed were to be controlled by several passions . . . —this orator may be fairly said to have no faith in the people; he rather believes that they are creatures of passion, and subject to none but base and selfish impulses. But now a second orator arises, a Chatham, a Webster, a Pericles, a Clay; his generous spirit

expands itself through the vast auditory, and he believes that he is addressing a company of high-spirited men, citizens. . . . When he says "fellow citizens," they believe him, and at once, from a tumultuous herd, they are converted into men . . . their thoughts and feelings rise to an heroical height, beyond that of common men or common times. The second orator "had faith in the people"; he addressed the better part of each man's nature, supposing it to be in him—and it *was* in him.[35]

The Whigs articulated their distinctive notion of statesmanship in their defense of the independence of Congress—especially the Senate—from presidential and party "influence." To the Whigs, the extension of executive authority under Andrew Jackson not only endangered the constitutional balance of powers but frustrated true statesmanship. The Senate, as one anti-Jackson newspaper observed, was supposed to be "a School for Statesmen." According to the Whigs, it was not merely to express the will of the people, it was to *refine* it. Slow and deliberative in its proceedings, the Senate was assigned by the Whigs the function of checking the rashness of public opinion, to which the popularly elected House was more directly responsive. And since their votes affected the welfare of the entire country, not just that of their constituents, senators had to behave as trustees of the national interest. Whigs therefore believed that senators should not be subjected to partisan pressures (such as instruction by state legislatures) which interfered with their freedom of action.[36]

Independence was an essential attribute in the senatorial statesman for another reason: it was necessary if he was to have the freedom to compromise. When the Whigs spoke of compromise, however, they often made an important distinction. To them, true compromise was a process of mutual adjustment and concession by which statesmen arrived at policies in the national interest—the politics of consensus-building. But Whigs acknowledged the existence of another type of compromise, practiced by the unprincipled and narrow-minded politician: expedient, piecemeal "log-rolling," in which selfish special interests were served without concern for the common good. Statesmanlike compromises evinced men's capacity for self-subordination in pursuit of the general welfare; log-rolling resulted from appeals to the appetites, mocking the republican faith in a community of interests.[37]

The style of the statesman made manifest the core values of Whiggery: moderation, self-restraint, rational persuasion, and a positive passion for the public good. These values served as a needed buffer for the tangible items in the Whig appeal; because of them, banks and publicly financed internal improvements were made palatable to men nurtured on the ideals of republicanism. By supporting Whig statesmen, Americans who hoped to benefit from government policies to promote economic progress could see themselves as virtuous citizens, linked together in republican community.

The history—and the failures—of the Whigs may be traced, in part, through their efforts to remain true to their ideal of statesmanship while functioning within a two-party system of politics. This is what the following chapters attempt to do. The thematic essays deal with certain aspects of the Whigs' appeal to their popular constituency; the biographical ones, with how some Whigs tried to realize their own personal visions of statesmanship. There is no pretense that this book exhausts all the varieties of Whig politics and belief. It may do no more than suggest the intellectual boundaries and limitations of the Whigs themselves. But I hope it will contribute to a fuller understanding of what kind of repository the Whig party served for Americans' fears and hopes.

CHAPTER 2

The Whig Party in the North:
The Rhetoric of Party Formation

T HE GREAT PROFUSION of studies on northern politics in the Jacksonian Era has created confusion rather than dispelled it. The more we seem to know about the Democratic and Whig parties in the free states, the more difficult it becomes to understand how, if at all, they linked the concerns of politicians with those of voters. Several historians have gone so far as to suggest that the main interests of the leaders of both organizations in the North had little to do with the concerns of their constituents. The former were preoccupied with economic policy, while the latter were mostly interested in ethnic and cultural issues.[1] Yet we know that both parties had the support of massive and intensely loyal followings in the North, as in the rest of the country.[2] It is therefore difficult to accept that they were as irrelevant to the concerns of the northern voting public as some of the literature might lead one to believe.

There was, of course, an obvious link between Jacksonian party leaders and followers—political rhetoric. But historians have recently shied away from the analysis of rhetoric, in part because of glaring errors by scholars who accepted partisan propaganda at face value. Some proponents of an ethnocultural interpretation of Jacksonian voting behavior have declared that the pronouncements of the Democrats and Whigs are not worthy of close consideration because they did not express the "real" views of the northern public.[3] Neither the naïveté of the past nor the cynicism of the present is acceptable, however. Partisan rhetoric may not perfectly reflect the opinions of voters, but it does provide clues as to what politicians believed would be comprehensible and appealing to their constituents. What we do need is a clearer conception of how rhetoric serves as a bridge between party leaders and followers.

Put most simply, the primary function of partisan rhetoric is to encourage support for a party and its candidates. With rhetoric, politicians try to revive the loyalties of the party faithful and sway new voters and members of the opposition over to their side. Partisan propaganda, especially when it is employed skillfully, is so useful a tool for party spokesmen because it gives voters a distinctive political *perspective*—an interpretive framework with which they can impart meaning to their choice of parties. Although not as intellectually complex or well-articulated as an ideology, a political perspective serves much the same purpose: it provides people with a shared outlook on the world, and thereby gives them a basis for common action.[4]

The reconstruction of a political perspective requires an unconventional approach to the analysis of partisan rhetoric. Traditionally, historians have simply described the positions enunciated by politicians, and assumed that voters based their choice of candidates upon them. But it is unlikely that, even in the highly politicized world of mid-nineteenth-century America, voters made a totally conscious, politically sophisticated judgment on each issue and candidate presented to them. The high levels of party loyalty would indicate that they used the party perspectives as the main determinants of how they voted. Hence, the specific *positions* taken in Whig rhetoric will not be the main subject of analysis here. Instead, I will concern myself primarily with the generalized assumptions, attitudes, symbols, and values employed by the Whigs in their presentation of specific issues and candidates. These things, taken together, comprised the distinctive perspective of the party, and thus provide the best evidence of what it meant to be a Whig.

This chapter will attempt to extract the distinctive perspective of the northern Whigs from their political rhetoric. Later chapters will explore the rhetoric of the southern Whigs. Because the perspective of the Whigs emerged over time, and incorporated elements from a variety of sources, the discussion of it here is placed within a narrative framework. Further, the Whigs developed and refined their rhetoric in an ongoing dialogue with their opponents, so no study of them would be complete without some consideration of the protean appeals of the Jacksonian Democrats.

[I]

It is impossible to trace the origins of the Whig party to a single time, person, or event. Perhaps the best place to start is with the presidency of John Quincy Adams, for in his administration one can detect the first glimmerings of what would become the outlook of the Whig party. Adams became President after the election of 1824, in which four candidates—Adams, Henry Clay, William H. Crawford, and Andrew Jackson—vied for the top spot. Party identities and issues were not at stake, as all the contestants were avowed Jeffersonian Republicans. In an apathetic contest—in some states, voter turnout was higher in local elections than in the national—Jackson received a plurality of the popular and electoral vote. Since no candidate had a majority in the electoral college, the outcome was decided in the House of Representatives, where, with Clay's backing, Adams was chosen.[5]

Because party loyalties and clearly defined issues were not involved in the 1824 election, Americans may have paid special attention to Adams' early pronouncements for clues to the tenor of his administration. In his inaugural address, Adams expressed a determination to create a nonpartisan regime, transcending old divisions. He declared that "the baneful weed of party strife" had been "uprooted," so it only remained for those who had "heretofore followed the standard of political party" to make "one effort of magnanimity, one sacrifice of prejudice and passion," that of "discarding every remnant of rancor against each other."[6] Adams' desire for an above-party administration was also evident in his appointments policies. At first he hoped to include in the cabinet his three rivals in the presidential election, but all except Clay spurned his overtures. Still, Adams persisted in the "amalgamation" policy. He appointed prominent Federalists to high posts, and he declined to make removals for partisan reasons. Adams even refused to fire officials, such as Postmaster General John McLean, whom he knew opposed his reelection and had appointed anti-administration subordinates.[7]

Adams also embraced policies of economic and social consolidation. In his first annual address to Congress, he declared that the federal government should exert an enlightened guidance over the nation's material progress. "The tenure of power by man," Adams avowed, "is in the moral purpose of his Creator, upon condition that it shall be exercised to ends of beneficence, to improve the condition of himself and his fellow-men." Casting aside the constitutional scruples of Madison and Monroe against federally financed internal improvements, he called for an ambitious national program to support the construction of canals and roads. Going beyond even the most ambitious schemes of such fellow nationalists as Clay, Adams also urged the Congress to establish a national university, a uniform system of weights and measures, an astronomical observatory, a Department of the Interior, and a reformed code of patent laws.[8]

Adams was publicly noncommital on the tariff and on land policy. But the views of the administration were revealed by Secretary of the Treasury Richard Rush. He, too, endorsed measures which would give the central government the power to exert some control over the nation's development. In a public report, Rush endorsed protection because it would foster industrialization by providing a home market for domestic manufactures. In another report, he deplored the flight of pioneers to the west for driving up workers' wages by draining eastern labor markets. This implied that steps should be taken to increase the price of the public lands, or to decrease the amount of western land being made available for settlement.[9]

The Adams administration's economic programs presumed a measure of elitism. In calling for central discipline over the nation's development, Adams exhorted the members of Congress to take a broad, long-range view of the general welfare, and not yield to the ostensibly narrow-minded concerns of the people. As he put it, statesmen should not be "palsied" by the will of their constituents, lest they doom the country to "perpetual inferiority." Adams' belief in the benefits of high-minded stewardship reflected his passionate faith in a homogeneous national interest which incorporated, while it transcended, all the country's diverse pursuits. "The great interests of an agricultural, commercial, and manufacturing nation," Adams asserted, "are so linked together that no permanent cause of prosperity to one of them can operate without extending its influence to the others."[10]

Adams' program was designed to reconcile the pursuit of economic modernization with the maintenance of republican values by keeping the United States at a "middle stage" of social development. On the one hand, its proposals to stimulate economic diversification and national self-sufficiency implicitly repudiated the traditional republican goal of agrarian simplicity. On the other hand, it aimed to avert the evils of class conflict and moral decadence Americans associated with material "progress" through enlightened political leadership and communal self-discipline. But a large number of Americans were dubious about Adams' claims to speak in behalf of the "national interest"; indeed, some doubted that there was such a thing. Adams' proposals consequently had the main effect of arousing a broadly based opposition that helped make his administration one of the most ineffectual in American history. Professional politicians, led by Martin Van Buren of New York, were alienated by the "amalgamation" policy because they wanted to use patronage to revive the Jeffersonian Republican party. States' rights men, especially in the South, were repelled by Adams' proposals to concentrate increased power in the federal government. And Americans of an egalitarian temper chafed at Adams' suggestion that a select elite, rather than the people themselves, knew best what course the country should take.[11]

For many of those made unhappy by the Adams administration, Andrew Jackson served as a rallying symbol. Jackson himself felt that he had been deprived of the presidency by a "corrupt bargain" between Adams and Clay, and he was determined to vindicate his personal honor and dignity. He thus became a hero for men who believed that the Adams administration's plans were nothing more than scheming to benefit privileged "aristocrats." Jackson's personal background also qualified him well for the role of an "anti-establishment" candidate. Of humble birth, he was a genuine self-made man, who lacked the polish of more seasoned politicians. He had made his public reputation as a military man, while his service in civil positions had been short and undistinguished. As a consequence, men who felt estranged from the traditional patterns of political and social privilege could identify easily with Jackson.[12]

Jackson's managers were content to rest their case in 1828 upon his personal appeal. On the major issues of the day, such as the tariff and internal improvements, they made vague and sometimes contradictory pronouncements.[13] Deprived of clearly defined issues, "the friends of Adams"—they were too poorly organized to constitute a true party—devoted much of their rhetoric to the personalities of the two candidates. This does not mean, however, that their campaign statements were devoid of meaning. In their portrayals of the two candidates, the President's supporters tried to project images of the contrasting ideals and values represented by Adams and Jackson. These images, in turn, provide some sense of how they envisaged themselves, the opposition, and the distinctive constituency to which they were trying to appeal.

Adams' supporters depicted the 1828 race, on the broadest level, as a contest between primitive passion and unrestrained appetite on the one hand, and "civilized" culture and discipline on the other. At their lowest and most scurrilous, they portrayed Jackson as an adulterer and mass murderer.[14] On a somewhat higher plane, they suggested that Jackson's life and military career had evinced a lack of regard for the law, civility, and morality. A group of Adams' "friends" in New York developed this argument at great length. They charged that Jackson had been implicated in Burr's treasonous conspiracy, engaged in "sanguinary duels," and shown "a laxity of moral principle" by acts of gratuitous cruelty on the battlefield. In like fashion, Jackson was said to be guilty of numerous abuses when he occupied positions of authority. He had suspended habeas corpus in New Orleans, and retained the suspension long after the defeat of the British. Worse, he had ordered the arrest of a member of the Louisiana legislature who had protested his conduct, and had imprisoned a judge and federal district attorney who had invoked habeas corpus in a case. Similarly, while leading federal troops in Georgia, Jackson had claimed the right to control the militia and ordered his men not to obey orders from the Secretary of War unless he issued them first. The New York Adamsites claimed that Jackson had also demonstrated a "tyrannical" disposition as military governor of Florida. In that capacity, he had imposed laws so objectionable that Congress had nullified them and returned all the penalties levied under their authority. The New Yorkers professed to see in this record of iniquities evidence that Jackson might well become another Caesar, who would bring down the fabric of republican government.[15]

Adams, of course, was portrayed by his "friends" as the very opposite of Jackson. He was a sober, cultured, and capable statesman, long seasoned by experience in diplomacy and government. Washington, Jefferson, Madison, and Monroe had all manifested their high opinion of Adams by appointing him to high positions. Further, Adams possessed great intellectual and reasoning powers, as made evident by his attainments as a scholar. Above all, he possessed an "unblemished private character," which he brought to his conduct of public affairs. To preserve the spotless reputation of their favorite, Adams' advocates rejected indignantly the Jacksonians' "corrupt bargain" charges. Clay had thrown his support to Adams in order to assure the election of the most capable candidate, and had been appointed Secretary of State in recognition of his own extraordinary abilities.[16]

The appeals of Adams' supporters had two basic presuppositions. They assumed that the presidency (and perhaps all high civil positions) should be reserved for statesmen of unique and proven talents, and that the standards of public morality should be those of private morality. These two notions, with their obvious roots in Puritan ideals of public stewardship, were reflected in the Adamsites' image of their constituency. The model Adams voter was, by their lights, a man of judgment, prudence, and restraint who respected established leaders and institutions. As a meeting of Adams' "friends" in Massachusetts put it: "we find that the sober, thinking, and especially the aged people, with the young men, who aim to advance themselves by diligence, industry, devotion to business in their calling, and attachment to principle, are almost unanimous for the administration." On the other side, the Adams men found arrayed those marginal men who, lacking firm moral and social roots, were attracted to the wild and ill-equipped Jackson— "the political managers, the unsuccessful politicians of all parties, the unreflecting, the adventurers."[17]

Adams' "friends" were adherents of a declining order of politics. Though they did not share the Federalists' notion of a clearly demarcated class hierarchy, they did cling to the Jeffersonian conception of a "natural aristocracy" of intellect and virtue. This was reflected in their tactics as well as their rhetoric. Rather than organize to reach voters directly, they mostly relied on local elites and committees of the President's "friends" to mobilize support. This put them at a considerable disadvantage against the Jacksonians, who had the more popular candidate and the more professional organization.[18] In the election, Adams made his strongest showing in politically conservative areas. The states he carried were former centers of Federalism and strongholds of moderate Republicanism: Delaware, Maryland, New Jersey, and all of New England. Adams also received 16 of the 36 electoral votes of New York, which chose its electors by congressional district. Jackson won everything else.

The election of 1828 demonstrated the liabilities of an overtly elitist appeal in American politics. The public was increasingly distrustful of political "establishments," as proved by the victory of Jackson, the political outsider par excellence. No longer would the republican certifications of long public service, scholarly attainments, and gentlemanly character be prime qualifications for high office. The opponents of Jackson were thus presented with the challenge of democratizing their appeal and returning the aspersion of "aristocracy" to "Old Hickory" and his party. But as the anti-Jacksonians moved to broaden their base, they would not discard all the themes of the Adams campaign. Indeed, the image of Jackson as a potential "tyrant" would prove serviceable to them. So, too, would the conception that Jackson represented the lawless elements of American society. Before these ideas could be employed effectively in political combat, however, they would have to be refashioned to suit the sensibilities of the mass electorate. How men dealt with this task constitutes, in good part, the story of how the Whig party and its distinctive political perspective came into being.

[II]

The "friends of Adams" was little more than an ad hoc collection of local notables, bound together loosely by friendships and personal correspondence. Never possessing much of a corporate identity, it dissolved after the debacle of 1828. Its successor as the main anti-Jacksonian organization was the National Republican party. With Henry Clay as their titular leader, the National Republicans shared much the same conservative, nationalistic outlook as the Adamsites. Their platform was Clay's "American System" of nationally financed internal improvements and a protective tariff. Such measures, they believed, would promote economic development by encouraging the exchange of goods between regions and the growth of manufactures. Further, by binding together the diverse interests of the country, they would hopefully promote national unity and harmony. Seeing the Union as a corporate, organic whole, the National Republicans idealized statesmen, such as Clay and Webster, who had a comprehensive perspective on the national interest. Conversely, they disdained party politicians for stirring up partisan conflict and pandering to the petty, immediate concerns of voters.[19]

The National Republicans, however, were not the sole non-Jacksonian party of the North. They shared that distinction with the Antimasonic party, whose formation was prompted by the disappearance and apparent murder in 1826 of William Morgan in western New York state. Morgan had threatened to publish a book revealing the Freemasons' secret oaths, rituals, and ceremonies, so it was widely believed that his misfortunes were due to Masonic skullduggery. When the authorities in New York seemed unresponsive to calls to investigate the Morgan case, a storm of controversy arose. Outraged citizens, despairing of obtaining satisfaction by ordinary means, organized to elect men who would press for effective action against the "monster order." The Antimasonic movement spread quickly beyond the borders of New York, prompting the formation of parties in all the northern states.[20]

Both as a party and a movement, Antimasonry was far more attuned to egalitarian sentiment than National Republicanism. It was no accident that astute anti-Jacksonian politicians, such as Thurlow Weed and William Seward of New York and Thaddeus Stevens of Pennsylvania, were early converts to the Antimasonic cause. Antimasonry arose from the widespread belief that the Freemasons, a self-constituted elite, had violated equality under the law by plotting to prevent the prosecution of Morgan's murderers and investigations of their secret activities. It also crystallized popular fears that the Freemasons conspired secretly to acquire a monopoly of public offices and to favor each other in business dealings.[21]

Antimasonry, then, was similar to the Jacksonian movement in its hostility to political elites and exclusive privilege. Indeed, where the Antimasons encountered political establishments dominated by National Republicans, as in Massachusetts and Rhode Island, many of them eventually became Democrats.[22] But most Antimasons seem to have felt little affinity for Jacksonian Democracy. For one thing, Jackson himself was a leading Freemason. More important, the Antimasons were hostile to strong organizational discipline like that exerted by the party "machines" being formed by Jackson's supporters in the northern states. Many of them were Arminian evangelical Protestants who believed that men should liberate themselves from social ties, such as exclusive party loyalty, that bound their consciences and inhibited their moral autonomy.[23] But no matter what their specific religious beliefs, Antimasons shared a revulsion against the centralized control they believed the Order exerted over its members. As they saw it, Freemasons renounced their moral independence when they joined the Order, even to the extent of agreeing to commit murder and conceal abominable crimes by fellow Masons.[24]

The Antimasons also objected to the Freemasons' violations of legal equality, as in their alleged protection of Morgan's murderers. Precisely because they valued the autonomy of the individual so highly, Antimasons ascribed special importance to the law as a device for regulating the interactions among men. Unlike the arbitrary mandates of the Freemasons, the law was public, uniform, and reasonably predictable. Thus, it protected the rights of the individual against encroachment so long as it was enforced impartially—something impossible when Freemasons dominated the political and judicial systems.[25] The Antimasons ascribed similar virtues to the Christian religion. Christianity taught its doctrines openly, and men were free to accept or reject them as their consciences dictated. Moreover, the ideals of Christ were universal in application. Christianity taught that men should extend their charity and love to everyone, while the Freemasons confined their "benevolence" to fellow-members of the Order.[26]

The Antimasons and National Republicans had great difficulty coalescing into an effective opposition to Jackson. Some National Republicans, with a certain aristocratic hauteur, expressed contempt for the "hack politicians" in the Antimasonic movement. Furthermore, some National Republicans, including Henry Clay, were Freemasons. The Antimasons, for their part, often found the National Republicans too "aristocratic" and as poisoned by Freemasonry as the Jacksonian Democrats.[27] There were, at the same time, some latent affinities between the two groups. Both shared a special concern for the maintenance of respect for the law—the National Republicans, because the law provided some semblance of order in a society where other cohesive forces (such as custom and tradition) were weak, the Antimasons, because it protected the rights of the individual. Both shared a distaste for centralized party discipline and organization. The Antimasons disliked these things for their limitations on individual conscience, while the National Republicans believed that they elevated to positions of power politicians of little ability and low social standing.

Nevertheless, the Antimasons and National Republicans found themselves working at cross-purposes as the election of 1832 approached. Leaders in both parties feared that Jackson could not be defeated unless they united behind a single candidate, but all attempts to arrange a nationwide coalition failed. The National Republicans nominated Henry Clay, while the Antimasons chose former Attorney General William Wirt. Neither man would withdraw in favor of the other, and there were zealots in both their camps—Freemasons who favored Clay and Antimasons who would not vote for a member of the "monster order"—who adamantly opposed any coalition. There were, however, fusion arrangements in New York, Ohio, and Pennsylvania. Moreover, even where the Antimasons and National Republicans failed to cooperate, they used similar arguments to justify themselves and arraign the Jackson administration. In 1832, therefore, we begin to find some of the rhetorical devices that would be used to justify the unification of anti-Jacksonian forces in the Whig party.[28]

The Antimasons and National Republicans took direct aim at the appointment policy of the Jackson administration. Upon assuming the presidency, Jackson had removed a large number of federal officials and replaced them with party loyalists. The proportion of presidential appointees he replaced during his terms in office was actually rather modest, somewhere between 10 and 20 percent of the total. But the number he removed was much larger than that by any previous President. Further, Jackson's partisan use of the patronage was a dramatic departure from the practice of the three Chief Executives who immediately preceded him.[29] Jackson justified his patronage policy as "rotation in office," which made government positions accessible to men of humble origins and prevented the growth of an aristocracy-in-office. The Antimasons and National Republicans professed to see it differently. Hoping to cast the aspersion of "aristocracy" upon Jackson and his party, they charged that rotation did not undermine privilege but instead created a new form of exclusiveness. It confined official appointments to men who were loyal to Jackson. For this reason, it resulted in the appointment of incompetents and sycophants who were willing to do Jackson's bidding. The administration compounded the evils of its patronage policies by bestowing printing contracts upon favorable newspapers and appointing their editors to government posts. These practices rendered the press subservient to President and party and resulted in the spread of partisan falsehoods throughout the country.[30]

Above all, the opposition parties condemned Jackson for placing himself above the law. With this charge, they tried to exploit the traditional republican fear of the tyrant who, driven by ambition and glory, destroys free institutions. The most glaring instance of Jackson's penchant for lawlessness, in the eyes of his critics, was his treatment of the Cherokee and Creek Indians of Georgia. These tribes had negotiated treaties with the United States which had assured their independence and sovereignty, but they had been subjected to attack by the government of Georgia, which wanted to clear their lands for white settlement. The Cherokees had appealed their case to the United States Supreme Court, which decided that Georgia had no jurisdiction over them. But rather than enforce the Court's decision, Jackson had ignored it. This, together with Jackson's removal of federal troops from Georgia, prompted the anti-administration parties to charge that the President had contemptuously violated the principle of equality under the law. They asserted, in addition, that Jackson had undermined the authority of the Supreme Court as the ultimate arbiter of the meaning of the Constitution and the law, and replaced it with his own arbitrary will.[31]

The anti-Jacksonian parties found additional evidence of the President's willfulness in his treatment of Congress. Jackson had invoked the veto more than any preceding president, and they decried his extensive use of such a device to frustrate the will of the people, as expressed by their elected representatives. Jackson had compounded this offense by vetoing legislation he objected to on "ordinary" grounds of expediency. Here, he departed from the practice of past presidents, who had reserved the use of the veto to nullify legislation they rejected for weighty, constitutional reasons. The President's opponents also took umbrage at the notion, proclaimed in his veto of the bill to recharter the Bank of the United States, that every federal official was sworn to support the Constitution "as he understands it." Echoing a complaint of Henry Clay, they argued that this notion would introduce "universal nullification" by allowing the President to substitute his judgment of constitutionality for that of the Supreme Court. If Jackson's whims were indeed superior to legal precedent, declared a group of National Republicans in Connecticut, "the Executive is clothed with a discretion, above and beyond all law. We hold our lives, our liberty, and our property at the will of one man, and that man as his whole life has proved, a very arbitrary one."[32]

The anti-Jacksonian parties also accused Jackson of weakening the people's attachment to the Union. His conduct in the Cherokee Indian affair, they asserted, had encouraged the nullifiers of South Carolina, who believed that every state could cancel the operation of federal laws within its boundaries. Moreover, Jackson had vetoed legislation that would bind the country more closely together. He had refused to sanction several internal improvements bills, citing strict constructionist objections to federal support of projects that lay entirely within the borders of a state. His veto of the bill to recharter the Bank of the United States had interfered with a unified financial system. Worse still, Jackson had lent no help to the cause of protection, which was necessary to spur the development of home manufactures, preserve the high wages of native workingmen, and provide American farmers with a larger domestic market.[33]

In the campaign of 1832, the Antimasons and National Republicans enunciated some of the themes that would be incorporated into the Whig perspective. The condemnation of Jackson as a "tyrant" crystallized the belief that stable republican institutions—the Constitution, the law, the Supreme Court, and the Union—were necessary and wholesome limitations on personal will. Freedom, in the emerging Whig perspective, did not simply mean the absence of restraints, as Jackson seemed to believe. Rather, it required voluntary acceptance of those restraints which assured that individual self-assertion was kept within reasonable boundaries, and was not contrary to the public good. What the anti-Jacksonians lacked in 1832 was a common sense of identity and purpose. So long as they remained divided by party labels, the opponents of Jackson would find concerted action extremely difficult. Many National Republican Freemasons would vote for Jacksonians rather than support candidates nominated by the Antimasons. Likewise, many Antimasons would refuse to back National Republicans who had the backing of Freemasons.

The division within the opposition, along with their superior political organization, gave the Jacksonian Democrats a considerable advantage in 1832. So, too, did the popularity of Jackson. Although he occupied the highest office in the land, Jackson still seemed a populistic figure engaged in combat against special privilege. Jackson's bank veto message (July 10, 1832) typified the spirit of his appeals to the people. On a variety of grounds, Jackson condemned the Second Bank of the United States proposed in the recharter bill as an institution which would benefit a select few at the expense of the general public. The bill proposed to grant the bank monopoly rights without giving the people a "fair equivalent" in return. He pointed out that the bill did not permit competition in the purchase of the bank's stock, or allow the people to receive the bank's notes. Westerners would suffer inordinately from recharter because they owned little stock in the bank, and would therefore have to make heavy interest payments on debts owed to stockholders in the East and Europe. By contrast, foreigners would benefit disproportionately from recharter because their stock, unlike that of American citizens, would not be subject to taxation by the states. Jackson summed up his objections in a forceful conclusion to the veto message in which he took his stand against "all new grants of exclusive privileges" and "the prostitution of our Government to the advancement of the few at the expense of the many."[34]

Despite its sweeping language, the bank veto message was cleverly drafted to appeal to a wide spectrum of opinion. Critics of paper money and the credit system could, of course, derive pleasure from its attacks on the special privileges of the bank. But so, too, could state bankers and entrepeneurs who disliked the restraints the bank imposed on the expansion of credit. Even advocates of a national bank could find something to like in the message. In one passage, Jackson implied that he would support the establishment of a central fiscal agency if it did not have some of the powers of the Bank of the United States.[35]

The anti-Jacksonian parties were no match for Old Hickory in 1832. Clay brought Kentucky into the National Republican fold, but he could not hold on to all the states Adams had carried four years before. Lacking Adams' regional appeal in New England, he lost Vermont to Wirt and Maine and New Hampshire to Jackson. Elsewhere, Clay carried only Delaware and Maryland. Except for South Carolina, whose legislature chose electors favorable to John B. Floyd, Jackson was victorious in every other state. He even won those (New York, Ohio, and Pennsylvania) where the Antimasons and National Republicans supported the same presidential ticket.[36]

[III]

The electoral catastrophe of 1832, more than any abstract argument, made a telling case for unity between the Antimasons and National Republicans. But the events of the winter and spring of 1832–33 confused rather than clarified the political scene. There was, first, the nullification crisis, during which the Antimasons and northern National Republicans rallied to the side of Jackson, who was determined to put down any rebellion by South Carolina. Then, when Clay brought forth a compromise tariff to conciliate the nullifiers, the Antimasons and northern National Republicans opposed it overwhelmingly. While the crisis of the Union estranged many northerners from Clay, some saw it as an opportunity for a realignment of the parties. In particular, Webster and some National Republicans in the northeast hoped to create a new party which would unite the opponents of nullification, both Jacksonian and non-Jacksonian, under the banner of the "Constitution and the Union."[37]

The project of a new unionist party collapsed quickly in the fall of 1833. Webster and his cohort were willing to unite behind Jackson only if he agreed to compromise on the bank issue by granting the national bank a temporary recharter. But Jackson showed no interest in such a scheme. Further, on September 26, he appointed Roger Taney Secretary of the Treasury, and Taney promptly ordered that after the month was over, federal money would no longer be deposited in the Bank of the United States. When Congress reconvened in December, Webster requested, through intermediaries, that the administration relent from its "war" on the bank. Jackson refused, leaving Webster and his allies with no alternative but to rejoin the opponents of the administration.[38]

The "removal of the deposits" (as it was somewhat inaccurately called) also helped revive the opposition to Jackson by giving new life to the issue of "executive usurpation." Critics of the President were quick to assert that the manner in which he effected the removal was a clear abuse of authority. The charter of the bank did not expire until January 1, 1836, and Congress had declared that the deposits were safe under its jurisdiction. Furthermore, federal law declared that the deposits were within the sphere of congressional authority. The Secretary of the Treasury could remove and transfer them, but he was required to provide the reasons for such actions to the Congress. But, charged the critics of the removal, Jackson had effectively bypassed this legal stipulation and seized control of public monies in violation of the spirit, if not the letter, of the law. Acting while Congress was not in session, he had removed a Treasury Secretary (William Duane) who had refused to remove the deposits, and replaced him with another (Roger Taney) who would submit to orders. Moreover, on September 18, Jackson had read to the cabinet a paper in which he accepted personal responsibility for the removal policy. The President's manner of disposing of the deposits also prompted cries of alarm among his opponents. He lodged them in banks specially selected by himself and his subordinates. The anti-Jacksonians condemned these institutions as "pets" of the administration, a new source of executive influence and corruption.[39]

The furor was exacerbated by the response of the Senate, where the anti-Jackson forces had a majority of seats. On December 2, 1833, Clay offered a resolution requesting that Jackson furnish to the Senate his papers on the removal. The resolution passed, but Jackson declined to comply with it. Then, on December 26, Clay offered in the Senate resolutions which censured Jackson. The first stated that by dismissing Duane and appointing Taney, Jackson had assumed powers not granted by the Constitution; the second, that the reasons Jackson gave for removing the deposits were "unsatisfactory and insufficient." Both censure resolutions passed the Senate in amended form on March 28, 1834. Jackson repudiated the censure, but the Senate refused to receive his Protest because it was worded "disrespectfully."[40]

In his speech advocating the passage of the censure resolutions, Clay made a vivid, if somewhat lurid, statement of the objections to Jackson's role. He condemned Jackson's assumption of control over the public money as a union of "the purse and the sword"—of military and financial power—that represented a menace to republican liberties. Indeed, an "elective monarchy" was emerging, and it was the duty of Congress to prevent it from seizing power. Clay warned that "We are in the midst of a revolution, hitherto bloodless, but rapidly tending toward a change of the pure republican character of the government, and to the concentration of all power in the hands of one man." If Congress did not act soon to counter Jackson's "usurpations," Clay predicted, disaster "will soon come on, and we shall die—ignobly die! Base, mean, and abject slaves—the scorn and contempt of mankind—unpitied, unwept, and unmourned."[41]

However dramatic they may have been, Clay's arguments were rather abstract. But the removal issue had a direct impact on the lives of many voters. In August 1833, Nicholas Biddle, president of the Bank of the United States, began to call in the bank's loans and restrict its deposit of notes. Biddle started this contraction in anticipation of the removal of the deposits, and he hoped it would result in an economic crisis which would lead the public to pressure Jackson for the restoration of the deposits and the recharter of the bank. The contraction had precisely this effect. Much of the country was hit by a severe recession, and committees of businessmen visited the President to plead with him to end his "war" on the bank. Jackson spurned all such requests, but his opponents still hoped to make political capital out of the removal issue. They defended Biddle's contraction as a necessary response to the withdrawal of government money from the bank and demanded that, failing recharter, the administration at least restore the deposits. The opposition looked forward to the New York city elections of April 1834 as the first important test of their position on the bank issue. Gotham was a Jacksonian stronghold, but it had been hard hit by the recession. Consequently, an anti-administration victory there would be evidence that the President had lost considerable support over the removal question.[42]

The results in New York City gave heart to the anti-administration forces across the country. Although the opponents of Jackson lost the mayoral contest by a narrow margin, they did manage to elect a majority of the members of the city council. More important, the New Yorkers had bestowed a new name upon the opposition to the President: "the Whig party."[43] With this name, they tried to evoke a set of historical associations identified with opposition to excessive executive power. So-called Country Party ideologues in eighteenth-century England had condemned the attempts of monarchs and their ministers to break down the independence of Parliament through patronage and other forms of corrupt "influence." The American revolutionaries had styled themselves "Whigs" after the English radicals who applied such criticisms to the court of George III. In the imperial policies of 1763–75, they had professed to see an insidious plot to export to America a whole pattern of royal and ministerial corruption designed to subjugate the colonies.[44]

But when the Whigs of 1834 employed Country Party imagery, it was in a manner quite different from that of the Whigs of 1776. Eighteenth-century republicans had condemned executive "influence" for undermining "mixed government." According to this conception, the ideal polity embodied a balance among the different orders of society—in the case of old England, the monarchy, nobility, and commons. Each order was to prevent abuses by the others, thereby preventing any from imposing its tyranny over the entire society. When the Founding Fathers had devised a national government for the United States, however, they had discarded the conception of mixed government and the assumptions underlying it. While they created a government of separate branches, they expressly stated that all authority was derived from the people. The separation of powers existed not to balance distinct social interests but to prevent the executive, the legislature, or the judiciary from encroaching upon each others' prerogatives. More, each department, so long as it retained its independence, was supposed to serve as a check on the others, and thereby protect popular freedoms against governmental "tyranny."[45]

This transformation in conceptions of government had profound implications for the "Whigs" of 1834. For in attacking Jackson's "usurpations," they could claim to be defending not only the prerogatives of Congress and the interests of the national bank, but the liberties of the people. In the immediate political context, the charge that Jackson was conspiring to undermine the separation of powers was a formidable justification for the unification of his opponents in a single party. It allowed Whig spokesmen to appeal to the Antimasons' fears about the subversion of individual freedom and the National Republicans' concern that personal self-assertion be limited by such institutional restraints as the Constitution and the law. What is more, the "executive usurpation" shibboleth enabled the Whigs to assert that because republicanism itself was in danger, the opponents of the administration should not be distracted by such divisive issues as Freemasonry and bank recharter. The multiple uses that Country Party symbols had for the critics of the removal of the deposits are well demonstrated by the remarks of Chandler Starr, a leading New York Whig:

> Bank or no Bank, Sir, it is a matter of small moment with us. We rally for
> the supremacy of the law, and in view of this high object, I would blot out

all the lines that have heretofore divided us. . . . Sir, I will forget, that there has been any contest between Masonry and Antimasonry, and would say to one and all, if there is any thing valuable in the free institutions for which our fathers fought and bled—if you would transmit this precious legacy unimpaired to your children, then resist these alarming encroachments of absolute power. The crisis is at hand, which determines whether we go the way of all Republics before us and submit to a military despotism or remain a free people.[46]

By imparting a shared identity and common purpose to the anti-Jackson forces, the Whig name provided them with a broad banner under which they could unite. Henry Clay conferred his approval on the use of the name on April 14, 1834, and it spread quickly across the country.[47] But the association of the Whig cause with the removal issue proved unfortunate. As Biddle continued his contraction policy into the spring of 1834, even many Whigs began to suspect that he was really responsible for the country's economic troubles. The Whigs' cause was further undermined when the House Ways and Means Committee uncovered evidence that Biddle had engineered the recession for political purposes. The opposition-controlled Senate appointed its Finance Committee, which was chaired by Webster, to make a separate investigation of the Bank of the United States. Predictably, it cleared the bank of responsibility for the panic. But the damage was already done. Under public pressure to give up the curtailment policy, Biddle finally relented, and began to expand the bank's operations. As if to confirm the charges made against him, the economy recovered quickly. And the Whigs, whose hopes had been so high in the spring, made a disappointing showing in the fall 1834 elections.[48]

The election results made it clear that the bank was a political liability for the Whigs. Even its most vigorous advocates, including Clay and Webster, gave up recharter and the restoration of the deposits as dead issues. But Country Party imagery applied to all the ways men could be influenced by a corrupt executive, not just by the use of money. Throughout the years 1834–36, the Whigs tried to arouse Americans to the dangers presented by Jackson's partisan use of the patronage. In the Senate, they supported legislation to limit the President's power to remove executive appointees, stressing the threat to the independence of officials if they could be removed summarily by the Chief Executive.[49] Senator Thomas Ewing of Ohio chaired a committee that uncovered evidence of massive corruption and mismanagement in the Post Office.[50]

The Whigs' most scathing denunciations of executive influence came in response to the Democratic National Convention of 1835, which nominated Van Buren for President. Pointing to the large number of presidential appointees at this meeting, they referred to it sarcastically as an "office-holders' convention," which had compliantly submitted to Jackson's choice of a successor.[51]

Although they denounced the Democratic convention, the Whigs may well have envied the discipline and unity it manifested. They held no national convention of their own—a decision that enabled them to trumpet their freedom from centralized control—and instead left the choice of candidates to local party meetings and legislative caucuses. Several candidates were widely considered by the northern Whigs, but only one, William Henry Harrison, aroused great interest and enthusiasm. Indeed, Harrison emerged as the anti-administration choice in all but two of the free states; Daniel Webster was the Whig candidate in Massachusetts, while Senator Hugh Lawson White of Tennessee headed the ticket in Illinois.[52] For a variety of reasons, Harrison was a good representative of what the Whigs wanted to project in 1836: an image of republican virtue and moderation, unsoiled by excessive partisanship. Although he had a long record of public service and professed to be an old-fashioned Jeffersonian Republican, Harrison had never become closely identified with any political party or faction. Hence, he was acceptable to the wide assortment of groups in the northern Whig coalition. Furthermore, Jackson had removed Harrison from the office of Minister to Colombia, a post to which he had been appointed by Adams. This made Harrison something of a hero to the opponents of party proscription. Perhaps most important, Harrison's public statements were sufficiently vague, yet appealing, to attract widespread popular support. While he espoused a return to uncorrupted republican government, he was noncommital when asked if he would approve the creation of a new national bank. He also declared that he favored federal financing of internal improvements, but only when the projects involved were of a "national" character.[53]

The Whigs professed to find much in Harrison's background and character that indicated he would be an incorruptible President. He came from an old Virginia family, and his father had signed the Declaration of Independence. His military record was long and distinguished, but—here the contrast with Jackson was implied—he had never been reckless or bloodthirsty on the battlefield. Even in his most famous and sanguinary campaign, the Battle of Tippecanoe, he had been a model of restraint. Harrison had also—again, unlike Jackson—served long and well in several civil capacities. As the Governor of the Northwest Territory and an Indian commissioner, he had disposed of large sums of public money without diverting a single cent. In addition, he had helped negotiate treaties with the Indians which had brought the United States sixty million acres of land. As a member of the national House of Representatives and Senate, Harrison had advocated such worthy causes as the improvement of the militia and the increase of veterans' pensions. A convention of Ohioans concisely stated the case for "Old Tip":

> in WILLIAM HENRY HARRISON, we view the gallant defender of his country in the hour of danger—the soldier who has suffered the privations, shared the toils, and breasted the dangers of savage warfare—a republican of the Jeffersonian school—and, *above all*, a statesman and patriot who will, if elected, be the President of *the Nation*, and not of *a party*—and make the offices what the Constitution designed them to be, *agencies for the benefit of the people, and not bribes with which to purchase votes.*[54]

In the Whigs' propaganda, the Democratic choice, Martin Van Buren, was the perfect foil for Harrison. Van Buren was the mastermind of New York's "Albany Regency"—America's first well-oiled political machine—and many Whigs thought he was largely responsible for the partisan spirit of the Jackson administration. To the Whigs, he was the personification of the worst evils of party politics—a manipulator who, without any personal distinction or fixed principles, was now to be promoted to the highest office in the land. Van Buren, declared a convention of Whigs in his home state, had a life "barren of all but petty schemes and discreditable intrigues." His career had likewise been marked by "a narrow and vindictive party spirit, an unrelenting proscription of opponents, and the politic distribution of the spoils." Therefore, "the fabric of Van Burenism" was not kept intact by "great principles," "binding ties of attachment," or "personal devotion." Rather, it was held together by the "promise of reward in the leader—the hope of spoils in his followers." But if there were "one successful blow at this system of corruption," the defeat of Van Buren, it would sink "into the dust."[55]

Although Van Buren won in 1836, the Whigs drew some encouragement from the election results. Running against the candidate of the majority party in a period of general prosperity, Harrison nevertheless carried seven states, four of which—Indiana, New Jersey, Ohio, and Vermont—were in the North. Moreover, he came very close to capturing Pennsylvania and Rhode Island. Harrison's lofty, statesmanlike stance, when contrasted with Van Buren's image as a party politician, had apparently attracted the support of a large popular constituency. Thurlow Weed was so impressed by Harrison's performance that he recommended that the Whigs accept him as their presidential candidate "by continuation" in the election of 1840.[56]

[IV]

Victory in 1836 may well have been a worse fate for a presidential candidate than defeat. Soon after Van Buren took office, the nation was shaken by a financial panic that quickly worsened into a wholesale depression. The panic of 1837 seems to have been due to a variety of factors. In the decade leading up to it, the American economy had exploded with growth, largely because of infusions of European investment. Much of this expansion, however, rested upon a shaky foundation of speculation, particularly in the public lands. When Jackson redeposited government funds in the "pet" banks, he worsened this situation, for many of these institutions made unsound loans. Furthermore, the demise of the U.S. bank as a government fiscal agency removed some of the restraints on the growth of credit. Then, in 1835, there were widespread crop failures. Farmers could not pay off their debts to merchants and speculators, who, in turn, could not discharge their obligations to the banks. Moreover, the crop failures decreased agricultural exports, diminishing the amount of specie brought into the economy by foreign trade. The economic situation worsened further in late 1836, when several financial houses in Great Britain failed, prompting English businessmen to withdraw capital from the American economy. Battered by severe contractionary forces in the economy, the banks of New York City suspended specie payments in May 1837, and every bank in the country followed their lead soon afterward. As the price of stocks fell sharply and unemployment increased dramatically, the nation entered a period of depressed economic activity which would last, with only brief interruptions, for six years.[57]

Jackson and his advisers had been alarmed by the boom of 1834–36, and had taken action to put a damper on speculation. In 1835–36, the Treasury imposed upon the deposit banks the requirement that they suppress the issuance of low-denomination notes. Prompted by a call from the President, several states enacted legislation to prevent the circulation of small notes. The administration also took action to assure that the deposit banks had adequate specie reserves to back the paper currency they issued. The culmination of the administration's contractionary policy was the "specie circular" of 1836, in which Jackson ordered that transactions in the public lands were to be conducted in specie.[58]

These actions by the Jackson administration did not prevent a financial catastrophe, and may even have hastened it by worsening the contractionary forces in the economy. In any case, the suspension of specie payments by the banks made them ineligible as depositories of government revenue. This compelled Van Buren to devise some new system for handling the public monies. His proposal, first offered to a special session of Congress called to consider the government's fiscal woes, was the so-called subtreasury plan. Under its terms, the federal deposits were to be removed from the private banks and placed in special government vaults. As amended in the Senate, the scheme also provided that the federal government would no longer receive the paper issues of private banks in payment of debts. These would have to be paid in specie or (in certain circumstances) federal notes.[59]

The subtreasury plan was more than a reflex response to an immediate problem. It was emblematic of a transformation in the ideological appeal of the Democratic party. Previous to it, the Democrats had been able to appeal to the proponents of both easy credit and hard money. Men in these two groups had supported Jackson's attack on central banking, though for quite different reasons: the easy money men, because the demise of the national bank might loosen the restraints on credit; the hard money men, because they saw the national bank as the foundation of the paper currency system. But the subtreasury was a victory for the Democratic advocates of a metallic currency. This was made clear by Van Buren's address to the special session of Congress. Although he disclaimed hostility to banks and the credit system, the President blamed the financial crisis on overtrading and speculation, which he attributed to excessive paper issues by the banks. This view was reiterated by other Democratic spokesmen, who agreed with Van Buren that the subtreasury would encourage the circulation of specie by withdrawing government support from the paper money system.[60]

The ascendancy of the hard money men within the Democratic party was most evident at the state level. In those states where the banks were too well established to be eliminated, the Democrats pushed for measures to restrain their issues of paper currency. A common Democratic reform in such states was the imposition of the requirement that the banks maintain a certain ratio between their specie holdings and paper circulation. In those states where the banks were less entrenched, and often responsible for speculative "wildcat" operations, the Democrats usually urged that they be closed down altogether.[61]

Besides its immediate implications for Democratic views on public finance, the subtreasury symbolized a distinct party perspective on the ideal relationship between the government and the economy. In his special session message, Van Buren expressly rejected schemes for federal relief for the people, declaring: "All communities are apt to look to government for too much."[62] This doctrine of government non-interventionism soon became a prime article of faith in the Democratic credo. It rested upon the belief in a "naturally" harmonious social order, which the government should not upset through legislative "meddling." In the Democratic view, the government's withdrawal of support from the paper money system would lead to a simpler and more equitable system of economic exchanges, based on the use of specie for ordinary financial transactions. Considered in this light, the "divorce" between the government and the banks represented a coherent Democratic attempt to reconcile the pursuit of economic progress with the maintenance of republican values. For while the Democrats did not believe that the hard money system would bring a return to the agrarian past, they did hope that it would assure that economic development would proceed more surefootedly, without undermining the ideal of a simple and stable republican order populated by virtuous producers. The Democrats cited several reasons for their faith in hard money. They claimed that, because it had a "natural," intrinsic value, a metallic currency would guarantee laborers a steady and reliable return for their work. In addition, since it was less prone to overissue than paper currency, specie would not stimulate booms and busts which made men's justly earned wages fluctuate in value. Most important to the Democrats in a moral point of view, specie, unlike paper, would not seduce men to pursue their fortunes through speculation rather than hard work.[63]

The Democratic turn toward hard money and noninterventionism alienated an important faction within the party, the so-called Conservatives. These men, who spoke for some of the entrepeneurial elements in the Democratic party, wanted Van Buren to retain the state deposit system, though with reforms to ensure that federal monies were placed in sound banks. Beyond their concern with the bank issue, the Conservatives saw the subtreasury as a sign of an ominous trend toward radicalism within the Democratic party. In their view, the "divorce" of the government from the banks was a dangerous abandonment of established institutions. They considered it the offspring of the doctrines of Democratic ideologues, known as "Loco-focos" in New York and "agrarians" elsewhere, who dogmatically opposed *any* ties between the government and the economy.[64]

But it was the Whigs who articulated the most elaborate and compelling arguments against the subtreasury and hard money. Indeed, the noninterventionist doctrine of the Democrats impelled them to develop a clear perspective on the proper role of the government in the economy. The importance of the debate over the subtreasury is suggested by the fact that the years 1837–38 saw the emergence of voting patterns in Congress, the state legislatures, and the mass electorate that would persist for years to come. Across the country, and at every level of government, Democrats and Whigs adopted clearly contrasting perspectives on the proper public response to the panic and ensuing depression.[65]

The Whigs, of course, found nothing to their liking in the subtreasury. Two of their major criticisms of the plan were that it would increase the power of the executive and promote the partisan interests of the Democrats. With such charges the Whigs hoped to revive their traditional County Party imagery and appeal to popular resentment of special privilege. The subtreasury, they argued, was not impartial or evenhanded; it did not represent abandonment of special interests. To the contrary, it would benefit federal officeholders, who, under its terms, would be paid in specie, not the depreciated paper currencies available to the people. Moreover, the subtreasury would augment the power of the President by increasing the number of patronage appointments he could make; there would, after all, have to be officials entrusted with the safekeeping of the public money. Even more ominous, the plan would give the President virtually direct control over the national treasury, enabling him to use it to promote the interests of himself and his party. For example, the Whigs hypothesized, Van Buren would be able to direct his political lieutenants to use public money to buy up the notes of a bank controlled by some of his opponents. Van Buren's men could then present the notes to the bank for payment, draining it of its specie reserves and forcing it to suspend operations.[66]

But most Whig attacks on the subtreasury concentrated upon the economic effects of the plan. The Whigs tried first to discredit the Democrats' explanation for the economic crisis and their response to it. They rejected Van Buren's argument that the panic had been caused by excessive speculation and overtrading. Instead, they blamed it on the Democrats' adoption of policies that were designed to discourage the expansion of the credit system and promote the use of hard money. Those policies, especially the specie circular, had drained the banks of the specie they needed to meet their foreign obligations. As citizens saw that the government no longer had confidence in the notes of the banks, they had withdrawn their deposits from them. Now, Van Buren proposed to totally abandon the banks by withdrawing the public deposits from them. This would contribute to the contraction of the economy even further by withdrawing metallic currency from circulation and locking it up in government vaults. Even worse, the people would hoard specie because its value would appreciate as its circulation diminished. As the amount of currency decreased, a drastic deflationary cycle would set in. Farmers would not be able to command the same return for their produce, and the wages of workingmen would fall. However, prices would not decrease at the same rate as domestic earnings because the expense of imported goods would not be affected by American financial policy. In addition, debts and mortgages would appreciate in value, increasing the burdens on those who had borrowed in the hope of a brighter future.[67]

The Whigs' criticism is less revealing as a set of explicit arguments than it is as a source for the study of implicit beliefs and assumptions. Above all, the Whig condemnation of hard money embodied a distinctive view on the effect of the credit system upon individual character. The Democratic explanation for the Panic of 1837 rested upon the notion that credit, especially in times of inflationary boom like the mid-1830s, was an evil temptation to extravagance. But to the Whigs, this was a libel on the virtue of the credit-seeking citizen, who was typically a young man just starting out in the world. Since, in the manner of all good republicans, he wanted to attain his "competence"—a farm or small shop—he had to borrow money. However, he could not obtain credit unless others had "confidence" in his good character; the credit system, then, created incentives to moderation, frugality, and thrift. The credit system also instilled public virtue in men of wealth. Rather than hoard their money selfishly, they invested it in projects of general benefit, such as canals, roads, and businesses which provided workers with jobs. Calvin Colton thus condemned "the no credit system" as "a quenching of the spirit of noble and generous confidence" and "a cramping of the expansive powers of sound public morality."[68]

Although it was couched in broad principles, the Whigs' defense of the credit system was far more attuned to the perceptions and experiences of men involved in the marketplace than the views of the administration Democrats. While the Democrats' criticisms of the paper money system hearkened back to such traditional republican ideals as simplicity and agrarian self-sufficiency, the Whigs' arguments presupposed an acceptance of the complex, interdependent relations created by modern finance. These relations rested upon the subjective foundations of mutual trust and public confidence; consequently, the Whigs could only conclude that calamity would result from the government's refusal to accept the paper money issued by the banks. Moreover, since they believed that the credit system was essential to the well-being of an advanced, "civilized" republic, the Whigs did not share the Democrats' faith in the beneficence of a more "natural" social order. To them, the hard money policy was a backward step in the progress of mankind, a reversion to barbarism. Without the credit system, businesses would have to shut down, men would lack incentives to improve their lot in life, and society would sink into stagnation. Furthermore, free institutions would be undermined, for the credit system promoted the widespread ownership of independent property, a sine qua non of republicanism. The Whigs pointed to contemporary examples to validate their arguments. Hard money countries, such as China, Greece, Russia, and

Saxony, were despotisms with primitive economies and rigid social structures.[69]

The Whigs' procredit arguments synthesized assumptions, values, and attitudes that can be traced back to the Adams administration. In their condemnations of the "divorce" between state and bank, the Whigs avowed, like the Adams men and National Republicans before them, the belief that the government had a responsibility to foster economic development. Likewise, the Whigs' idealization of a commercial republic, with credit as one of its cornerstones, was a logical outgrowth of the vision embodied in Clay's American System. Perhaps the most significant element of continuity in the procredit argument was its portrayal of the psychological makeup of the model citizen. That portrayal, which reflected the Whigs' idealized conception of themselves, placed a premium on a character trait always valued highly by the opponents of Jackson, the capacity for self-restraint.

But the procredit argument was more than a rehash of well-worn ideas. It brought together familiar appeals and gave them an immediacy and popularity they had not possessed before. Above all, it enabled the Whigs, so often stigmatized in the past as "aristocratic" defenders of special privilege, to portray themselves as the true champions of equal opportunity. The "Address to the People" of the New York Whig Convention of 1838 shows this clearly:

> It accords with the republican spirit of our institutions to give to all our citizens, as far as possible, equal means and opportunities of acquiring property. A system of credit, which enlarges the currency, furnishes these means; and it is the only mode by which they can be furnished, and by which competition can be produced. . . . We maintain that every poor man who desires an adequate reward for his labor is interested in maintaining a credit system which will furnish that reward, and in denouncing any and every measure that is calculated to enhance the value of coin, and thus diminish the number of his employers; that every young man whose fortune is yet to be made by his industry can have no hope of success through any other means, than through the credit which his character may enable him to obtain, and that to close upon him the avenues which have conducted so many to prosperity would be as disastrous to the country as it would be unjust to the individual.[70]

The Whigs' identification of their cause with the banks and the credit system entailed some political risks. This was illustrated by the fate of the subtreasury bill. In the special session of Congress and the two regular sessions following it, the measure was defeated by coalitions of Whigs and Conservative Democrats. The need for the subtreasury was obviated in May 1838, when the banks began to resume specie payments and the economy experienced a mild recovery. But late in 1838 the banks again suspended specie payments, and the economic situation worsened. Under these circumstances, the banks were widely blamed for causing the distress, and support for the administration grew. Bolstered by increased majorities in both houses of Congress, the administration Democrats were finally able to pass the subtreasury bill in June 1840. Van Buren signed it on July 4, 1840, and party spokesmen heralded it as "a second Declaration of Independence."[71]

There was another good reason for the Whigs to be wary of the bank issue; they did not agree on the best way to revive the credit system and restore public confidence. Some, led by Clay and Webster, proposed the creation of a new national bank. Others, remembering how the old bank had become a political liability, preferred to avoid committing themselves to any specific plan. Moreover, the Whigs wanted to win over the Conservative Democrats, who advocated the restoration of the state deposit system. The Whigs' desire to attract the broadest possible support influenced their choice of a presidential candidate and campaign strategy in 1840. Largely owing to the machinations of such pragmatic northern politicians as Seward and Weed, they passed over Henry Clay as the Whig nominee. Not only was Clay closely associated with the bank, he had clashed too often in the past with various groups the northern Whigs wanted to attract in 1840—Antimasons, Democrats, and antislavery men. The Whigs turned instead to Harrison, whose strong performance in 1836 and fuzzy positions on the issues recommended him as a man who could appeal to the maximum number of voters. The Whigs also adopted no national platform, allowing local party organizations and candidates the greatest possible flexibility in their campaign pronouncements.[72]

Historians have long relished retelling the story of the Whig campaign of 1840, with its panoply of log cabins and cider barrels. What tends to be forgotten, however, is that the Whigs did, after all, address some of the genuine concerns of the electorate. If the Whigs' strategy in 1840 was opportunistic, it could be so only because it expressed a vaguely formulated consensus among all the elements opposed to the Van Buren administration. There was, first of all, the issue of the character of the two candidates. As in 1836, the Whigs hailed Harrison as a simple and honest citizen-soldier—a Cincinnatus taken from his plow—who would restore the republic to pristine purity. In Harrison's own statements and those of his supporters there were promises to sweep the spoilsmen out of office and to prevent official interference in elections. Harrison also pledged to serve only one term—and thus eliminate the major inducement for a President to meddle in politics, the desire for reelection—and to use the veto only when he thought a bill was unconstitutional or had been drafted in haste.[73]

The Whigs, of course, found nothing to praise in Harrison's opponent, President Martin Van Buren. Having denounced "Little Van" as a ruthless politico and master spoilsman in 1836, they now found their worst fears confirmed by his policies as Chief Executive. Although he was more subtle and devious than Jackson, Van Buren, too, had tried to expand the scope of executive power through various types of influence. He had suggested the subtreasury plan, which would give him direct control over the public monies and increase the patronage. He had also devised the evil scheme, presented under the name of Secretary of War Joel Poinsett, to create a nationwide militia directly under his control. Most symptomatic of Van Buren's corruption, in Whig eyes, was his use of the emoluments of office to deck the White House in regal splendor, as if to express disdain for the people. This contempt was evident, too, in Van Buren's rejection of all proposals to help relieve the suffering masses.[74]

But the economic issue was the major preoccupation of 1840. The Whigs offered no single nostrum for dealing with the country's woes, and some offered no nostrum at all. But in virtually all their pronouncements, there was one major theme: the government had to revive credit and restore public confidence through measures of "relief." The noninterventionist policy symbolized by the subtreasury was an abandonment of the people and a selfish measure to benefit the President and his clique of spoilsmen. Thus, the cause of republican restoration was the same as that of financial relief. Whig economic policies might well propel the country more rapidly into an uncharted future, but men were assured in 1840 that a vote for Harrison was a vote for republican virtue. The victory of Harrison, predicted a convention of Connecticut Whigs,

> will be the triumph of reform. It will be a sure pledge that the balance of the constitution is to be restored; that the imperial power of the Executive

shall be brought within safe limits; that the government shall be once more administered, not for the interests of a portion, not for the emolument of office-holders, but for the common welfare of the whole people.[75]

[V]

With the banners of relief and reform held aloft proudly, the Whigs rode to victory in 1840. In his one-month tenure as President, Harrison evinced his determination to implement the principles the party had enunciated in the campaign. In his inaugural address, which was studded with references to the history of the classical republics, he avowed that he would have a high-minded administration, partial to no section or special interest group.[76] Although he removed large numbers of Democratic officeholders and replaced them with Whigs—a policy rationalized with charges of Democratic corruption—Harrison tried to minimize official meddling in politics. In a circular issued to his department heads, he declared that the payment of political contributions or assessments by a federal appointee would be a cause for his dismissal. The circular also ordered officials not to intervene in elections or to receive compensation in return for their services to a party.[77]

Harrison responded to the Whigs' desire for relief legislation by calling a special session of Congress to consider remedies for the nation's economic crisis. But he died before the Congress convened and was replaced by John Tyler. In the special session, congressional Whigs manifested their disdain for the Democratic doctrine of noninterference in the economy. By party-line votes, the House and Senate passed a bill abolishing the subtreasury, which was signed by Tyler. Things became more troublesome when the Whigs turned to *positive* measures of relief. The Whigs passed a bill to establish a new national bank, but it was vetoed by Tyler. The measure was modified and passed again, only to meet with another veto. Then, in the regular congressional session of 1841–42, the Whigs pushed through legislation to increase the tariff and distribute land revenue among the states. Tyler balked at this combination of policies, and only accepted a tariff bill after Congress agreed to drop distribution.[78]

Tyler's actions were a direct challenge to the Whigs' desire for measures to spur economic recovery. Under the challenge of crisis presented by his obstructionism, the Whigs forged a stronger unity behind a coherent party platform. After the two bank vetoes, a special session of the Whig congressional caucus virtually read Tyler out of the party.[79] In the regular session of 1841–42, Whig congressmen voted with near-unanimity for party measures designed to stimulate the economy. Looking toward the 1844 campaign, the Whigs rallied to the cause of restoring a national currency, preserving the tariff of 1842, and distributing the federal revenue among the states. Above all, they rallied to the standard of the man most responsible for promoting these proposals, Henry Clay.[80]

Considered simply as a set of party "positions," the program embraced by the Whigs comprised a rational and coherent response to the problem of economic recovery. A national currency would help revive the credit system; the tariff would protect manufacturers and the wages of workingmen against cheap foreign competition; and distribution would enable the states to pay off their debts without levying direct taxes. But the Whig platform was more than a collection of discrete "positions"; it embodied a distinctive perspective on the American economy and the government's proper relation to it. It presumed an acceptance of the morality of a marketplace society, based on mutual trust and public confidence. It envisaged a more self-sufficient and diversified economy, in which domestic rather than foreign manufacturers would supply Americans with an increasing proportion of their industrial goods. Most important, the Whig platform assumed the existence of a national government which would foster and harmonize the diverse interests of the country.

The Whigs, then, envisaged a continually expanding and diversifying economy. But they placed this compelling vision of the future within a framework of civic values. It was essential that they do this, for the Whig platform could be criticized—and was by many Democrats—as an assault on republican ideals. The credit system might promote extravagance and materialism, qualities incompatible with traditional republican "virtue." Similarly, industrialization might produce a degraded and dependent working class without landed property, the ideal basis of civic attachment. Many Whig spokesmen were content to reassure voters that their proposals presented no threat to the vision of an agrarian republic. Indeed, they argued that the wealth created by an expansionary economy would enable young men and the poor—or at least the worthy and industrious among them—to acquire independent property. They also claimed that factory workers need not fear permanent dependency because the abundance of cheap land in the United States ensured that they would be able to purchase a homestead with only several years' savings.[81]

Some Whig spokesmen went further, and revised the ideal of "virtuous" citizenship to suit the requirements of industrialism and capitalism. In the pronouncements of these men, the definition of "virtue" was divorced from its traditional association with material self-sufficiency and transformed into a more recognizably modern, purely subjective quality. This Whig conception of "virtue" still implied moderation, self-discipline, and an aversion to dependency; but these qualities were lifted out of an agrarian context. Instead, "virtue" was defined as a state of mind which could be possessed by men living in any type of society, including those dominated by the marketplace and industrialism. Some Whigs even praised modern economic institutions for instilling "virtuous" personality traits in the men they affected: workers had to be disciplined and methodical at their machines, capitalists had to attend constantly and regularly to their affairs because of fluctuations in the economy, and young men-on-the-make had to be industrious and continent if they were to obtain credit.[82]

This distinctive conception of "virtue" was evident in the images of the two parties' constituencies that were devised by Whig propagandists. In Whig rhetoric, the distinctive "virtue" of the party's followers was their capacity for self-restraint, which enabled them to rise in the world by dint of individual effort. By contrast, from this perspective, the typical Democrat was deficient in "virtue" because he could not control his passions and appetites. Realizing that he had no hope of mobility because of his weaknesses, the Democrat opposed Whig measures to foster economic progress because he envied those who might benefit from such legislation. Hence, the Democrats preferred to "level downward" rather than "level upward." D. Francis Bacon made a characteristically Whiggish assessment of the moral characters of the two parties: "Those who labor in poverty, with intelligence, honesty, virtue, and HOPE, are Whigs, ten to one; those who labor not, or labor in ignorance and vice, and in despair of improving their condition under any system of government are [Democrats]—a hundred to one." The "virtuous" self-repression of Bacon's stereotypical Whigs also included a respect for the sanctity of the right of possession. They realized that they could not "improve" themselves unless property was secure. The Whigs were

> the bulwark of the men of possession against Agrarian and destructive legislation, against the desperate and Revolutionary enemies of Law and Order, giving thus more protection than they received or asked. They protected the *possessions* of others, and only sought protection for their hopes.[83]

Because of the emphasis they placed on the subjective nature of "virtue," the Whigs ascribed special value to those institutions which instilled self-restraint in the individual. There were three agencies on which they laid primary responsibility for maintaining the moral basis of a capitalistic society: the churches, the schools, and the law. Each of these institutions propagated the salutary lesson that people had to curb their passions, and subject them to internal and external controls. They did this by threatening sanctions. More, they established guidelines on how individuals should conduct themselves in public. For such reasons, Whig spokesmen exhorted audiences to "revere" the institutions which inculcated "virtue," and made possible an orderly society composed of autonomous, self-directed individuals.[84]

The Whigs' belief that the government should try to shape the conduct of citizens was one of their most important differences from the Democrats. With their belief in the noninterventionist state, the Democrats opposed meddling in people's private lives. To them, the freedom of the individual from coercion was the highest value, and the government should largely confine itself to maintaining law and order. Once men were freed from excessive control, the "natural" social order would emerge, and men would "spontaneously" pursue their own best self-interest. Social reformers and the Whigs, however, seemed to believe that they knew how other men should behave, and were intent on imposing their will.[85]

But the Whigs themselves were not entirely united on how large a role the government should play in regulating the lives of citizens. While they agreed that it was desirable to instill the capacity for self-restraint, they split over the question of whether the government should try to coerce conformity to their ideal of the "virtuous" personality. The southern Whigs, of course, had no interest in coercive social legislation; it implied that the authorities could intervene in the relationship between the master and the slave.[86] The northern Whigs, however, disagreed among themselves on how far the state should go. This disagreement reflected their different estimates of the pervasiveness of modern mores in northern society. To those Whigs who believed that modern institutions and mores were indeed strong and pervasive, coercion was unnecessary. To those Whigs who were more concerned with the fragility of the social fabric, state intervention to maintain public order often seemed inevitable.

One issue which revealed such a disagreement was the so-called immigrant problem. By no means were the Whigs' attitudes on this question simply an expression of religious and ethnic group hostilities. They reflected, rather, certain conflicts within the Whig perspective. Operating within the framework of certain shared ideological commitments, the Whigs had a fundamentally ambivalent view of the immigrant. On the one hand, they agreed that immigrants were a positive factor in American "progress" because of the cheap labor they provided for the country's farms and factories. Hence, the Whigs tended to oppose measures that might discourage immigrants from coming to the United States.[87] On the other hand, the Whigs were also generally agreed that the less assimilable immigrants—particularly the Germans and Irish Catholics—were lacking in private and public virtue. Instead of voting disinterestedly upon a well-informed notion of the common good, they voted the welfare of their group, often at the direction of machine politicians and priests. They were also deficient in self-restraint, as evident in their proneness to drunkenness and violence.[88]

Where northern Whigs parted company was over how the "immigrant problem" should be rectified. Nativist Whigs advocated the enforcement of conformity to Anglo-Saxon Protestant norms. Immigrant children, they argued, should be taught in schools that used the King James Bible and textbooks which argued that there were indissoluble links between enlightenment, Protestantism, and republicanism. Laws should also be enacted to extend the naturalization period, and to guarantee that those of foreign birth would have long familiarity with American institutions before they could vote. Nonnativist Whigs argued for a less coercive approach. They believed that American society had an intrinsic capacity to assimilate newcomers which made unnecessary measures of cultural compulsion. William Seward shared this belief, which he manifested in his proposal, as Governor of New York, to extend state aid to New York

City's Catholic parochial schools. Seward and like-minded Whigs also believed that immigrants would be most easily absorbed into the American political system if they learned to exercise the privileges of citizenship. They accordingly opposed extending the naturalization requirement and supported statutes which permitted aliens to vote after a short period of residency in the United States.[89]

But it was the issue of slavery that revealed the deepest fissures within the northern wing of the Whig party. Slavery was so divisive a problem for the northern Whigs because it presented them with a confict in values. They wanted to promote economic development, and slavery was clearly incompatible with their vision of an advanced capitalistic economy. With virtual unanimity, northern Whigs condemned slavery as a backward and regressive institution which deprived the slave of control of his own person, stigmatized labor, and undermined the incentives to self-improvement.[90] But slaves were a form of property, and respect for property rights was a prime tenet of Whiggery. Furthermore, government action against slavery might endanger the Union, and Whigs believed fervently that the preservation of the Union was essential to social cohesion. Thus, when slavery became a national issue, the ensuing debate laid bare important ideological differences among the northern Whigs. On the one side, there were those who placed paramount importance on order, stability, and intersectional cooperation; on the other, those who placed a higher value on moral and economic "progress." These differences were so pregnant with significance for the fate of the Whig Party that they require more than a synoptic discussion. Rather, they call for the analysis of the lives and beliefs of the two men who, in the opinion of their contemporaries, spoke most eloquently for the opposing principles within northern Whiggery, Daniel Webster and William Seward.

CHAPTER 3

Daniel Webster:
Conservative Whig

THE WHIGS were the party of legislative leadership, and the principal art of the classic legislator was oratory. The Whigs had many distinguished orators, but by general consent Daniel Webster stood above all the rest. Indeed, there was something spellbinding about Webster, both on and off the public platform, that prompted his admirers to praise which seems extravagant today. Some classed him in the same ranks as Charlemagne, Dante, Hercules, Antaeus, Michelangelo, and Pericles. Others, despairing of human comparisons when trying to describe his prodigious powers, evoked images of Niagara Falls or the groundswell of the ocean. Perhaps the most common epithet applied to Webster in his lifetime was "God-like."[1]

Why did people think of Webster in this way? Clearly, much of the man's magnetic appeal was derived from the simple, elemental fact of his appearance. Webster *looked* like an extraordinary figure, the very prototype of the born leader. Although, at five feet, ten inches, he was not especially tall, he seemed to tower over more massive men. There was much to be awed by in his countenance: the swarthy complexion that earned him the nickname "Black Dan"; the strong, broad shoulders and cavernous chest; the massive, high-domed head, topped by jet-black hair; the black eyes—blazing, some said, like furnaces—beneath cavernous brows; and the massive yet expressive mouth Thomas Carlyle compared to that of a mastiff.[2] Completing the image of grandeur was the full Revolutionary dress Webster wore on public occasions—dark blue coat with gilt buttons, buff vest, and white neckcloth. Henry W. Hilliard, recalling the first time he saw Webster in the Senate, wrote that "as he sat in his place, surrounded by his peers, it seemed as if the whole weight of the government might rest securely on his broad shoulders."[3]

Webster also impressed many of his contemporaries with his style of speaking. In this, he was a welcome contrast to the spread-eagle posturing typical of his colleagues. Customarily, Webster would begin his speeches in a low but audible tone, "calm, deliberate, and unimpassioned," but "never wanting in dignity." Avoiding sweeping gestures, he would rely on modulations of his voice to communicate the emotions appropriate to his message, only occasionally punctuating his more impassioned statements with upward and downward thrusts of the hand. The most important weapon in Webster's arsenal was his voice. According to Henry Cabot Lodge, it was "low and musical in conversation; in debate it was high but full, ringing out in moments of excitement like a clarion, and then sinking to deep notes with the solemn richness of organ-tones."[4]

Yet many of Webster's admirers rarely, if ever, saw him or heard him speak. Webster's fame as an orator was sustained by his immense talents as a literary artist. The published versions of his speeches were carefully crafted and often extensively revised before they were sent to the printer. They were noteworthy, in an age of verbosity, for their lucid arguments, in which they were far superior to the emotional outpourings of Clay and the metaphysical exercises of Calhoun. "Mr. Webster," as one of his eulogists declared, "was remarkable for penetration and comprehensiveness, for analysis, clear arrangement and statement. He would fix his large powers on a subject as he fixed his large burning eyes upon an object. He would look into a subject, look through it, around it, master it."[5]

There were, then, substantial grounds for the massive reputation Webster enjoyed in his time. It is nevertheless evident that the Webster persona did not guarantee—indeed, it may have precluded—widespread personal affection for its author. Although he was an eager aspirant to the presidency, Webster always suffered from the burden of being an "unavailable" candidate. He sought the Whigs' nomination in 1836, 1840, 1848, and 1852, but failed on each occasion.[6]. There are several conventional explanations for Webster's apparent lack of popular appeal. His reserved and often lofty public demeanor, it has been claimed, repelled men who interpreted it as an "aristocratic" air of superiority. There is no doubt that Webster lacked the common touch, and that the image he cultivated was more that of a living national monument than of a fallible, flesh-and-blood human being. His efforts to arouse public sympathy—as when he cried, during the 1840 presidential campaign, about his siblings who had been born in a log cabin—always seemed contrived. Webster's relationship to the populace was well described by Francis Grund: "Though respected and admired throughout the country, he is not beloved—no, not even by his own partisans. Mr. Webster knows the laws of his country; but he is less acquainted with the men who are to be governed by them, and possesses none of those conciliatory and engaging qualities which insure personal popularity."[7]

Webster's public esteem may also have been limited by his political philosophy and connections. He began his career as a Federalist, and throughout his life was arrayed on the side of the conservative, propertied elements of the northeast. Moreover, there was a certain lack of audacity in Webster that kept him out of touch with public opinion. Unlike Clay, he could not express the aspirations of the people because he did not share them. As Francis Lieber put it, Webster "had no instinct for the massive movements of his kind . . . he had . . . no eye or heart for the embryo elements of the new day."[8]

Perhaps the most damaging problem for Webster was the immense (and well publicized) disparity between the almost superhuman image he tried to project and certain patent realities of his life. Webster lived extravagantly, spent money profligately, and was dependent upon periodic subscriptions from wealthy businessmen to maintain his opulent style of life. Furthermore, his career was marked by drastic reversals of political position which seemed to be dictated by expediency and the needs of his wealthy supporters. All this suggested to some that, for all his formidable abilities, Webster lacked the strength of character usually associated with genuine conviction. Nathaniel Hawthorne thus characterized Webster ("Old Stony Phiz") as "a man of mighty faculties and little aims, whose life, with all its high performances, was vague and empty, because no high purpose had endowed it with reality."[9]

Yet some men saw virtues in the very qualities that seemed to limit his popularity. Webster's inconsistencies, for instance, were defended by his admirers as the necessary adjustments of a statesman to change; while he always adhered to the same principles, Webster was wise enough to see that new circumstances called for new policies. Similarly, Webster's refusal to live by the politician's code of affability was cited as evidence of his respect for the public. Having a high regard for the intelligence of the people, he did not believe that they would be flattered by fawning affection. Neither, with his genuine concern for the welfare of the nation, would Webster submit to party dictates. "If sometimes he felt himself fretted by the reins of party leaders, it was because, in his sagacity as a generous statesman, he preferred the interests of the whole to the dictation of a few."[10]

In the eyes of his admirers, Webster's aloofness indicated that he somehow stood apart from, and above, the clamorous partisanship of democratic politics. While the politicians engaged in their low tricks, Webster remained stolid and reliable—"a sort of balance wheel in the political machine to keep its action regular and steady." According to the mystique that grew about Webster, his talents were best displayed in a crisis. Then, like some wise and benevolent guardian, he would give direction to a nation which had lost its way. "One felt," recalled S. K. Lothrop, "that so long as he lived, come what would, there would be one among us mighty enough for any emergency that might happen to the country . . . and whose influence on public affairs and public opinion would be felt, whatever might be his station or office."[11]

Even Webster's foibles had their part in the image of the "God-like Daniel." Consider the case of Emerson. Although Emerson generally disdained politics and often accused the Whigs of timidity and stodginess, he seems to have been awed by Webster. Yet he was not ignorant of Webster's many lapses. As he wrote to Carlyle, Webster "has his own sins, no doubt, is no saint, is a prodigal." Emerson also had no difficulty seeing through Webster's facade of public rectitude: "His Christian religion is always weak, being merely popular . . . one feels every moment that he goes for the actual world, & never a moment for the ideal." But Emerson chose to interpret Webster's transgressions as evidence of inner resources; if Webster yielded to his appetites, it was not for weakness of will, but because he possessed them to a superhuman degree. Webster, Emerson conceded,

> has not this or that fine evangelical property. He is no saint, but the wild olive wood, ungrafted, yet by grace; but, according to his lights, a very true and admirable man. His expansiveness seems to be necessary to him. Were he too prudent a Yankee, it would be a sad deduction from his magnificence. I only wish he would not truckle. I do not care how much he spends.[12]

It is suggestive of the nature of Webster's appeal that he should have been admired by both political conservatives and an independent intellectual such as Emerson. For these men, different as they were, shared deep misgivings about mass party politics. The conservatives were disturbed by the premium it seemed to place on demagogy and partisanship, while Emerson was repelled by its submergence of individuality. Independence, intellect, and a certain critical detachment from the will of the majority were the last qualities sought out in the politician. But it was precisely these qualities that Webster possessed to a superlative degree, or so his admirers believed. In his role as a shaper of public opinion, Webster somehow gave voice to the ideals which should govern civic life. Once having cast Webster in the part of the transcendent statesman, his admirers were predisposed to elevate his failings into signs of strength; heroes, after all, are supposed to personify qualities we admire in ourselves. They therefore dismissed Webster's private frailties as venial rather than mortal sins. To them, the important thing was that in his *public* capacity, Webster sublimated the forces within himself into service for the common good.

The idealized image of Webster, then, may be regarded as a projection of the yearnings of men who felt estranged from mass democratic politics. But there was substance to the Webster persona; it was not merely a mirage. Webster consciously assumed and played the role of the disinterested statesman, and men found his performances credible because he applied to them his considerable natural talents. Yet, in becoming a spokesman for the highest ideals of the American republic, Webster established a high standard of expectation in his followers. Thus, when he deviated seriously from the requirements of his public role, the results were calamitous for his reputation. In both its heroic and tragic aspects, Webster's life has much to tell us about the limitations of personal leadership in a democracy.

[I]

Daniel Webster was born January 18, 1782, in Salisbury, New Hampshire, a small settlement in the Merrimack Valley. Two years later, the Websters moved three miles to Salisbury Lower Village, where Daniel spent his childhood and adolescence. The dominant influence upon him in these years was his father Ebenezer, who maintained a farm and a tavern on the family homestead. Ebenezer Webster was a classic case of the social mobility made possible by war and political upheaval. Although he was descended from a long line of undistinguished farmers and had never received a formal education, Ebenezer had achieved considerable local eminence as an officer of militia in the French and Indian War and the Revolution. In civilian life, he was rewarded with such positions of prominence as his friends and neighbors could bestow: justice of the place, delegate to the state convention that ratified the federal Constitution, elector in the first presidential election, and representative in the state assembly. Ebenezer had good reason to be thankful for the republic, as it enabled men like himself to rise. His loyalties, naturally enough, went to the Federalists, the party of national authority and political conservatism, and he transmitted to his family a fierce devotion to the party and person of George Washington.[13]

Daniel, Ebenezer's youngest son and the seventh of his eight children, proved unsuited to chores on the family farm, preferring to play and recite patriotic tales and passages from the Bible to visitors at his father's tavern. Seeing that the boy possessed intellectual promise, Ebenezer decided that he should have the rare (and expensive) privilege of an advanced education. At age fourteen, after sporadic instruction at several local schools and academies, Daniel was sent to the prestigious Exeter Academy, where he studied for a term. A neighborhood minister gave him some additional preparation before he was dispatched to Dartmouth College in 1797. Here, Daniel chose the law as the career best suited to his desire for fame and intellectual distinction. Upon graduation from college, he served an apprenticeship to a Salisbury lawyer, Thomas W. Thompson, which was interrupted by a stint of school-teaching in Maine. In 1804 Webster moved to Boston to complete his legal training and secured a clerkship in the office of Christopher Gore, a prominent attorney and Federalist politician. The next year he returned to New Hampshire to establish a law office at Boscawan, near the family homestead. After his father's death, he handed over to his brother Ezekiel control of his law business and the family farm, and moved (May 1807) to the thriving New Hampshire seaport of Portsmouth.[14]

Webster's political career took off rapidly in his new home. The local Federalist elite welcomed him into their ranks, and his party's popularity in Portsmouth increased dramatically after the Republican-sponsored Embargo and War of 1812 cut off its profitable transatlantic trade.

Webster was elected to the House of Representatives in 1812 and reelected two years later, but his two terms as a New Hampshire congressman were full of frustration. A member of a small and impotent minority in the House, he was little more than an obstructionist and carping critic of the Madison administration. When the War of 1812 ended suddenly and without injury to American interests or prestige, Webster was left in a bind. The war had nearly ruined Portsmouth's economy, so it no longer provided him with the profitable legal work he needed. Furthermore, Webster's service in Congress had made him ambitious for national prominence, and New Hampshire was too modest and provincial a state for a politician with such aspirations.[15]

In 1816 Webster moved to Boston, where he hoped to begin his career anew in a larger theater for his ambitions. The city proved hospitable. The Federalist party of Massachusetts was dominated from Boston by a small elite of businessmen who were willing to pay handsomely for his legal and political services. Men of culture as well as of wealth, they readily welcomed Webster into their homes and allowed him to invest in their enterprises. Their political ideas were soundly conservative: although they had relinquished the ideal of leadership by a closed, aristocratic elite, they still sought a government of the "natural leaders of society," set apart by wealth, fine breeding, and educational achievement. By their own lights, they were high-minded custodians of the public good, who manifested their civic consciousness through political leadership, philanthropy, and patronage of learning and the arts. With his oratorical talents and adaptable conservatism, Webster was amply qualified to be their spokesman. For the most part, he served their interests well as a United States congressman (1823–27) and senator (1827–41, 1845–50).[16]

The supreme irony of Webster's early career was that he spent it, for the most part, as a critic of the enlargement of federal power. The man who would become the ablest spokesman of American nationalism started out as a defender of states' rights and strict constructionism. In this role, Webster was only representing the will of his constituents. The citizens of Portsmouth, like those of other maritime communities in New England, wanted to avoid war with Great Britain. When efforts to avert conflict failed, Webster was reduced to opposing legislation to facilitate the prosecution of the war effort. Although he did not advocate New England's secession from the Union, Webster implied that it might be a legitimate last resort if federal policies continued to be injurious to the interests of his section. In his private correspondence, Webster praised the proceedings of the Hartford Convention as "esteemed, moderate, temperate & judicious." Long after the end of the War of 1812, Webster had to defend himself against charges that he had supported the disunionist cause.[17]

Even for a time after his move to Boston, Webster continued to speak from a narrowly sectional position. This was especially true of his opposition to the Republican-sponsored tariff of 1816. Although this measure was only mildly protective in its effects, it was anathema to the shippers and shipbuilders of New England, who feared the loss of transatlantic trade if Americans produced their own manufactures. In an eloquent speech at Faneuil Hall in 1820, Webster stated the anti-protectionist case most forcefully. He claimed that he was not opposed to manufactures *per se*. What he disliked was legislation to artificially stimulate them at the expense of other interests in the community, such as commerce and agriculture.[18]

Webster's early particularist leanings were wholly consistent with his Federalist convictions. Although, like many other young Federalists, he adopted some of the popular campaign methods of the Republicans,[19] Webster still adhered, for the most part, to orthodox Federalist ideology. His ideal republic was that of the older generation of Federalists: a polity without arbitrary power or inherited privilege, but having a clearly demarcated hierarchy of classes and mass deference to a governing elite. There was nothing in such an ideal that was inherently incompatible with the expansion of federal power. Indeed, it was the Federalists who, desiring to attach men of wealth to the central government, had led the movement to create the first Bank of the United States and enact the first protective tariff. But once the federal government was captured by the Republicans, the Federalists—particularly in New England, their last bastion of power—retreated to a particularist position. Centralized power, after all, could be used to subvert the power of established elites as well as to buttress it.[20]

From Webster's perspective, Republican policies presented a clear danger to the established distribution of power in New England. Jefferson's Embargo, the War of 1812, and the postwar tariff were all injurious to the economic interests of the Federalist elites, most of whom derived their wealth from the transatlantic trade. An even more

profound threat was the Republicans' exaltation of the sovereign people
and their resort to divisive party politics. The Republicans, with their
penchant for "democracy," mocked the Federalists' faith that an ordered
social hierarchy and mass deference were the keystones of republican
government. "The path to despotism leads through the mire and dirt of
uncontrolled democracy," wrote Webster in 1802. Sometimes, in his fear
of unchecked popular rule, Webster tended toward the apocalyptic. In
1807, when Federalist fortunes were at a low ebb, he feared that "our
Country is growing corrupt at a rate, which distances the spread of every
other." Even in so relatively calm a year as 1816, Webster complained of
the "great anxiety" accompanying the "good prospect" of the nation.[21]

The main axiom of Webster's Federalist ideology was the proposition,
taken from the classical republican theorist James Harrington, that
"Power *naturally* and *necessarily* follows property." From this thesis,
Webster derived the notion that political power in a republic should be
in proportion to the possession of property. The propertyless, lacking
the proverbial stake in society, should be denied an active role in civic
life, Webster argued, because they might sell their votes to patrons or
support demagogues. Men of wealth, by contrast, should be entrusted
with authority because they had the sense of responsibility that comes
with roots in the community. Furthermore, they could not be corrupted
easily. Webster most fully expounded these ideas at the Massachusetts
Constitutional Convention of 1820–21. There, it was proposed that the
state senate should be apportioned on the basis of population. But
Webster argued successfully for the retention of the existing system of
apportioning seats in the senate according to taxable property, asserting
that it protected property rights against assault by popular majorities.
Some of Webster's arguments against the promotion of manufactures
were couched in similar terms. Industrialization, he warned, threatened
to create a propertyless working class, a rootless and turbulent group of
citizens who would be a constant menace to republican institutions.[22]

Changes in Massachusetts and in the nation as a whole compelled
Webster to change his positions and accommodate his ideology to new
circumstances. The spread of universal white manhood suffrage made an
anachronism of his vision of a government restricted to men of property.
The exclusion of foreign trade during the War of 1812 led to the
mushroom growth of American manufacturing and the rise of a new
class of wealthy industrialists. New England was especially affected by the

last development, which helped reshape the elites of the region when the new manufacturers and their children began to marry into the families of Boston's merchant princes. Moreover, the deprivation of the transatlantic carrying trade during the war with Britain had compelled many of the New England shippers and shipbuilders to branch into manufacturing. Accordingly, by the mid-1820s, many members of Boston's elite had considerable investments in certain industries, particularly textiles, and were petitioning Webster to support high tariffs. The new elite of industrialists had other needs and demands, too. In order to amass the huge amounts of capital needed to finance their mills and factories, they increasingly resorted to the corporate form of organization; consequently, they wanted their company charters to be secure against legislative encroachment. In addition, they were dependent upon trade with other regions of the country—particularly the South, which supplied the mills with raw cotton—and thus wanted a national financial system which would supply them with easy credit and a reliable medium of exchange.[23]

In short, the emergence of political democracy and industrial capitalism had made obsolete the provincial and defensive conservatism of Webster's early Federalist phase. Formerly, Webster and other New England conservatives had been afflicted with a siege mentality. They wanted desperately to preserve as much as possible of a distinctive regional culture and social structure. By the 1820s, an increasing number were looking outward, seeking to create a national legal and political environment conducive to capitalist development. The beliefs to which they would give their allegiance would be adapted to the new conditions—dynamic, expansive, and "progressive" to reflect an America transformed by economic growth and surging with democratic aspiration. Yet the men whom Webster represented remained "conservative" in their desire to preserve those values from the past which they believed underwrote a stable social order: unity, harmony, and most of all, respect for property. It was Webster's lot, as the foremost spokesman of New England conservatism, to articulate an ideology which would reconcile his sponsors' hopes for material "progress" with their yearnings for the reassuring certainties of the past.

Webster began his role as a spokesman for the new conservatism in his status as a constitutional lawyer. In the Supreme Court headed by the Federalist John Marshall he found a branch of the federal government which accepted his view that the national authorities should uphold corporate privilege. In the Dartmouth College case (1818), the Court concurred with his argument that corporate charters were contracts whose inviolability was protected by the Constitution against "impairing" state legislation. A year later, in *McCulloch v. Maryland*, the Court agreed with Webster that the branches of the Bank of the United States could not be taxed by state legislatures. The power to tax, declared Marshall, was the power to destroy; so levies on the congressionally created national bank were an unacceptable infringement of federal supremacy. The Court ruled in accord with Webster's arguments once again in *Gibbons v. Ogden* (1824). It determined that the New York legislature could not grant a monopoly to a steamship company which carried passengers between New York and New Jersey; such action violated the constitutional provision making the federal government the sole regulator of interstate commerce.[24]

Still, the decisions of the Marshall Court were of limited usefulness in creating favorable conditions for capitalist development. Their function was to inhibit unfavorable state restraints. Webster and the interests he represented wanted more: state and federal legislation which would actively foster business growth. This objective would have to be sought through ordinary legislative channels, where it would be subject to public scrutiny and debate. Furthermore, in an era of widening popular involvement in politics, it was bound to become a lively subject of political controversy. Webster was hence compelled by the exigencies of democratic politics to reach beyond the narrow circles of elite opinion, and address his arguments to a mass audience.

Webster's arguments for the fostering state rested on the same belief as his Federalism: that in a republican polity, power and property should be united in the same hands. What changed was the manner in which Webster applied this conviction to American conditions. As a Federalist, he had assumed that there was an hierarchy of distinct classes, demarcated, in good part, by their possession of various amounts of property. There could be mobility between these classes, but it was severely limited, in practice, by strong social sanctions (such as ridicule) against those who pretended to rise above their appointed station in life. Those who were upwardly mobile (such as Webster himself) had their new status validated by the stratum into which they had risen, and were expected to adopt its distinctive ways.[25] In place of this clearly stratified picture of society, Webster substituted a far more fluid one. There were no distinct social classes in the United States, he argued, because the abundance of opportunity allowed men to rise (or fall) in accordance with the abilities they brought to "the race of life." This argument rested upon the assumption that there were unique conditions in the United States which made it possible for even the humblest American to attain a decent "competence." Over the years, Webster enumerated several factors to which he attributed his countrymen's happy fate: the absence of inherited privilege, inheritance laws which periodically broke up large estates, the abundance of cheap land, and the availability of free education. All these things, according to Webster, made possible the widespread diffusion of property among white adult male Americans.[26]

Webster thus became a fervent disciple of the gospel of American exceptionalism. The gospel painted a happy picture of social conditions in the United States, but it was no invitation to complacency. To the contrary; for Webster and other spokesmen, it was a call to activism. For if power and property *could* be brought together in the hands of a great number of Americans, what was the function of an enlightened republican government but to insure that the two *were* united? Webster hence defended the public promotion of capitalist development because it would diffuse the possession of property and thereby give an ever-larger proportion of Americans a stake in society.[27]

Webster's argument for the promotional state had direct relevance to his defense of Whig economic policies. For instance, Webster advocated high tariffs with the claim that they protected the high wage levels in America against ruinous foreign competition, enabling native workingmen to achieve their propertied independence.[28] Likewise, he praised the credit system for providing poor men with the capital they needed to purchase their own farms, shops, and homes.[29] He also argued that the government should underwrite and regulate the paper issues of the banks in order to prevent the fluctuations in their value which robbed workers of the just returns of their labor.[30] Corporate charters should be immune from political intrusions, because corporations enabled businessmen to raise the capital needed to operate mills and factories which provided laborers with remunerative employment.[31] Webster also lent his voice to the cause of publicly financed internal improvements. He asserted that such facilities helped diffuse property by linking farmers and artisans to the remote markets in which they could sell their goods and produce at the highest prices.[32]

But even as Webster adapted classical republicanism to the conditions of Jacksonian America, he remained concerned with the maintenance of public order and civic virtue. As a Federalist, he had been able to assume that individuals had a given "place" in the social hierarchy, for which there were prescribed modes of conduct, enforced by external agencies of control. However, having glorified the mobile, self-sufficient individual as the basic unit of American society, he could no longer make this assumption. What, then, would prevent the United States from degenerating into a scramble of selfish individualists, seeking their own aggrandizement without regard for the public good? Webster's response to this anticipated problem was to project a new ideal of the model citizen, the man who disciplined his appetites because he had internalized self-restraint. This ideal was not atomistic. Like other Whigs, Webster believed that the traditional agencies of social control, such as the family, church, and school, could help instill the character traits of the autonomous personality in children and adults. He also favored inspiring in the people a "reverence" for the law, as the law provided checks on the human propensity toward violence and licentiousness.[33]

But internalized self-restraint could only tell men what they should *not* do. Webster realized that in a fluid society, where there could be few stable or lifelong attachments, men would feel a special need for a positive symbol that would provide them with a sense of shared purpose and identity. He found that symbol in the thing Americans most obviously had in common—the Union. In the preservation of the Union, Webster also found a cause which would justify the subordination of individualism to the needs of the social organism. The premises of Webster's nationalism, which he articulated in response to Calhoun's doctrine of nullification, are summarized easily. The Constitution, which created the Union, had been ordained and established by the people, acting in their sovereign capacity, and was not simply a compact among discrete states. The Constitution was therefore the supreme law of the land, and the federal government acted immediately and directly upon the individual citizen, not through the agency of the states. The last resort in cases of dispute over the respective limits of state and national power was the federal judiciary. The people, acting as a sovereign body, were within their rights to dissolve the Union if they felt the central government had become tyrannical. But they could do so only through revolution, not by the interposition of state power against federal authority. Consequently, no state could nullify national legislation.[34]

This, of course, was only the intellectual framework of Webster's nationalism. What gave his ideas their sustaining power was not so much Webster's powers as a logician but his ability to muster in their defense a rich body of emotive symbols and associations. Webster realized that national loyalty was highly subjective, and that the Union would be "nothing" if the people saw it merely as a conglomeration of interests; they had to think of it as more than "a bond without affection." Since the Union rested on "fraternal feeling," it was held together by "unseen . . . chains"; so it was the duty of the statesman to constantly remind Americans of their shared ideals and heritage. As Webster avowed in 1848, it was the main aim of his career to make Americans *"one people, one in interest, one in character, and one in political feeling."*[35]

Webster's nationalism was a passionate faith, but it also had its foundations in grainy, substantial fact. Webster invoked the image of a corporate, organic Union to justify the use of federal power to create a nation consolidated by ties of common economic interest. By the same token, Webster hoped, through the nation-state, to harmonize republican virtue with the free pursuit of material interest: he wanted Americans to feel that, by promoting capitalist development, they were not only benefiting themselves but contributing to the common good. Webster thus argued forcefully for the notion that there was a national "harmony of interests." While he conceded that the states had a wide diversity of concerns, he avowed that "these several interests, if not identical, are not therefore inconsistent and hostile. Far from it. They unite, on the contrary, to promote an aggregate result of unrivalled national happiness."[36]

The various strands of Webster's nationalism were best brought together in the speech which did the most to make him a major national figure, the "Second Reply to Hayne." This address, delivered over parts of two days (January 26 and 27, 1830), is indeed admirable as a summation of Webster's views. But it also illustrates how much Webster's nationalism was an outgrowth of the aspirations, needs, and values of New England's capitalists. Its background is suggestive; the controversy provoking Webster's marathon effort grew out of a proposal by Senator Samuel A. Foot of Connecticut that the survey and sale of the public lands be stopped temporarily. Thomas Hart Benton, senator from Missouri, rose to denounce this as a scheme to hold down the wages of eastern workingmen by discouraging migration to the West. Senator Robert Y. Hayne of South Carolina joined in Benton's protest and suggested that the revenues from the sale of the lands might be a "fund for corruption" to break down the sovereignty of the states. Webster, who was arguing a case before the Supreme Court, heard this exchange while on a visit to the Senate chamber. It disturbed him, for it might portend a coalition of agrarian interests, in which the South would support cheap land for the West in exchange for western backing of a reduction in the tariff. Such an alliance would isolate New England, so Webster was anxious to avert it.[37]

In his first reply to Hayne (January 14, 1830) Webster provided a factual, at times technical, defense of New England's position. He denied the charge that the East had been "illiberal" toward the West in its land policies. Historically, New England congressmen had been more supportive of cheap land than their southern counterparts. Webster confessed that New Englanders considered the public lands an important source of government revenue. But this was not because they wanted to impose some evil "consolidation" upon the Union. Rather, they wanted to use the land proceeds to finance internal improvements which would bind the states more closely together. Shifting to the subject of the tariff, Webster pointed out that New England now supported high protective duties because past tariffs—most of them backed by the South and the West—had forced his region to invest heavily in manufacturing. Toward the end of his speech, Webster insinuated an allusion that served to divert the debate from land policy and the tariff to the broader issues of nationalism and sectionalism. Rebuking those who claimed that New England was hostile to the West, he pointed out that a New Englander, Nathan Dane, had written the Northwest Ordinance, which had excluded slavery from the Northwest Territory.[38]

Hayne took Webster's bait. He charged that Webster had attacked slavery and the southern way of life. A loyal Calhounite, he also tried to rebut Webster's nationalism with a vigorous assertion of the doctrine of state interposition.[39] But by going along with the terms of Webster's reply to his first speech, Hayne had fallen into a trap, helping to shift the focus of debate from the land issue—a potential bridge between the South and the West—to the subject of the nature of the Union. With this topic foremost, Webster was able to drive a wedge between the South and the West and thereby avert the political isolation of New England. Part of Webster's strategy was to remind westerners of the commitment they shared with New Englanders to an economy based on free labor. He alluded again to Nathan Dane's authorship of the Northwest Ordinance, under which the northwestern states had prospered. He made an invidious comparison between Kentucky and Ohio, and suggested that the former would have benefited from the ordinance's prohibition of slavery. Furthermore, under the ordinance the Northwest had been provided with schools modeled after those of New England, which had diffused knowledge and morality among the settlers. In order to press home the sectional significance of the ordinance, Webster analyzed the congressional vote on the measure. Southern congressmen had been heavily opposed to it, while northern congressmen had been virtually unanimous in favoring it.[40]

Webster added an appeal to economic nationalism. Here, his argument was straightforward: if New Englanders wanted economic legislation at national expense, it was because they wanted all Americans to share in the benefits of capitalist development. With this argument, Webster hoped to dispel the notion that Yankees were solely concerned with their own selfish interests. He also hoped to appeal to westerners and southerners who wanted nationally financed internal improvements. He made a significant choice of concrete examples: he asserted that New Englanders would favor internal improvements in Ohio or South Carolina, even though they had no direct interest in them, because they viewed the states "not as separated, but as united." "We do not," Webster intoned, "impose geographical limits to our patriotic feeling or regard; we do not follow rivers and mountains, and lines of latitude, to find boundaries, beyond which public improvements do not benefit us."[41]

After an elaborate exposition of his views on the Union and nullification, Webster launched into a passionate peroration. The implied message of his imagery was a conservative one: the Union was the only means of reconciling liberty with order. Webster did not believe that any other bond could overcome the forces dividing the American people, so he denounced nullification and secession as forms of political suicide. Without the Union, the most important restraint on men's passions would be removed, unleashing anarchy and chaos. A disunited

America thus brought to Webster's mind nightmares of "States dissevered, discordant, belligerent; . . . a land rent with civil feuds, or drenched, . . . in fraternal blood!"[42]

[II]

Webster's nationalism was more than the centerpiece of his ideology; it was also a personal political stratagem. Webster hoped to leave behind his early reputation as a spokesman for particularistic interests. Webster, the guardian of the Constitution and the Union, was clearly a more appealing figure than Webster, the obstructive Federalist. The overwhelmingly favorable response to the Second Reply to Hayne, even in the South, showed clearly the popular appeal of Webster's new role.[43] Yet the stance of national statesman also had its drawbacks. The most serious was that it reinforced Webster's predilection for a style of politics that placed a premium on personal reputation and individual accomplishments. Such a style made sense in the light of Webster's conservative outlook, which exalted the independent statesman, unfettered by party ties. But parties and partisanship were on the rise in the United States of the 1830s, and Webster's personal leadership made him seem too unreliable to the general voting public and professional politicians. In the very hour of his greatest triumph, Webster was laying the ground for future defeats.

Webster's first experiment with above-party politics came shortly after the War of 1812. He was quick to realize that the conclusion of the war had placed the Federalists in a hopeless minority position, and that they could only hope to exert much influence through an amalgamation with the Republicans. Unfortunately for Webster and his party, Monroe was willing to accept a fusion arrangement only on Republican terms. He welcomed the support of Federalists, but would not favor them with appointments to office.[44] By 1824, things had changed. The Federalists were even weaker than before, but the Republican party had broken up into factions supporting four different presidential candidates. Anticipating an indecisive vote in the electoral college, Webster advised his Federalist colleagues to remain neutral in the election so that they could play a pivotal role in a presidential contest in the House. Events transpired as Webster had predicted, and he played a key role in securing some of the Federalist support which helped elect John Quincy Adams.[45]

Webster's triumph soon soured. To be sure, Adams shared his desire for a nonpartisan administration and did not discriminate against Federalists in his appointments policy. Webster himself attained great influence as one of the administration's spokesmen in the House of Representatives and (beginning in 1827) the Senate. But because of Adams' political ineptitude and his disdain for even the rudiments of party discipline, his administration was a disaster. Adams' defeat in 1828 should have been a lesson in the irrelevance of nonpartisan, consensual political ideals. Instead, Webster attributed the loss to "private disagreements and individual personalities." He became, along with Clay, a leader of the new National Republican party, but reconciled himself to the role of partisan spokesman by condemning the Jacksonians as factious partisans. Still underestimating the strength of party loyalty, Webster believed that the Democratic coalition would collapse quickly because it was based on devotion to a magnetic leader. This did not happen, and the Democrats' strength made it imperative that the opposition close ranks. But Webster chafed under the weight of party discipline, especially when it required that he subordinate his ambitions to those of Henry Clay. In 1831, his spirits buoyed by the response to his Second Reply to Hayne, Webster tried to promote himself as an anti-administration presidential candidate. Knowing that Clay, a Freemason, would never be accepted by the Antimasons, he wrote to Charles Miner, an Antimasonic leader in Pennsylvania, suggesting that the National Republicans and Antimasons might unite behind a non-Masonic presidential candidate. Miner jumped at the hint, and replied that Webster would be an ideal "Union" choice. But the National Republicans were intent on nominating Clay, and nothing came of Webster's scheme.[46]

His "union" plan having collapsed, Webster was confined to the role of mouthpiece for the National Republicans. He continued to condemn the Democrats for blind partisanship, opposed Van Buren's nomination as ambassador to Great Britain, and joined Clay in pressing Nicholas Biddle to request the recharter of the national bank in 1832. He denounced Jackson's veto message as a demagogic document that was contemptuous of Congress, evoked class hatred, and lacked logical power or appeal to "respectable" men. Sensing, however, the great popularity of Jackson's message condemning the bank, Webster feared that his antiveto speech was "too *forensic*" for a mass audience.[47]

The fury of Webster's phillipic against the bank veto might have led some to think he had become a loyal partisan. It was not so. Webster was still enamored of the idea of creating a "Union party." He revived this project shortly after the 1832 elections, prompted by the nullification crisis. Throughout the winter of 1832–33, Webster worked hand in glove with his old nemesis Andrew Jackson to help put down the rebels in South Carolina. At a December 1832 meeting in Faneuil Hall, he praised Jackson's vigorously nationalistic proclamation to the people of that state. In Congress, he opposed any concessions on the tariff to propitiate the nullifiers, and he served as Senate floor leader for the administration's Revenue Collection ("Force") Bill. When Calhoun enunciated the theory of nullification in the Senate, it was Webster who, after some prodding by Jackson, delivered the most eloquent response.[48]

Despite Webster's efforts, the nullification controversy was settled on terms that were not to his satisfaction. Webster considered the compromise tariff an unjustified concession to South Carolina—in effect, a reward for its bad behavior—and it estranged him from Clay. Furthermore, he did not think that the settlement had conclusively ended the threat of nullification. In the spring of 1833 Webster believed that the nullifiers were hatching new disunionist plots, and he hoped that the issue of the Union would help to unite his supporters with Jackson's. There were, as it turned out, opportunities for Webster and Jackson to flatter each other's self-esteem. Webster induced his friends in the Massachusetts legislature to officially invite Jackson to the Bay State. The President accepted, and his tour became a personal triumph largely because the senator had arranged a favorable reception. While Jackson toured Massachusetts, Webster made a journey through the West, where he found unionist sentiment strong and Jacksonian politicians personally congenial. In July, Webster met with former Secretary of State Edward Livingston, soon to leave the country as the new minister to France. At the time, some believed that Livingston, speaking for Jackson, offered Webster a high post in the administration, perhaps even at the cabinet level. This is unlikely, but it is certain that Livingston expressed Jackson's thanks for Webster's help in the nullification crisis.[49]

Webster's coalition idea, however, did not reckon with the intensity of Jackson's antipathy for the Bank of the United States or the power of

Democratic party loyalties. Although Jackson decided in early 1833 that the government would no longer deposit its funds in the U.S. bank, he delayed the announcement of this decision until September. Webster feared that Jackson might take this step, but throughout the spring of 1833, he indulged the vain hope that it might be avoided.[50] Even after Jackson ordered the removal of the deposits, Webster tried to arrange a compromise with the administration. When the Senate convened on December 12, 1833, the anti-administration forces constituted a clear majority. However, Webster and nine other opposition senators (seven of whom were from New England) voted with the Democrats to delay the scheduled vote on committee assignments until December 16. Felix Grundy, senator from Tennessee, met with Jackson to relay Webster's offer of a bargain: administration support of a bill to recharter the bank for five years, in exchange for help in organizing the Senate committees. Vice President Van Buren was present at the meeting, and argued forcefully against the proposed arrangement. He declared that an association with so staunch a Federalist as Webster would blur party lines and confuse the party faithful; so, too, would any compromise on the bank issue. Apparently swayed by these arguments, Jackson instructed Grundy to turn Webster down. Webster thus had no choice but to join the incipient Whig party. His reward was the chairmanship of the Senate Finance Committee.[51]

Webster remained a staunch Whig throughout the period 1834–40. He found, however, that party fidelity did not bring him the prize he craved so badly. He wanted the nomination in 1836, but his chances collapsed after a convention of Pennsylvania Antimasons passed over him in favor of William Henry Harrison. Webster was thereafter reduced to being the Whig candidate in only his home state.[52] Webster again sought the nomination for the 1840 race, but his candidacy never caught fire, and he withdrew in June 1839 while on a tour of Europe. Nevertheless, he helped determine the eventual nominee by preventing Clay from gaining early commitments from New England delegates to the Whig national convention. When the Whigs met, Webster's former supporters helped swing the nomination to Harrison.[53]

Webster's reward for his services to the Whig cause was his appointment as Secretary of State by Harrison. From this post, Webster apparently hoped to consolidate a position of party leadership independent of Clay, and perhaps establish himself as Harrison's heir apparent. When Clay and Harrison fell out over the issue of calling a special session of Congress, Webster was the natural beneficiary of the President's ire against the assertive Kentuckian. In his appointments policy, Harrison consistently favored Webster's recommendations over those of Clay.[54] Harrison's death badly dispirited Webster, for he feared that the new President, John Tyler, would be an instrument of Clay. It turned out otherwise. Tyler bristled at Clay's attempt to commit him to a scheme for a powerful new national bank, and gave his tacit support to a more modest proposal devised by Secretary of the Treasury Thomas Ewing. Webster sided with the President, promoting support for the Ewing bill through private correspondence and anonymous editorials in the *National Intelligencer*, the semiofficial organ of the Whig party. When Clay and his supporters pushed their own bill through Congress, Webster, who feared a party blow-up, joined the other members of the cabinet in urging Tyler to sign the bank bill. But the President rejected his advice.[55]

After Tyler vetoed the bank bill on August 16, Webster worked hard to prevent a split between the President and the congressional Whigs. At a cabinet meeting on August 18, Webster and Ewing asked Tyler what type of bank he would find acceptable. They extracted the outlines of a plan for a national bank centered in Washington, with unlimited power to create branches in the states. However, the bank would not have the power to discount promissory notes, which Tyler feared would enable it to corrupt state politicians. The President then asked the two secretaries to see Senator John MacPherson Berrien of Georgia and Congressman John Sergeant of Pennsylvania, chairmen of their respective houses' finance committees. Tyler instructed Ewing and Webster to tell the two what sort of bank bill would, "in their opinion," receive the presidential signature. However, they were not to profess to speak in Tyler's behalf or to commit him to any specific plan. Ewing and Webster followed the President's instructions. Shortly before a new bank bill embodying the President's suggestions was submitted to Congress, Webster met with Tyler to review the proposal. Tyler suggested two changes which were readily accepted by the Whigs in Congress: the bank was to be known euphemistically as a "fiscal agency" (the "bank" title now had bad connotations), and its capital was to be less than Ewing and Webster had proposed.[56]

A bank bill which incorporated Tyler's suggestions was introduced in

the House on August 20. While Congress debated the bill, Tyler chafed
under attacks from the Clay Whigs for his veto of the first bank proposal
and began to resent claims that he was pledged to sign the new bill as a
party measure. On August 23 he appeared at Webster's office and
complained at length of congressional insults to his dignity and
independence. The next day he asked for Webster's help in securing a
delay of further consideration of the bank bill. Webster, whose political
fortunes were by then closely tied to those of the President, agreed. He
wrote a public letter asking Massachusetts senators Isaac Bates and Rufus
Choate to help secure a postponement. But it was too late. The bank bill
had already passed the House, and the Whig senators decided to force
Tyler's hand. The President responded with another veto.[57]

Tyler's clashes with Congress over the bank issue illustrated one of the
fundamental weaknesses of the Whig party, its inability to define a
positive role for the presidency in its relations with the legislative branch.
They also demonstrated how the Whigs' condemnations of party
regimentation brought into their ranks men such as Tyler, who would
not submit to even a minimal degree of partisan direction. But to the
overwhelming majority of the Whigs' national leaders, Tyler's obligation
with regard to the second bank bill was clear. The measure was the
keystone of the party's program for economic recovery, and Tyler was
duty bound to sign it. Accordingly, the second bank bill caused a furor.
Tyler was repudiated by a meeting of the Whig caucus, and every
member of the cabinet except Webster resigned. In a public letter
explaining his reasons for remaining in the administration, Webster
claimed that the cabinet resignations only made matters worse for the
party and that there was still a chance of enacting a new bank bill in the
next session of Congress. More, he shared Tyler's views in his special
area of responsibility, foreign policy. These reasons were plausible to a
degree, but political considerations certainly influenced Webster's
decision to stay. He undoubtedly did not want to sacrifice his independent position in the party to the leadership of Clay. Indeed, it is likely
that he saw the whole bank affair as a scheme by Clay to isolate and
embarrass both himself and the President. Tyler saw it that way, and was
determined to have his revenge on "Prince Hal." In an interview on
September 11, Webster asked Tyler: "Where am I to go, Mr. President?"
Tyler's response was noncommital: "You must decide that for yourself,
Mr. Webster." Webster, interpreting this as an invitation to stay, replied:

"If you leave it to me . . . I will stay where I am." Tyler then sprang forward and said: "Give me your hand on that, and . . . I will say to you that Henry Clay is a doomed man from this hour."[58]

Webster's decision to stay in the cabinet was a political gamble. One source of satisfaction for him was that he had the support of the Whigs in his home state. But even they made it clear that Webster should remain only until he had negotiated a settlement of the disputed northeastern boundary between the United States and Canada. Robert C. Winthrop, an important Massachusetts Whig, warned Webster that he should not "permanently" tie himself to the President, for it was clear that Tyler would eventually meet with the *"disesteem"* of all the Whigs.[59] Webster had different plans. He hoped to use his position in the administration to promote his personal popularity and perhaps encourage a realignment of the parties. Now that the administration was isolated from the most partisan Whigs, he wanted to rally to its side those independents who deplored the excesses of "partisanship." Thus, in an editorial he appealed to "the great community of American Freemen" to judge the President's acts "free from the malign influences of party spirit."[60]

Webster knew that rhetoric alone would not bring the administration popular support. He and the President would have to establish a record of substantial accomplishments. When Congress convened again in December 1841, Tyler submitted his own bank plan for its approval. This so-called "exchequer," which Webster helped devise, was designed to meet the desires of men who believed in the need for a central financial institution but feared the powers that might repose in a new national bank. The exchequer would not have a charter, and its affairs were to be supervised by an independent board of commissioners. Congress was to be free to expand or contract its operations; however, it would not be able to make loans or engage in commercial speculations.[61]

While Congress considered the exchequer, Webster worked hard in his own sphere, diplomacy. His greatest accomplishment was a settlement of the boundary dispute with Canada. The importance Webster attached to this agreement is indicated by the morally questionable means he employed to achieve it. Early in his talks with the British envoy, Lord Ashburton, he accepted as a basis for the negotiations a map of dubious authenticity which had been discovered in the Paris archives. This map had a red line which supposedly demarcated the U.S.-

Canadian boundary agreed to by the American and English negotiators in 1783. After a treaty had been drafted, Webster gave some State Department money to a shady adventurer, F. O. J. ("Fog") Smith, with which he was to bribe the editors of several newspapers in Maine who were critical of the proposed settlement.[62]

Tyler and Webster learned, to their pain, that party lines were not to be scrambled so easily as they hoped. Although it had the support of some Democrats and anti-Clay Whigs, the exchequer scheme was buried in committee. When it finally came up for a vote in Congress in 1843, it was defeated by a wide margin. Similarly, the Webster-Ashburton Treaty, which passed the Senate by a large margin, did not bring Webster a large popular following. Many Democrats, led by Lewis Cass, denounced it as unduly favorable to Great Britain. As word leaked out of some of the shady methods Webster had used to secure approval of the treaty, it became a personal embarrassment for him. A congressional investigation cleared Webster of culpable wrongdoing, but the information it collected damaged his reputation.[63]

Ignoring the entreaties of his Whig friends in Massachusetts, Webster decided to remain in the cabinet after he completed the negotiations with Ashburton. He could not rejoin the Whigs without submitting to Clay's leadership, which would have been humiliating after the events of 1841. Webster read the returns of the 1842 elections, in which the Whigs did poorly, as a vindication of his position. The Whigs even lost the governorship of Massachusetts, normally staunchly Whig, and Webster attributed this result to the state party's endorsement of Clay for President at its September convention. Webster therefore saw reason to hope that a realignment of parties might yet occur. Supposing that "the Whig Party may be regarded as now broken up," he predicted that a "vast portion of the moderate & disinterested" in both parties would "join in support of the President."[64]

Instead, party lines held. More, Tyler's plans did not coincide with Webster's. Tyler wanted to be elected to the presidency in his own right, and when his independent stance failed to attract a large popular constituency, he began to woo the Democrats. This estranged him from Webster, who did not like Tyler's appointment of large numbers of Democratic partisans to positions in the State Department. There were other causes of friction. Tyler resented what he saw as Webster's attempts to take credit for the exchequer plan, and Webster did not share Tyler's desire for the annexation of Texas. In February 1843 Tyler let it be known through an intermediary that he wanted Webster to resign; he expected "*nothing*" from the Whigs, and the continued presence of "Black Dan" in the cabinet prevented him from "massing" the support of Democrats. Webster tried to secure from Tyler an appointment as minister to England, which would have removed him from the cabinet with a minimum of public embarrassment. But Edward Everett, who held that post, refused to step aside. On May 8, 1843 Webster offered his resignation, and it was accepted by Tyler.[65]

Still, Webster hoped to carve an independent niche in American politics. On May 18 he delivered an extraordinary speech in Baltimore, in which he broached a plan for reciprocal tariff reductions with Great Britain. This plan was an outgrowth of a project Webster had suggested to Tyler when he was still in the State Department. The reciprocal tariff agreement was to induce Great Britain to use its influence to persuade Mexico to cede northern California in return for the American government's assumption of Mexico's foreign debts. In addition, the United States would treat Great Britain liberally in the negotiations over the Oregon boundary. This elaborate plan was aimed at several large constituencies: merchants who wanted lower duties, western annexationists who wanted California, and holders of Mexican debts. Tyler, however, was more interested in the acquisition of Texas, and threw cold water on Webster's proposals.[66]

His grand diplomatic scheme having been repudiated by the President, Webster decided that his only hope for a political future was with the Whigs. But he wanted his reunion to be managed gracefully. Fortunately for Webster, the situation was favorable. The Whigs of Massachusetts were still hurting from their defeat in 1842 and were eager to accept him back in return for his help on the stump. Accordingly, in September 1843 Webster made a speech at Andover in which he signified his return to party orthodoxy by reiterating traditional Whig positions on the tariff, internal improvements, and banking. By December Webster was offering Clay his assistance in the approaching presidential election.[67]

[III]

Clay's defeat in 1844 was a decisive check to the Whigs' drive for economic consolidation. More, the Polk administration embarked upon

a course of territorial aggrandizement which would make slavery the
dominant issues in American politics. This shift in the political agenda
created immense difficulties for Webster. Slavery presented him with the
problem of reconciling his devotion to the preservation of the Union
with the values of a free society—openness, liberty, and social mobility.
Webster struggled manfully to resolve this problem on terms that would
be acceptable to a majority of Americans in both the North and the
South. His failure to do so was symptomatic of the crisis the slavery issue
created for conservative northern Whigs, torn between their commitment to a free society and their dedication to the maintenance of social
harmony within the framework of the nation-state.

Webster began his political career as a harsh critic of the "peculiar
institution." He denounced slavery as a blight on society, opposed the
Missouri Compromise because it did not exclude slavery from the entire
West, and condemned the African slave trade. What is most significant
about these early antislavery actions of Webster is that they did not arise
from egalitarianism or humanitarianism. With his belief in an hierarchical society, Webster had no desire for sweeping changes in
American social arrangements; he tolerated slavery (though he did not
like it) as part of the system of stratification. What Webster did object to
was the disproportionate political power which slavery gave the South
and the party dominating southern politics, the Jeffersonian Republicans. In 1804 he endorsed a proposed constitutional amendment to
repeal the clause which allowed slaves to be counted as three-fifths of a
person for purposes of apportionment. Webster asked, with a facetious-
ness that suggests a lack of deep moral revulsion, why property in slaves
should be represented when that in cattle was not?[68]

As Webster's conservatism was transformed in the 1820s and 1830s, so
was his position on slavery. The change was twofold. On the one hand,
Webster was obliged to condemn slavery even more aggressively, for
slavery was incompatible with the America of openness and opportunity
he celebrated in his speeches. Slavery was a relic of the past, a denial of
every man's freedom to rise or fall according to his capacities. On the
other hand, Webster had exalted the preservation of the Union as the
highest good. Hence, Webster had to reassure the South that he would
not support attacks upon its institutions which violated the Constitution
and might lead to the dissolution of the Union. The Second Reply to
Hayne was a hallmark in Webster's articulation of his new position on

slavery. Hayne charged him with having attacked slavery, but Webster protested, "I did not utter a single word which any ingenuity could torture into an attack on the slavery of the South." Webster confessed that he shared the North's view that slavery was "one of the greatest evils, both moral and political." However, he would leave the question of how to deal with it to "those whose right and duty it is to inquire and to decide"—namely, the people of the southern states. Webster made one sacrifice of his earlier antislavery views on the altar of national harmony. He would no longer "countenance" changing the three-fifths clause of the Constitution—"it is the original bargain, the compact; let it stand."[69]

There were limits, nonetheless, as to how far Webster would go to conciliate the South. He did not, for example, approve of the suppression of basic constitutional freedoms simply to assuage the ire of southerners angered by abolitionists. Webster declared that Congress was legally "bound" to receive abolitionist petitions so long as they requested measures which were "clearly" constitutional, including the abolition of both slavery and the slave trade in the District of Columbia. It was his position that, if they were worded courteously, such petitions should be "respectfully" received and read, and referred to the appropriate congressional committee. Webster added that, in his judgment, the North was "unanimous" in its opposition to interfering with slavery within the states, but "perhaps equally unanimous" in the belief that it would be constitutional to abolish slavery in the nation's capital. In any case, public opinion must be allowed to express itself in a free society. It was not "the part of prudence," Webster warned, to reject petitions from those whose real motives were "less than praiseworthy"—i.e., those who wanted to interfere with slavery in the states. To do so would give such petitioners just cause to complain that they had been treated unfairly.[70]

Webster's position on the petition question was not without its elements of political calculation. Webster seems to have perceived that political antislavery was on the rise in the 1830s, and that the petition issue had given the abolitionist movement some respectability by tying its cause to that of free speech. In January 1838 he ventured the opinion that "the Anti Slavery feeling is growing stronger and stronger every day. . . . " While he avowed that he would not accept anything that would violate the rights of the states or slaveholders, he declared that "it is our policy, in my opinion, most clearly, not to yield the substantial truth, for the sake of conciliating those whom we can never conciliate, at the expense of the loss of the friendship & support of those great masses of good men, who are interested in the Anti-Slavery cause."[71]

But the petition question was of transitory importance, and it did not fundamentally affect the relationship between the North and South. The issue of the expansion of slavery presented Webster with a sterner test. By the very nature of his ideological position, Webster had to oppose the expansion of slavery. With his commitment to an economy based on free labor, he could not support any measure which might tend to perpetuate slavery and increase the political power of slaveholders. In more immediate and practical terms, Webster feared that congressmen from new slave states would oppose the national economic legislation he wanted so badly, particularly a protective tariff. However, Webster did not want to estrange the South, which might strain the Union and harm his chances for the presidency. Accordingly, he constantly reassured southerners that he did not regard their section as a subordinate part of the country and that he would oppose any attack upon slavery within the states.

Webster first fully articulated this position in 1837. At the time there was much talk of annexing the newly formed Republic of Texas. Webster spoke forcefully against such a step, declaring that it would contribute to the enlargement of slave territory in the United States, something no American should desire. But he also took pains to assure the South that he had no desire to meddle with its domestic institutions. When Texas reemerged as an issue in the 1840s, Webster played an important part in the controversy. During his stint as Secretary of State, Tyler and Waddy Thompson, the presidential representative to Mexico, had expressed interest in annexing the Lone Star Republic. Webster gave their proposals a cold reception. While visiting Washington in January 1844, Webster learned from his successor in the State Department, Abel Upshur, that the administration was negotiating to acquire Texas. Disturbed, Webster proceeded to muster public opposition. He persuaded Joseph Gales to run anti-annexation editorials in his *National Intelligencer*. Webster also induced several friends to introduce in the Massachusetts legislature resolutions condemning the expansion of slavery.[72]

Having helped arouse opposition to Texas annexation, Webster tried to make political capital of the issue. He realized that Texas was the fulcrum with which he could restore himself to a pivotal role in the Whig party after his flirtation with Tyler and third-party politics. In Massachusetts, the annexation question prompted the formation of a faction of Whigs who categorically opposed the acquisition of Texas, the so-called Young Whigs. The beliefs of these men clashed with those of the dominant Whig faction, led by Webster's nemesis, Abbot Lawrence. Lawrence and his followers did not want to agitate Texas for fear that doing so would harm the presidential candidacy of Henry Clay. Webster exploited the Texas issue to gain the favor of the Young Whigs and to create for himself a major role in the inner councils of the Massachusetts party. The defeat of the Texas treaty in the Senate (June 8, 1844) temporarily blunted the edges of the annexation question. Nevertheless, Webster emphasized it, and its implications for the future of slavery, as he stumped the North for Henry Clay in the fall of 1844.[73]

Clay's defeat by the annexationist Polk guaranteed that Texas would remain an important issue. It was also a blow to the Lawrence faction, which had worked energetically for Clay's nomination and election. Determined to exploit the favorable political situation, Webster encouraged the Whig majority in the Massachusetts House of Representatives to reaffirm its opposition to the expansion of slavery. He also helped plan an anti-Texas meeting at Faneuil Hall in January 1845. Webster's success at reestablishing himself as a Whig leader was confirmed in the same month, when the state legislature elected him to the United States Senate. Despite Webster's objections, the resolution annexing Texas passed the Senate. But Webster agreed with the Young Whigs that the acquisition should be opposed to the bitter end. When Texas applied for formal entry into the Union in December 1845, Webster was among the diehard opponents of its admission.[74]

Although Webster spearheaded the anti-Texas movement, his anti-annexationism differed sharply from that of the Young Whigs. The Young Whigs saw opposition to slavery's expansion as part of a thoroughgoing attack on southern society and institutions. They believed that the enlargement of slave territory was the only way the "slave power" could continue to dominate and oppress the nonslaveholders of the South. If slavery were contained in a fixed area, the slave population would grow too large to be supported and controlled by its owners. It would then have to be freed by the slaveholders, who would thereby lose the basis of their disproportionate economic and political power in the South.[75] But Webster, with his regard for things established, had no desire to undermine the position of the slaveholding elite, many of whom were Whigs. Webster also feared that attacks on the South would endanger the southern Whigs' support for nationalistic economic legislation and jeopardize his attempts to promote himself as the Whig presidential candidate in 1848.[76]

Webster's differences with the Young Whigs were clearly defined in the political controversies created by the Mexican War. Webster opposed the war, which he said had been provoked deliberately by Polk. But he refused to agree with the "Conscience Whigs"—the new name assumed by Massachusetts' antislavery Whigs—that steps should be taken to stop the American war effort. Webster rejected the Conscience Whigs' argument that supplies should not be sent to American troops because the continuation of the war might lead to the acquisition of territory from Mexico. No matter how improper the war may have been, it was the duty of the responsible statesman to stand by the country's fighting men. Neither did Webster join in the Conscience Whigs' condemnations of the war as the outcome of a plot to extend slave territory. When strongly worded antislavery resolutions were introduced at the Massachusetts Whig convention in September 1846, Webster appeared arm in arm with his old foe Abbot Lawrence to argue against their passage.[77]

In Congress, Webster tried to pursue a course that would satisfy his antiwar constituents without alienating the South. He attacked the Mexican War primarily on legal and constitutional grounds, saying that Polk had used questionable means to draw the United States into the conflict. He denied charges that the war was the result of a "slave power conspiracy." When the Wilmot Proviso was first debated in the Senate, Webster remained silent. But he was vocal in his support of the proposal by Senator John MacPherson Berrien of Georgia that the United States renounce all possible territorial acquisitions from Mexico. Webster's argument for the "no territory" policy was largely philosophical: the country was large enough, and territorial expansion might tear it apart. There were distinct political advantages for Webster in supporting Berrien's proposal. By sidestepping the issue of slavery's expansion, it promised the best of two worlds: Webster could claim that "no territory" prevented the enlargement of slave lands without suggesting that the South was an inferior part of the Union. Nonetheless, Berrien's plan did not prevail. With the failure of the "no territory" stratagem, Webster felt compelled to vote for the more controversial Wilmot Proviso. However, he continued to oppose territorial expansion, and voted against the Treaty of Guadalupe Hidalgo, which ended the Mexican War and brought the United States vast new lands.[78]

Webster's moderation did not prevent the polarization of Whig politics in his home state. The Conscience Whigs remained adamantly opposed to the war, territorial expansion, and slavery. The Lawrence faction—dubbed "Cotton Whigs" by their foes because of their support by textile industrialists—wanted to maintain close and cooperative relations with the southern Whigs. Webster's presidential candidacy was a casualty of the hostility between the two sides. The Conscience Whigs gave Webster only lukewarm support, while Lawrence worked behind the scenes to subvert his candidacy. Webster received the support of both factions at the Whig national convention in 1848, but neither expected nor desired his nomination. Lawrence wanted Webster's support for his vice presidential candidacy on a ticket headed by Zachary Taylor, while the Conscience forces were seeking his backing in case they bolted the convention. Neither group got what it wanted. Taylor was chosen as the Whig candidate for President, but Lawrence was passed over for the second spot in favor of Millard Fillmore. Taylor's nomination prompted the Conscience Whigs to leave the convention and join the Free Soil party, but Webster did not follow them. After a lengthy period of public silence, he sullenly "acquiesced" in the nomination of Taylor.[79]

[IV]

Taylor's victory in the election left Webster in a rather isolated position within the Whig party. The Cotton Whigs were clearly in control of things in Massachusetts, as Abbot Lawrence was given control over the state's federal patronage. And the Conscience Whigs, with whom Webster had worked to undercut Lawrence's influence, were now mostly located in another party. Webster tried to bypass the state Whig leadership through direct meetings with the President, but found that this did not work. Although Taylor was "pleasant and conversable," he was also headstrong. Webster's lack of influence in the administration became painfully evident when he tried to secure for his son Fletcher an appointment as federal district attorney for Boston. Despite his energetic efforts, the post was given to George Lunt, an ally of Lawrence.[80]

Webster's estrangement from the Taylor administration provides a necessary backdrop for explaining his actions in the crisis of 1850. This is not to say that his differences with the President "caused" his behavior; it is clear, though, that the political situation inclined Webster to act independently of the administration. Like Clay, he had little reason to support the policies of a man who had, in effect, repudiated his guidance. But through support of an intersectional compromise, both Webster and Clay could hope to recover some of their lost preeminence and help restore the Senate as the center of power in the Whig party.

There were other factors which inclined Webster to favor compromise. He had always been amenable to a pragmatic and flexible approach to the problem of the expansion of slavery. So long as it seemed that slavery *would not* enter the territories, Webster did not care much about the methods that might be used to keep it out. Webster's pragmatism, in turn, reflected his own lack of deep moral outrage at the evils of slavery. One reason some men were adamant over the extension issue was that they were so revolted by slavery that they *had* to feel it was being checked somewhere. Unable, for constitutional reasons, to impose limits upon slavery within the states, they projected their moral animus into the debate over its presence in the national domain.[81] Webster, however, did not share such moral urgency. Indeed, one of his major complaints throughout the crisis of 1850 was that the lengthy debates over slavery were preventing the consideration of tariff legislation.[82]

Perhaps the most important factor which predisposed Webster to favor compromise was his deep temperamental conservatism. To Webster, unlike the free soilers in the Whig party, slavery was essentially an institutional problem, to be resolved by gradual means that would not upset the social order. The Union was a necessary means to preserve American liberties within a framework of order. Webster could therefore support compromise as an immediate necessity to secure the long-range ends the Union would bring, including the eradication of slavery. In a letter to the Reverend William Henry Furness, Webster wrote that he could not "cooperate in breaking up a social and political system, on the warmth, rather than the strength of a hope that, in such convulsion, the cause of emancipation may be promoted." Slavery would be abolished,

Webster predicted, by "the mild influences of Christianity, the softening and melting power of the Sun of righteousness" rather than "the storms and tempests of heated controversy."[83]

Webster did not want to offend the large numbers of free soilers among the northern Whigs. He would act only under the press of urgency, when men began to look to him for a sense of direction. When Clay visited him on the evening of January 21, 1850, he agreed "in substance" with the Kentuckian's plan, which he believed "ought to be satisfactory" to both the North and South. The Wilmot Proviso, he declared, was "no shibboleth" for him.[84] Yet for the next six weeks, while opinion polarized for or against Clay's plan, Webster remained publicly silent. Throughout most of this period he was confident that the Union was safe and that California would be admitted as a free state without difficulty. He would speak only if—and when—he was needed.[85]

The event which seems to have precipitated Webster into action came on February 23. That day, in an interview with Alexander Stephens and Robert Toombs, President Taylor apparently spurned all suggestions of compromise. When the two Georgians declared that the South would rebel against any federal attempt to prevent Texas from laying claim to part of New Mexico, Taylor threatened to hang them as traitors. This shocked southern congressmen, especially those who were Whigs, for it indicated that the President was implacably opposed to concessions to the South. After talking with several southern politicians who had heard about Taylor's tirade, Webster wrote to his son that he was "broken with anxiety." By March 1 he was prepared to deliver a major address to present his views.[86]

Webster's famous speech of March 7, 1850, was, above all, an attempt to strike a balance between conflicting points of view. By achieving such an equipoise, Webster hoped to articulate a position acceptable to a nationwide constituency. The speech began with Webster adopting the familiar persona of the statesman standing above sectional strife: "Mr. President, I wish to speak today not as a Massachusetts man, not as a Northern man, but as an American. . . . I speak today for the preservation of the Union. 'Hear me for my cause.' " In the first part of his address, Webster tried to reduce the emotional intensity of the debate over slavery with a plea for moderation and mutual forbearance. His rhetorical strategy was to discuss slavery as a matter of institutions, laws, and customs rather than as a question of absolute principles. Webster

pointed out that slavery had existed "from time immemorial"—among
the ancient Jews, Greeks, and Romans—and that Jesus and his apostles
had not spoken against it. All this he saw as proof that slavery had deep
historical roots, and that its abolition could not come through a radical
break with the past. Webster thus rebuked those who were "too
impatient to wait for the slow progress of moral causes in the
improvement of mankind." Men forgot that it had taken eighteen
hundred years for Christianity to spread its beneficent influence across
the western world.[87]

Applied to the United States, the historical analysis counseled modesty
on the part of both the critics and defenders of slavery. At the time the
Constitution was adopted, there had been "no diversity" of views on
slavery; South as well as North, all Americans agreed it was an evil. No
provision had been made for its abolition because the Founding Fathers
had believed it would be abandoned eventually as uneconomical and
inefficient. But the invention of the cotton gin, which made possible
large-scale cotton cultivation, had reversed the tide of history and proved
them wrong. As slavery had spread in the South it was being abandoned
in the North, causing the polarization of sectional opinions on the
institution. The North, basing its economy upon free labor, now
condemned it as a terrible social blight, while an increasing number of
southerners praised it as a "positive good."[88]

Having brought the discussion of slavery down to his own day,
Webster next addressed the most pressing issue: how should the country
deal with the possible existence of slavery in the Mexican Cession? Here,
Webster urged submission to the will of God, which worked fortuitously
in favor of freedom. He argued that African slavery "as we regard it" was
excluded by natural causes from California and New Mexico. It was a
"fixed fact" he declared, that both areas were "destined to be free"
because their arid and mountainous topography would make slave labor
unprofitable. (An unstated—and invalid—assumption of Webster's
argument here was that slavery was only suitable for large-scale
cultivation of staple crops.) Accordingly, Webster declared, he would not
vote for the Wilmot Proviso, which would "uselessly . . . reaffirm an
ordinance of nature" and "reenact the will of God." Given the mandate
of Divinity, which was far more authoritative than any human law, he
would put in no law "for the mere purpose of a taunt or reproach"; its
only function, in current circumstances, would be "to wound the pride

of the South." He would favor positive legislative bars on the spread of slavery only where they promised to accomplish some "substantive good."[89]

Webster's position on the Mexican Cession was designed to appeal to men in both sections. To the North, Webster said that nature and fate were on the side of free soil; to the South, that he would not insult its civilization through demeaning national legislation. Webster next tried to balance the grievances of the sections against each other. He conceded that the South had the right to complain about abolitionist attacks and the inadequate enforcement of the constitutional clause which required the return of fugitive slaves. The first complaint could not be dealt with through legislation, as free speech was protected by the Constitution. The second could, and Webster pledged his support for a more effective fugitive slave law. The North, too, had its legitimate grievances. It had the right to complain of the practice southern seaports had of imprisoning black seamen from northern ships. The South, Webster warned, should take steps to remedy this wrong. More important, northerners were properly appalled at those southerners who attacked the free labor system and claimed that slaves were better off than northern workingmen. Such assertions Webster dismissed as utter nonsense. No men were more upright than the free laborers of the North. On this matter of opinion, however, there could be no redress through the law. One could hope only to "allay the agitation, and cultivate a better feeling."[90]

In his conclusion, Webster suggested, as he had in the past, that the Union was the only security for American peace and prosperity. Declaring that he heard talk of "peaceable secession" with "distress and anguish," Webster compared it to the notion that the planets could leave their orbits without causing a cosmic "convulsion." Peaceful disunion was an "utter impossibility," for the North and South could never agree on how to divide up the army, navy, and public lands. Moreover, the attendant loss of central authority would result in a *"two-fold* war," in which not only the sections, but the slaves and their masters, would be pitted against each other. Webster exhorted all Americans to escape from the darkness of disunionism in favor of the sunlight of liberty and Union.[91]

The March 7 speech met with a massive response. Webster reported that he franked out thousands of copies to meet the public demand, and thousands more were printed and distributed by some of his wealthy supporters. If Webster's correspondence is any guide, he did succeed at defining a position whose appeal transcended sectional lines. A large number of conservative northern Whigs rallied to him. Webster, they wrote, had effectively rebuked the agitators and demagogues in both sections.[92] Webster also received much support from northern businessmen, many of whom had been threatened with a loss of orders from the South if the antislavery forces were not put down.[93] Perhaps most gratifying were the favorable responses his speech met with in the South. His southern correspondents echoed a common theme: Webster had strengthened the procompromise forces through his refusal to pander to antislavery "fanaticism." The March 7 speech apparently had such a moderating influence upon southern opinion that several historians have assigned it a major role in spiking the guns of the secessionist movement.[94]

Important representatives of religious opinion, especially in the more conservative Protestant denominations, also supported Webster's position. They shared Webster's view that those who would mitigate the wrongs of slavery must work within the established social order. Slavery was an integral part of the Christian tradition: the Bible did not condemn it, and the Mosaic code had made provision for it. The best way to deal with its evils was to follow the example of Moses and the ancient Hebrews, who had encouraged the religious education of slaves as a preparation for their gradual emancipation. The religious conservatives also agreed with Webster's criticism of those who advocated defiance of the obligation to return fugitive slaves. Such proponents of law-breaking had forgotten that Christ had enjoined civil obedience upon his followers and that Saint Paul had directed a runaway slave to return to his master. These examples showed that the individual, no matter how righteous his cause, must accept limitations on his conscience, for the alternative would be chaos. The truly good man sought to persuade others by good works and example, and tried to create the conditions for the gradual and peaceable change of institutions.[95]

The favorable responses of businessmen, southerners, and conservatives to Webster's arguments were predictable. But Webster's speech was also a bid for the sympathy of antislavery men, and in this respect it was a failure. The roots of this failure were ideological in nature. Webster's legalistic and melioristic philosophy of social change was ill suited to the temper of the most articulate critics of slavery. Mostly members of a younger generation, they did not share Webster's concern about the disintegration of a hierarchical society and felt less anguish over attacks upon established institutions. More comfortable with the individualistic ethos of entrepeneurial capitalism, they felt it most important to remove the fetters, both literal and figurative, on personal liberty. They were therefore unmoved by Webster's pleas for compromise and regarded his advocacy of a gradualistic approach to the problem of slavery as an abandonment of principle. Those who had confused Webster's views with their own struck at the Senator with particular ferocity, charging him with having elevated the rights of Mammon above those of humanity in the March 7 speech. Whittier described Webster as a fallen angel, Sumner compared him to a "fallen star," and Emerson wrote that his "understanding only works truly and with all its force when it stands for animal good; and that is for property."[96]

The individualistic premises of the antislavery intellectuals were also evident in the arguments of those who attacked the theological underpinnings of Webster's plea for compromise. Mostly members of the evangelical churches or the reform branch of the Unitarian movement, such men repudiated Webster's thesis that Christian teachings called for an ameliorative approach to the problem of American slavery. They declared that slavery in the United States in the mid-nineteenth century was far different from the human bondage described in the Bible. American slavery lacked the mitigating features of Hebraic slavery, which had required the religious training of all slaves and provided for their release from bondage after a specified period. American slaves were denied control over their persons, deprived of education and religious instruction, bought and sold without regard for the breaking up of families, and deprived of all the rewards of their labor. Worse yet, the morals of slaves declined because they were denied the civilizing effects of religious life and because their marriages were not sanctified. Domestic slavery also had deleterious effects on the morals of slaveholders, for it allowed them unrestricted access to their female slaves, whom they saw as objects for the indulgence of their sexual appetites.[97]

Webster's critics thus asserted that, because of its total assault on the individual personality, American slavery was not amenable to ameliorative remedies. This concern for the preservation of the integrity of the individual was evident, too, in the arguments of those who repudiated Webster's claim that Americans were morally obligated to help return fugitives from slavery. Some, using a phrase of William Seward, appealed to the "higher law" of God, which enjoined moral obligations transcending those of the Constitution.[98] Others distinguished between the injunction to obey the Constitution and the requirement to obey laws passed under its aegis. Men of this persuasion declared that the Constitution was (in the words of one of them) "a PRO-LIBERTY compact," and denied that there was a binding duty to obey laws (such as the Fugitive Slave Law) which were contrary to its essential meaning and purpose.[99] But no matter what their specific position, those who denounced Webster's arguments on religious grounds agreed that moral responsibility was ultimately an individual, not a collective matter. God would punish individuals for deliberate wrongdoing; so the duty of obedience did not absolve men of the obligation to act accordingly to the dictates of conscience.

Perhaps the most disturbing evidence of northern unhappiness over the March 7 speech was the response of Edward Everett. Everett was a faithful protégé of Webster, and he shared the Senator's abhorrence of sectional strife. When he wrote in a critical vein, Webster was bound to heed him. The import of Everett's letter was that Webster had gone too far to conciliate the South. Everett pointed out that the fugitive slave bill of Senator John Mason of Virginia, which many believed Webster had endorsed in his speech, would be unacceptable to the North. This was because the bill denied alleged fugitives the right to a jury trial in the state where they were apprehended. Everett's remarks did not go unheeded by Webster. In the pamphlet version of the March 7 speech, he revised his comments on the fugitive slave issue to suggest that he would support Mason's bill only if it were amended to his satisfaction. On June 3 he introduced amendments designed to meet the objections Everett had described. They were later moved by Senator Dayton of New Jersey, but lost, 11–27.[100]

Although Webster's speech provoked great furor and debate, it had notably little effect on his fellow members of the Senate. Of the northern Whigs in that body, only James Cooper of Pennsylvania, who was locked in a struggle with free soil Whigs in his state, endorsed Clay's compromise plan. It was not the power of Webster's rhetoric but the death of President Taylor on July 9 that helped shift the odds in favor of intersectional conciliation. The new President, Millard Fillmore, favored Clay's proposed settlement and chose a procompromise cabinet headed by Webster. From his new position as Secretary of State, Webster helped promote the passage of the compromise measures. When Fillmore needed a public message on the New Mexico boundary problem, Webster suggested that a carefully worded endorsement of the settlement should be inserted in the document. The President agreed, and Webster, in consultation with some friends, drafted the message accordingly.[101] Webster also acted to suppress the the anticompromise elements within the Whig party. He urged the President to deny patronage to free soil Whigs and saw to it that federal business was withdrawn from hostile party newspapers in his home state.[102]

Once the compromise bills were passed, Webster played an important role in ensuring the enforcement of the most controversial one, the Fugitive Slave Law. Although this law did not suit Webster's own convictions—it did not assure accused fugitives a jury trial in the state where they were captured—Webster was determined to see that it was observed. In his mind, enforcement of the law was a token of good faith to the South, a reassurance that its constitutional rights were being respected. Implementation of the law also accorded with Webster's political instincts. If he could associate opposition to the Fugitive Slave Law with law-breaking, he could muster additional support for the compromise among conservative northerners.[103]

Webster's focal role in the enforcement of the Fugitive Slave Law was also related to the measure's controversial status in Massachusetts. Boston had long been a refuge for fugitive slaves, some of whom had become respected citizens of the community. Furthermore, in 1842 the state legislature had passed a Personal Liberty Act which stated that Massachusetts would not aid in the return of fugitive slaves. But the Fugitive Slave Law created special federal commissioners to effectuate the capture and return of runaways, in effect bypassing the state law. This disturbed many citizens, who feared that their state might become a scene of slave-snatching.[104]

Webster, nevertheless, was determined to see that the law was upheld in Massachusetts. He was personally offended when respectable Bostonians prevented a black couple from being returned to their owner, and when an alleged fugitive was rescued outside a federal courtroom by free blacks and spirited outside the country. Webster insisted that such fugitives be captured, and he recruited some of the best legal talent of Massachusetts to help prosecute them. He also warned the uncooperative federal district attorney for Boston, George Lunt, that he was expected to bring in convictions. When another accused fugitive, Thomas Sims, was captured, Webster came to Boston to see that the law was prosecuted vigorously. In order to prevent Sims' seizure, the federal court house in Boston was guarded by three hundred police and surrounded by iron chains suspended several feet above the ground. Sims was tried, convicted, and sent back to his master.[105]

Webster's close association with the compromise and enforcement of the Fugitive Slave Law did not endear him to the strong antislavery element in the northern Whig party. Webster, however, did not believe that the hostility of members of his own party would require him to change allegiances. Rather than accept opposition from within the party, he hoped to remodel it to suit his own views. Disgusted by the free soil leanings of the Whigs in his own state, he asked Everett to make a speech at the Massachusetts Whig convention of September 1850 which would "nationalize" the state party. But the Massachusetts Whigs, who were hard pressed by a coalition of Democrats and Free Soilers, repudiated the Fugitive Slave Law in their platform.[106]

The strength of anticompromise sentiment among the Whigs in Massachusetts and other northern states did not lead Webster to revise his views. He believed that demagogues were agitating the issue to improve their political fortunes and that most Whigs would support his position if they were freed of such deceptive influences. From this he concluded that if the "nationalization" of the Whig party failed, the alternative would be the formation of a new national party, which would leave the disunionist agitators in a hopeless minority.[107] Webster first broached this idea in October 1850, prompted by his experience of cooperating with Democrats to help secure the passage of the compromise bills. After his failure to convert the Massachusetts Whigs, Webster took direct action to promote the creation of a new political coalition devoted to preserving the "finality" of the compromise. When the State Whigs nominated an anticompromise man, Robert C. Winthrop, as their candidate for the Senate in 1851, Webster repudiated their decision. More, he indicated to friendly Whigs that he would be willing to accept a Union Democrat as the new senator. But Charles Sumner, a Free Soiler, was elected to the Senate seat instead. Webster also tried to promote coalition politics in Connecticut and Pennsylvania, but was unsuccessful in both states.[108]

Still, Webster persisted in the Union party idea. At his urging, a Union convention met at Faneuil Hall in November 1851 to nominate him for the presidency. The meeting was a clear rebuke to the state Whig party, which had lost the last two elections in Massachusetts despite its embrace of antislavery principles. The platform of the convention appealed to the members of both major parties while it astutely avoided the issues which had traditionally divided them. Its only principles were fidelity to the Constitution and the law and acceptance of the "finality" of the compromise; a ticket headed by Webster was to be the vehicle for advancing them.[109] But the realignment anticipated by the convention never happened. As he had done so often in the past, Webster had badly underestimated the strength of party loyalties and overestimated the power of his own reputation. What is more, the Union plan was inherently flawed. Its premise was that the compromise measures were the chief issue in American politics. But because the measures functioned well, most men felt little urgency about taking special steps to guarantee their "finality." Contrariwise, if the settlement of 1850 had not succeeded in quelling sectional tension, support of it would not have been a political asset. In light of the compromise's evident—though hardly universal—success at muting the slavery issue, Webster and his cohort seemed hardly justified in their effort to make "finality" the fulcrum of American politics.[110]

When the bankruptcy of the Union party idea became apparent, Webster turned to pursuit of the Whig presidential nomination. Unfortunately for Webster, neither he nor his friends had learned any lessons from past defeats. They expected Webster to win at the Whig convention simply on the strength of his accomplishments and reputation. It came as rude shock to them that the first choice of the procompromise Whigs was not their man but President Fillmore. Neither did Webster and his proponents feel the need to develop a strong organization to woo delegates. Instead they distributed copies of the Secretary's speeches across the country, obviously in the faith that his rhetorical powers would win supporters. When this failed to make many converts, Webster attributed the problem not to outdated methods but to a lack of effort on the part of his supporters.[111]

The bitter harvest of the Webster campaign's failures was reaped at the

Whig convention. Webster received only 29 votes on the first ballot, while Fillmore had 133 and General Winfield Scott 132. Webster's support came almost entirely from New England, while Fillmore commanded virtually the whole vote of the South, and Scott enjoyed support from a preponderance of the northern delegates. Fillmore's presence in the race was itself evidence of Webster's political weakness. The President had been kept in the race, though somewhat reluctantly, because the southern Whigs thought he would be the strongest candidate in their section. Despite his championship of the compromise, Webster, with his Federalist background and New England origins, was not considered an "available" candidate by the southerners.[112]

Although his base of support was paltry, Webster hoped for victory. His strategists believed that he would emerge as a compromise choice when the Fillmore delegates saw that they could not carry New York and Scott's delegates realized that their man was unacceptable to the South.[113] Instead, the convention deadlocked for more than forty ballots. During a weekend recess, the Fillmore managers tried to strike a bargain with the Webster camp: if Webster were able to muster forty votes, Fillmore would swing his votes to him. If not, Webster was to give his support to Fillmore. But Webster would not agree to the second part of this arrangement. He wanted a "decent vote" so he could "retire without disgrace."[114] Finally, just before the convention was to reconvene, Webster decided to withdraw and request his delegates to vote for Fillmore. But even this self-sacrifice was unavailing. As it turned out, Webster had underestimated the extent of antisouthern feeling even among his own supporters. Some of these men believed that Webster's association with the compromise measures, especially the Fugitive Slave Law, was a political liability. However, they thought that by supporting Webster and refusing to throw their votes to Fillmore, they could assure Scott's nomination. Then, they would be able to blame Webster's defeat on the faithlessness of the South and reestablish good relations with the antislavery Whigs. Hence, when Webster withdrew, enough of his delegates shifted to Scott to give him the nomination on the fifty-third ballot.[115]

When the results of the convention became known to Webster, he was embittered. Still clinging to the belief that he should have won the prize, he attributed his defeat to the "folly" and "infidelity" of his supporters at the convention.[116] He returned home to his estate Marshfield—as it turned out, for the last time—in September 1852. Although seriously ill, he was hounded by friends and politicians, some of whom wanted him to become an independent presidential candidate, while others insisted that he should back Scott. Through it all, Webster tried to maintain a philosophical calm and reserve. He would neither encourage nor discourage the movement for an independent candidacy; as for Scott, he could not endorse a man who had prevented him from being nominated and elected for President. Webster elaborated upon his political views in private conversations with his confidant Peter Harvey. He predicted that the Whig party would collapse soon after the upcoming elections, and he advised Harvey to vote for the Democratic presidential candidate, Franklin Pierce.[117]

Perhaps the most revealing part of Webster's conversations with Harvey was his explanation for the belief that the Whig party was doomed. Webster declared that the Whigs had sabotaged themselves by passing over principled statesmen such as himself in favor of "available" military men.[118] This opinion was obtuse and self-serving, but it would have been unjust to expect a more detached assessment from Webster. Raised upon essentially aristocratic political ideals, he could never accept the submergence of personal leadership required by modern politics. But in an era of mass democracy and party organization, Webster's personalized political style was both anachronistic and self-defeating. If Webster's career had any "theme," it was that the politics of personality gave free rein to vanity and selfishness. Unable to subordinate his will to that of a party, Webster was constantly caught up in his own capacious ambitions. He was a practitioner and victim of what Richard Hofstadter has called "the code of proud and jealous notables." Lincoln and Seward, prototypes of the younger generation of professional politicians among the Whigs, came to see this clearly. Years after the collapse of the Whig party, they told Gideon Welles that Clay and Webster had been "hard and selfish leaders, whose private personal ambition had con-tributed to the ruin of their party."[119] Perhaps the most that can be said of Webster's contribution to American politics is that he showed men like Lincoln and Seward how not to conduct themselves in public life.

Daniel Webster died on the morning of October 24, 1852. The event was cause for widespread lamentation and inspired warm memorials from friends and admirers across the nation. But the tribute which may tell the most about Webster's enduring power over his contemporaries came from a former ally turned critic, Ralph Waldo Emerson:

> Nature had not in our days, or, not since Napoleon, cut out such a masterpiece. He brought the strength of a savage into the height of culture. He was a man in equilibrio. A man within & without, the strong and perfect body of the first ages, with the civility & thought of the last. . . . And what he brought, he kept. Cities had not hurt him, he held undiminished the power & terror of his strength, the majesty of his demeanor[.]
>
> He had a counsel in his breast. He was a statesman, & not the semblance of one. Most of our statesmen are in their places by luck & vulpine skill . . . Webster was there for cause: the reality; the final person, who had to answer the questions of all the faineants, & who had an answer.[120]

Coming from such a source, this was praise Webster would have valued and appreciated.

CHAPTER 4

William Seward and
the Politics of Progress

A SEEMING PARADOX has dogged the reputation of William Henry
Seward. His name may sometimes evoke the image of an idealistic
statesman, who defied the South in the name of a "higher law" and the
"irrepressible conflict." Yet it may also bring to mind a less flattering
picture, that of a manipulator and temporizer, prone to trimming his
ideological sails to the winds of public opinion. Both portraits of Seward
are preserved in the historiography of the antebellum period, and the
contrast between the two has provoked a lively debate on their respective
merits.[1]

Few historians, however, seem to have appreciated the significance of
the fact that Seward was well aware that he had to perform a difficult
public role. Very early in his political career, for example, Seward wrote
to his wife:

> I shall, from the force of constitutional bias, be found always mingling in
> the controversies which agitate the country. Enthusiasm for the right and
> ambition for personal distinction are passions of which I cannot divest
> myself, and while every day's experience is teaching me that the former is
> the very agent which must defeat the latter, I am far from believing that I
> should be more happy were I to withdraw altogether from political
> action.[2]

Even at the height of his influence as a member of the United States
Senate, Seward wrote to a close personal friend:

> As for personal considerations I do not often speak of them[,] because no
> man can speak wisely and perhaps no man need expect to be believed if he
> speak sincerely—I am buoyant in the conviction that henceforth the cause

with which I have been connected [antislavery] is to go on more
successfully than ever. It will vindicate my past. I shall not compromise
that past. If I ever was ambitious after the fashion of other men I did not
know it. I have been chastened by vexations and mortifications until I have
given up all aspirations and seek nothing more than to close my term here
(of which on no account would I accept a renewal) with the reputation
that I have acquired[,] be it more or less.[3]

Seward's protestations of disinterest were in part a reflection of the
uneasy relationship between his private and public lives. Like many
antebellum politicians, Seward discovered that a career in politics
required a considerable sacrifice of financial security and personal
happiness. Often in debt, and repeatedly accused by his wife of
dereliction of domestic duties, Seward was understandably stung by
charges that he was a self-seeking opportunist.[4] But Seward was
especially sensitive to such criticism because he thought of himself as a
statesman of vision who had shouldered a great moral burden. A firm
exponent of the gospel of progress, he nevertheless found himself at
odds with the majority of the American public when he insisted that the
United States would have to undergo a wholesale regeneration before it
could rise to its deserved position of preeminence in the world.
Specifically, he maintained that the country could never fulfill its destiny
if it excluded entire classes of men from the rights and duties of
citizenship. Accordingly, he took upon himself the thankless task of
championing the interests of free blacks, slaves, and immigrants.

Yet Seward felt the pull of ambition and the constraints of the possible,
and he realized that he could never accomplish his objectives if he were
an "impracticable" visionary or single-minded fanatic. So he equivocated
and evaded when he felt it was necessary. Rather than "agitate" public
opinion, Seward typically waited for events to prepare the people to heed
his voice. Explaining his part in the "division of labor" between the
reformer and the statesman, he wrote:

I am indeed worth little to the cause of political justice by myself alone, but
I hope to serve and advance it by persuading some portion of my
countrymen to adopt and maintain it also. When I seem unmoved and
inactive, you rightly conclude it is only because I am keeping steadily in
view a coming occasion and opportunity to move and act, as I think, more
wisely and effectively. I will not deny . . . the confession that my life is
chiefly dedicated to the advancement of a reform which I think cannot be
hastily or convulsively made.[5]

But Seward was also sometimes swept by gusts of honest indignation which caused him to defend the oppressed—as when he undertook the defense of William Freeman, a mentally deranged black man accused of murder. In such instances, Seward felt the brunt of public displeasure. Yet he always retained his optimistic faith in the ultimate wisdom of the people and the beneficence of the historical process. "Progress" may have been an ineluctable desideratum to Seward, but he learned early in life that "the road of progress is not always clear and direct."[6]

[I]

William Henry Seward was born in the tiny hamlet of Florida, Orange County, New York, on May 16, 1801. Sickly, introspective, and bookish, the young William decided that he wanted to be a lawyer, and his father encouraged him in this ambition. After suitable preparation at an academy, he was dispatched, at age fifteen, to Union College in Schenectady, where he excelled as a student. Upon graduation in 1821, he read law in Goshen and in New York City. In the latter, he lived the life of a bon vivant, acquiring the catholic cultural tastes and intellectual interests which characterized him throughout his career.[7]

The central figure of Seward's childhood and early manhood was his father, Samuel Sweezy ("Harry") Seward. A man of considerable ability and versatility—at various times he made his living as a physician, farmer, land speculator, shopkeeper, and judge—"Harry" Seward was a commanding figure within the modest precincts of Florida. Accustomed to receiving the respect and deference of his neighbors, he seems to have tyrannized his family, which, besides his wife and five children (one daughter died shortly after birth) included several slaves. His relations with his three sons were especially difficult. Two left home after quarrels, while William came into conflict with his father when, as a college student, he had himself fitted for an expensive suit. Harry Seward refused to subsidize his son's taste for sartorial elegance, and the impecunious William fled to Georgia, where he assumed a teaching post at a rural academy. Pursued by threatening notes from his father, he returned to New York only after desperate entreaties from his mother.[8]

But William rebelled against the authority of his father without rejecting it. Like Harry Seward, "Little Bill" was an adherent of the Bucktail faction of New York's Republican party and an opponent of the Erie Canal. Although in retrospect, Seward pictured himself as a determined foe of slavery from his youth, there is no evidence that his father's slaveholding inspired in him any intense aversion. His decision to take up residence in Georgia, for example, was hardly the act of someone with an abiding hatred for southern mores. One of the primary concerns of Seward's later life was, however, suggested by the title of his college valedictory: "The Integrity of the American Union."[9]

It was not until the mid-1820s that Seward's political outlook began to assume a more recognizable form. This transformation is partly traceable to several changes in Seward's circumstances. In 1823 Seward moved to Auburn, a small town on the eastern edge of New York's "infected district," where the Bucktail Republicans and their policies would soon become unpopular. From his travels in the vicinity of Auburn, which was located near the eastern terminus of the Erie Canal, Seward acquired direct knowledge of the beneficial effects of internal improvements on the communities along their path. His convictions on this issue and others also seem to have been affected by his marriage to Frances Adeline Miller, the daughter of Auburn's foremost citizen, Judge Elijah Miller. Judge Miller, a former Federalist, was a devoted admirer of DeWitt Clinton and John Quincy Adams, and his political heroes soon became Seward's. His daughter, a woman of unusual intelligence but conventional moral sensibilities, seems to have played a decisive role in awakening her husband to the evils of slavery. Throughout his career, she encouraged him in his verbal aggressions upon the "peculiar institution."[10]

By far the most important figure in directing Seward's ambitions toward politics was Thurlow Weed. It was in 1824 that Seward first met this engaging newspaper editor and politician from Rochester, and the political fortunes of the two soon became inseparably linked. Although Weed operated in the penumbra of Seward's public presence, earning himself the sobriquet "the Magician," no great mystery surrounds his relationship with his political partner. In Weed, who shared Seward's interests in literature and the theater, Seward found the ideal companion to relieve the loneliness and uncertainties of the pursuit of power. In the rough division of responsibilities that obtained between the two men,

Seward rallied the troops with partisan principle, while Weed was the political Mephistopheles, engaging in the unholy arts of party management. Together, they made the progression, in the 1820s and '30s, from the Adams party to the Antimasons to the Whigs.[11]

[II]

Seward never issued an extended exposition of his political creed, but a relatively consistent body of beliefs may be pieced together from his speeches and writings as a state senator (1831–34), governor of New York (1839–43), and United States senator (1849–61). At the heart of those beliefs was an undeviating faith in the virtues of republican government under the auspices of the American Union. The American form of republicanism, Seward believed, vindicated the dignity and worth of the individual. Unlike monarchies and aristocracies, which relied on fraud and force, the American republic rested on the voluntary consent of the governed and guaranteed each citizen a maximum of rights. Similarly, the federal structure of the United States government preserved citizens from the extremes of centralized despotism and chaotic localism which haunted Old World regimes. Under the federal system, each state yielded to the central government only those powers which were necessary to maintain the Union as a whole, while reserving those needed to secure public order and individual freedom. In like fashion, the separation of powers among the branches of the federal government protected Americans against tyrannical excesses by either the people or their chosen officeholders.[12]

Seward believed that the American system of free labor, with the independent artisan or freeholder as its central figure, was the expression of republicanism in the material realm. A man who worked to fulfill his own needs and those of his family felt exalted because he served no master but himself. He could be a good citizen because he thought and acted in his own behalf, not that of a despotic monarchy or exploitative aristocracy. Respecting the freedom he possessed, he would not be prone to deprive others of its advantages for fear he might lose them himself.[13]

Had the foregoing been the whole of Seward's outlook, his political creed would have been virtually indistinguishable from the eighteenth-century republicanism from which it was derived. But Seward was very much a man of his times. His public stance represents, in large part, an attempt to adapt the traditional republican world view to the realities of the antebellum United States. Seward was particularly impressed by the reciprocal relationships between political freedom and material aspiration in the dynamic, capitalistic society he saw around him. To him, "civil liberty" was only one of the conditions of individual happiness, and it was "desirable chiefly because it favors the social advancement which is the ever-fulfilling destiny of mankind."[14] "Give men freedom," he argued, and "they will demand improvement as the natural means of gratifying their rational desires."[15] Some Americans may have been distressed by the spectacle of simple republicans being seduced by the allure of wealth and upward social mobility, but not Seward. Indeed, he maintained that, by demonstrating that men could be both prosperous and free, a wealthy United States would be a stronger United States. If the citizens of a republic were satisfied with their material circumstances, they would more readily give their free consent to the government. And if they were happy and loyal, other peoples would want to join or emulate them, giving despots reason to quake on their thrones.[16]

Seward believed that private enterprise could never, by itself, propel the United States into the company of the world's most advanced economic powers. It was hence one of his cardinal tenets that the federal government had an important role to play in promoting the nation's economic development. Through protective tariffs, it could foster underdeveloped industries, such as iron and textiles, and combat the effects of recessions. It could aid or subsidize projects which were beyond the means of private enterprise but which would redound to the general welfare—a large merchant marine, an Atlantic cable, the dredging of rivers and canals, and the construction of a transcontinental railroad. Most important, by granting civic equality to the foreign born, it could attract to the United States a massive pool of inexpensive labor to man the nation's factories and till its fields. Seward also believed that the central government could help ensure that the fruits of prosperity were distributed equitably among the population. For example, it could open the national domain to men of humble means by granting free land to settlers in small plots and by placing legal curbs on the accumulation of large estates.[17]

Seward was well aware of the objections to his ambitious proposals, but he had ready rejoinders to his critics. He dismissed southern charges that protective tariffs and federally financed internal improvements would serve special sectional (i.e., northern) interests. Rather, such policies would benefit the whole country by fostering the development of a national marketplace and an intersectional "community of interests."[18] He scoffed at nativists who argued that immigrants should not be granted civil rights because they lacked the qualities of good citizens. Seward claimed that, since the foreign born were attracted to the United States because of its many freedoms and advantages, they were eager to be assimilated into the national mainstream. To deny immigrants political equality would "exclude a large and considerable portion of the members of the state from participating in the conduct of its affairs." This would be a deplorable situation in a country based upon the free consent of the governed.[19] Responding to those who feared that the elements of material progress—immigration, industrialization, and urbanization—might create a class of the permanently poor, Seward exalted the ability of the nation's public schools to promote social mobility. "What is the secret of aristocracy?" he asked one audience. "It is, that knowledge is power. . . . What makes *this* man a common laborer, and the *other* a *usurer—this* man a slave and the *other* a tyrant? Knowledge."[20]

Seward was not unaffected by the traditional republican fear of the corrupting effects of wealth. Like many of his contemporaries, he was concerned that Americans might become so engrossed in the pursuit of prosperity that they would lose sight of their duties as citizens and exemplars to the world. He did hope that the common school would help future citizens acquire a "feeling for the public good."[21] But Seward was apprehensive that his own generation was incapable of the patriotic self-sacrifices exacted from the heroes of the Revolution. Consequently, he continually exhorted Americans to measure up to their duty to demonstrate that men could be both morally responsible and free. The American people had a mission—

> to take up the cross of republicanism and bear it before the nations, to fight its earliest battles, to enjoy its earliest triumphs, to illustrate its purifying and elevating virtues, and by our courage and resolution, our moderation and our magnanimity, to cheer and sustain its future followers

through the baptism of blood and the martydom of fire. A mission so noble and so benevolent demands a generous and self-denying enthusiasm. Our greatness is to be won by beneficence without ambition.[22]

By the same token, Seward charged himself with the responsibility for serving the welfare of future generations as well as his own. As a "statesman," he was well aware that "every important measure of government in which he may be engaged is in some degree the result of causes anterior to his own existence, and may be productive not only of consequences immediately affecting himself and his contemporaries, but of others pervading the whole state and as distant as its dissolution."[23] As a prophet of progress, he realized that "the tenure of human power is on condition of its being beneficently exercised for the common welfare of the human race."[24] He also appreciated the wisdom of the notion that the awesome power to shape the nation's destiny should be exercised temperately and responsibly. Seward had no patience with "innovators," who believed social advance required precipitate, root-and-branch change. Although it was "inexorable," the "law of progress" did not "require changes of institutions to be made at the cost of public calamities, or even of great inconveniencies."[25]

But education and exhortation were not enough, in Seward's view, to secure the blessings of republican government in the United States. So long as slavery existed in the country, there would be a blot on the fair frame of her free institutions. Slavery violated every precept on which the country had been founded. In place of the moral absolutes of the natural rights philosophy, which affirmed the inviolable equality of all men, slavery substituted the rule of force. It declared that one class in society could arbitrarily seize control of the lives and labor of another, and use the power of the state to preseve their uniquely privileged position. Worse yet, by underpinning the "aristocratic" advantages of a special elite, slavery raised an impediment to the nation's advancement. Since the slave labored out of compulsion and his master had no incentive to engage in productive work, "the whole amount of social labor" was diminished wherever slavery existed. To compound this problem, slavery discouraged initiative in nonslaveholding whites by attaching higher social status to the ownership of human chattel than to entrepeneurship. Together, the enslavement of blacks and the degradation of free labor inhibited the development of the "spirit of improvement" Seward found rampant in the North. Wherever he traveled in the South, Seward noted that cities, commerce, and industry—all the elements of a "progressive" civilization—were in a backward state.[26]

Southern society, in Seward's mind, recalled the worst features of the decadent regimes of the Old World. Like other forms of "aristocratic" rule, slavery thrived on ignorance and a low level of aspiration among the masses. Although an educated and ambitious slave might be a more skilled and efficient worker, the lords of the lash feared that he might question the Divine dispensation of his low status. Likewise, the slavocracy feared that an assertive class of nonslaveholding whites might contest their supremacy in state and society. Public education was therefore discouraged in the South, and even temperate discussions of the disadvantages of slavery were forcibly suppressed by the authorities. "There is nowhere in any slaveholding state personal safety for a citizen even of that state itself, who questions the rightful domination of the slaveholding class."[27]

In addition, slavery bred aristocratic habits of mind throughout white society. Seward observed that even in the North, slavery had created racial prejudice, which led whites to suppose themselves inherently superior to all blacks, no matter what their social status. In the North as well as in the South, slavery thus impeded the ideals of a modern republic, in which every man's position was a function of his ability and achievements. Although Seward himself did not foresee the total assimilation of the "African race" into American society, he considered the denial of civic equality to blacks a gross injustice. He argued that black Americans should be granted equal opportunities in education and the equal protection of the law, and allowed to become citizens after a period of tutelage. Such policies would at least concede to blacks the right to their own livelihood and the power to maintain their position through the ballot box. If whites were not willing to make even such modest concessions, they should at least help transport freed blacks to where they could live in freedom and dignity by themselves.[28]

Seward considered the slaveholders' regime and the Democratic party natural allies. To be sure, he realized that the Jacksonian-era parties were not polarized over the slavery issue—there were many Whig slaveholders and many antislavery Democrats. But Seward believed that the Democrats, by standing against "progressive" economic measures, were invariably, if not always wittingly, the servants of the slave power. They opposed the use of the federal land money to promote mass education, which would be a solvent of "slavocratic" power. They opposed federally financed internal improvements, thereby preventing the construction of canals and roads which would be "highways for the escape of bondsmen." And they opposed the enactment of high protective tariffs, which would permit American free labor to demonstrate its superiority to unfree labor, both foreign and domestic.[29]

The Democrats' aggressive foreign policies increased Seward's disgust with the party of Jackson. Seward was no foe of expansionism; indeed, he seems to have believed that the United States would eventually embrace all of North America.[30] But he wanted the extension of American power by peaceful rather than warlike means, with the country drawing adjacent territory within its boundaries by force of example, not arms. An expansionist war, he believed, would only result in the subjugation of unwilling peoples and discredit the American republic in the eyes of the world. The Mexican War was such a conflict, and Seward found it doubly disgusting because he thought it was provoked to provide room for the expansion of slavery. It confirmed his belief that, in Democratic hands, the United States government served the interests of slavery, not freedom.[31]

When Seward sought to translate his convictions into practice, his model of principled statesmanship was John Quincy Adams. To Seward, Adams was "not of this generation, but of the past, spared to hear the voice of posterity."[32] He was a living rebuke to Americans grown morally slack and complacent, a bracing reminder of the resolve of the Founding Fathers to erect a model republic on American shores. A man of unimpeachable principles, Adams pricked the consciences of Americans by his heroic and disinterested struggle for the reception of abolitionist petitions by Congress. "No visionary and no enthusiast," but a practical statesman, he had been an early champion of the policies which Seward believed were necessary if the United States were to become a world power. Adams' combination of Yankee idealism and practicality inspired Seward throughout his career, from his years as an obscure state legislator to those as Lincoln's Secretary of State.[33]

There was one major respect, however, in which Seward differed from his mentor: from first to last, he was a good party man. Hardly a magnetic figure—he was short of stature and had a stooped figure, a large nose, and a husky, indistinct voice—Seward belonged to the younger generation of Whig politicians who attained office through political acumen and organizational skills rather than personal charisma. More, through the bitter experience of repeated defeat at the hands of the New York Democrats in the 1820s and '30s, Seward learned the salutary virtues of party loyalty and discipline. Parties, in Seward's view, were necessary to present alternative policies to the public. Through them, men could concert their efforts and discipline the errant, ensuring that government officials would fulfill their campaign pledges. Seward believed that one issue dominated political debate at any time, and that only two parties could develop around it. This was because an issue "always has two sides, a right side and a wrong side, but no third or middle side." The party whose position on the dominant issue suited the public was the majority party; the other criticized its abuses and mistakes so that it might in turn win the popular favor. Third parties might introduce new issues into the partisan dialogue but they either disappeared after serving this purpose or supplanted one of the major parties.[34]

Much of Seward's thought on the subject of party may be dismissed as moralistic and simplistic. Seward seems to have accepted party conflict more out of recognition of its inevitability rather than out of a belief that it was desirable. Neither does he seem to have realized that the differences between parties are seldom reduceable to a single issue. Seward's failure to fully acknowledge the divergence of views *within* parties was reflected in the difficulties he experienced when dealing with Whigs who did not share his "progressive" views. But he does seem to have had a relatively sophisticated understanding of the solidaristic functions of party loyalty. Seward perceived that parties were important agencies for disciplining and organizing public opinion, so that it might be effectively expressed. Partisanship was to him no evil but an indispensable feature of mass democracy. In an 1848 speech, for instance, Seward listed the "relation of party" along with those of the army, church, and family, as a form of social attachment instituted by God:

> Through these relations, and not otherwise, we must seek our own happiness and serve our country and our race. The custom which attaches sanctity to each of these relations is the moral sense of mankind, which justly and severely condemns apostacy and infidelity. A change of such relations may sometimes be excusable, and occasionally necessary, but

even in such cases it is always unfortunate, and except for weighty causes, is always unjustifiable. Versatility and caprice are defects—vices. Perserverance and fidelity are among the chief elements of elevated character, and are indispensable to usefulness.[35]

[III]

Seward's political credo brought advanced Whig thought to a philosophical culmination. But when Seward set out to implement his beliefs during his tenure as governor of New York, he discovered that there were Whigs as well as Democrats who did not share his vision of social progress. When he led New York into an ambitious plan of internal improvements, he plunged the state heavily into debt, prompting the legislature to stop all projects which were already in progress and levy a tax to finance future construction. When he refused to use the full force of the state against antirent disturbances in the Hudson River Valley, he drew the ire of Democrats and conservative Whigs, who branded him an enemy of law and order. When he proposed that state educational funds be extended to parochial schools in New York City, he was condemned by nativists within his own party as an ally of papists and an unprincipled monger in Catholic votes. And when he refused to return to Virginia three free blacks accused of aiding the escape of a fugitive slave, he drew harsh criticism from the Democratically controlled legislature and provoked southern threats of commercial retaliation against New York.[36]

But Seward was not deflected from his course by the hostile responses to his actions as governor. Rather, they confirmed his belief that he was a disinterested statesman in the van of progressive opinion. He defended his zealous internal improvements program with the argument that it would promote the future prosperity of New York. As for the burden of debt incurred by the state, that would be easy to discharge once the new transportation facilities increased tax receipts by promoting commerce and raising land values.[37] Responding to his nativist critics, Seward denied that his parochial school plan was designed to attract Catholic votes. He only wanted to ensure that the children of Catholics would receive a worthwhile education so that they would become good citizens.[38] Similarly, Seward declared that he had treated the antirenters leniently because they had rebelled against a backward and oppressive system of land tenure.[39] As for his conduct in the affair of the fugitive slave, that was justified on the ground that the law of nations, which regulated relations between the states, did not recognize slavery.[40] When Seward prepared to leave office, leaving a din of controversy in his wake, he wrote to a friend that he regretted that "My principles are too liberal[,] too philanthropic . . . for my party."[41]

Seward's resolve was strengthened by the largely favorable northern response to his principled stand in the Virginia fugitive's case. Seward's militant stand during that affair established him as a leader of political antislavery, but it tended to obscure his moderate view of the proper tactics to abolish slavery. Unlike some abolitionists, who proposed a frontal assault on slavery wherever it existed, Seward refused to countenance direct interference with slavery in the states. Believing that the Union provided a stable framework for securing the "blessings of liberty" to all Americans, Seward rejected such a course because it would probably result in the secession of the southern states. Moreover, he believed that slavery could be eliminated gradually and peacefully by containing its expansion and offering slaveowners compensation for emancipating their human chattel.[42]

While Seward was sustained by the faith that freedom was destined to win its contest with slavery, his confidence in the easy triumph of liberty was somewhat shaken in the mid-1840s. His misgivings were prompted by the annexation of Texas, the Mexican War, and the failure of a referendum for black suffrage in New York in 1846.[43] Paradoxically, it seemed that the regressive forces in American society had a sense of purpose that was lacking in their "progressive" opponents. "Freedom," Seward lamented, "is in harmony with our system of government, and with the spirit of the age, and is, therefore, passive and quiescent." Slavery, however, "is in conflict with that system, with justice, and with humanity, and is therefore organized, defensive, active, and perpetually aggressive." Accordingly, in the late 1840s Seward began to take upon himself a positive and assertive role in checking the advances of slave power. Specifically, he hoped to lead a revival of the spirit of liberty which had inspired the Founding Fathers, strengthening the resolve of the North to resist the expansion of slavery. In Seward's view, such a moral crusade would serve a dual function. It would vindicate the superiority of the progressive free labor society of the North, but also prove that northerners had not been rendered so corrupt and complacent by prosperity that they no longer valued freedom.[44]

But Seward's fervor was tempered by his recognition of the political realities within which he had to function. He feared that, by forcing the slavery issue upon the Whig party, he might divide and destroy it without serving the cause of antislavery or that of his own advancement. And, unlike many men in both major parties, he denied that an advantageous moment for injecting antislavery into national politics had arrived by 1848. Thus, although the Free Soil party mounted a national campaign that year, Seward adhered to the Whig party despite the fact that its presidential candidate, Zachary Taylor, was a slaveholder. He explained this decision in a speech before a meeting of Cleveland, Ohio, Whigs. Insisting that the Whig party was the best hope of the opponents of slavery, he dismissed Taylor's slaveholding and service in the Mexican War as "ephemeral" and "immaterial" issues. What mattered was that Taylor, unlike the Democratic candidate, Lewis Cass, "stands on the same ground which General Harrision held, that the rightful authority of the legislature to pass all laws which do not contravene the constitution as established judicially or by legislative precedents."[45] Seward's implication was clear: since the North had a majority of seats in Congress, Taylor's victory would be tantamount to a victory of the antislavery Wilmot Proviso.

Of course, this was a clever (if somewhat disingenuous) exploitation of the Whig battle cry of congressional independence, turned to the advantage of a man in a squeeze. But Seward realized that this shopworn appeal was not enough to satisfy the fervently antislavery Whigs of Ohio's Western Reserve. Rather than directly respond to Taylor's critics, however, he tried to distract attention from the general's slaveholding by upbraiding northerners for their own role in racial discrimination. New Yorkers, he pointed out, withheld the vote from "the race we have emancipated." Ohioans were "guilty in the same way, by a system of black laws, still more aristocratic and odious." The Constitution, with its fugitive slave and three-fifths provisions, also implicated northerners in the crime of sustaining slavery. The North, then, had to put its own moral house in order, and the force of public opinion could call it to the task:

> Constitutions and laws can no more rise above the virtue of the people than the limpid stream can climb above its native spring. Inculcate, then,

the love of freedom and the equal rights of man, under the paternal roof;
see to it that they are taught in the schools and in the churches; reform
your own code—extend a cordial welcome to the fugitive who lays his
weary limbs at your door, and defend him as you would your paternal
gods; correct your own error, that slavery has a constitutional guaranty
which may not be released, and ought not be relinquished. Say to Slavery,
when it shows its bond and demands the pound of flesh, that if it draws
one drop of blood, its life shall pay the forfeit. Inculcate that free states can
maintain the rights of hospitality and of humanity; that executive authority
can forbear to favor slavery; that Congress can debate; that Congress at
least can mediate with the slaveholding states, that at least future
generations might be bought and given up to freedom; and that the
treasures wasted in the war with Mexico would have been sufficient to have
redeemed millions unborn from bondage.[46]

After presumably arousing the consciences of the Cleveland Whigs
with this declamation, Seward pleaded for "the spirit of moderation and
benevolence, and not of retaliation and fanaticism" to create conditions
which would "soon bring the parties of the country into an effective
aggression upon slavery." Casting himself in the role of prophet, Seward
declared that in every great work of moral regeneration, "preparation"
was necessary. Through self-reformation, the North would prepare the
way for a national campaign to end slavery. "God works out his
sublimest purposes among men with preparation," observed Seward.
"There was a voice of one crying in the wilderness, 'Prepare ye the way,'
before the Son of man could come. There was a John before Jesus, there
was a baptism of the Holy Ghost and of fire."[47]

Seward's thesis of "preparation" was one of those appeals by which he
maintained a delicate balance between the claims of principle and
expediency. Shortly after the 1848 elections, however, Seward was
elevated to the United States Senate, a forum from which he hoped to
help lead Americans to fulfill their duty to rehabilitate the republic. The
time was most apposite for him to perform this role, for Congress was to
debate the status of slavery in the territory won in the Mexican War. Even
before the new Congress convened, Seward established himself as a
major factor in the controversy. Through his close friendship with the
brother of the incoming President, Colonel J. P. Taylor, he obtained an
entrée into the inner councils of the administration. Before long, he was
acting as an unofficial emissary between the cabinet and the Senate, and
actually sat in on sessions of the former body. Hence, when the President

proposed that California should be admitted into the Union as a free state, his decision was widely attributed to Seward.[48]

Taylor's plan for California precipitated a heated debate in Congress. On the eve of the controversy, Seward wrote to a friend: "I am alone, in the Senate, and in Congress, and about in the United States, alone. While adhering faithfully to the Whigs, I dare to hold on to the disallowed rights of disenfranchised men and classes. I must stand in that solitude, and maintain it, or fall altogether."[49] Seward adhered to this position of solitary eminence even as he saw the "tame, indolent, pusillanimous" forces of the North shrink from controversy and the "malcontents of the South" threaten secession.[50] Although he probably hoped that the territorial crisis would prompt the creation of a new antislavery party under Whig auspices—a party in which he would certainly play a leading role—Seward disclaimed any motives of self-aggrandizement. He cherished the belief that, as a champion of liberty, his "views and opinions" were "entirely disconnected from personal interest."[51] In preparing an oratorical vindication of his position, Seward plotted an ambitious course. He would do nothing less than "demonstrate the certain deliverance of the continent from slavery to be inevitable, and the dissolution of the Union to be impossible."[52]

Webster's March 7 speech roused Seward to respond. Freedom had not yet had a voice in the Senate, and Seward, anxious to forestall compromise, leaped into the breach. His speech on the California question, delivered on March 11, 1850, was probably expected to be a forthright defense of administration policy. Instead, it was a long, tortuous, and occasionally profound philosophical disquisition. Seward began by defending California's application for immediate statehood without the normal expedient of a transitional territorial stage. The application was only irregular because there was no congressional enabling act. More important, California's immediate admission was vital if the United States was to fulfill its mission as the harbinger of republicanism and economic progress. The New World was appointed for the "maturity" of mankind, assigned by God to demonstrate "the development of self-government operating in obedience to reason and judgment." The eastern states were to "renovate" Europe and Africa, and the Pacific coast states were to do the same for Asia. It was essential, therefore, that California be admitted as quickly as possible, lest it decide to become an independent country or ally itself with a foreign power. For this reason, Seward announced that he would be willing to accept the admission of California as a slave state if such a concession were necessary to ensure its entry into the Union.[53]

But this last assertion presented a purely hypothetical case, designed to dramatize the urgency of California's admission as a state. In fact, Seward saw no need to make concessions to the forces of slavery. He thus repudiated Calhoun's call for a constitutional amendment to guarantee an "equilibrium" between the free and the slave states by giving the South the power to veto national legislation. Such an amendment would "convert the Government from a national democracy, operating by a constitutional majority of voices, into a federal alliance, in which the minority shall have a veto against the majority." In any event, Calhoun's proposal would only cause future conflict, for every "political" equilibrium had to rest upon a "physical" equilibrium. The free states would continue to outdistance the slave states in population and political power because the North had a higher rate of natural increase and received most of the immigrants from abroad. Inevitably, the growing northern majority would demand that its mores and institutions prevail nationwide despite any artificial "equilibrium" which statesman might try to contrive.[54]

For similar reasons, Seward attacked Clay's proposed compromise scheme. He rejected "all legislative compromises" as "radically wrong and essentially vicious." They were evasions of issues, for they conjoined matters that should be considered separately, on the basis of their own merits, and committed men to policies which might prove to be premature. Seward proceeded to enumerate his objections to some of the provisions of Clay's plan. The Fugitive Slave Law was an act of folly; the people of the North would not comply with a law requiring them to assist in the return of runaway slaves. The suggested abolition of the slave trade in the District of Columbia was also unacceptable, for it would foreclose the future possibility of voluntary emancipation by a vote of the residents of the city. Seward objected especially to Clay's suggested compromise on the issue of slavery's presence in New Mexico and Utah. He argued that Congress had no "arbitrary power" over these territories, which were held in common by the entire nation. The Constitution, to be sure, was silent on the specific issue of how the national domain should be organized with respect to slavery. But the general principles of the Constitution, along with Divine Law, entailed upon statesmen the moral obligation to promote the advancement of freedom wherever possible:

> The Constitution regulates our stewardship; the Constitution devotes the domain to union, to justice, to defence, to welfare, and to liberty.
>
> But there is a higher law than the Constitution, which regulates our authority over the domain, and devotes it to the same noble purposes. The territory is a part—no inconsiderable part—of the common heritage of mankind, bestowed upon them by the Creator of the universe. We are his stewards, and must so discharge our trust as to secure, in the highest attainable degree, their happiness.

It was "the most alarming evidence of our degeneracy," Seward avowed, that Congress even debated the territorial issue. When confronted with the same problem, the Founding Fathers had devoted the Northwest Territory entirely to freedom.[55]

Seward's "higher law" appealed to a popular Whig notion, that the statesman had a special duty to exercise enlightened stewardship over the nation's present in order to ensure the future fulfillment of the common good. But some procompromise Whigs, led by Webster, claimed that positive federal action to exclude slavery from the territories was unnecessary because their climate, which was unsuited to plantations, would achieve the same end. Seward dismissed this argument. There was no climate which was "uncongenial to slavery, and few where it had not existed in one form or another." Slavery was indeed a regressive institution, doomed to ultimate extinction, but the "indolence" of its opponents, not economic necessity, determined whether it would expand. Neither, Seward declared, was the territorial crisis simply due to the agitation of the public mind by party conflict, as Clay had suggested. It was due rather to the "distracted" state of the parties, which had become feeble and disunited because they rested upon expedient compromises, not the direct confrontation of important issues.[56]

Seward also rejected the most potent argument of the advocates of compromise, the prospect that the failure of a bisectional agreement would lead to disunion and civil war. He dismissed the expressed fears of such conservative Whigs as Webster that the corporate unity of the country was too fragile to survive sectional conflict. Confident that the bonds of nationality were strong enough to withstand political shocks, Seward had no patience with warnings that the Union was in danger.

Despite all the heated political rhetoric, nothing actually endangering national unity had happened. Southern congressmen had met, a majority had endorsed Calhoun's militant "Southern Address," and the southern state legislatures had issued "conventional responses" to this manifesto. Furthermore, even if there were a secessionist movement, it would quickly collapse. The "conservative" husbandmen of the "rural republic" would reject such a rash course of action. More important, the nation was bound together by ties of mutual interest and intercourse— "steam navigation," "steam locomotion," and "telegraphic communications." The Union was hence indestructible, and "would rise again in all its just and magnificent proportions tomorrow," the day after being "dashed to atoms by the whirlwind, the lightning, or the earthquake." "This nation," Seward declaimed, 'is a globe still accumulating upon accumulation—not a dissolving sphere."[57]

The issue, then, as Seward saw it, was whether statesmen would try to run athwart the mandates of progress, of which the rising tide of antislavery sentiment was the clearest expression. Statesmen would be wise to confront the problem in 1850, and not run the risk of future convulsions, which would be inevitable if Calhoun or the compromisers had their way. Congress could still decide "whether the Union shall stand, and slavery, under the steady, peaceful action of moral, social, and political causes, be removed by gradual, voluntary effort, and with compensation, or whether the Union shall be dissolved, and civil war ensue, bringing on a violent but complete and immediate emancipation."[58]

With these prophetic words, Seward exposed the nub of the territorial issue. He was asking, in effect, that the federal government assume responsibility for the gradual elimination of slavery, both by preventing its expansion and by providing for compensation. Seward's speech also presented the procompromise Whigs with special difficulties, for it suggested that there was an inherent contradiction between the Whig ideal of social and economic progress and the preservation of national unity. Seward's "higher law" pointed in the direction of a single national social system, based uniformly on free labor. But to the advocates of compromise, the imposition of northern institutions upon the South could never be achieved peacefully. Even moderate southern spokesmen were appalled by Seward's speech; in effect, the New Yorker was asking them to surrender exclusive control over their peculiar institution.[59]

Conservative Whigs were no friendlier. To them, Seward was no statesman at all. The true duty of the statesman in the present crisis, as they saw it, was to balance prudently the claims of conflicting social interests. The national duty to promote freedom, which Seward had invoked, was important, but it became a subordinate consideration when the Union was in immediate danger of dissolution. Indeed, the preservation of the Union was essential if American liberties were to be kept within orderly bounds, so to conservative Whigs, Seward's "higher law" seemed subversive of the social order. If men adopted this unwritten standard, what was to prevent them from flouting the law when they chose? Thus, to Henry Clay, Seward's March 11 speech invoked "Wild, reckless, and abominable theories, which strike at the foundations of all property, and threaten to crush in ruins the fabric of civilized society."[60]

Even several members of the administration were dissatisfied with Seward's speech; President Taylor himself was reported to have branded it too "ultra."[61] The crowning blow to Seward was Weed's response. He suggested that Seward would have done better if, instead of waxing philosophical, he had delivered a forthright defense of Taylor's policies in California and the territories. Weed feared that the "higher law" had galvanized northern conservatives behind the Clay compromise.[62] But there were also favorable responses. Antislavery men reported that Seward's speech had strengthened their determination to oppose concessions to the South.[63] Seward himself was proud of it; replying to Weed's criticism, he wrote that the speech contained "nothing I could afford to strike out or to qualify." He had eschewed an open commitment to Taylor's plan in order to maintain his "disinterested" public role:

> Reflection upon [the speech] . . . however, does not yet satisfy me that a declaration of adherence to the President's plan would have been added to my argument, without utterly destroying my freedom. For then the question would have been 'To what use the argument, the conclusion is enough and is not a deduction from the premises.' And the charge, so made for a dozen years, of insincerity[,] would have been adopted by the malignant of all parties and all factions, and could never have been removed.[64]

Seward was stung by criticism of the "higher law," but he was partly responsible for the conflicting and hostile interpretations of the meaning of the concept. Several months after the March 11 speech, for example, he declared piously in the Senate that when he invoked the "higher law," he meant no more than that there was a "Sovereign Ruler of the Universe." But at the same time, he cited a quotation from Algernon Sydney that could be interpreted as conferring approval upon the defiance of certain laws: "If it be said that every nation ought in this to follow their own constitutions, we are at an end of our controversies; for they ought not to be followed, unless they are rightly made; they cannot be rightly made if they are contrary to the universal law of God and nature."[65] Seward compounded his problems with procompromise men by not disclaiming the support of antislavery men who seized upon the "higher law" slogan to justify disobedience of the Fugitive Slave Law. In fact, he accepted the dedication of a book that urged noncompliance with laws which were contrary to the "higher law" of God.[66] Even at his most "disinterested," Seward could not resist the temptation to pluck the political fruit of other men's misapprehensions of his ideas.

[IV]

Seward did, however, attempt to clarify his position on the territorial issue. In his speech of July 2, 1850, he embraced Taylor's plan as a practical alternative to the Wilmot Proviso. In the same address, Seward reaffirmed his desire to regenerate the republic by committing it to a policy of favoring freedom over slavery. Quoting Bolingbroke, he declared it a "sound maxim" that "every government is perpetually degenerating toward corruption, from which it must be rescued at successive periods by the resuscitation of its first principles and the reestablishment of its original constitution."[67] But one week after the day on which these words were uttered, President Taylor died. This led to the accession to the presidency of Millard Fillmore, Seward's chief nemesis in New York politics. Shortly afterward, Clay's plan was broken up into its constituent parts, and each of the compromise bills was passed separately by Congress and signed by President Fillmore. Seward despaired at this turn of events, but there was nothing he could do to change it.[68]

Fillmore's conduct as President naturally aroused intense hostility among the followers of Seward. This animosity achieved expression at the New York state Whig convention in September 1850. Seward men dominated the conclave, and passed a resolution praising their hero for his conduct in the Senate. The President's admirers, who became known as "Silver Grays," bolted the convention because they considered this action a rebuff to their chief. Fortunately for the New York Whigs, the breach was not irreparable. In 1851 they patched up an arrangement in which the Seward forces agreed to respect the compromise as the law of the land, while the Fillmore men conceded their opponents' right to agitate to change the law by legal means.[69]

But disagreement over the merits of the compromise of 1850 still split the Whig party in New York, as in the other northern states. The seriousness of the intraparty rift was revealed in the race for the Whig presidential nomination in 1852. In that contest, the proadministration forces supported the presidential claims of either Fillmore or Webster. Seward and Weed, however, backed General Winfield Scott, and succeeded in obtaining a majority of the New York votes at the Whig convention for their man. Half of the Scott delegates at the national convention (including a majority of those from New York) refused to vote for a platform resolution endorsing the compromise of 1850. The resolution nevertheless passed, but Scott was nominated after the Fillmore and Webster men failed to unite on a single candidate. Scott then proceeded to alienate many southern Whigs by coyly accepting the nomination "with the resolutions annexed," a declaration that avoided explicit support of the compromise. Scott compounded his problems through his close association with Seward and Weed, who encouraged him to pursue actively the growing number of Irish Catholic and German immigrant votes. Nativist Whigs were disgusted by this strategy, which may have lost Scott more votes than it won.[70]

Scott went down to disastrous defeat in 1852. Seward witnessed the Whig debacle with a mixture of weariness and disgust, but he was already looking forward to the reorganization of the parties. The Scott candidacy, insofar as it had Seward's hallmark, may have pointed toward the type of party he wanted to see emerge: a party which would unite antislavery men and immigrants, though perhaps at the expense of alienating nativists and the South.[71] Seward's hopes for the emergence of a new party may have rested upon the realization that many northerners' acceptance of the 1850 settlement was of an extremely conditional nature. Webster and other advocates of the compromise had declared that positive federal exclusion of slavery from the territories was unnecessary because climate would keep slaveholders out of the territories. This was an important point, for to many northerners, the confinement of slavery would lead to its eventual extinction.[72] But if the policy of confinement were to be reversed, then members of the northern public would believe that a movement was afoot to perpetuate slavery, and thus call for a policy of positive exclusion. This was precisely how many Americans of the North responded to the passage of the Kansas-Nebraska Act in 1854. By explicitly repealing the Missouri Compromise, this measure opened the unorganized northern section of the Louisiana Purchase to slavery. It understandably aroused a storm of protest throughout the North, and Seward was one of its most articulate critics.[73]

Partly because of the uproar over the Kansas-Nebraska Act, the Whig party began to collapse in the mid-1850s. But Seward's departure from it was somewhat belated. In New York, the Whig party was kept intact through the 1854 state legislative elections, for Weed believed that it was the only political vehicle through which he could secure Seward's reelection to the Senate. Once that objective was accomplished, Seward led the New York Whigs in dissolving their organization, and fusing with the anti-Nebraska Republican party. As a Republican, Seward rededicated himself to the task of arousing freemen to the dangers of slavery. He was a leading critic of the policies of the Pierce and Buchanan administrations in Kansas. In an 1858 speech, Seward described the contest between slavery and freedom as an "irrepressible conflict," at the end of which slavery would either be a national institution or would be extinguished.[74] Yet even before this address was delivered, Seward had professed the belief that slavery had been doomed by the defeat of the proslavery Lecompton Constitution. In the struggle to block congressional approval of that document, he declared, northern public opinion had been sufficiently aroused to check any further aggressions of the slave power.[75]

Seward's newfound confidence in the imminent victory of freedom was accompanied by a moderation of his antislavery rhetoric which may have been designed to help him secure the Republican presidential nomination in 1860. But Seward was deprived of the leadership of the party he had done so much to bring into existence. For all the astute management of Weed, Seward had acquired too many liabilities as a leader of "progressive" Whiggery and Republicanism. Conservative Republicans were put off by his "radical" rhetoric, former Democrats objected to his economic views, and nativists were repelled by his attitudes toward immigrants. The Republicans instead turned to Lincoln, who had not given too many hostages in his Whig phase.[76] Thus, in Seward, the political code of "availability" could claim yet another statesman as a victim.

CHAPTER 5

Henry Clay and
the Politics of Consensus

M ORE THAN ANY OTHER MAN, Henry Clay won the hearts of the
Whigs. Clay inspired such devotion that, as James Parton re-
marked, "men shed tears at his defeat, and women went to bed sick with
pure sympathy at his disappointment." Nathan Sargent recalled that on
the day after news of Clay's defeat in the 1844 presidential election
reached Philadelphia, a Whig stronghold, "It was as if the first-born of
every family had been stricken down." Even in condemnation, Clay's
foes conceded the immense power and appeal of his personality. One
critic, writing in opposition to Clay's championship of the compromise
of 1850, estimated ruefully that "Something like half a million people,
more or less, in these United States, think that they were begotten by
Henry Clay, and must implicitly obey or reverently follow him."[1]

Clay's popularity is easily documented but very difficult to explain.
Perhaps the main reason for the elusiveness of his appeal is that it rested
upon qualities of personality which had to experienced personally in
order to be appreciated fully. When men tried to account for their
admiration of Clay, they usually wrote first of his "ardor" and
"impetuosity." Clay was a passionate, warm-tempered man who seems
to have conveyed his enthusiasm to almost everyone he touched. Even
jaded politicians and journalists were moved by the dramatic intensity
with which he would pursue—and usually win—the approval of a crowd
or audience. There was, to be sure, a less attractive side to Clay's
emotional nature. Clay was sometimes carried away by his passions into
personal asperities and fits of anger, particularly after political dis-
appointments. But Clay's uglier moments were usually redeemed by his

generous nature. As Robert C. Winthrop noted, Clay was rarely slow in explanation or apology, and he never bore "malice or resentment" toward anyone.[2]

Clay was also gifted with an exceptional ability to win the affection—or at least the grudging admiration—of others. There are many testimonials to his winning ways. Maybe the most striking was that of Calhoun, who was not given to avowals of affection: "I don't like Clay. He is a bad man, an imposter, a creature of wicked schemes. I won't speak to him, but, by God, I love him!" One of Clay's biographers, who knew his subject personally, wrote that he had an "intuitive knowledge of character" and a "skill and delicacy" with which he "adapted" himself to the "peculiarities" of others. Much of this was simply a talent for flattery. As Thurlow Weed put it, he sent men away charmed because he made them think that he was charmed by them. But there was a more subtle element which men described as a "magnetism" or "fascination," as if it were an unfathomable force. "You subsided," wrote Henry Grattan, "into the sphere of his attraction."[3]

The impression that Clay's leadership was derived largely from qualities of personality is reinforced when one considers his other attributes. Some of his contemporaries, such as Benton and Webster, were able to command respect through sheer physical presence. Clay was not fortunate in this respect. Grattan wrote that his features were "common-place, and by no means prepossessing," while Adolph de Bacourt compared his appearance to that of an English farmer. Clay was slender in frame, with an unusually large head, an aquiline nose, and gray-blue eyes. His forehead was high, framed by black hair which was usually combed back and which became perceptibly grayer with age. Clay's only remarkable feature was his mouth, which was so large that it was said that he could rest one side while kissing with the other. Mobile and expressive, it was his chief means of conveying his passing moods. The one truly impressive aspect of Clay's appearance was his height—at six feet, he could look down on most of his opponents literally as well as figuratively.[4]

If Clay was hardly a dashing figure, neither could he lead men by force of intellect. There was much truth in James Parton's gibe that he explored nothing to its depth except a game of whist. Clay's intellectual barrenness is most palpably evident in his speeches. Observers attributed his success as an orator to the passion of his delivery, the rich sonorities of his voice, and his use of gestures and mannerisms to punctuate his major points. But almost all agreed that in print, his productions were shallow, disjointed, and lacking in logical clarity. Robert Winthrop was only repeating a common opinion when he wrote that Clay's works "will not be consulted, like Webster's for profound Constitutional arguments or convincing logic, nor yet for brilliant metaphors or illustrations."[5]

When Clay's personal traits, attractive and unattractive, are taken into account, the impression is left that none of them, either singly or together, can explain the man's remarkable popularity. For the qualities of personality do not in themselves account for the appeal of a historical figure; what must also be explained is why people responded to him in the ways they did, and why they admired the particular attributes he possessed. If the Whigs' adulation of Clay seems mysterious today, it may be because he served a certain symbolic function for his party that no longer satisfies the yearnings of Americans.

A cursory examination of the evidence suggests that Clay did indeed have a crucial symbolic role for the Whigs—that of the statesmanlike pacificator and mediator, whose life was consecrated to the preservation of the Union. Those who sought to explain why Clay was so well adapted to this role found their explanation in his ability to master the particular tensions of his own life. These tensions, in turn, seemed to mirror the distinctive strains of life in antebellum America. Clay combined the courtliness and gentility of his home state, Virginia, with the hearty familiarity of his adopted state, Kentucky. He was a slaveowner, but condemned human bondage, and championed the cause of freedom throughout the Western Hemisphere. Devoted to the advancement of material progress, he still enunciated the lofty ideals of the Founding Fathers. A man of intense emotional fervor, he disciplined his passions in service to the public good.[6]

There was, then, much more than superficial truth in James Parton's observation that "the great compromiser, was himself a compromise."[7] Not only did Clay establish himself as a major public figure through his talents as a conciliator; he came to represent the Whig ideal of harmonious balance through self-mastery. And because the collective and individual dilemmas of antebellum Americans seem so well personified in Clay, his life and career can tell us much about the society and the party in which he played so important a part.

[I]

In his lifetime, Clay was often hailed as a "self-made man"—a phrase, not coincidentally, that he helped popularize. There are elements of truth in such characterizations, but it is important to remember that they were not simply celebrations of unfettered individualism. If Clay's life was often taken as a vindication of the individual's ability to rise, so, too, was it seen as an example of how free institutions created an open field for the development and display of talents.[8] Moreover, some of the facts of Clay's early life patently do not fit the image of a rugged individualist lifting himself out of poverty without assistance. His parents, to whom he was born on April 12, 1777 in Hanover county, Virginia, were hardly destitute; at the time of Henry's birth they owned a small tract of land and several slaves. Neither was his family of low social standing. Although little is known about his father, John Clay, it has been established that he was a respected Baptist preacher. Shortly after the Reverend Clay's death in 1781, Henry's mother married Captain Henry Watkins. From a financial point of view, the match was a good one. Between them, the Watkinses owned a 464-acre estate, a farm, and eighteen slaves.[9]

Despite the relative wealth of his mother and stepfather, Henry received only three years of formal schooling, and worked from an early age at odd jobs in a mill and a Richmond retail store. Local tradition preserved memories of him in these years as "the Mill Boy of the Slashes," riding barefoot atop a horse as he went about his errands. Clay's admirers would later exploit this image to promote their hero as a man who had surmounted humble beginnings through hard work. But life seldom imitates party propaganda, and good luck, along with well-situated sponsorship, had a large role in advancing Clay's fortunes. When he was fifteen, his stepfather secured him a clerkship to the Chancellor of Virginia's Court of Chancery, George Wythe, an eminent jurist who had tutored Thomas Jefferson and signed the Declaration of Independence. Through his association with Wythe, Clay came to know Robert Brooke, Virginia's attorney general. Under Brooke's direction, Clay received the rudiments of a legal education and began to polish the oratorical skills which would later serve him well in courtrooms and legislative halls.[10]

Clay was admitted to the Virginia bar in 1797 and soon afterward moved to Kentucky. In the open environment of his adopted state, his talents blossomed. Although Clay was not deeply learned in the law, jurors liked his familiar and ingratiating style of advocacy, and he quickly became one of Kentucky's leading trial lawyers. A marriage to Lucretia Hart, daughter of Thomas Hart, one of Lexington's leading citizens, helped increase his wealth and consolidate his social standing. Soon, Clay began to purchase large tracts of land outside Lexington, which he combined into his beautiful estate, "Ashland." Political preferment came quickly and easily. He was elected to two terms (1803–6) in the Kentucky legislature, and in 1806, when he was only twenty-nine, he was chosen to fill an unexpired term in the United States Senate. Subsequently, he returned to the Kentucky legislature, where he served as Speaker of the House for three years (1807–10), until he was chosen for another unexpired Senate term. In 1810, Clay was elected a congressman, and, although he was only a freshman member, selected Speaker of the House—because, it was said later, only he could tame the rambunctious John Randolph. In his intermittent terms as Speaker (1811–14, 1815–20, 1823–25) Clay made the office a position of immense power.[11]

Clay began his political career as a zealous Jeffersonian, and maintained throughout his life an ardent belief in Republican principles. But his Republicanism, reflecting as it did the "frontier" setting of early Kentucky, was of a special kind. Like other Republicans, Clay was dedicated to the principles of individual liberty, economical government, and states' rights. But he was also devoted to government promotion of the economic development of his state; the "Old Republican" gospel, with its agrarian suspicion of commerce and manufacturing, had no appeal for him. And it was with considerable reason that Clay saw no incompatibility between Republican principles and his promotional activities. In an underdeveloped state such as Kentucky, with its abundant untapped resources and relatively fluid social structure, the fostering of economic growth could be defended credibly as not merely favoritism for a privileged few but a necessity for the prosperity and well-being of all. There were also some particular elements of the Kentucky economy that required fostering by the government. The Bluegrass region, where Clay took up residence, was a major growing area for domestic hemp, which required protection against competition from cheaper, dew-rotted Russian hemp. Moreover, Kentucky, like other western states, had a deficiency of specie because many of its citizens used hard money to purchase manufactures shipped in from the East. For this reason, there was widespread sentiment in Kentucky for the development of both banks and local manufactures.[12]

It was in Kentucky that Clay refined his talents as a booster, broker, and promoter. Clay himself shared in the entrepeneurial zeal prevalent in Kentucky, as evidenced by his experiments with hemp-growing and the raising of new breeds of cattle and sheep at Ashland. He was also a hotel proprietor, a director of the Bank of Kentucky, and a founder of the Madison Hemp and Flax Spinning Company. As a state legislator, Clay helped create a congenial climate for business in Kentucky. He championed the creation of the Kentucky Insurance Company (founded in 1802), which was endowed with some of the powers of a bank, and he helped secure a charter for the partly state-owned Bank of Kentucky in 1806. A proponent of internal improvements, Clay also encouraged the formation of the Ohio Canal Company and served on the state legislative committee overseeing the clearing of rivers and the construction of roads. In 1809, when Kentucky textile manufacturers complained of poor markets, he introduced a bill calling on all members of the legislature to wear garments made within the state.[13]

Clay's promotional enthusiasm was also displayed in the United States Congress. He introduced bills to encourage the use of domestic hemp by the American navy, give bounties to home manufacturers, and finance the construction of internal improvements. The one apparent exception to Clay's probusiness orientation was his opposition to the rechartering of the First Bank of the United States in 1811. Yet a reading of his explanation for this action reveals that Clay was not opposed to banking per se. Instructed by the Kentucky legislature to vote against recharter, Clay asserted that the state banks were sufficient to meet the country's financial needs, and that "misconduct" by the national bank might subvert them. He also charged that the national bank was an unconstitutional monopoly which might create a "splendid association of favored individuals" operating independently of the government.[14]

The manner in which Clay accommodated Republican principles to his promotional schemes is most clearly revealed in his speech on domestic manufactures. From this address (April 6, 1810), it is evident that Clay envisioned manufacturing within the frame of an agrarian-based economy—agrarian in most of its productive activities and in its civic ideals as well. Clay denied that he intended to convert the United States from an agricultural to a manufacturing nation. He only wanted protection for such manufactures—chiefly "necessities" which could be made in small shops, mills, and homes—as would make the United States financially independent of Europe. Agriculture, Clay conceded, would always be the major source of wealth in America, and domestic manufactures would help it maintain its supremacy by providing it with an enlarged consumer market. In any case, protection would be only a temporary expedient, maintained until the country attained material self-sufficiency. Clay minimized the danger that manufacturing might create a dependent and morally degraded working class. Manufactures, rather, would improve the morals of the nation, as the use of machinery made possible the employment of unskilled laborers who would otherwise live in idleness.[15]

[II]

The process by which Clay integrated his promotional schemes into his visionary "American System" was a long and tortuous one. It is clear, however, that the decisive event impelling Clay to formulate the system was the War of 1812. Clay, of course, was one of the most zealous proponents of war with Great Britain, and he played an important role in swinging Madison into the prowar camp. Like many other Republicans, Clay envisioned the war as an opportunity to open up export markets for American agriculture, from which native farmers had been excluded by British commercial restrictions. This concern was consonant with Republican ideology, for it grew out of the fear that if American farmers were denied outlets for their surpluses, they would be idle and unemployed—conditions that would undermine their virtue and independence.[16] But the war did not prove to be an unambiguous victory for free trade. As one of the negotiators of the Treaty of Ghent, Clay was irked by Great Britain's refusal to open its ports to American exports. He also worried—justifiably, as it turned out—that the British would dump their manufactures on the American market, and thereby destroy the home industries built up during the war. In the hope of providing American farmers with an enlarged domestic market and protecting manufacturers against ruinous British competition, Clay pushed vigorously for the moderately protective tariff enacted in 1816.[17]

The war experience contributed in other ways to Clay's advocacy of economic nationalism. The condition of American finances during the war, when many state banks refused to honor one another's notes and some suspended specie payments for lack of sufficient reserves, made him a convert to the cause of a new national bank. Repressing his states' rights scruples, Clay declared that such an institution was needed to provide controls on the loans and discounts of the state and local banks. The primitive condition of American transportation facilities had also become painfully evident during the war, and Clay pushed hard for federal financing of internal improvements. He helped guide through the House legislation that authorized the use of the bonus and dividends paid to the government by the new Bank of the United States to finance new roads and canals. When Madison and Monroe vetoed such bills, claiming that they were unconstitutional, Clay rebuked them vehemently. Dismissing the Presidents' strict constructionist sensibilities, Clay argued passionately that internal improvements were necessary to diffuse information throughout the country, promote the circulation of trade, and create a community of interests between the sections.[18]

Clay's vigorous advocacy of economic nationalism is easily recognized in his postbellum speeches and voting record. Less obvious is the fact that Clay wanted to extend the benefits of commercial republicanism beyond the boundaries of the United States, to embrace much of the Western Hemisphere. When rebellions against Spanish rule broke out in Latin America, Clay pressed for diplomatic support of the rebels. He envisioned that independent South American republics would provide the United States with new sources of raw materials and markets for its manufactures. In his vision of the future, the United States and Latin America would constitute a self-sufficient, interdependent trade area, bound together by common financial ties and by a common devotion to republicanism.[19]

Latin America, however, failed to live up to Clay's expectations in either respect. Thus Clay began, especially after 1820, to envision an internal balance of trade and diversification of pursuits as the foundations of American nationality and economic independence. His views crystallized during the acute financial panic and depression that began in 1819. Clay attributed the crisis to the American economy's overreliance on agriculture, particularly the cultivation of staples for export; if the country had a larger industrial base, and therefore a larger consumer market, it would not have been so seriously affected by the convulsions in the world economy after the War of 1812. Specifically, the United States would not have experienced so massive a buildup of agricultural surpluses—and thus increased agricultural unemployment—once the war was over, and the Europeans could return to growing their own foodstuffs. The Europeans had flooded the American market with cheap manufactures, and thereby deprived domestic laborers of work. This, too, Clay saw as justification for the protection of home manufactures. Clay envisioned further troubles ahead if the economy was not diversified. The native population was increasing at four times the rate of the European, so American farmers could not rely on foreign markets being large enough to absorb their surpluses. For this reason alone, it would be necessary to create an increased domestic consuming market by diverting a larger proportion of American workers into non-agricultural pursuits.[20]

As the War of 1812 and Panic of 1819 receded into memory, and Americans became more concerned with their own well-being rather than the requirements of collective independence, Clay's arguments for the American System shifted in emphasis. He increasingly stressed how the American System would widen avenues of individual opportunity by harmonizing particular interests with the national good. Each of the main parts of the system—the protective tariff, federally financed internal improvements, and (with the recharter controversy of 1832) a national bank—fit neatly into his vision. The tariff would provide laborers with jobs, farmers with markets, and consumers with cheaper manufactured goods. Canals and roads would make trade cheaper and more convenient, and also open up new lands for cultivation by farmers. And a national bank would provide the safe and reliable medium of exchange and easy credit with which Americans could conduct commercial transactions. In an almost rhapsodic passage, Clay summarized his vision of how the system would merge all private pursuits into a harmonious, organic whole: "The truth is, that the System *excites* and *creates* labor, and this labor creates wealth, and this new wealth communicates additional ability to consume, which acts on all the objects contributing to human comfort and enjoyment."[21]

In its grandeur and sweep, the American System typified the visionary qualities that made Clay so compelling a figure to many Americans. Through the system, Clay imparted an aura of romance to the pursuits of a country whose main business was business. Born out of Clay's fervent faith that economic development could be harmonized with the precepts of republicanism, it presumed that the nation's entrepeneurial energies should be garnered under the direction of enlightened statesmen and businessmen. But to many Americans, this vision was inherently flawed, as it required the subordination of the popular will to the demands of privileged elites. In an era of increasing "democratic" ferment, such charges would gain in both frequency and currency. Ironically, the American System, which was to help unify the national existence, would itself become a source of dissension.

An episode which dramatized the political liabilities in Clay's vision was the so-called Relief War in Kentucky. In Kentucky, as in other states, there was a great speculative boom after the War of 1812, fueled in part by the expansive fiscal policies of the Second Bank of the United States. When panic came in 1819, the bank foreclosed ruthlessly on debtors and demanded specie payments from the depleted state banks. A Relief party was formed in response to calls for release from such onerous exactions. It carried the elections of 1820, and induced the legislature to pass a replevin law providing for a maximum of two years' stay on the execution of debts. In addition, the Relief-dominated legislature created a new Bank of the Commonwealth, which was empowered to issue notes backed by the mortgage security of the state. These notes were loaned out to Kentuckians to help them pay their debts, but were rejected by many creditors and depreciated in value. Then, in 1824 the Kentucky Court of Appeals declared the Replevin Law unconstitutional. In response, the legislature created a new Court of Appeals; "Old Court" and "New Court" parties arose to support the decisions of the rival judicial bodies. Finally, after "Old Court" victories in the elections of 1825 and 1826, the "New Court" was liquidated.[22]

Although Clay took no active part in the Relief War, it had enduring consequences for his political career. During the controversy, Clay sided privately with the Old Court, but avoided committing himself publicly. In the disputed presidential election of 1824, the New Court majority in the legislature instructed Kentucky's congressional delegation to vote for Jackson. Clay, who had obtained the overwhelming popular support of his state in the election, disregarded the instructions, and instead supported John Quincy Adams. Further, the Adams administration tended to favor Old Court men over New Courters in patronage appointments. Such things were not forgotten by the leaders of the New Court. Amos Kendall, Francis Preston Blair, and William T. Barry—all prominent New Court men—organized a Jackson party in Kentucky, which carried the state for him in the 1828 elections. Later, they would serve as influential advisers of Jackson and important actors in the Bank War. Clay would carry Kentucky again when he was a presidential candidate, in 1832 and 1844, but with much smaller percentages of the vote than in 1824. The opposition to his candidacies would be concentrated in the former centers of pro-Relief sentiment.[23]

[III]

The Relief War was part of a larger transformation in American society, in which the ideal of consensual government under elite guidance came increasingly under attack. In that transformation, Clay arrayed himself on the "conservative" side, with deleterious effects on the rest of his public career. His enemies cast him in the role of an advocate for special interests who, despairing of achieving his goals in the open, resorted to the low arts of manipulation. Clay's reputation for deviousness was compounded by the alleged "corrupt bargain" whereby he gave his support to the presidential candidacy of John Quincy Adams in exchange for the Secretaryship of State. The shifting nature of American politics also had consequences for Clay's statesmanship. In his advocacy of the American System, Clay had attempted to concretize the ideal of a national interest, superior to and yet incorporating all local and individual interests. But with the disintegration of that ideal, Clay often found himself reduced to the role of a broker among contending factions and groups. Hence, the central irony of Clay's statesmanship: having advocated economic consolidation as a basis for national unification, he established his reputation as a Union-saver partly through his willingness to compromise some of the policies which lay at the heart of the American System.

The devolution of Clay's statesmanship and its consequences for the American System are most apparent in the history of protective tariff legislation. To Clay, protection was the centerpiece of the American

System: indeed, when he first used the phrase in 1824, it was in a Senate speech defending protection against the "British" policy of free trade. The protectionists, under Clay's guidance, succeeded in imposing a moderate tariff in 1824. But they were confronted by a rising tide of critics, mostly from the southern states, who decried import duties as an unjust tax upon agrarians to "artificially" foster northern manufactures. The chorus of opposition grew louder as the states of the Deep South became more deeply involved in the cultivation of staples for shipment to Britain and came to see tariffs as an impediment to the export trade. The antiprotection movement achieved its greatest preponderance in South Carolina, where there arose a movement pressing for state nullification of (supposedly) oppressive customs duties.[24]

The nullification movement in South Carolina gained new converts in 1828, when Congress enacted the so-called Tariff of Abominations. Although this measure did raise most tariff duties, Clay, who was Secretary of State at the time, rued its passage. He regarded it as the offspring of a plot by Jackson's followers to saddle the Adams administration with responsibility for a set of tariff schedules that was unpopular in both New England and the South. Nevertheless, Clay was determined that South Carolina should not exploit the objectionable features of the legislation to undermine the principle of protection. Returning to the Senate in 1830 as the prospective presidential candidate of the National Republican party, he hoped to bring forth a scheme which would avert a crisis without sharp reductions in the tariff. On January 11, 1832, Clay proposed his compromise plan: he suggested the lifting of duties on goods that did not compete with American products, and the imposition of prohibitive duties on competitive goods. The nullifiers, however, objected to this proposal. For one thing, it would not contribute toward the objective of eliminating the national debt; for another, it did not sacrifice the principle of protection. Also objectionable to the nullifiers was Clay's concurrent project of distributing among the states the revenue from the sale of the public lands. Clay conceived of this scheme in order to bypass states' righters' objections to direct federal funding of projects within the states, such as internal improvements, common schools, and the southern movement to colonize free blacks. But opponents of protection feared that, by draining off federal revenue, distribution might create pressure in the future for increases in the tariff.[25]

Clay's tariff and distribution bills passed the Senate, where the anti-administration forces had a majority of the seats. But they were stalled in the Jacksonian House, which passed instead a bill, devised by Treasury Secretary Louis McLane, which provided for small reductions in the duties on unprotected articles. When this bill reached the Senate, Clay and his colleagues amended it to restore many of the protective features of their own plan. Under pressure from the administration, the Senate receded from its amendments. Nonetheless, in its final form, the compromise tariff bill of 1832 contained no major concessions to the nullifiers. It provided for only an average one-quarter reduction of the duties on protected goods. Understandably, Clay considered it a victory for the American System.[26]

Events in late 1832 impelled Clay to shift his ground. Jackson won the presidential election by a massive majority, and Clay did not carry a single state south of Maryland and Kentucky. Moreover, the nullifiers swept the elections in South Carolina, and enacted an Ordinance of Nullification on November 24. The situation was complicated further by the actions of President Jackson. In his annual message in December 1832 Jackson embraced policies that would have effectively dismantled much of what remained of the American System—he proposed that the government divest itself of its stock in the Bank of the United States, abandon federal financing of internal improvements, and cede the public lands to the states in which they were situated. Then, in his Proclamation to the People of South Carolina, Jackson denounced the theory of nullification and enunciated his belief in the supremacy and indivisibility of the Union. But in an obvious administration move to propitiate the nullifiers, Congressman Gulian Verplanck, Democrat of New York, proposed a bill to reduce tariff levels to those of 1816 within two years.[27]

All these events created a new political framework within which Clay had to function. His defeat in the presidential election made it clear that he had to widen his popular constituency, especially in the South. The Verplanck tariff presented a clear danger to the protective principle, while South Carolina's threat of nullification and Jackson's angry response gave him an opportunity to play the peacemaker. Fortunately for Clay, Calhoun did not want Jackson to take credit for settling the crisis, while he was willing to share it with his colleague from Kentucky.[28]

It was against this backdrop that Clay tried to devise a compromise settlement of the tariff issue. While visiting Philadelphia in December 1832 he met with a committee of manufacturers and politicians, and concocted a plan to retain the existing tariff duties until March 3, 1840, and then lower all of them to a uniform, *ad valorem* level. But this scheme was unacceptable to the protectionists in Congress, and Clay shelved it. After tensions intensified further, and Jackson brought forth his Revenue Collection ("Force") Bill to compel South Carolina to pay tariff duties, Clay introduced a new plan. He hoped it would satisfy both the administration and the nullifiers, yet avert an even more drastic tariff reduction by the incoming session of Congress. Specifically, the Clay compromise proposed that tariff duties be reduced gradually over a nine-year period, beginning July 1, 1833, until they were all at a uniform 20 percent level, assessed *ad valorem*, on July 1, 1842.[29]

The speech in which Clay offered his compromise tariff contains a masterful statement of his philosophy of statesmanship and "mutual concession." There was, above all, an appeal for consensus, based upon solicitude for the interests of the Union. Clay rejected an immediate and wholesale abandonment of protection, arguing that such a step "would bring ruin and destruction on the whole people of this country." Only a "mutual accommodation" among the contending parties would prevent this evil, or the even greater misfortune of a violent confrontation between the federal government and South Carolina. After outlining his plan, Clay conceded that many might find in it "some reasons for objection." Protectionists would complain that it lowered tariff rates too much, while the nullifiers would say that it did not lower them enough. While admitting that there was such "loss and gain" in his measure, Clay argued that it would be shared "among our countrymen." Thus, it was "founded on that great principle of compromise and concession which lies at the bottom of our institutions." Clay confessed that he believed South Carolina had been "rash, intemperate, and greatly in the wrong. . . ." But he disavowed any desire to estrange her from the other states. To achieve the desired amity, he called for the suppression of "party feelings and party causes," and a genuinely nonpartisan consideration of his compromise, which he had fashioned to serve "the vast interests of the united people."[30]

Clay further elaborated his philosophy of compromise in response to anticipated criticism. Expecting the charge that he had abandoned protection, Clay responded that it was better to make small sacrifices in the present than risk drastic ones in the future. Furthermore, his plan would remove the tariff from politics and "place it on a bed of security and repose for nine years, where it may grow and strengthen, and become acceptable to the whole people." As for those who charged him with yielding to nullification, Clay offered the counsel of reason; moderation often required compromise with wrong so that right could prevail in the future. As he asked baldly: "Is it not the duty of every man who aspires to be a statesman, to look at the naked facts as they really are?" Above all, Clay's appeal was for the return of conditions which would restore a favorable climate for statesmanlike politics, based on a true national consensus, unclouded by divisive emotions:

> ... I count upon the good effects resulting from a restoration of the harmony of this divided people, upon their good sense, and their love of justice. Who can doubt, that when their passions have subsided, and reason has resumed her empire, that there will be a disposition throughout the whole Union, to render ample justice to all its parts.[31]

Despite these appeals to lofty sentiments, Clay knew that the passage of his plan would require some down-to-earth politicking. Calhoun was at first cool to Clay's proposal, but became more supportive after the spread of rumors that he might be arrested as a traitor if the nullification crisis lasted much longer. The protectionist forces presented Clay with more difficulties. Led by Senator John Clayton of Delaware, they insisted that a provision establishing home valuation of imported goods be added to Clay's bill when it reached the Senate floor. Since exporters, whose invoices usually provided the basis for assessing duties, tended to undervalue their products, this amendment effectively raised duties an average of 5 percent. Clay, who needed some protectionist support if his proposal was to pass, acceded to Clayton's request. The administration, lacking an alternative scheme, offered no resistance to Clay's measure, and it passed the House and the Senate. On the last day of the congressional session, it was signed by Jackson.[32]

Placed somewhat in eclipse by the tariff controversy was Clay's distribution proposal. Nevertheless, distribution was of vital importance to Clay because it might be used to justify future increases in the tariff. Moreover, it would help finance at the state level projects Clay liked—internal improvements, common schools, and the colonization of free blacks. Clay conceived his plan in opposition to those of Thomas Hart Benton and John C. Calhoun. Benton suggested that the lands first be offered to settlers at a uniform price, with those remaining unsold being offered on a graduated scale of declining prices; Calhoun, that the lands be ceded to the states in which they were located. Clay suggested that the lands be sold at auction, with the remainder going at the standard rate of $1.25 an acre. As a concession to the West, he proposed that 15 percent of the proceeds be given to the states in which the lands lay, with the remainder being distributed among the states in proportion to their representation in Congress.[33]

Clay's distribution scheme was an astute piece of political log-rolling, designed to appeal to a multitude of constituencies in both the older and the newer states. It obtained the support of both houses of Congress, and reached the desk of Jackson on the last full day of his first term, March 3, 1833. But Old Hickory did not want to see implemented a measure which would reflect credit on an old foe, and he pocket-vetoed it.[34] Interest in distribution was revived several years later, but under unfortunate circumstances. When the federal debt was retired in 1836, the pressure for distribution intensified, for it could no longer be claimed that land revenues were needed to pay off the government's past obligations. A distribution bill consequently passed both houses of Congress, and was signed by Jackson. Three installments of the federal revenue were distributed to the states, but much of it was squandered on ill-advised internal improvements projects, contributing to the speculative boom of the mid-1830s. With the arrival of financial panic and depression in 1837, and the resultant depletion of the national treasury, further distribution of federal funds was halted at the request of Van Buren.[35]

The tariff and distribution reemerged as significant issues in 1841. Clay and other Whig leaders in Congress wanted to employ both to stimulate economic recovery. But in order to achieve their objectives, they had to engage in bargaining which thwarted their original intentions. A new distribution bill passed the special session of Congress, but only after a series of concessions to special interest groups. In order to placate westerners, the Whig leaders were compelled to accept preemption, which allowed settlers the right to claim 160 acres of public land and buy it at the minimum government price, free of competitive bidding, when it was opened to purchase. In order to satisfy debtors, who were an especially powerful interest group in the Northeast, the Whig leaders had to support a bill that provided for voluntary and compulsory individual and corporate bankruptcies. After this measure passed the Senate, it was tabled in the House; it passed the latter body only after the western Whigs received pledges of support for distribution from their eastern colleagues. Then, in order to placate the fears of the southern Whigs, who were concerned that distribution might cause higher tariff schedules, the Whig leadership agreed to amend the distribution bill to provide for the suspension of distribution if tariff duties exceeded 20 percent.[36]

The *dénouement* of all this legislative maneuvering unfolded in the regular session of Congress that convened in December 1841. Fearful that the government might lack needed revenue, the Congress passed in June 1842 a provisional ("little") tariff bill which postponed for a month the final (July 1) decrease of duties provided for in the compromise bill of 1833. In the same measure, it ordered distribution to proceed. Tyler vetoed the "little" tariff, complaining that its provision on distribution was contrary to the prior action of Congress and that its protective provisions violated the compromise of 1833. The Congress responded by passing a "permanent" tariff bill which provided for distribution. It, too, was vetoed by Tyler. Concerned that the government might be on the verge of bankruptcy unless a new tariff was implemented, the Whig congressional leadership decided to discard distribution and pass an "incidentally" protective tariff which raised duties to an average level of 30 percent. This arrangement lost some Whig votes in the South and West, where distribution was popular, but it gained the votes of enough protariff northern Democrats to pass both houses of Congress. This left Tyler in an awkward position. He had stated that he would accept "incidental" protection so long as it was not coupled with distribution, which made federal revenues fluctuate and might provide justification for a higher tariff in the future. The new bill met Tyler's specifications, and, not wishing to appear inconsistent, he signed it on August 30.[37]

Failure and frustration also dogged Clay's efforts in behalf of his third pet economic scheme, a national bank. On this issue, however, the key problem was not so much log-rolling as Clay's clumsy maneuvering for political advantage; when it came to the bank, Clay himself demonstrated a profound disregard for high-minded statesmanship. The national bank project was not at first part of the American System, but

Clay incorporated it during the bank crisis of 1832. Clay, along with Webster, urged Nicholas Biddle to seek the recharter of the Bank of the United States that year, even though the charter was not due to expire until 1836. Clay probably—and correctly—anticipated a veto of the bank bill, which he hoped would alienate the bank's supporters among the Jacksonian Democrats, particularly in the crucial state of Pennsylvania. Clay was too clever. Jackson vetoed the recharter bill but still won a sweeping victory. He even carried Pennsylvania. In the congressional session after the presidential election, some anti-administration leaders saw hopes of passing a short-term recharter bill that would be signed by Jackson. But Clay pressed for a long-term recharter and spurned all efforts at compromise, effectively ensuring the demise of the bank as a national institution.[38]

In 1838–39, as Clay maneuvered for southern support of his presidential candidacy, he edged away from close association with the national bank idea. Indeed, there is some evidence that one condition for the states' rights Whigs' support of Clay was his assurance that, if elected, he would not press aggressively for the creation of a new central bank. But once he was denied the Whig nomination, Clay felt free to place his own definition on the meaning of a Whig victory. In a speech at Taylorsville, Virginia, during the 1840 campaign, he listed a new national bank among the objectives that should be sought by a Whig regime.[39]

When Harrison took office, Clay began to press him for a special session of Congress. Harrison, offended by Clay's onslaught, refused these entreaties and instructed Clay to confine himself in the future to written communications. Harrison eventually conceded the special session, but only after Secretary of the Treasury Thomas Ewing warned that the government might go bankrupt without new sources of revenue. By the time the special session convened, Harrison was dead.[40]

John Tyler's ascendancy put Clay in an ambivalent state of mind. As he wrote to Francis Brooke: "If the Executive will cordially cooperate in carrying out the Whig measures, all will be well. Otherwise, everything is at hazard." He may have taken heart when, in an unofficial inaugural address, Tyler declared that he wanted a "constitutional" reform of the financial system to restore a sound currency. Clay may have seen further cause for hope when, in an address to the special session of Congress, Tyler said that he would yield to the initiative of "the immediate representatives of the States and the people" on financial matters. While reserving the right to employ the veto, Tyler added that he did not believe any act of Congress would justify its use. Clay did not hesitate to step forward and define the course the Whigs in Congress should follow. A week after the President's message, he offered resolutions outlining a program of economic recovery. The establishment of a new national bank was high on his agenda.[41]

It soon became clear, however, that Clay would not have his way without resistance. Secretary Ewing drew up a plan, apparently with the President's approval, that did not meet with Clay's approval. It provided for the creation of a new central bank headquartered in Washington, D.C., which could only establish branches in states where both houses of the legislature approved them. Clay, who was chairman of the Senate Finance Committee, was intent on pushing through his own bill. It, too, did not propose to create a bank with all the powers of the old Bank of the United States. To meet the objections of states' rights Whigs who doubted that the national government could create a bank outside federal jurisdiction, Clay also suggested the creation of a bank centered in the nation's capital. However, it would have had virtually unlimited branching powers. Only the negative vote of both houses of a state legislature, registered in the first session after the passage of his bill, could prevent the erection of a bank branch within a state's jurisdiction. Even this concession to states' rights sensibilities was stripped of much of its meaning by a provision that the state veto could be overridden by a simple majority vote of both houses of Congress.[42]

Clay's bill passed the Congress, but was vetoed by Tyler. In his veto message, Tyler objected not only to its state branching provisions but to the power it gave the national bank to loan promissory notes within the states. However, this power was necessary if any national bank was to exert some control over the issues of the local banks; what is more, it was included in Ewing's plan as well as to Clay's. Fortunately, Tyler seems to have forgotten this objection to the Clay bill, so Ewing and Webster were able to patch up a compromise bill which apparently met with the President's approval. Clay helped steer the new measure through Congress, but he also taunted Tyler for the bank veto and claimed that the President was committed to support the new bill as a party measure. He added the charge that Tyler was under the influence of a "cabal"—a "corporal's guard"—which was urging him to obstruct further Whig legislation. Clay's verbal thrusts were probably calculated to irritate

Tyler, who, in good Whig fashion, prided himself on his principled independence from party pressures. As Clay had defined the issue, Tyler could not win no matter how he dealt with the new bank bill. If he signed it, he would be submitting to party rule; if he did not, he would be a traitor to his party. Tyler took the latter path.[43]

The bank controversy showed Clay at his most unattractive. Even close political friends, such as Secretary Ewing, questioned his motives. Many believed that he had acted deliberately to create a schism between the Whigs in Congress and the administration and to promote himself as the Whigs' presidential candidate in 1844. What saved Clay from further doubts was Tyler's seeming vacillation and treachery, along with the widespread feeling that the country needed a centralized financial system. Still, Clay was subjected to charges that he was the "dictator" of the Whigs, and felt compelled not to appear to be laying down a "party line" for others to follow. He resigned from the Senate, his departure preceded by a speech in which he begged forgiveness from those who might have found his manner arrogant and overbearing.[44]

With the conclusion of the Whig Congress of 1841–42, Clay's American System was virtually moribund. The Whigs had failed to establish a new national bank, and would never have an opportunity to devise another. A new tariff had been implemented, but with lower duties than Clay wanted, and only after the Whigs had sacrificed distribution. What is more, in order to secure the passage of the original distribution bill, Clay had been forced to accept preemption, which undermined the use of the lands as a source of revenue. The failure of the Whigs to implement the American System was indicative of how the standard operations of party politics could frustrate a systematic, long-range approach to the problem of economic recovery. It revealed, most embarassingly, that in the absence of a thoroughgoing party consensus, Clay's politics of "mutual concession" easily degenerated into log-rolling and petty personal squabbling.[45]

[IV]

So far, the discussion has been confined to Clay's statesmanship, as exhibited in the field of economic policy. And it was to this field that Clay's talents as a broker were best suited. The policies embraced in the American System were, after all, superlatively matters of degree—how much federal aid to internal improvements, how powerful a national bank, and what amount of protection for manufactures. Because most Americans did not believe that such issues raised fundamental questions as to how they should conduct their lives, they were subject to the ordinary legislative processes of give-and-take. Moreover, there was sufficient ambiguity in the American System for northern and southern Whigs to read their divergent social ideals into it. For the Whigs of the North, it would stimulate economic progress, and thereby create the preconditions for a modern national economy based uniformly on free labor. But the Whigs of the South believed, with some justification, that it would create an interdependent national economy, of which the slavery-based labor system of their section would be an integral part.

Clay was required to exercise a different order of statesmanship when slavery became a matter of national political debate. The slavery issue did raise important questions as to how men should conduct their lives and organize their social arrangements. To Clay, his task as the Great Pacificator was to reconcile the differences between the sections within the framework of the Union. His philosophy of intersectional compromise therefore presupposed a national consensus that the preservation of the Union was a goal of transcendent importance. The difficulty of Clay's role was that it compelled him to leave ambiguous the ideals and objectives which the Union was supposed to subserve. Hence the fragility of his accomplishments as a peacemaker; the settlements he arranged were not true compromises at all, for they did not resolve the differences between the sections, but obfuscated them. Hence, too, the transitoriness of those "compromises" once the divergent social ideals of men in the two sections were articulated in political debate. Clay's art of "mutual concession" then proved unequal to the task of settling differences. And with the discrediting of "Union-saving" as the proper task of the statesman, there naturally came a considerable devaluation of Clay's place in history.

Clay began his public career as a harsh critic of slavery. Shortly after he moved to Kentucky, he wrote two newspaper articles urging that the state's constitution be amended to provide for the gradual abolition of slavery. Although Clay's arguments were not heeded by the state constitutional convention of 1799, they nevertheless provide evidence of his early opinions of slavery. Primarily, Clay condemned slavery as incompatible with the republican ideal of a free, happy, and harmonious society based on uncoerced labor. Slavery, he asserted, deprived human beings "of all the rights which make life desirable." In a powerful passage, he evoked the terror and degradation slaves felt upon being bought and sold, their families split apart, with "all the tender and endearing ties of nature . . . broken asunder and disregarded. . . ." He condemned slavery, too, for removing the incentives for the slaveowner to engage in productive work. In Clay's words, slavery injured the master by "enabling him to live indolently, and thus contracting all the vices generated by a state of idleness."[46]

Clay's criticism of slavery was derived from the philosophy of natural rights. "The rights of man," as Clay put it, "must always be the same. The same reasons urged by the present, might have been urged by the past, and may by the future generation[s] in favor of their liberty." Yet there was an important qualification to Clay's idealism. Like Jefferson, Clay amended his commitment to natural rights in order to take account of social utility. Immediate, unqualified emancipation was unfeasible, Clay declared, because it would sacrifice the freedom and happiness of everyone in pursuit of an illusory ideal of liberty: "Thirty thousand slaves, without preparation for enjoying the rights of a freeman, without property, without principle, let loose upon society, would be wretched themselves, and render others miserable." But the liberation of the children of the slaves, Clay asserted, was "exempt" from this objection. Consequently, he urged that a program should be established to gradually emancipate the offspring of slaves and provide them with an education to "qualify them for the exercise of the rights of a citizen."[47]

Despite its concessions to practicality, Clay's original position was certainly an advanced one for its time. He was advocating, in effect, the creation of a biracial society in Kentucky within the space of a single generation! Although most Kentuckians at the time probably professed a dislike of slavery, few were prepared to translate their antislavery ideals into practice. Ultimately, it was Clay who adapted to prevailing preconceptions rather than the reverse. By 1800, he owned three slaves; four years later, he owned eight. As Clay developed closer ties to the society of slaveholders, his view of emancipation changed. This was most evident in his zealous support of the colonization movement. Clay participated in the founding meeting (December 28, 1816) of the American Colonization Society and served as one of its original vice presidents. He became president of the ACS in 1836, upon the death of the first occupant of that office, James Madison.[48]

Clay's support of colonization was evidence of a profound transformation in his social philosophy. No longer did Clay conceptualize the slavery issue within the framework of natural rights. Rather, he conceived of it in the manner appropriate to a man who has adjusted himself to a society without fully accepting its working arrangements. The concern for the liberty and welfare of the slaves remained, but it was now hedged in by a philosophy of gradualism, organicism, and institutionalism. The most striking change in Clay's outlook was the abandonment of the ideal of a biracial society. Apparently persuaded by experience that whites would never accept freed blacks as equals, Clay supported the colonizationists' proposal that freedmen be sent to Africa. Thus, Clay no longer believed (or assumed) that men's racial prejudices could be overcome easily by experience or education. Neither, with his increased acceptance of prevailing mores, could he contemplate more drastic means of promoting interracial harmony. He now saw racial prejudice as something existing independently of the hierarchical relations between blacks and whites—as an ineradicable bias which could not be diminished simply by elevating the condition of blacks.[49]

There were other conservative implications to Clay's support of colonization. The plan was, by its very nature, incremental and gradualistic. Clay conceded that it might take several centuries to remove totally the American population of slaves and freed blacks. It also presented no danger to property rights. Emancipation was to be by the voluntary effort of the slaveholders, with perhaps some financial incentives being offered for their participation. Most important, colonization would not, in its advocates' eyes, threaten social peace, stability, or harmony. As the colonizers saw it, one of the signal virtues of their cause was that, unlike abolitionism, it did not propose to unleash upon the country legions of freed blacks who might be angry and resentful over their former condition of servitude. For this very reason, Clay claimed that colonization removed one of the major obstacles to emancipation. Slaveholders would surely be more willing to free slaves if they knew that by doing so they would not contribute to interracial warfare.[50]

Although it represented a capitulation to white prejudices, Clay's support of colonization was also expressive of his continued belief in the essential humanity and dignity of the slave. One reason Clay believed that emancipated slaves would rebel against their former masters was his conviction that slaves, "as rational beings like ourselves," would resent their former captivity. Apparently, Clay never accepted the myth of the "naturally" submissive slave. Yet here, too, his conservative outlook was evident. As George Fredrickson has pointed out, one reason for the ascendancy of racist thinking was the need many Americans felt to reconcile racial prejudice with egalitarianism; by classifying blacks as irremediably and inherently inferior, they could justify slavery and racial discrimination without sacrificing the ideal of a society of equal (white) men. If Clay did not feel such a drive for cognitive consistency, it may have been because he conceived of society as an hierarchy of differentiated groups and classes possessing various degrees of freedom. Colonization was wholly consistent with such a conception, for it presumed a model of social relations that included notions of custodianship and mutual responsibility. Such a model may appear attractive when contrasted with the crude racism promulgated by some proponents of the view that slavery was a "positive good." Yet it should also be painfully evident that colonization evaded rather than confronted the problem of racial adjustment in a professedly democratic society. It is indeed sobering to reflect that, by the 1830s, colonizationists such as Clay were the only influential critics of slavery remaining in the South.[51]

The inadequacies of the colonization movement are evident not only in its social philosophy but in its practical accomplishments. The number of American blacks shipped by the ACS to its African colony of Liberia in any single year never even remotely approached the number of blacks added to the population by natural increase or smuggling. Clay was well aware of this, but explained that colonization was only a pilot program, which would grow in size after it received government subsidies. Yet Clay never explained why colonization should succeed through government financing when relatively few slaveholders expressed an interest in it, let alone participated. Neither was Clay much disturbed that the colonization movement was supported by men who believed that exporting free blacks would actually strengthen slavery by removing potential inciters of slave revolts.[52]

Clay's own conduct was testimony to the limitations of his personal commitment to emancipation. Even while he supported colonization,

Clay continued to increase the number of slaves he owned, which reached a maximum of sixty in 1846. More striking, Clay never colonized any of his own human chattel, though he did provide in his will for the emancipation and colonization of those born after January 1, 1850. Clay's treatment of his slaves provides additional testimony to the limits of his social vision. Although he was generally a benevolent and caring master, he ordered the imprisonment of one slave who sued for her freedom. With all his good intentions, Clay could never totally disengage himself from the valuations of a society in which power, wealth, and social status were derived largely from the ownership of human beings.[53]

Additional aspects of Clay's ideological position may be derived from his views on the place slavery occupied within the structure of the Union. Clay's antislavery principles indicated an affinity with the central belief of free soilers—that slavery should be branded an undesirable institution and efforts be made to contain its expansion. But Clay's devotion to social stability and intersectional comity indicated a different course, one which rejected invidious distinctions between the economies, cultures, and values of the North and South. Clay's struggle to balance these two conflicting imperatives was evident in the controversy over Missouri's admission to the Union. Clay argued that it was wrong to impose conditions upon the admission of a new state, save for the constitutional requirement that it have a republican form of government. He therefore opposed Congressman James Tallmadge's proposal that, as a condition of its acceptance, Missouri should be required to prohibit the further introduction of slaves into its territory. Similarly, Clay rejected Tallmadge's suggestion that Missouri should be obliged to free at age twenty-five the children born to its slaves after its entry into the Union. Clay also opposed the admission of Maine so long as it was proposed that conditions be imposed upon Missouri. In order to reconcile these positions with his antislavery principles, Clay enunciated the "diffusionist" theory made popular by Jefferson—that the territorial expansion of slavery would mitigate its hardships by relieving the press of population upon the land and food supply of the older slave states.[54]

Clay's part in the Missouri crisis may be derived from his voting record and speeches, as reported by others. He voted with a near-unanimous South to admit Missouri as a state without conditions, and played no part in securing the passage of the so-called First Missouri

Compromise. By this arrangement Missouri was admitted as a slave state, Maine as a free state, and slavery was prohibited in the unorganized part of the Louisiana Purchase north of 36° 30.' But when Missouri placed in its state constitution a clause forbidding free blacks and mulattoes to settle within its boundaries, Clay joined those who condemned the provision. He helped obtain the passage of a congressional resolution declaring that Missouri had violated the clause of the Constitution which guaranteed the citizens of any state—including, in the case of some states, free blacks and mulattoes—the rights and immunities of all other states. Yet Clay also claimed that the obnoxious constitutional clause was no reason for excluding Missouri from the Union. He reasoned that it was null and void because Missouri's legislators would have to swear an oath of fealty to the federal Constitution. In the hope of putting the Missouri controversy to rest, Clay induced the House to form a Committee of Thirteen, with himself as chairman. The committee, following Clay's lead, issued a report stating that Missouri could not pass laws unacceptable to Congress. But the full House rejected this report. Then, Clay suggested a "compromise" stating that Missouri had been admitted into the Union on the same grounds as the other states, and that no act of Missouri would be construed as contrary to the Constitution. This formula, which actually settled nothing, was accepted by the Congress and Missouri.[55]

As with Clay's other "compromises," the Missouri settlement raises serious questions as to Clay's reputation as a conciliator. On the issue of Missouri's admission, Clay actually took a distinctly prosouthern position, which was rejected by the vast majority of northern congressmen. With regard to the clause in Missouri's constitution, the formula he fashioned was nothing but a masterpiece of ambiguity which evaded the substantive issue. On no grounds, then, had Clay succeeded in defining a genuine consensus between the sections.[56]

Clay's stance on slavery became increasingly uncomfortable when extremely polarized positions emerged in the 1830s. In a sense, abolitionism and the defense of slavery as a "positive good" were both symptomatic of the democratization of American politics. As has already been pointed out, the belief in the inherent inferiority of blacks—and thus, their suitability for permanent subordination—grew out of the need to reconcile egalitarian ideals with the realities of slavery and racial discrimination. Abolitionism, too, reflected the democratic ferment of the Jacksonian era. It was based on the conviction that the promise of human equality and brotherhood could—and should—be extended to blacks as well as whites. Clay had no use of either of these extremes. He charged the abolitionists with reckless disregard for established institutions and the rights of the states. Likewise, he condemned the adherents of "positive good" theories for their acceptance of brutality and abandonment of the republican ideal of equality.[57]

The abolitionist agitations of the 1830s obliged Clay to translate his convictions into actions. Clay's response to abolitionism was premised upon several assumptions: that, above all else, the Union must be preserved; that slavery, though not a positive good, must be respected as a domestic institution of the southern states; that slavery should not, so far as possible, be a subject of national political debate; and that free institutions should not be sacrificed or compromised, except in cases of manifest danger to the public peace and safety. Some of the implications of these assumptions were revealed in Clay's response to the problem of how to deal with abolitionist literature in the federal mails. Calhoun wanted Congress to make it illegal for postmasters to deliver materials forbidden by the laws of a state, but Clay demurred. While he agreed that antislavery publications were potentially dangerous, especially when they incited rebellion, Clay denied that they were an appropriate subject of federal legislation. There was no constitutional authority for the central government to enact laws which implemented state legislation that suppressed mail deliveries. Neither, Clay avowed, should the government be conceded the power to decide what mail should be delivered. If such a power existed, the federal authorities would be able to compel northern postmasters to suppress proslavery propaganda. Clay urged instead a policy of federal neutrality, which would allow local officials to intercept and destroy "incendiary" mail when it entered its state of destination. This was in fact the policy followed by southern postmasters under the provisions of the Federal Mails Law of 1836.[58]

Clay took a similar, moderate tack on the question of how Congress should deal with petitions requesting abolition in the District of Columbia. Clay favored their reception and referral to the appropriate congressional committees, which, Clay declared, should reject them "respectfully," with a statement of reasons. He suggested several such reasons: the people of the District of Columbia did not want abolition; Maryland and Virginia would not have ceded the land of the district if they had anticipated the abolition of slavery there; and that abolition in the district would cause additional anxiety in the South, prompting future repression of the slave population. To Clay, his approach tempered principle with prudence. While it acknowledged the constitutional right of petition, it separated the cause of civil liberties from that of abolition.[59]

Strive as he might to occupy a middle ground, Clay repeatedly found himself pulled between the poles of pro- and antislavery sentiment. In the 1830s, he tended to deal more harshly with the abolitionists, perhaps because abolitionism represented a clearer danger to established institutions. It is certainly true that, since abolition represented an unqualified manifestation of some of the antislavery principles he had always enunciated, Clay had to dissociate himself from it if he was to retain his political standing in the South. The delicacy of his position was most evident in 1838–39, as he angled for the southern Whigs' support for his presidential candidacy. In December 1837 Calhoun presented in the Senate six resolutions which stated in unqualified terms that the federal government must do nothing which even implied toleration for criticism of slavery. Clay voted for four of the resolutions, but induced the Senate to alter the other two. In amended form, the resolutions comprised a relatively moderate platform on the proper relationship between the federal government and slavery. They called upon Congress to reject petitions which advocated the abolition of slavery within the states, denied that the federal government could interfere with the interstate slave trade, and repudiated as "inexpedient" the abolition of slavery in the District of Columbia and the territory of Florida. The resolutions made one purely symbolic concession to the abolitionists. Petitions requesting abolition in Florida and the nation's capital should be received by Congress because they urged policies within the sphere of federal authority.[60]

Still, Clay seems to have believed that the six resolutions were not enough to satisfy men who thought that he was temporizing on the slavery issue to attract antislavery support. For on February 7, 1839, he delivered a blistering attack on the abolitionists. Clay's arguments were addressed to the North as well as the South, and they pointed to the Achilles heel of abolitionism, the notion that blacks and whites would live in harmony after an emancipation of the slaves. Clay charged that, because they favored emancipation without colonization, the abolitionists favored an amalgamation of the races; only through racial mixture could whites and blacks resolve their differences. A more likely prospect, however, was that emancipation would bring intensified racial conflict. Freed slaves would flood the North, compete with white laborers, and drive down their wages, or the country would be convulsed by interracial warfare as blacks and whites sought to preserve the purity and separateness of the races. This astringent blast at the abolitionists may have helped Clay among the southern Whigs at the national party convention. But it also disturbed such northern politicians as Seward and Weed, who believed Clay had gone too far in his attacks. The political maneuvers of these men eventually deprived Clay of the Whig nomination.[61]

The Texas annexation question again presented Clay with the problem of defining the proper relation between national authority and slavery. And it did so with much greater force than the mail and petition issues, which were largely matters of abstract "rights." Because it affected the concrete balance of power, Texas annexation raised some bewildering perplexities for Clay. Should new slave territory be incorporated into the Union, and thereby create the danger of upsetting the equilibrium of sectional interests within the country? Could the problem be handled through the ordinary means of give-and-take compromise, or was a different approach necessary? Were there some grounds on which a true national consensus on the matter could be established?

Clay's answers to these questions were in his famous "Raleigh Letter," published in the *National Intelligencer* of April 17, 1844. He adduced many arguments against the immediate annexation of Texas. But all of them were informed by a central thesis: that the Union was an organic, indivisible whole, not a bundle of conflicting interests which had to be kept in a rough equilibrium through territorial acquisitions. Clay attempted to convey this vision of intersectional harmony by concentrating on anti-annexation arguments which might appeal to men on both sides of the Mason-Dixon line. He pointed out that the national honor might be tarnished if the United States appeared to be embarking on an aggressive, expansionist course. He raised the danger that annexation might provoke war with Mexico, which had not renounced its claims to Texas. Clay also adverted to the prospect that other powers might enter such a conflict on Mexico's side if they thought the United States had set out to spread slavery. In any event, Clay suggested, southerners' hopes that they might benefit from annexation were probably chimerical. Only part of Texas was suited to slavery, and if Texas were subdivided—a not unrealistic prospect in view of its immense size—it would probably yield three free states and two slave states.[62]

There was enough ambiguity in Clay's stand for him to embrace annexation under hypothetical conditions that would not endanger the Union. This proved useful once it became clear that Clay's anti-annexationism was unpopular in the South. In his two "Alabama letters," Clay reiterated his opposition to immediate annexation, but in a manner more suited to southern sensibilities. He disavowed personal opposition to *eventual* annexation, and pointed out that, as Secretary of State, he had opposed ceding American claims to Texas in return for the acquisition of Florida from Spain. He also retreated from some of the harsher language of the Raleigh letter, and declared that he would give annexation "favorable" attention if it were approved by Congress. Implicit in this idea, however, was the assumption that annexation should receive substantial bisectional support. Clay clearly implied that annexation should result from a treaty with Texas, and such an agreement would require the approval of two-thirds of the Senate.[63]

But with all his maneuvering, Clay lost in 1844. It has been common, both in his time and since, to attribute his defeat to his position on Texas. Clay's opposition to annexation, it is said, hurt him in the South while northerners were made unhappy by the equivocations of the Alabama letters. There may be some truth in this argument, but it must be qualified by a consideration of the context in which the Texas issue presented itself. The failure of the Whigs to implement their program in 1841–42, along with the economic recovery of 1842–43, diminished the importance of the parties' differences on financial issues. Hence, the Whigs experienced limited success when they tried to divert attention from Texas to such traditional issues as the tariff and banking. The importance of this factor is highlighted when it is recalled that the 1844 defeat was one for the Whigs as a *party*, and not just a personal defeat for Clay. Whig congressmen in both North and South, who were presumably freer than Clay to adapt their positions on Texas to local opinion, did poorly in the elections of 1844–45. The Whigs gained no seats in the House of Representatives, where they had lost their majority in the mid-term elections of 1842–43, and they lost control of the Senate.[64]

The 1844 election revealed other stresses in the Whig party. Above all, it showed how the Whigs' position as a minority party often impelled them to engage in expedient political tactics which were contrary to their national, long-range interests. In New York City, the local Whig party fused with the Native American party out of fear that it might not otherwise be able to win. This decision backfired when the nativists failed to deliver much-needed votes to the Whig ticket, and it repelled many naturalized voters who might have been willing to vote for Clay. Many observers believed that the resulting loss of immigrant votes was sizable enough to have swung the narrowly contested race in New York to the Democrats. Clay himself attributed his defeat in large part to "the influence of the Native American question, uniting against the Whigs all the new Catholic immigrants."[65]

But if the 1844 election did not turn entirely upon Texas, it was nevertheless true that the issue revealed deep strains within the Whig party. The danger that new acquisitions might further intensify those tensions led Clay, like many other Whigs, to oppose the Mexican War and the policy of territorial aggrandizement. Clay's polemics against the war were based on traditional Whig principles—dislike of excessive presidential power, the desire for a culturally homogeneous nation, and the yearning for greater national unity. Clay declared that there would have been no war except for Texas annexation—which, of course, he had opposed—and that Polk had justified American involvement with the "palpable falsehood" that Mexico had caused the fighting. He invoked the danger of future "insurrection" and "rebellion" if alien Mexicans and Indians were brought into the Union, for such groups lacked the moral restraint and public virtue required in the citizens of a republic. Most important, Clay pointed to the danger that the Union might be "dissevered or "dissolved" if the sections quarreled over whether slavery should be allowed in territory acquired from Mexico.[66]

Clay's antiwar stand, with its appeal to lofty Whig ideals, was no doubt calculcated to appeal to a broad national audience. Even though he would turn seventy-one in 1848, Clay was looking again toward becoming the presidential candidate of his party. The emergence of

Zachary Taylor as a popular choice for the Whig nomination probably impelled him to take extraordinary steps to promote his candidacy. In the conclusion of a speech at Lexington, Kentucky, on November 13, 1847, Clay offered two resolutions which, in his view, should express the Whigs' stand on the war. The first resolution reaffirmed the "no territory" policy. It called upon the country to renounce the desire to dismember Mexico by any means. The second resolution declared that the United States must specifically and "emphatically" disclaim the desire to gain territory "for the purpose of propagating slavery, or introducing slaves from the United States, into such territory."[67]

This second resolution was controversial in Whig circles. Some southern Whigs, such as Robert Toombs, condemned it as pandering to abolitionists.[68] Conversely, the Lexington speech seems to have gained Clay considerable support among the northern Whigs. Indeed, Clay came to the Whig convention with the majority of the votes of delegates from the free states. But his strength on the first ballot was largely illusory. Much of it was due to sentiment and the antislavery Whigs' lack of a strong alternative candidate. The party pros in both sections, including such old Whig stalwarts as John J. Crittenden, Abraham Lincoln, and Alexander Stephens, regarded Harry of the West as "unavailable." Thus, Clay's support at the convention evaporated rapidly, and Taylor was nominated overwhelmingly on the fourth ballot. With characteristic impetuosity but considerable accuracy, Clay branded the nomination a fraud and an abandonment of Whig principles. He refused to endorse or campaign for Taylor, and used illness as a pretext not to vote in the November elections.[69]

Clay's poor performance in 1848 was partly due to his under-estimation of the extent of the South's attachment to slavery. If Clay needed any further evidence of the intensity of this attachment, his home state provided it the next year. In a letter to Richard Pindell dated February 17, 1849, Clay proposed that the Kentucky consitutional convention whose delegates were to be elected later in the year should consider some plan for the emancipation and colonization of the state's slaves. Clay outlined his own scheme: all slaves born in Kentucky in or after a given year (Clay suggested 1855 or 1860) were to be freed at age twenty-five and required to work three more years. The wages they earned in this period would finance their transportation to an (unnamed) colony. The offspring of these emancipated slaves would be apprenticed without wages, and then hired out for three years to support the cost of their transportation.[70]

As William R. Brock has written of the Clay plan, "Gradualism could hardly have been more gradual." Under Clay's terms, emancipation would not begin until 1880 or 1885, and every existing slave in Kentucky would remain in lifetime bondage. Yet even this was too radical for Kentucky, a relatively moderate slave state. Clay led the formation of an emancipation party which hoped to elect delegates to the state constitutional convention. The party was not committed to any specific plan, but Clay's preeminent role in it meant that his scheme received the most attention. Despite its prestigious leadership, the party was swamped at the polls, and failed to elect a single delegate. Indeed, the presence of the emancipation movement may have helped provoke a strong proslavery reaction in Kentucky. The state convention voted to retain all of Kentucky's laws protecting slavery, make the emancipation of slaves more difficult, and prohibit the immigration of free blacks into the state. Most significant, it proposed a new clause to the state constitution which read: "The right of property is before and higher than any constitutional sanction; and the right of the owner of a slave, and its increase, is the same and is as inviolable as the right of the owner to any property whatever." The only gauge we have of the popular response to these actions was the popular vote on the new constitution, and it was overwhelmingly favorable.[71]

Kentuckians may have rejected Clay's advice on slavery, but they still saw him as the man best equipped to resolve a national crisis. Thus, late in 1849, in the midst of the controversy over the admission of California, Clay was elected to the Senate by the Kentucky legislature. On January 29, 1850, he presented eight resolutions which comprised a comprehensive settlement of the problems vexing the country. In a speech of February 2 Clay explained the reasoning underlying his proposals. He accepted Taylor's plan for the admission of California as a free state, which he said he would favor under any circumstances. But he proposed to couple it with other measures to restore harmony to the country. One of his resolutions read that slavery did not exist in the Mexican Cession, and probably would not be introduced there. This was an implicit concession to the South, for it represented an abandonment of the

Wilmot Proviso. Yet it seemed to be of substantive benefit to the North, since it apparently accepted the abolition of slavery in the new territories by Mexican law.[72]

Some of Clay's resolutions pertained to problems that did not grow out of the status of slavery in the territorial acquisitions from Mexico. Anxious to avert a forceful confrontation between Texas and the federal government, Clay proposed that some settlement be devised of the dispute over the border between New Mexico and Texas. To obtain support for such a scheme from the American holders of Texas bonds, he proposed that the federal government assume part of Texas' debts. As in the past, Clay repudiated abolition in the District of Columbia. However, he urged the suppression of the slave markets in the capital because they had become odious in the eyes of the country. To assuage southern concern about the movement of slaves across state boundaries, Clay asked for a stronger fugitive slave law and a disavowal of any federal intent to interfere with the interstate slave trade.[73]

In Clay's eyes, his set of resolutions was the means to restore the normal, accommodative processes of American politics. The chief threat to those processes, according to Clay, was the North's material and political preponderance over the South, which it wanted to use in a policy—the immediate, unqualified admission of California—which would symbolize its supremacy. Compromise would help restore a more harmonious frame of mind to the country. It would remove from politics issues which polarized Americans, and open the way for a more manageable politics of adjustment among a plurality of contending, but not mutually irreconcilable, interests. Given the obvious—and increasing—disparity between the power and the wealth of the sections, Clay described the North's acceptance of his compromise as a token of generosity and good feeling. He urged the North, in his words, to yield on certain points because they involved only matters of principle, while the South had at stake "the social fabric, life, and all that makes life desirable and happy."[74]

Clay's arguments in 1850 marked a subtle shift in his philosophy of compromise. Previously, Clay had championed "mutual concession" to reconcile conflicting points of view within the framework of the Union. And Clay had always kept in mind a substantive vision of the type of Union he desired—one of diversified yet interdependent pursuits, all linked together in organic unity. But in 1850 the contours of this vision grew more obscure, as Clay championed an almost mystical reverence for the Union. In his pleas for an uncritical—almost unthinking—devotion to the Union, Clay implicitly conceded that the Union could be preserved only by obscuring the ends it was supposed to serve. In this light, compromise became almost a metaphysical principle. As Clay put it, life itself was a compromise between life and death, and the immoderate pursuit of pure ideals asked too much of frail humanity. The problem with such appeals was that in a period of crisis men are most aware of the principles by which they want to live. Antislavery politicians, led by Seward, condemned the compromisers for wanting to abandon the national commitment to freedom, while proslavery men condemned them for indifference to the interests of slavery.[75]

A detailed account of the fate of Clay's compromise measures would be inappropriate here. But several aspects of the circumstances of the passage of the bills require comment, for they are indicative of some of the problems of Clay's approach. When Clay first introduced his resolutions, he did not suggest that they should be reduced to a single piece of legislation. Rather, he wanted to see them embodied in separate bills which would be considered on their respective merits. However, some southern proponents of compromise, led by Senator Henry Foote, Democrat of Mississippi, feared that a California admission law might pass without any concessions being made to the South. Thus, when his resolutions were referred to the special committee of thirteen, Clay, as chairman, was subjected to intense pressure to combine them in a single measure. Clay agreed, though with some reluctance, to bring together several compromise bills. The omnibus proposal that emerged from his committee coupled the California bill with legislation on New Mexico and Utah and a tough fugitive slave law drafted by Senator John Y. Mason of Virginia. But when it reached the Senate floor, the strategy behind it backfired. Senators refused to vote for proposals favorable to their own section when they were combined with measures of benefit to the other section. The politics of "mutual concession" apparently did not work very well when men's definitions of the common good were mutually contradictory.[76]

Fate, luck, and some astute politicking rescued Clay's bills from disaster. Taylor's death and Fillmore's accession brought to power an administration favorable to compromise. Then, on August 7, after some elaborate legislative maneuvers, the omnibus was broken up. The provisions dealing with California, New Mexico, and fugitive slaves were sheared off from the Utah territorial bill, which passed easily. Clay was angered by this result, which he saw as a potential calamity for compromise. Drained physically by his strenuous efforts, he left Washington to recuperate at Newport. In his absence, Senator Stephen Douglas of Illinois pursued a new strategy to secure passage of the compromise bills. He realized that all of them would pass if they were voted upon individually, for each would receive overwhelming support from congressmen in one section, and a small number of supporters and absentees in the other section would tip the balance in its favor. Although this strategy sacrificed the principle of bisectionalism, Douglas believed that it was the only one which would work. He was right. Each compromise bill was carefully shepherded through Congress, passing both houses by narrow margins, and signed by the President.[77]

The method of passing the compromise bills, then, belied the very idea of compromise. Because there was no vote on the compromise as a whole, it could not be said to represent a consensus, arrived at through mutual agreement. Indeed, if the compromise had been considered as a unit, it would have received very little support. But the piecemeal method of passage, while it proved eminently practical, left a legacy of problems. Above all, it assured that there would be substantial numbers of men in both sections—chiefly antislavery Whigs in the North and anticompromise Democrats in the South—who felt no obligation to uphold the entire settlement. In the settlement of 1850 lay the seeds of future controversy.[78]

There were additional problems with the compromise bills. In the form in which they passed Congress, they were altered to be more favorable to the South than Clay had originally intended. Texas received more territory, the fugitive slave bill was toughened, and the disposition of slavery in New Mexico and Utah was left to their legislatures, with no mention of its current status in either territory. The territorial bills also contained ambiguities which would create problems in the future. For one, they left unresolved the question of whether New Mexico and Utah could exclude slavery during the territorial stage, or had to wait until they applied for statehood. This evasive tactic would not, as it turned out, prove effective in squelching the territorial issue, for it would reemerge in the Kansas-Nebraska controversy of 1854. Furthermore, the bills provided that disputes over slavery within New Mexico and Utah could be referred, as a last resort, to the federal courts. That this was no solution would be shown by the Dred Scott case.[79]

But in 1850 all these problems were buried in the legalistic language of the compromise bills. The nation seemed to issue a collective sigh of relief after their passage, and Clay joined in the general celebration. Evasions had succeeded in quieting controversy in the past; so why not again? Despite deteriorating health and advanced age, Clay made advocacy of the settlement a personal cause. After the adjournment of Congress, he returned to Kentucky and spoke before the state legislature on the need for intersectional harmony. When Clay returned to the Senate in December 1850, he delivered an impassioned speech urging that the President be given the power to call out the militia to enforce the fugitive slave law.[80]

Still in declining condition, Clay visited Havana and New Orleans in the spring of 1851, but failed to recover his health. When he returned to Washington in December 1851, he yielded to pressure from the Democratic governor of Kentucky and resigned from his seat in the Senate. Although he wished to spend his last days at Ashland, his ailments and poor weather precluded such a move, so he spent the winter and spring of 1852 in Washington. He died there on June 29, 1852, attended only by his son Thomas, an end which seems sadly inappropriate for so thoroughly social a creature.[81] Within two years of Clay's death, the delicate framework of compromises he had helped erect, and the Whig party along with it, began to collapse. It was a sorry commentary on the career of one who had given so much of himself to the cause of the Union. But when we recall that Clay had said that the need for compromise arose from the weakness and insufficiency of humanity, it may seem a fitting one.

CHAPTER 6

Southern Whigs and
the Politics of Statesmanship

THE TWO-PARTY SYSTEM of the Old South has been, and remains, one of the least explored problems in American history. Perhaps the main reason for this neglect is the belief that the South's unity in defense of its special interests (especially slavery) precluded serious political debate. One eminent proponent of this notion wrote more than a generation ago that "party conflict south of the Potomac, from nullification to the late 1840's, had the hollow sound of a stage duel with tin swords."[1] More recently, several historians have uncovered evidence which indicates that there were in fact substantive ideological differences between the parties of the Old South. The southern Whigs and Democrats of the Jacksonian era, it appears, disagreed about the same national issues as their counterparts in other parts of the country. Moreover, many of them resisted the sectionalization of the party system in the divisive 1850s.[2]

A recognition of the strength of partisan loyalties in the Old South prompts questions as to how the broad principles of the major parties were made relevant to the special concerns of southern voters. The antebellum southern Democrats, members of a party rhetorically dedicated to states' rights and strict construction, may perhaps be considered the protectors of the Old South's distinctive interests. But the southern Whigs cannot be explained away. As Charles G. Sellers pointed out, the Whigs, who commanded the support of about one-half of the southern electorate in the Jacksonian era, had a more liberal view of the powers of the federal government than the Democrats, at least in economic matters. Needless to say, this fact hardly comports with the traditional portrait of a monolithic South united by hostility to national "consolidationism."[3]

Unfortunately, Sellers was far more adept at delineating southern Whiggery than he was at accounting for it. Sellers argued that the Whig party in the South was controlled by "the commercial groups of the cities and the towns, with their allied lawyers and editors."[4] This contention, which Sellers backed up with statistical evidence, provided the basis for his thesis that the southern Whigs represented the economic interests of bankers, merchants, professionals, and their clients in the planter class. But there is a difficulty with this notion. Businessmen and urban professionals were about as numerous among the leaders of the southern Democrats as their Whig counterparts.[5] Sellers therefore fails to demonstrate that southern Whiggery expressed the needs of distinct occupational or economic groups.

Sellers' "explanation" of southern Whiggery has a yet more serious flaw; it presupposes that the Whigs' partisan allegiance was simply a "reflection" of their financial interests. Party loyalty, however, is seldom so simple a phenomenon as such an argument suggests. There may indeed have been economic and social conditions which predisposed men to become Whigs, but these do not provide a complete, self-sufficient explanation of what it meant to be a Whig.[6] It is also necessary to comprehend the distinctive assumptions, attitudes, and values—the perspective—shared by the southern Whigs. Only then will it be possible to understand how they perceived their "interests," pecuniary and otherwise, and translated those perceptions into their choice of party.

[I]

Before 1833, the southern opposition to Jackson was weak and poorly organized. There were, to be sure, pockets of support for the anti-Jacksonian parties in the South, mostly in areas populated by voters who hoped to benefit from the nationalistic economic legislation promoted by the Adams men and the National Republicans. In Maryland, western North Carolina, and western Virginia, Jackson's opponents sought federal support for local internal improvements projects; in hemp-growing Kentucky and rice-growing Louisiana, they advocated protection of home-cultivated staples against cheap foreign competition; and in commercial centers scattered throughout the South, they supported the recharter of the Bank of the United States.[7] However, the supporters of Adams and Clay in the South did not define their objectives in narrowly economic terms. Like their northern counterparts, they were philosophical conservatives, intensely attached to established republican institutions. In their appeals to the public, they denounced Jackson as a usurper and demagogue, who bred disrespect for the Constitution and the laws through his arbitrary abuse of presidential power.[8] But such denunciations did not meet with the assent of many voters in the South, for the Adams "friends" and National Republicans were ineffectual in most of the southern states. Apparently, Jackson and the policies he pursued before his reelection—his veto of internal improvements bills which he claimed violated strict constructionist principles, his support of Georgia in its dispute with the Cherokee and Creek Indians, and the bank veto—were overwhelmingly popular in the South.[9]

It was events that transpired after Jackson's reelection which prompted the formation of substantial anti-administration parties in the South. The first of these events came on December 10, 1832, when Jackson promulgated his "Proclamation to the People of South Carolina" in response to the Carolina "Ordinance of Nullification." The proclamation asserted that the citizens of South Carolina owed primary allegiance to the federal government. Moreover, the administration backed up the theory of this document with the Revenue Collection ("Force") Bill, which many southerners thought was intended to empower the President to compel South Carolina's adherence to the Union.[10]

Needless to say, Calhoun and the nullifiers were appalled by the putative consolidationism of Jackson's response. But so were many southerners who opposed the claims of South Carolina but objected to the nationalistic doctrines of the President's proclamation. Yet Jackson had only begun to trample upon the Jeffersonian sensibilities of southerners who had previously seen him as a champion of states' rights and strict construction. In September 1833, he ordered the removal of the government's deposits in the Bank of the United States and their redeposit in the so-called pet banks. These actions alienated not only southern supporters of the bank (or some alternative type of national bank); they repelled opponents of the bank who considered the removal of the deposits a "usurpation" of congressional prerogative. The southern opponents of the President therefore applauded the decision of the majority of the Senate to censure Jackson for not consulting Congress on the removal issue. But the Jacksonians were not to be outdone by the opposition. They initiated a successful grass-roots campaign which pressured state legislatures to instruct United States senators to vote for the expunging of the censure resolutions.[11]

The immediate import of these controversies was obvious: the presidency had become a vital, initiatory force in American politics. Seeing himself as the personal representative of the will of the American people, Jackson would not brook opposition by a special state convention (the Ordinance of Nullification), a Treasury Secretary (to the removal of the deposits), or the Senate (the censure resolutions). Furthermore he would resort to extraordinary measures, bypassing established centers of power, to have his way.[12] To southerners fearful of a powerful and intrusive federal government, Jackson's "usurpations" presented a new danger of concentrated, irresponsible power, unbound by constitutional or statutory restraints. But a "despot" can only be a "despot" if other men surrender their wills to his. In the eyes of his disparate southern opponents, Jackson was able to act in an arbitrary manner only because he had the support of a personal political "machine" with extensions in the states. The working components of this machine, they believed, were slavish "collar men" who had sold their republican birthright for a mess of patronage. Lacking merit or distinction, these political nobodies had joined in Jackson's train because of his fame. Knowing that they had no claims upon the loyalties of the people, these sycophants had spread the blight of partisanship to Old Hickory and his party. So, if Jackson retained the popular regard despite his "usurpations," Whigs reasoned that it was because his followers aroused the masses to a frenzy, intimidating public officials to fall into line behind the President. As a North Carolinian lamented: "Politicians aware of the influence of Jacksonism nourish it for their *own support* and protiction [sic] and endeavor to spellbound [sic] every subject by the magic of a name."[13]

The Whig party in the South, then, arose out of the same concerns as northern Whiggery—fear of unrestrained executive power, abhorrence at Jackson's perceived lawlessness, and revulsion against corrupt party influence. However, the southern Whigs' anxieties, unlike those of their northern colleagues, were coupled with concerns about the preservation of state sovereignty and the protection of slavery. Behind their fear of mass party rule lay the apprehension that an unfettered majoritarian democracy, without any restraints of "principle," might well violate the minority interests of the South. This anxiety was most evident in the Whigs' desire to uphold the Senate's independence against the inroads of executive and party influence. Since all the states were represented equally in the Senate, and the free and slave states were the same in number, southerners traditionally looked to that body as a guardian of their rights within the Union. But if the Senate could be controlled by means of instructions, patronage, and the public money, then its ability to serve such a function would be threatened. It would certainly be no barrier against a "despotic" northern majority agitating a popularity-seeking President to oppress the South.[14]

Southerners distressed by the style of leadership of Jackson and his followers commonly looked to Henry Clay for a more reassuring alternative. Clay, after all, was a political counter to Jackson throughout the controversies that followed the President's reelection. During the nullification crisis, Clay's voice had counseled reason and moderation. Rather than factiously side with either of the contending parties, he devised a settlement in the interest of the whole country, "patriotically" compromising the principle of protection in order to preserve national harmony. Further, he had removed the tariff issue from politics, where it had stirred up acrimonious debate.[15] During the controversy over the removal of the deposits, Clay warned that, once they were in the coffers of the pet banks, federal funds, along with the patronage, would be a source of party influence in state politics. At first, this charge may have seemed unjustified. But many southerners were persuaded of its truth once they saw the Democrats induce state legislatures to wield the club of instruction over the heads of members of the Senate. Echoing Clay, they began to call for limitations on "executive influence" in order to preserve the constitutional checks on presidential power.[16]

In short, the opponents of Jacksonian "usurpations" in the South found a congenial set of values epitomized in Clay's style of leadership. When partisan and sectional controversy raged, Clay resorted to rational persuasion instead of threats; he appealed for harmony rather than acrimony; and he evoked men's patriotism in preference to agitating the asperities of party spirit.[17] As symbolized by the statesmanship of Clay, the Whig party seemed to offer security against the worse features of Jacksonian Democracy. To its southern followers, the Whig party stood for the protection of sectional rights against factious partisanship, respect for the restraints of the Constitution and the law, and adherence to "principle" over the pursuit of popularity. Above all, it represented the settlement of controversy through the reconciliation of differences—the politics of consensus-building—rather than the appeal to force. These ideas were shared by the northern Whigs, and thus formed a potential bridge between the sectional wings of the Whig party. But the Whigs were only a loose amalgam of state parties in the early years of their organization (1833–35). It remained to be seen whether the Whigs could function as a truly national party.

[II]

The 1836 presidential election was the first test of the Whigs' ability to function on a nationwide basis, and they failed it dismally. Clay, already a two-time loser, declined to be a candidate, and the Whigs could not unite behind the other aspirants for the mantle of party leadership. Although there were several attempts to call a national convention to choose an official party ticket, many Whigs refused to submit to "dictation" by such a conclave. Lacking a practical alternative, the Whigs ran three presidential candidates (William Henry Harrison, Daniel Webster, and Hugh Lawson White) in their separate bailiwicks. By this strategy, they apparently hoped to throw the election into the House of Representatives, where there might be a Whig majority.[18]

This scheme was a mixed blessing for the Whigs. On the debit side, it enabled the Democrats to condemn them as political "aristocrats" who were attempting to prevent the choice of the President by the people. Some southern supporters of Van Buren suggested that if the Whigs controlled an election in the House, they would choose an extreme nationalist (such as Webster) who would be offensive to the South.[19] But the Whigs' plan did enable them to pose as a party of free men, who had not (as had the Democrats) compliantly accepted the handpicked candidate of the President and his "officeholders' convention." It had the added virtue of opening the way for the Whigs to run as their southern presidential candidate Senator Hugh Lawson White of

Tennessee. Replete with flowing locks and magisterial pomp, White was the epitome of the senatorial statesman. His statesmanlike qualities were cast into sharp relief because he had recently been one of Jackson's closest confidants, and had to withstand harsh attacks by Old Hickory after he embarked on his independent campaign for the presidency. His skillfully cultivated public persona was that of a martyr to the cause of liberty, who had risked his political career through his candidacy. Thus, by voting for him, southerners could issue their own declarations of independence from Jacksonian party influence.[20]

White's pronouncements rang all the standard changes upon the Whig battle cry that the Jacksonian party was composed of servile placemen following the dictates of the President. White denounced them as a "mere faction," a conglomeration "composed of men belonging to every sect, having no common bond of unity save that of a wish to place one of themselves in the highest office known to the Constitution." They united behind a single candidate because they wanted "all the honors, offices, and emoluments of the government" distributed among themselves. Once in office, these spoilsmen "become dependent upon the quarter's salary for food and clothing," and their positions were their "only means of obtaining a livelihood by honest means."[21]

Worse yet, White asserted, the placeman's parasitism was "communicated" to the members of his family and their various "connections." White claimed that "they know the situation of the officer, he and they talk it over in the family circle; they sympathize with him and all know the feelings of the executive will be the more kind towards him in proportion to his influence among his friends; and the result will be that in most cases they will settle down in the conviction that it is most wise to think and vote as the President wishes." And there was always the danger that federal spoilsmen would command the support of the public, expanding the scope of partisan dependency:

> Society, from the very situation of the officer, will suppose him a better judge of the fitness of a man for the presidential chair than he would be if he were a private man; besides that, many will know that the officer will have it in his power to do them good turns in his office if they can secure his good opinion.[22]

These utterances of White were given a special immediacy and appeal by his assertion that he was a victim of Jacksonian willfulness. White claimed that, like many southern apostles of Jefferson, he had supported Jackson in 1828 and 1832 because the Old Hero had espoused traditional Republican principles and programs. Among these he included: the distribution of the proceeds of public land sales among the states, the curtailment of executive power and patronage, the suppression of party spirit, and the appointment of federal officers solely on the basis of merit. But, White charged, Jackson had betrayed his campaign pledges once he was securely in power. Moreover, he had tried to arrogate power into his hands so that he could dictate the choice of his successor. White declared that in his own case, he had incurred the wrath of Jackson and the spite of his sycophants when he began his independent candidacy. Yet despite his personal ties to the President, White would not yield:

> I feel that I was not intended to be the *slave* of any man or set of men—that I have some mind, and that the author of my existence intended that I should form opinions as to *politics* and *religion*, and freely and fearlessly act upon them, without being intimidated by what either man or devils can do.[23]

In the southern Whigs' propaganda, the Democratic candidate for President in 1836, Vice President Martin Van Buren, was the perfect foil for White. As depicted by his southern opponents, Van Buren personified the dangers the new system of party politics represented to the special interests of the South. A meeting of Whigs in Orange County, North Carolina, sounded the leitmotifs of the White campaign's indictment of "Little Van." Van Buren, it pointed out, was no statesman. He was a mere politician, the head of New York's corrupt "Albany Regency" and a notorious trimmer. Accordingly, he had no record of great achievements by which his true attitudes toward the South might be judged. But a quick survey of his public record was enough to give southerners cause for dismay. Throughout his career in politics, Van Buren had followed what seemed to be the most expedient course of action. In 1812, he had backed the Federalists' favorite, DeWitt Clinton, in his presidential candidacy against the beloved Madison. As a state senator, he had voted to instruct New York's United States senators to oppose Missouri's admission as a slave state, and he had supported the enfranchisement of some free blacks. As a member of the national Senate, Van Buren had sustained the tariff of 1824 and masterminded the "tariff of abominations." He had only begun to court the South when the prospect of the presidency loomed before his eyes. But despite his professions of solicitude, especially on the subject of slavery, he had not changed. It was still Van Buren's "well known character" to "go *with the majority* wherever he can find it (whether right or wrong)," a quality particularly dangerous in the light of the growth of abolitionism in the North.[24]

By contrast, the Orange County Whigs saluted White as a "statesman of firm and liberal principles." Throughout his career, he had "uniformly supported the interests of the planting states." White had opposed the tariffs of 1828 and 1832, condemned the Second Bank of the United States, urged economy in government and pushed for the reduction of the powers and patronage of the executive. Most important, as a staunch son of the South, White could be counted upon to oppose abolitionism at every opportunity. The Orange County Whigs pointedly asserted that since the executive had great power to squelch the agitation of the slavery issue—as illustrated by the Post Office's recent disposal of abolitionist literature sent to the southern states—it was very important to "have a President who is with us on this great question."[25]

[III]

In the 1836 presidential election the Whigs demonstrated that, running on a regional basis (rather than merely in the separate states), they could roughly match the Democrats' vote-getting power in the South.[26] But the appearance of disarray the Whig party presented to the American public in 1836 highlighted the lack of discipline within its ranks. Even with their regional strategy, the Whigs were foiled in their scheme to throw the election into the House. However, they may have soon come to view this setback as providential. The panic of 1837 and the ensuing depression provided the Whigs with the national issues around which the sectional wings of the party could coalesce. The Whigs' resolve to make political capital of the nation's financial woes was strengthened by the defection of the Conservative Democrats from the side of the administration. The southern Conservatives and Whigs, like their northern counterparts, joined in denouncing Van Buren's sub-treasury scheme as an abandonment of government responsibility for the public good. Instead, it made the federal government the servant of selfish partisan interests. To support these contentions, the Conservatives and Whigs pointed out that the administration plan would insulate government officials from derangements of the economy. Under its provisions, the Treasury would receive and disburse monies only in specie or in federal notes, not in the depreciated bank paper available to the general public. Both the Conservatives and the Whigs suggested that this was why the party of politicians and spoilsmen liked the subtreasury. Dependent on government salaries, Democratic officeholders surely wanted their wages paid in stable coin or paper backed by the credit of the central government.[27]

The subtreasury was not an unmitigated boon for the Whigs, as Calhoun and some of his followers rejoined the Democrats over the issue. Calhoun, who had cooperated informally with the Whigs since the nullification crisis, acclaimed the subtreasury as the only sound solution to the country's financial problems. Sounding a refrain that would be repeated by other southern Democrats, he asserted that the "divorce" between bank and state would free the federal government from dependency upon northern capital. Calhoun also warned southerners that if the subtreasury were defeated, the Whigs would try to create a new national bank, an abominable engine of consolidation. Calhoun added that he was siding with the Democrats because he wanted to preserve an equitable balance between the legislative and executive branches. The "federal" Whigs, by contrast, wanted a despotism of the Congress, which would impose its will upon the entire country without regard for the Constitution, the laws, and the rights of the states.[28]

The alliance between the Calhounites and the Democrats helped clarify the ideological distinctions between the southern wings of the major parties. They clearly differed over whether the federal government had the responsibility to uphold public confidence in the banks—the Whigs (along with the Conservative Democrats) affirming the existence of such a responsibility, the Democrats denying it. But the southern Whigs' views on the banking issue did not represent an abandonment of their concern that executive power and party patronage were threats to state sovereignty. According to them, the maintenance of public confidence in the banks was essential to prevent the enlargement of partisan "influence." The subtreasury, the Whigs claimed, was nothing more than a "Treasury Bank," whereby Van Buren would acquire direct control over the people's money, a power he would employ to undermine banks owned by his opponents. Congressman Waddy Thompson of South Carolina pressed this argument with particular vehemence. He declared that if the federal government were conceded the power to manipulate or destroy the banks, which it would have under the subtreasury, than it would also be granted the ability to meddle with other state institutions, including slavery.[29]

The southern Whigs' solicitude for the particularist sensibilities of their fellow southerners was also evident in their gingerly handling of the question of how the federal government should help restore confidence in the credit of the state banks. Although some supported the creation of a new national bank independent of the executive, most avoided committing themselves to such a scheme.[30] Several even proposed banking plans which were fashioned to minimize the South's reliance on northern capital.[31] But the majority of southern Whig spokesmen did not offer or support any particular system of public finance. They preferred instead to denounce the subtreasury as a corrupt device to augment presidential power and party influence at the expense of the people's freedoms and the sovereignty of the states.[32]

[IV]

The subtreasury served well as one of the Whigs' primary targets in the demagogic log cabin campaign of 1840. With virtual unanimity, Whigs condemned it as a partisan monstrosity clearly detrimental to the national good.[33] They declared that the downfall of Van Buren and his system of influence would restore true republican government, in service to the people. Once the members of Congress were no longer subject to executive dictation, they would be free to legislate in the interest of the entire country rather than that of a mere party. The Whig standard-bearer, William Henry Harrison, also took pains to assure the public that he would not try to impose his will upon the Congress. When asked whether he would approve the chartering of a new national bank, he announced tortuously: "There is not in the constitution any express grant of power for such purpose, and it could never be constitutional to exercise that power, save in the event, the powers granted to congress could not be carried into effect, without resorting to such an institution."

But, true to the Whig gospel of legislative independence, Harrison avowed that "the executive should not by any act of his forestall the action of the national legislature," and he promised to respect the judgment of Congress on the bank issue.[34]

Despite Harrison's espousal of traditional Whig principles, the southern Whigs had some reason to feel uneasy about their party's obfuscatory tactics in 1840. Henry Clay, their choice at the national convention, had lost because of the opposition of northern Whigs who might not be solicitous of southern interests if they dominated a Harrison administration. Moreover, the Whig ticket had been chosen by a conclave of politicians, as if in emulation of the methods of the Democrats. Could southerners entrust their special concerns to the candidates chosen by such a body, whose majority had evidently placed "availability" above adherence to principle during the balloting for the presidential nomination?[35]

Whig propagandists asked southerners who might have felt such misgivings to examine the careers and characters of their candidates for President and Vice President. Both were touted as principled statesmen who would uphold the interests of the whole country, including the South. John Tyler of Virginia, their second entry, fit the conventional mold of the senatorial statesman. Like several other members of his species, he had resigned from the national Senate rather than submit to instruction by a Democratically controlled state legislature. He was the perfect complement to Harrison, a statesmanlike general in the line of Cincinnatus and Washington. The Whigs assured southerners that they could take special comfort in the fact that Harrison, like Tyler, was a son of Virginia. They also pointed out that "Tip" had remained sympathetic to southern concerns even after he moved west. As a congressman from Ohio, he had voted with the South to admit Missouri into the Union as a slave state, and had lost his seat as a result. By this martyrdom, he had demonstrated that he was no factious northern man. And even on matters where he disagreed with most southerners, such as his support of high tariffs, there was every assurance that Harrison would respect the letter of the Constitution when enforcing the decisions of Congress. At the very least, he would practice economy in government, obviating the need for excessive duties on imports.[36]

According to the Whigs, no such faith could be invested in Van Buren. They dredged up all the charges they had made against the "Sly Fox" in

1836 and liberally garnished them with references to some of his actions as President. The southern Whigs tried to make great political hay out of Van Buren's decision to sustain a legal judgment against Navy Lieutenant George Mason Hooe which had been based on the testimony of two slaves. They claimed that this judgment established a precedent contrary to the laws of the southern states, which declared that the testimony of slaves against free men was inadmissible in court. Secretary of War Joel Poinsett's militia plan (which the Whigs attributed to Van Buren) was pronounced a menace to states' rights because it would create military jurisdictions cutting across state lines and pave the way for a standing army controlled directly by the President. The Whigs cited the Democrats' actions in the case of several disputed elections to the House of Representatives as another reason to suspect the states' rights professions of the administration party. The New Jersey legislature had certified that the Whig candidates had won the contested seats, but the Democratic majority in the House had overridden its decision.[37]

But southern champions of the Whig ticket claimed that all these issues faded into insignificance before the preeminent question, the maintenance of republican virtue. As a Whig spokesman explained, Harrison's election would regenerate the republic by returning it to the hands of a statesman would would place the national interest above all else:

> We do not so much want state rights or any particular policy as integrity, honesty in our rulers. It is the fair form of virtue we should first impress on our Institutions. Let virtue's bright image be first reflected from our redeemed institutions—for no people were ever yet free who had not a rigid morality as the grand pillar of their political institutions. Elect Gen. Harrison—the wise and virtuous Harrison—and we shall hear no more . . . of incompetent and unworthy men being promoted to office . . . the primeval simplicity of by-gone days will return to bless the country— the pure days of the republic will be upon us once more.[38]

Of course, one advantage of emphasizing the putative statesmanship of Harrison was that such a stratagem allowed the Whigs to evade specific commitments on the policies they would implement once in power. However, this evasiveness could backfire easily. Since the Whigs did not stand upon a party platform, there was nothing to prevent conflicts within their ranks over what measures they should enact in office. Certainly, most Whig leaders would have denied the potential for such conflicts. They were content to claim that a Congress freed of executive influence and dominated by Whigs would enact legislation in the national interest. According to Whig spokesmen, Harrison would veto only legislation which was unconstitutional or which had been passed in undue haste; thus, there was little chance for clashes between the executive and legislature. The likelihood of collisions between the President and Congress was further reduced by Harrison's professed belief that the Chief Executive should defer to the wisdom of the national legislature. Indeed, the leaders of the congressional Whigs must have basked in glory when they heard their views on legislative supremacy echoed in Harrison's inaugural:

> it is preposterous to suppose that a thought could for a moment have been entertained that the President, placed at the center of the country, could better understand the wants of the people than their own immediate representatives, who spend a part of every year among them . . . bound to them by the triple tie of interest, duty, and affection.[39]

The accession of Tyler to the presidency caused no great alarm among the Whigs' congressional leadership, for the new President echoed Harrison's views on the proper relation among the branches of government. The Whigs in Congress were even able to maintain a publicly conciliatory stance toward Tyler after he vetoed their first national bank bill, for it apparently violated Tyler's states' rights principles. But Tyler's second bank veto was another matter. The second bank bill had been drawn up to satisfy the constitutional scruples of Tyler and was passed on an almost strictly party line vote. Consequently, when Tyler vetoed it, his professions of standing upon lofty principles were drowned out by Whig cries of treachery. His "independence" seemed mere willfulness, his "principles" pretexts for obstinacy. Few southern Whigs, no matter what their private views of the bank bills, embraced Tyler's cause; only 3 of 55 in the House stuck by the President when he was read out of the party. But, perhaps out of fear that grass-roots southern Whigs might be alienated by their treatment of Tyler, a states' rights southerner, the Whig leadership assigned key roles in the expulsion process to congressmen from below the Mason-Dixon line. Senator Willie P. Mangum of North Carolina presided over the meeting of the Whig caucus that expelled Tyler, and Congressman John

Pendleton Kennedy of Maryland drafted its "Address" to the American people and a lengthier *Defence of the Whigs*.[40]

Understandably, both the "Address" and the *Defence* tried to persuade the Whig faithful that Tyler's refusal to yield to a party majority was contrary to the requirements of true statesmanship. To those who pointed out that the Whigs had not run on a platform in 1840, the "Address" replied that the Whigs had not needed a platform that year. Their policies, it claimed, had been brought before the public for twelve years with "unexampled devotion" and "were illustrated by the precepts and practice of the most eminent and patriotic of our citizens in every form by which they were able to address themselves to the intelligence of the people." Of course, the political principles to be derived from the Whigs' "precepts and practice" were necessarily ambiguous. It was only natural in a country as large and diversified as the United States that political notions "should be subject to occasional modifications, dependent upon local influences." But this was no reason for the obduracy of Tyler. In fact, the heterogeneity of the Whig coalition made it all the more necessary that the party "move together in a spirit of mutual concession and accommodation of sectional difference of opinion." In 1840 the Whigs had

> felt a proud consciousness that in the patriotism of the party all such differences would vanish, and that the demands of an enlarged welfare would be met and fulfilled, through the virtue of that spirit of compromise and forbearance, that liberal and comprehensive sentiment of self-denial and concession, which rests at the heart of our confederacy, and which constitutes the living principle of our Union.[41]

But Tyler had frustrated the best hopes of the Whigs. Why had he pursued such a perverse and destructive course? The Whigs could not, of course, impute principled motives to Tyler's actions. If they had done so, it would have been impossible for them to adduce lofty reasons for his expulsion. *The Defence of the Whigs* therefore charged that Tyler had surrounded himself with a clique of mercenary politicians in the first months of his administration. Seeing that they stood no chance of preferment under future Whig presidents, the members of this new "Kitchen Cabinet" had inflated Tyler's ambition to seek a second term. They realized that the Whigs had ruled out more than one term for the President, and that Tyler would therefore have to ingratiate himself with the Democrats; hence, they had induced him to veto the bank bills. But the Democrats, too, had recognized the contemptible duplicity of Tyler. After playing upon his vanity and lust for power to frustrate the Whigs, they had abandoned him to a pitiful "corporal's guard" of supporters.[42]

[V]

After the Tyler trauma, the Whigs still presented themselves as a party of statesmen selflessly devoted to the national interest. But through their difficulties with Tyler, the Whigs learned a valuable lesson. If they were to function as a stable element in a two-party system, it was necessary for individuals to subordinate their views to the cause of party unity.[43] Party loyalty in effect became for the Whigs, as it was for the Democrats, an expression of the highest patriotism. Yet the Whigs still felt the need to believe that their party served worthier purposes than the opposition. One way they maintained this faith was by continuing to denounce their foes—the Tylerites as well as the Democrats—as self-interested factions of spoilsmen and "despots." Another way was through the cult of Henry Clay. In Clay, Whigs professed to see "the highest moral and intellectual qualities of the *Statesman*—courage, elevation of character and elevation of views; a nobleness of and generosity of nature that attracts confidence, and can inspire enthusiasm; the spirit of persuasion and the spirit of command combined."[44] It was especially important that the Whigs be perceived in the South as the party of statesmanship, selflessly dedicated to the interests of the entire country. For only then could many southern Whigs be good party men without feeling that they might be false to the minority interests of their section.

CHAPTER 7

The Southern Whigs and Economic Development

W HEN THE southern Whigs rallied behind Clay after the Tyler fiasco, they joined forces behind his economic program as well. Not only did most Whig congressmen from the South vote for the Kentuckian's proposals; they espoused and defended them on the stump. To be sure, sectional appeals did not entirely disappear from the rhetoric of the southern Whigs. But party spokesmen made a deliberate effort to downplay them. The injection of the Texas annexation question into the 1844 campaign was bewailed by the Whigs of the South, who feared the sectionally divisive effects of the issue. Throughout the campaign, they tried repeatedly but without much success to make economic policy the main topic of debate.[1]

The southern Whigs' embrace of economic nationalism has long puzzled historians. One scholar has described it as "The Great Aberration,"[2] a phrase which suggests that it was a deviant episode in the history of southern Whiggery. It should be noted, however, that even after their supposed metamorphosis, the southern Whigs defended their support of party measures with arguments pitched to the special sensibilities of their section. For example, many justified the levying of duties on imports with the argument that its primary objective was to raise needed government revenue. Aware that the protection of manufactures had long been condemned as oppressive to the South, they described protection as a merely "incidental" effect of Whig tariff legislation.[3] Moreover, there were clear limits to the southern Whigs' willingness to support national economic legislation. When the Whig tariff of 1842 was modified in a manner favorable to northern manufactures and separated from a provision requiring the distribution of federal revenue among the states, it lost considerable support among Whig congressmen from the South.[4]

But the southern Whigs' regard for the distinctive concerns of their section should not obscure the fact that they believed there were important differences between themselves and the southern Democrats. Indeed, their willingness to provide extenuating arguments for Whig policies indicates that their primary loyalties were to the party and what they thought were its basic objectives. Their fidelity to Whiggery meant, in turn, that they pursued their goals within a national frame of reference—i.e., that they were more interested in making common cause with Whigs in other parts of the country than with their fellow southerners in the Democratic party.

What did the southern Whigs believe distinguished them and their northern colleagues from the Democrats? Above all, Whigs defined their differences from the Democrats in terms of certain ideals, beliefs, and assumptions which comprised their distinct perspective on politics and society. Most important, Whigs presupposed that every polity was a harmonious entity with a single, overriding interest—the common good—which was distinct from, yet incorporated, the interests of every social group. The Whigs believed that it was the special duty of the statesman to ascertain the common good, and that he could do so because of his high-minded and disinterested devotion to the general welfare. The statesman appealed to the people in their status as *citizens*, who were obligated to subordinate their own concerns to the needs of the polity. In this respect, he was unlike the politician, who pandered to voters' immediate and self-serving conceptions of their interests, often at the expense of dividing and undermining the republic.[5]

The Whigs also had grave reservations about the spread of partisanship and party conflict. These phenomena were promoted by the Jacksonian Democrats, who implicitly (and sometimes explicitly) repudiated the Whigs' faith in an organic harmony of social interests. The acceptance of the legitimacy of competition between parties, after all, implied the recognition of conflicting interests in the polity—or at least of contrasting definitions of the common good. Mass political parties also interposed their own interests between the citizen and the state. The partisan's passionate devotion to his party, Whigs feared, imperiled his ability to make a rational judgment of what measures would contribute to the general welfare. It may therefore have been an important psychological requirement for the Whigs that they believe their party was led by statesmen, for only then could they feel like true citizens.[6]

The Whigs' political perspective reflected their desire to uphold the corporate and organic ideals of republicanism in an era of rapid change. It appealed, naturally enough, to conservatives who were repelled by the Democrats' rhetoric of class warfare and party conflict. But because it incorporated some of the most cherished ideals of republican ideology, the Whigs' outlook had broad popular appeal. Like the Democrats, the Whigs seem to have craved the supposed purity and unity of the early republic, and this craving seems to have fed upon their innate realization of the hopelessness of satisfying it.[7]

[I]

The Whigs' perspective on the government's proper role in the economy was first clearly elicited by the panic of 1837. The southern Whigs' explanation of the crisis and their proposals to remedy it closely paralleled those of their northern colleagues. They attributed the distress to Jacksonian "experiments" with a hard money currency which, they charged, had undermined public trust in the paper-issuing banks. They also asserted that the subtreasury plan would worsen the contraction of the economy by withdrawing the public money from circulation. Concomitantly, the Whigs called for federal policies which would restore the people's confidence in the credit system, and restraints upon the expansion and contraction of the paper money supply to prevent inflationary "booms" and deflationary "busts." At the state level, the Whigs defended the banks against assaults by radical, hard money Democrats who wanted to suspend their operations altogether.[8]

Although the southern Whigs did not agree upon any single scheme for reviving the economy in the late 1830s, they were virtually unanimous in affirming that the federal government was responsible for supporting the credit system. This consensus arose from their conviction that credit, when subject to salutary governmental controls, was a good thing. There were several ways in which the paper money system contributed to the common good. It promoted republicanism by providing young men and the poor with the means of attaining their "competence." It prevented wealth from being selfishly hoarded by its owners, and instead kept it in constant circulation. These procredit arguments provided the foundations for another Whig thesis, that the interests of social classes in an advanced, commercial society were organically interlinked and mutually harmonious. While hard money Democrats condemned bank investors as an "aristocracy" who lived off the fruits of speculation rather than physical labor, the Whigs praised them as public benefactors. Through the credit system, the wealth of such men could be mobilized in sufficient quantities to finance projects which were beyond the resources of individuals, but which served the general welfare—bridges, buildings, and canals. Moreover, the opportunities for upward mobility created by the credit system assured that wealth would constantly change hands, preventing the development of an exclusive American aristocracy.[9]

The southern Whigs' defense of the credit system, like that of their northern counterparts, was based on moral and psychological assumptions which were attuned to the requirements of the marketplace. It presupposed, above all, that men had the internalized self-discipline necessary in a commercial economy, with its many temptations to extravagance and ill-advised speculations. Indeed, from the Whig perspective, the credit system was a school of character because it bestowed its rewards on frugality, moderation, and self-restraint. Only men with such qualities received the "confidence" of creditors, and only they had the steadiness and application to make a fortune from their borrowed assets. The Whigs consequently ridiculed the Democrats' hard money policies as a throwback to "Spartan" republicanism, which proposed to make men virtuous by reducing them to poverty. According to them, such policies would actually lower private and public morality by removing the incentives to individual virtue. A Whig pamphleteer praised countries with abundant credit because in them "integrity and industry avail their possessor and have their reward," but deplored the moral condition of those with hard money economies. In such nations, there was "no incentive to moral ambition," and "in this condition man must necessarily drag out a miserable life of licentiousness, vice, and crime." More, a commercial economy based on credit promoted republican liberty by elevating men's estimation of their own worth:

> The effect of commerce, indeed, is to liberalize, enlighten and improve
> mankind. It adds to the wealth and comfort, and in this way conduces to

the physical and intellectual improvement, and the consequent respectability of the human race. In fine, it places man in that condition, in which
he feels the dignity of human nature and the consequence of himself. And
until you do place him in this condition, he can never become an aspirant
for freedom. Hence it is, that the nations which have been most liberalized
by the civilizing, elevating influences of commerce, have been most
imbued with the spirit of liberty.[10]

The national bank controversy of 1841 subjected the southern Whigs'
commercial principles to a stern political test. Although they had
enthusiastically embraced the banking system, most of the southern
Whigs had previously avoided committing themselves to support of a
new national bank, in part out of fear of being charged with "Federalism" by the Democrats. Because of this anxiety, southern Whigs also
took great pains to prove that a national "fiscal agency" was not contrary
to states' rights or strict constructionist principles. Several demonstrated,
with an impressive show of evidence, that the establishment of the first
Bank of the United States had been supported by most southern
Jeffersonian Republicans. The southern Whigs also made much of the
fact that Republicans from the South had played leading roles in the
creation of the second bank. President James Madison, a Virginia
Republican, had proposed its establishment, which had been supported
by the majority of the southern Republicans in Congress. By contrast,
most northern Federalist congressmen had voted against the chartering
of the second national bank.[11]

The southern Whigs also tried to refute Democratic charges that a
central bank would reduce the economy of the South to "colonial"
dependence upon northern capital. They deplored such assertions for
suggesting that the interests of the sections were mutually incompatible,
and tried to demonstrate that the South, like the rest of the country,
would benefit from a national financial system. Several claimed that
without a central bank, southerners would suffer from discriminatory
rates of exchange between the sections. They pointed out that northern
merchants received a premium on the price of imported goods shipped
to the South from northern ports. This state of affairs would continue
and perhaps even worsen if there were no central fiscal agency to provide
the country with a single currency of uniform value. Henry Clay made a
somewhat similar argument to several audiences during a tour of the
South in 1844. He appealed to nationalistic sentiments and resentments

in support of his contention that the southern states shared the nation's interest in a new national bank. Clay argued that the strongest opposition to a central bank came from British "monied and commercial interests" operating through Wall Street. These interests knew that without such a bank, the United States—especially its less developed regions, the South and the West—would be dependent upon them for capital, and that they would be able to charge Americans exorbitant rates of interest. But a federal bank, Clay prophesied, would free the United States from this dependency and provide southerners with easier and cheaper credit.[12]

[II]

Although the Whigs continued to defend banking at the state level after 1844, they virtually abandoned proposals to create a new national bank in the wake of Clay's defeat. But they remained consistent in their support of Whig tariffs. Southern Democrats were quick to attack such measures as special class legislation, whereby northern manufacturers were enabled to plunder the agrarian consumers of the South. Their Whig counterparts were equally quick to decry such claims for suggesting a fictitious incompatibility between the interests of the sections. In a protariff speech, Congressman Robert Toombs of Georgia protested Democratic "efforts to prejudice the south against the north, or the north against the south." The people of both sections, he avowed, "have a common interest as well as a common history. The blood that was mingled at Yorktown and at Eutaw cannot be kept at enmity forever, and the time as come when the whig of Bunker Hill is the same as the whig in Georgia." In a similar defense of Whig tariff legislation, Senator John MacPherson Berrien, also of Georgia, told a Boston audience that "I have endeavored to implant in the minds of all the people of Georgia, that—distant as they may be from portions of the country—the whole country is their country, and that they have a great and deep interest in whatever concerns the prosperity of the whole country."[13]

Congressman Alexander H. H. Stuart of Virginia articulated forcefully the corporate conception of the Union which underlay the southern Whigs' support of tariff legislation. Addressing his colleagues in Congress, he avowed:

> In my opinion, it will be found, if we take a comprehensive and statesmanlike view of our whole Confederacy, that there is in truth no

necessary conflict of interest between the North and the South, or the East and the West. The very diversities of soil, of climate, of population and of production, which at the first might be supposed to create antagonistic interests, are, when rightly considered, the most fruitful sources of strength and union and harmony. . . . We should look at the great interests of the nation, not as something separate and distinct from each other, but as constituting parts of a grand system, intimately connected together, wisely fitted to each other, and when properly brought into action, working harmoniously together, and mutually giving and receiving nutriment and support.[14]

Of course, the southern Whigs were not content to defend tariff measures with abstract arguments on the nature of society. There were concrete reasons why the national interest would be served by the imposition of duties on certain imports. Many favored such a policy because the stimulus it would afford domestic manufacturing would make the United States less dependent upon Europe, especially Great Britain. Appealing to American hatred of foreign influence, Congressman John Bell of Tennessee urged the wisdom of protection because it would "tend materially to reduce and cripple the energies" of the countries "with whom we have any considerable commercial connections." Sargeant S. Prentiss of Mississippi and "Parson" William G. Brownlow of Tennessee agreed that, so long as Americans relied upon the British for manufactured goods, they would be "slaves" of a despised foe. For this reason, Thomas L. Clingman, Congressman from North Carolina, echoed Whig charges that the free trade Democrats were the "British party," who would undo by economic means what the Revolution had accomplished in the political realm.[15]

Some southern Whigs developed a sectional variation upon this theme of liberating the United States from economic subserviency to Great Britain. They pointed out that the British were increasingly relying upon India for their supplies of raw cotton, and thus could not be relied upon in the future as a market for the South. Several even suggested that Great Britain might attempt to "abolitionize" the southern states by suddenly cutting off its cotton imports. It was therefore in the interest of the South that it build up the northern textile industry. Northern manufacturers, as citizens of the same country, could at least be trusted not to make war upon southerners' "peculiar institution."[16]

But this appeal was uncharacteristic of the southern Whigs' arguments for the tariff; most of them subsumed southern interests under the rubric of the national interest. The southern Whigs were especially fond of the notion that the industrialization of the North would promote an intersectional harmony of interests by creating a larger consumer market for southern agricultural goods. If northerners needed the products of southern farms, and southerners needed northern customers, neither would even contemplate disunion. The southern Whig press quoted approvingly a group of Mississippi planters who predicted in 1844:

> If the system of affording adequate protection to American industry be perservered in for but a few years, all the great interests of the country will become so blended and so dependent one upon another, that all attempts, whether of abolitionists or of abstractionists, to destroy our beloved Union, will be laughed to scorn for centuries to come.[17]

The Augusta, Georgia, *Chronicle* employed some counterfactual reasoning to emphasize the importance of the northern consuming market. If manufacturers did not prosper, northern workingmen would be driven out of work, migrate west, and become farmers. Inevitably, this would result in a glutted market of farm produce; worse yet, since farmers ordinarily made their own clothing, there would be less demand for southern cotton and wool. The *Chronicle* concluded:

> Every man retained in the factories of Lowell, or in the furnaces of Pennsylvania, is a customer of the farmer and planter, and every man driven from them to seek the west must of necessity become a rival. Wherever men are enabled to combine their exertions, their labor becomes more productive, and they become larger consumers. Wherever they are forced to fly from each other, their labor becomes less productive, and they become smaller consumers.[18]

And what of the effects of the tariff upon consumer prices? Southern Whigs conceded that the exclusion of cheap imports might temporarily increase the expense of home manufactured goods. But in short order, the stimulus afforded domestic industry by protective duties would result in a countervailing increase in the supply of inexpensive American manufactures. In fact, native-made products would probably be cheaper than the European variety because they would not have to be shipped great distances. To validate these assertions, southern Whigs often cited price figures for the period following the enactment of the 1842 tariff. These statistics demonstrated, they maintained, that the measure had not imposed a great hardship upon the American buying public.[19]

Passionately committed to the idea of a national harmony of interests, the southern Whigs often presented themselves as the champions of the welfare of northern workingmen. Repeating a standard party refrain, they advocated the passage of Whig tariffs because they would vindicate the right of the American worker to the fruits of his labor. Without protective duties, southern Whigs claimed, cheap imports would compel native manufacturers to lower their employees' wages to the dismally low levels paid European laborers. For this reason, declaimed Congressman Daniel M. Barringer of North Carolina, the Whigs' tariff proposals manifested the virtues of republican institutions in America, which enabled every man to rise to the limits of his capacity. Senator Berrien added his vigorous assent to this sentiment, declaring that there was nothing wrong with favoring the industrious working poor of the United States over the idle "pauper labor of Europe."[20]

It may seem incongruous for southerners to assert the dignity of free labor when their own society rested upon slaves. But most southerners believed that slavery placed all white men upon a level of equality because it established race, not class, as the basis of social distinctions. It was therefore easy for southern Whigs to praise the tariff for exalting free (i.e., white) labor; to them, such praise implied no criticism of slavery as a system. Robert Toombs showed this in his own protariff argument. Pointing to the fact that Calhoun made an exception to his free trade principles when it came to sugar grown in Louisiana—which was cultivated by slaves—Toombs charged the South Carolinian with placing a higher value on slave labor than free labor. Protection, after all, was a form of preferential treatment. But if any labor was entitled to special consideration, Toombs contended, "it is the labor of freemen. It is the labor of the hardy mechanic and plain workman, in what he manufactures for home consumption." Toombs' implication was clear: the Whigs, not Calhoun and the Democrats, were the true advocates of the interests of the white workingman.[21]

[III]

The protariff arguments advanced by the southern Whigs were premised upon the assumption of a sectional division of labor: the North was the manufacturing section, the South, the planting section. However, a considerable number of southern Whigs favored the promotion of industry in the South itself and thought that the tariff would help their cause. Among these men there were strident critics of southern economic backwardness who claimed that slavery was a severe impediment to the material uplift of their section. But with few exceptions, such Whigs were hamstrung by their attachment to a stable and harmonious social order. Fearful of slave revolts and the massive dislocations which a general emancipation might entail, they did nothing that directly undermined slavery. Often themselves slaveowners, they could appreciate the concerns of the planter class as well as its formidable political power. Thus, while antislavery southern Whigs developed penetrating critiques of involuntary servitude, they never matched them with realistic programs for its elimination. They shared in a virtually universal southern consensus that slavery should be dealt with by the South on its own, and they proposed no more radical a solution to the problem than that slaveholders participate in the colonization movement.[22] The presence of vocal critics of slavery among the southern Whigs was significant in one respect, however. It made it easier for the antislavery Whigs of the North to support their party, believing that its southern wing hoped to ameliorate the condition of the slaves or even to eliminate slavery altogether through the economic "redemption" of the South.[23]

Yet it is unlikely that most southern Whigs saw any necessary or desirable connection between the economic revitalization of the South and the subversion of slavery. The views expressed by a Whig newspaper in Georgia seem to have been typical of those held by a majority of southern party members:

> Slaveholders must demonstrate in a large way, and by visible results, that slave labor is as profitable to you and as useful to the world, as free labor is at the North or can be at the South—that it is not inimical to common schools, the improvement of the soil and the progress of manufactures. . . . Our sectional movements are taken for weakness in this regard. The whole matter will turn in the end on the pivot of dollars and cents. We can only prove our view by attaining prosperity.[24]

Southern Whigs made a strong case for the thesis that the industrialization of the South would actually serve the interests of the planter class.
Owing largely to the overproduction of cotton, the first half of the 1840s
was a period of financial hardship for most of the staple growers of the
South. Whigs argued sensibly that the promotion of the nonagricultural
sectors of the southern economy would aid the cause of economic
recovery. For one thing, if capital were diverted into manufacturing, less
cotton might be grown, relieving the glut which depressed prices; for
another, a larger southern working class would provide an increased
consumer market for the produce of the farms and fields.[25]

But the southern Whigs had much broader and more profound
concerns than the profits of planters. Most of all, they wanted to
strengthen that harmony which they believed was the "natural"
relationship between social classes. The effectiveness of the Democrats'
appeals to the populace gave them particular cause for worry. In the
South, Jacksonian rhetoric seemed to pander to the resentments of the
so-called poor whites, who hated the aristocratic pretensions and lordly
manners of the better-established planters. The Democrats' crusades
against the banks and its attempts to eliminate the "federal basis" of
representation in several southern state legislatures also appeared to be
keyed to the sympathies of this element. To the Whigs, the poor whites'
support of such schemes was evidence of their particular susceptibility to
manipulation by politicians who tried to stir up class conflict. In fact, the
southern Democrats were no menace to the social order; like their
counterparts elsewhere, they only wanted to minimize government-
sanctioned privilege. But the southern Whigs, who wanted to protect
such privilege, were loath to see or admit this. It was more convenient for
them to perceive and depict the Democrats as reckless demagogues and
disorganizers who might even attack slavery if votes were to be won by
doing so.[26]

The poor whites to whom the Democrats appealed presented the
Whigs with a dilemma rooted in the social structure of the South. They
were condemned to poverty—and thus to feelings of estrangement and
resentment—so long as they disdained manual labor. But their disdain
seemed to be derived from the stigma slavery placed upon all work with
one's hands. How, then, in the absence of an effective program of
emancipation, could they be uplifted socially? Some southern Whigs saw
industrialization as one way out. Through the useful, productive, and

well-paying jobs they provided, factories would help transform impoverished southern whites into industrious, discipled, and presumably contented workers. Some southern industrialists also took special steps to ensure that their employees were models of virtue. For instance, Daniel Pratt, a prominent Alabama manufacturer and Whig, established a model factory community in his "Prattville" which was patterned after similar towns in the North. He provided neat and trim homes for the inhabitants, whom he encouraged to come in family units rather than as isolated individuals. Liquor was not permitted within two miles of the center of town, and there were churches in which Prattvillers learned the benefits of abstemious living. Schools inculcated habits of industry and thrift in operatives' children while their parents worked.[27]

Southern Whigs promoted industrialization as a politically inocuous solution to another problem at least partly attributable to slavery—the flight from the South of small farmers displaced by the plantation system.[28] Whigs from areas hard hit by this difficulty declared that the exodus would continue unless would-be migrants were given new and remunerative forms of employment, such as factory work.[29] For similar reasons, southern Whigs were enthusiastic about Henry Clay's proposal that some of the federal revenue distributed among the states should help finance internal improvements. With canals and railroads linking them to the marketplace, isolated and impoverished farmers who might otherwise have to emigrate would be able to prosper on their native soil. Uplifted financially with the help of the government, they would become reliable, sedentary, and tax-paying members of their communities.[30]

[IV]

Although the southern Whigs presented themselves as guardians of public virtue, their economic programs were contrary to traditional republican precepts. Those precepts taught that the ideal "virtuous" republican was a self-sufficient freeholder, able to determine the interest of the whole polity because he was dependent upon no one for his livelihood. Equally important to the preservation of the citizen's virtue, according to classical republican ideology, was that he not become so involved in the pursuit of material goods that he lose sight of the public good. These spartan and pastoral ideals were incarnated in the gospel of the Old Republican ideologues of the Democratic party. The Old Republicans condemned large-scale industry for reducing workingmen to dependency upon manufacturers and tariffs for plundering the nation's virtuous husbandmen. Worse still, declaimed the agrarian radicals, policies which artificially stimulated economic growth threatened to create an effeminate and corrupt breed of Americans. The bane of "luxury" always endangered the health of republics, and its dangers were multiplied when wealth was obtained through manipulation and legerdemain. Only the moral discipline exacted by honest industry, the Old Republicans preached, could keep men virtuous.[31]

In the case of some southern Democrats, a commitment to pristine republicanism amounted to a rejection of modernity itself. To these men, the Whigs' promotion of a diversified economic system threatened to make an anachronism of the ideal of an agrarian republic. Such exponents of simplicity also prophesied that as Americans consumed more, they would succumb to the evils of luxury and lose that hardihood of character required of the good citizen. In the South, the most agrarian region of the country, charges of this sort were especially damaging. Many southerners had come to believe that their section had a distinct "civilization" based on rural values, and they feared that it might be undermined by commercialism and industrialism.[32]

Confronted with the old-fashioned republicanism of their critics, southern Whigs found themselves in a quandary. They would not forswear the benefits of material progress, yet neither did they want to relinquish principles and moral preferences they had been taught to cherish. Some, of course, were not aware of any difficulty. Others tried to reconcile traditional ideals with modern realities. Perhaps the most illuminating statement by men in this second category was that of Congressman Everett H. Ewing of Tennessee. Speaking in opposition to a Democratic move to lower tariff levels, Ewing conceded that there were those who believed that "it would be better for us to remain a simple agricultural people, with few wants and appetites, and with fewer of the luxuries and appliances which have become common to the rest of the world." Ewing did not think that this point of view was reasonable, however. It was impractical to think that the United States, with its many commercial contacts abroad, could avoid being affected by such influences. Furthermore, the experience of classical republics, upon which the Old Republicans and free trade Democrats based their theories, was not applicable to the middle of the nineteenth century:

> Homilies may be read about the evils of luxury, about the decline and fall of people and of empires through its baneful influence, about their overthrow by the simple, and hardy, and barbarous people upon their borders. Cincinnatus and Cato, Lycurgus and Solon, may be held up to our view as splended exemplars of the good old times when man was in his prime, and indulgence was held little better than an offence against the just laws of his nature. To all this it may be answered, that, among the ancient nations, civilization, refinement, and a general diffusion of intelligence, had no real existence; that there existed few, if any, of the checks and balances of modern society; that with luxury necessarily came vice, and, with indulgence, not unfrequently the grossest sensuality. The complicated web of modern civil society had no exemplar in ancient times, nor can any fair comparison be instituted between the states of the people in these distant periods.[33]

Ewing's comments provide a key to understanding how the Whigs revised classic republican civic ideals to the requirements of a commercialized society. Firmly enmeshed in "the complicated web of modern civil society," their model citizen had his virtue preserved through an elaborate system of social controls which ensured he would be "intelligent," "civilized," and "refined."[34] This notion was most explicitly stated by Senator Reverdy Johnson of Maryland. He argued that the Whigs' tariff of 1842 was fundamental to American prosperity, which was in turn essential to the institutions which maintained public morals—chiefly, the churches and the schools. Thus, to eliminate the tariff, and in the process reduce men to a condition of want, would be to subvert both private and public virtue. The poor had little use for education and religion because they had no hope for the future and were thoroughly engrossed in the business of merely staying alive. In the depths of their despair, many of them resorted to vice and crime to sustain themselves.[35]

The Whigs' conception of virtue was reflected in their perceptions of themselves and their opponents. From their perspective, the Democrats were the party of "French liberty"—like the Jacobins, they conceived of freedom simply as the absence of restraints. Impatient not merely with external controls but with the fetters of law and precedent, the

Democrats attacked all manner of things established. In Mississippi, they advocated the repudiation of legitimate bonded debts; in Rhode Island, they supported a rebellion against the state constitution; in the South, they allied with nullifiers who threatened to divide the Union if Texas was not annexed from Mexico; and throughout the country, they were associated with Loco-focos and "agrarians" who denounced banks and wanted indiscriminate social leveling. In the Whigs' view, the Democrats' seeming disregard for vested institutions marked them as the party of licentiousness. By undermining the wholesome barriers against mob rule, they might reduce the country to anarchy and pave the way for its submission to a despot. The Whigs, by contrast, saw themselves as the party of "regulated liberty"; they believed that men could only be free if they sublimated their appetites, and subjected them to rational discipline. This was the freedom appropriate to a "civilized" republic, in which the special virtue of the citizen was his capacity for self-restraint. The Richmond *Whig* thus argued that while the Whigs might be wrong in supporting certain economic policies, "but supporting, as they do, Liberty regulated by law—a republicanism alike removed from licentiousness and despotism—they are far preferable to the political enthusiasts, in whose footsteps follow the destruction of private rights, and the establishment of anarchy and tyranny."[36]

Like their northern colleagues, the southern Whigs believed that there were certain institutions which helped propagate virtuous character traits—the legal system, religion, and public education. But perhaps because of the relative paucity of common schools in the South, they placed a special emphasis on the last of these. It was axiomatic, many Whigs believed, that an ignorant people would follow unprincipled demagogues who pandered to their resentments. A well-regulated education, however, would inculcate a strong sense of civic responsibility in children, making them into sober and law-abiding citizens. Citing Montesquieu on the necessity of virtue in a republic, Congressman William Cost Johnson of Maryland asserted that Americans "must sink into ignorance, into anarchy, or into despotism, if they have not the means and facilities of early and progressive education." Congressman Thomas L. Clingman of North Carolina expressed a similar faith. He endorsed Henry Clay's proposal that some of the federal revenue should be earmarked for the support of common schools "so that our voters hereafter may understand their rights as inhabitants of this free

Republic, and no longer be the victims of the arts of demagogues." Such sentiments were apparently so widespread that Judge Benjamin F. Porter of Alabama asked rhetorically: "Is it necessary, at this day, to remind you, or to enforce by argument, that the foundation of our government is virtue, that virtue springs from education, and that a state of ignorance is the worst of all states, a state successfully of superstition, barbarity, despotism, crime?"[37]

Public education would also help combat the rigid stratification of social classes. Southern Whigs claimed that common schools were an important agency for awakening and developing the talents of poor children. Congressman Kenneth Rayner of North Carolina, for instance, exhorted the Congress to vote to distribute money for the support of common schools among the states in order to "bring to the service of his country many an indigent youth that might otherwise have passed through life unknowing and unknown. . . . You will enable each State to establish a moral garden within its limits for cultivation of many a mental flower that might otherwise 'waste its sweetness on the desert air.' "[38]

Southern Whigs also believed that public education contributed to the harmonization of social classes. Because children were supposedly mixed together in common school classrooms without regard to their parents' social status, public education served to lower some of the psychological barriers dividing the rich from the poor. Since students were graded by performance and ability in the common school, it promoted the republican ideal of equal opportunity. "Civis," writing in the Raleigh *Register*, celebrated the fact that "There is a democracy of feeling connected with a common school, which forbids every kind of preference except that of personal merit, and which brings all upon a level in duties to be preferred." To combat feelings of class envy, there also had to be a "levelling down of all feelings of rank by birth or fortune"; so "Civis" urged wealthy parents to send their offspring to publicly funded schools.[39]

With their great faith in the republicanizing effects of education, it was only logical for Whigs to think that the fortunes of their party were directly linked to the enlightenment of the populace. Education, they believed, would bring the Whig ideals of private and public virtue to the ignorant and undisciplined votaries of Jacksonian Democracy. The Whigs could not triumph, asserted a Whig newspaper in Augusta, Georgia, until "education dispels the darkness from the sequestered

regions, where common schools, churches, newspapers, and post-offices
are far between. In these is the home of the unadulterated Democracy in
Georgia." Likewise, after the Whigs' disastrous rout in the 1852 elections,
the Raleigh *Register* consoled itself with the observation that

> It is one of the most conclusive demonstrations of the unity of
> Locofocoism and Demagogueism [*sic*], that wherever ignorance prevails,
> there that party holds its impregnable majorities. . . . we feel assured that
> schools will prove the effectual ally of Whig doctrines, the wholesome food
> that will finally give health to the whole body politic, drive out the evil
> spirit of Locofocoism, and make the American Republic no longer an
> experiment, but a glorious truth, a magnificent and proud certainty, based
> upon an imperishable foundation, and destined to bless the world through
> ages upon ages, yet to come.[40]

[V]

The southern Whigs' support of federal assistance for the material
development of the country was only sustainable in a congenial political
climate. In the early 1840s, when they became full converts to economic
nationalism, their prospects of success seemed good. Intersectional
tensions were at a low ebb, so many southerners were willing to
cooperate with northerners in supporting nationalistic legislation. The
then-current depression increased support for proposals to restore the
financial health of the nation through schemes of public finance. The
Whigs' distribution plan was popular, as states hard hit by the crisis in
the economy were anxious for help in paying their debts and financing
their school systems and internal improvements. The severity of the
economic downturn for southern staple-crop farmers made them
increasingly receptive to the Whig argument that manufacturing would
provide them with enlarged markets and new capital outlets. And, as if to
confirm the wisdom of Whig policies, the passage of the tariff of 1842
was followed by a period of general recovery.[41]

But events were unkind to the Whigs. Tyler vetoed their bank and
distribution bills, while the Polk administration reestablished the sub-
treasury and helped bring about the demise of the tariff of 1842. Furthermore, the failure of economic disaster to follow the passage of the
subtreasury and the Walker tariff belied the Whigs' claims that a national

financial system and high tariff were vital to prosperity. In the general upturn of the mid-1840s, agricultural prices also rebounded. This made it less sensible for southerners to invest in risky industrial ventures when they were almost assured of quick returns in staple production. Most important, the sectional crises which began in the late 1840s made it difficult for southern Whigs to claim that there was an intersectional harmony of interests. By the 1852 elections, a substantial number of southern Whigs had abandoned their party's nationalistic economic programs. Many were also prepared to abandon the party itself if its northern wing refused to endorse the "finality" of the compromise of 1850.[42]

Of course, the southern Whigs did not lose all interest in the promotion of material progress. What did tend to disappear was the national frame of reference. No longer eager to strengthen a federal government which might be used by the northern majority to oppress the South, they increasingly called upon southerners to raise themselves by their own bootstraps. Having largely abandoned the tariff, they urged that special incentives be given to southern industrialists, including measures to discourage southern purchase of goods from the North or abroad.[43] Some also advocated the use of education to strengthen southern unity. These men urged that "Yankee" influences be purged from southern classrooms by employing teachers born and trained in the South who would use texts which were "sound" on sectional issues.[44]

These strategies were not endorsed by all the southern Whigs.[45] And most of those who did endorse them wanted to preserve the Union, not destroy it. An economically self-sufficient and internally unified South, these Whigs argued, would have a stronger bargaining position vis à vis the North in any future controversies affecting slavery. Because it could apply economic pressure to wring concessions from northern politicians, it would not have to resort to drastic political remedies, such as the threat of secession. Southern Whigs felt compelled to add, however, that if separation were to become necessary, an autarchic South could contemplate the prospect without fear of catastrophe. It was one indication of the heightened sectional consciousness in southern politics that they should think they were obliged to make such a statement.[46]

By relinquishing their support of nationalistic economic policies, the southern Whigs gave up much that had previously distinguished them from their opponents. Many southern Democrats found acceptable the idea of *state* aid to private enterprise because it did not require an activist federal government, and could be promoted as a prop of southern rights.[47] Yet differences remained. Many southern Whigs retained the civic consciousness which had shaped their critique of the Democracy, and they remained wary of the "demagogic" agitation of sectional issues. The American (Know-Nothing) and Constitutional Union parties appealed to many southern Whigs, it appears, because they gave voice to a yearning for the restoration of comity in America, under the aegis of high-minded statesmen. In addition, southern Whigs could support these parties without abandoning their faith in the essential harmony of American society. The Know-Nothings and Constitutional Unionists argued alike that the crises of the 1850s were largely due to irresponsible fanatics and agitators who inflated the significance of relatively minor or purely symbolic issues. The major spokesmen of the two parties found unacceptable the idea that there were fundamental disparities between the interests of the sections.[48] It is revealing, however, that the Know-Nothings and Constitutional Unionists avoided committing themselves to constructive programs for directing the nation's material development. The differences between the outlooks of most voters in the North and in the South—no matter how factitious—effectively barred them from advancing such programs. Neither the Know-Nothings or Constitutional Unionists could afford to project ambitious visions of the nation's future, because by doing so they would have raised troubling questions about the place of slavery. Partly for this reason, both parties were weak and fitful offspring of Whiggery, fated to live short lives destitute of accomplishment.

CHAPTER 8

Alexander Stephens: States' Rights Whig

A S IRRELEVANT as it might seem to the crass realities of antebellum politics, the role of the statesman was an eminently practical one for its Whig adherents. The statesman, after all, governed his public conduct by an "ethic of responsibility."[1] His table of virtues did not consist of Platonic absolutes, to be implemented without concern for their worldly consequences; his zeal for "improvement" was tempered by a scrupulous regard for time-honored traditions, usages, and institutions. In times of trouble, he did not resort to chimerical "experiments" or easy expedients, surrendering the "calm and dispassionate conclusions of wisdom and experience to the sudden outbreaks of popular feeling."[2] Neither, however, did the statesman disregard the will of the electorate. Rather, it was "his duty to bow in obedience to the sober judgment of the people, after reason and reflection have regained their dominion."[3]

But for all their professions of statesmanship, the Whigs always had great difficulty in reconciling principle with practicality, reality with the ideal. They might claim to venerate established institutions, but there was a "peculiar institution" which was morally repellent to most northern members of the party.[4] The southern Whigs knew that, given the intensity of antislavery sentiment among the Whigs of the North, their northern colleagues could not appear to be unduly solicitous of special southern concerns. Accordingly, the southern Whigs did everything in their power to exclude slavery from the forums of national debate. Yet, as Whigs, they were obliged to uphold programs which had long been branded with the taint of "Federalism" in the South. Hence, when questions relating to slavery did come under the purview of the nation, they demanded that their counterparts in the North act like statesmen; having forsaken the path of expediency themselves, they felt justified in calling upon the northern Whigs to take the high road of self-sacrifice and mutual concession.[5] But for many northern Whigs, any action which seemed to compromise with the radical evil of slavery was anything but "principled." So when the southern Whigs appealed to the statesmanlike impulses of their northern associates—demanding that they make the choice between "cotton" and "conscience"[6]—they often unwittingly contributed to the dissolution of their party. Such were the perplexities of being both a southerner and self-styled statesman.

Some of the problems of southern Whiggery are illustrated by the career of Alexander Stephens. With monotonous regularity before the Civil War, Stephens asserted that, because it was outmanned and outarmed, the South could secure concessions from the North only through appeals for justice and the politics of principle.[7] But as he reiterated this position, Stephens became trapped in a perverse, inverted logic. His demands for the protection of southern rights within the Union became more strident as the prospect of the actual assertion of those rights became progressively more abstract and theoretical.[8] Like many antebellum southerners, Stephens was a captive of the republican assumption that power was insatiably aggressive and thus always a menace to liberty. He feared that if the North were conceded the power to contain slavery, it would inevitably deprive the southern states of the freedom to control their own domestic institutions.[9]

More, Stephens' concern with the maintenance of the South's rights, which was shared by southern politicians in both parties, reflected his section's code of honor. That code, with its touchiness in matters of personal dignity and self-respect, was the natural outgrowth of a social system in which an entire class of human beings was consigned to permanent inferiority. For a white southerner to accept insults to his self-esteem meant nothing less than being lowered to the level of a slave. Since the code declared that exemption from slavery was the basis of human dignity it buttressed the racial basis of equality in the South and the solidarity of white southerners of all social classes. Indeed, the southern concern with the maintenance of honor was so basic to sectional unity that it entered into national politics. There, it translated into the demand that the South—whose interests were equated with those of the slaveholding class—must be treated equally with the other sections of the Union. Anything else would mean its reduction to "slavery." To Stephens, the preservation of southern "honor" was certainly involved in the territorial issue. Unlike other southern spokesmen, Stephens did not think that there was any realistic prospect that slaveholders would take their human chattel into national lands. He believed that most settlers of the West would come from the North and would exclude slavery from the territories by local legislation. He nevertheless insisted that at the *national* level, no government action should place limitations upon the expansion of slavery; Stephens condemned the free soil policy embraced by most of the northern Whigs as an insult to the South. But by insisting upon "rights" which he himself considered nugatory, Stephens contributed to the intensification of the sectional dispute. In the process, he unwittingly helped propel it onto a battlefield where the hard realities of power counted most.[10]

[I]

Alexander Stephens[11] was born in 1812 in rural Wilkes County (later Taliaferro), Georgia. From the beginning of life, he lived with adversity. Born frail and sickly, he was early denied the emotional sustenance which might have made easier the bearing of his physical ailments. His mother died only three months after his birth, and the woman his father married two years later apparently had little maternal feeling for her charge. Stephens' only adult recollection of her was that "between me and my stepmother there never did exist much filial affection." Alexander's father evidently did not dispense much "filial affection" either. By all reports, Andrew Stephens was a humorless, hard working, and intensely pious schoolmaster-farmer who inspired a mixture of reverence and fear in his children. Subscribing to the Calvinist notion that work disciplined the soul, he assigned Alexander a large share in the family chores despite the boy's frailty. As a consequence, Stephens' early education was episodic, consisting (by his fourteenth year) of only twenty-four months in several crude provincial academies and Sunday schools.[12]

Whatever security the young Stephens may have experienced on the family homestead came to an abrupt end in 1826, when his father and stepmother died of influenza within a week of each other. After this calamity, the Stephens children were parceled out among their adult relatives. The fourteen-year-old Alexander was dispatched to the home of a maternal uncle and spinster aunt in Washington, Georgia. Here, he had his first great stroke of luck. While attending religious instructions, he came to the attention of several Presbyterian clergymen and laymen, who were impressed by his intelligence and moral earnestness. Hoping to make a minister of the intense young man, but without a firm vocational commitment from him, they helped finance his education at Franklin College (now the University of Georgia) at Athens. However, in his junior year Alexander realized that he was not suited to the clergy, and he repaid his sponsors from his share of the Stephens estate. Although he was an outstanding student, and never joined in the youthful escapades of his less dutiful classmates, this decision left him without a vocation; in the rough-and-tumble Georgia of 1832 his B.A. with the graduating honor of "the Latin and English salutary" was not a very marketable commodity. Like thousands of young men of the nineteenth century fresh out of college, Stephens had little choice but to teach young schoolchildren. But after a year and a half of wrestling with his youthful charges, some of whom were stronger than himself, Stephens decided on a new career. He moved to Crawfordville, a small town only three miles from his birthplace, where he read law for several months in the county court house, passed the bar examination, and established a legal practice.[13]

Stephens prospered as a lawyer—his forensic talents were of great value in the Georgia judicial system[14]—and he quickly became known as a man of affairs in Crawfordville. Stephens' record of courtroom victories also attracted the attention of the bench and bar of northern Georgia. He established many useful contacts in his new profession, some of which ripened into close friendships. Stephens became especially attached to an impetuous but respected attorney two years his senior, Robert Toombs, with whom he would later serve in the state legislature and national House of Representatives.[15] Following the social route laid down for southern gentlemen of his time, Stephens invested his legal earnings in a large plantation on the outskirts of Crawfordville, and in 1841 he began to buy slaves to farm it. As he ascended the social scale, Stephens began to assume the manners of a cultivated aristocrat—refined in tastes, gracious and benevolent toward his social inferiors, yet almost pathetically eager to requite insults to his hard-won "honor" through the code duello.[16]

Stephens' rise to wealth and station was rapid, if not meteoric, but by no means was it easy. "Slight and sickly, with a shrill voice and the face of a lad grown prematurely old"—Varina Howell Davis said he was like "one born out of season"—Stephens had to overcome physical as well as social barriers to attain success.[17] The constant butt of (often unintentional) slights because of his appearance, and chronically plagued by agonizing physical ailments, Stephens often succumbed to moods of self-pity and melancholia.[18] His entire life reflected the unremitting struggle to overcome despair and make assets of the most obvious handicaps. "The secret of my life," Stephens confided to his half-brother Linton, "has been—*revenge reversed*":

> That is, to rise superior to the neglect and contumely of the mean of mankind, by doing them good instead of harm. A determination to war against fate; to meet the world in all its forces; to master evil with good, and to leave no foe standing in the rear. . . . What have I not suffered from a look! what have I not suffered from the tone of a remark, from a sense of neglect, from a supposed injury—an intended injury! But every such pang was a friction that brought out the latent fires. My spirit of warring against the world, however, never had in it anything of a desire to *crush* or *trample*; no, only a desire to get above them, to excel them, to enjoy the gratification of seeing them feel that they were wrong; to compel their admiration.[19]

The fact that Stephens had to surmount many obstacles to attain fame and fortune certainly had great political value. In Stephens, the common folk of Georgia sensed they had a man who instinctively understood their own struggles to make good.[20] Stephens reciprocated his constituents' affection, but he was no egalitarian. Like many self-made men, he disdained the "lazy, careless and indolent" who did not live up to his own exacting standards of self-discipline and self-reliance.[21] More, Stephens was deeply imbued with a hard-boned Calvinist piety— probably acquired from his father and early religious training—and his perception of depravity in others was untempered by a recognition of ordinary human frailty in himself. An ascetic beyond the requirements of his faith or the work ethic (he never married, and his private life probably would have done credit to a monk), Stephens was disgusted by the "moving principles" of the unreflective mass of mankind, "sensuality and *sexuality*." Crawfordville had only a few hundred inhabitants in the mid-1830s, but it provided Stephens with ample fodder for his reflections on the "follies" of mankind: the "village crowd" lounging about the courthouse, one man seducing another's wife during a revival meeting, couples dancing the waltz, and the "strolling *vagabonds*, drunken filthy wretches" who attended the circus when it visited town.[22]

When Stephens raised his eyes from the corruptions of men in the particular to the accomplishments of mankind in general, his spirits lifted. The prodigious signs of material progress in his age affirmed the power of reason to make "the laws of nature subservient to the uses and purposes of man." In railroads, canals, telegraphs, and steam-driven ships and presses, Stephens saw the tools of humanity's liberation from ignorance and insular prejudices. But did such things guarantee the moral uplift of the human race? Stephens had his doubts. Man had mastered inert matter with intellect, but in affairs of state, the lower appetites prevailed:

> Politics and government, in my opinion, have in the main, since the formation of human society, been at war with the best interests of man. Government, place and power have always been the prizes which those have sought and struggled for, who have strong passions and mean propensities—those in whom the animal and brute qualities of our nature triumph over the refined and intellectual. Hence, those who contend for the prize of government resort to all sorts of means to arouse the worst and basest animal passions of the low and vulgar, to get them, as ministering devils or demons, to accomplish their purposes. The good of the people— the elevation, or even comfort, to say nothing of the happiness, of the masses of mankind—seldom enter into the minds of those who ambitiously aspire to rule.[23]

Throughout his public career, Stephens searched restlessly for the political company of men whom he believed led by rational persuasion. His social ideal was that of a class impervious to the corruptions of wealth and power, an "aristocracy" of "*honor, principle, good breeding*, and *education*," not one of "wealth and fashion, etc."[24]

Stephens certainly accounted himself a member of this Jeffersonian "aristocracy of nature."[25] Statecraft is, of course, the preeminent calling of "natural aristocrats," and Stephens evinced an interest in public affairs shortly after he took up residence in Crawfordville. He first declared publicly his political convictions in Fourth of July orations in

1834 and 1835. Unfortunately, there is no reliable text of the first speech, which seems to have been a restatement of traditional states' rights principles.[26] But we do have Stephens' own synopsis of the second: "My sentiment offered was—Nominative Conventions. Dangerous inroads upon Republican simplicity, and utterly inconsistent with the unrestricted exercise of that free choice in the selection of their officers, which constitutes the dearest right of free men."[27] These views placed Stephens on the side of those who protested against the use of machine politics by the Democratic party to secure the presidential nomination of Martin Van Buren. Accordingly, Stephens aligned himself with the State Rights party of Georgia, which had been formed in 1833 to protest Jackson's threat to coerce South Carolina, and which supported Hugh Lawson White for President in 1836.[28] A loosely organized faction of anti-Jacksonian politicians which existed only at the state level, Georgia's State Rights party had no direct ties to the Whig party of the North. Stephens' private musings of 1834 and 1835 indicate that, like many other State Righters, he did not find palatable the economic nationalism of the northern Whigs. Although he wrote in his diary that he abhorred the Proclamation and thought Jackson had acted "precipitantly" in removing the deposits, Stephens added that he was willing to dismiss such reservations in light of the "vile" opposition to the Old Hero. Moreover, he considered the Bank of the United States such a "reptile" that he could swallow any scruples about the methods Jackson used to squash it.[29]

If Stephens had a strong common bond with the northern Whigs in the mid-1830s, it was his deep distaste for populistic politics and demagogy. This became evident in 1836, when he stood for a seat in the Georgia legislature. Throughout the campaign that year, Stephens was criticized by his opponents for speaking at a county meeting against the formation of a vigilance committee to punish "abolitionists" who were suspected of circulating antislavery petitions and propaganda. Taking the high road, Stephens had urged his hearers "to stand by the supremacy of the law," and let the courts deal with the abolitionists. Although the county committee followed this advice, Stephens' position was not a popular one to take in Georgia in 1836, only a year after northern abolitionists had showered the South with antislavery literature.[30] But Stephens disdained majoritarian democracy, and believed firmly that popular rule should be tempered by respect for the procedural protections of the law. Throughout his career, he feared that popular commotions could lead to revolution, and he always urged good sense and moderation.

Despite his stand on the vigilance committee issue, Stephens won election to the state legislature, and held his seat for several terms.[31] As a state legislator, Stephens strove to advance the commercial interests of Georgia's prosperous cotton-growing Black Belt, in which his own constituency was located. A fiscal conservative, he was a vocal critic of state policies which he felt were injurious to commercial banking and the credit system.[32] He was also a zealous proponent of state aid to internal improvements projects which aimed to create new trade outlets for Georgia's planters.[33] In addition, Stephens pushed vigorously for increased state aid to common schools, arguing that public education would contribute to the exploitation of Georgia's native intellectual resources.[34]

It is tempting to see signs of the incipient Whig in Stephens' actions as a state legislator. Stephens' interest in commercial development, state aid to private enterprise, and widened educational opportunities were all characteristic of Whigs throughout the country. There is no evidence, however, that Stephens was interested in the promotion of material "progress" at the national level. Indeed, he was involved in the movement to obtain direct trade routes between the South and Europe, which would have minimized the economic ties between the northern and southern states. Moreover, on issues which concerned slavery, Stephens was a dogmatic champion of states' rights and southern interests. He would not abide northern "meddling."[35] And when the Georgia State Righters began to move toward affiliation with the nationalistic northern Whigs, Stephens protested. On July 4, 1839, he announced his support of a quixotic movement to nominate the old nullifier and ex-Governor of Georgia, George Troup, for the presidency. Sounding very much like an ideological purist, he urged the State Righters to be a "Spartan band" opposed to both major parties—"the one is a known enemy, the other a traitor to our cause." Stephens denounced the Whigs as rank Federalists, but reserved his harshest philippics for the Democrats. It was the Democrats, after all, to whom southerners had looked for the protection of states' rights. Instead, the party had been "the Judas-like traitors by whom, for the spoils of office, the Republicans had been deceived and betrayed." They had professed free trade, but had been willing to force a tariff upon South Carolina at the point of a bayonet. They had professed retrenchment and economy, but Van Buren had increased the federal budget from $11 to $40 million per annum. They had cried for a divorce between bank and state, "when their whole object was to divorce public money from the banks, it is true, but to their own pockets." And, crime of crimes, the Democrats had clasped "ultra Federalists" and abolitionists in their promiscuous embrace. Yet they and the Whigs were "courting" Georgia, "and never was a fair maiden more artfully allured by the wiles of seduction than was the integrity of the State now assailed by these political suitors."[36]

These were powerful words, indicative of the anguish Stephens and southerners like him felt about becoming involved in a national, nonprogrammatic two-party system. Stephens' lengthy denunciation of the Democrats does indicate that he had accepted the Whigs' indictment of the Jacksonians as untrustworthy friends of the South because of their opportunism. One historian has gone so far as to suggest that Stephens and the other Troupites were fully prepared to support an acceptable Whig ticket in 1840. In his view, the Troup-for-President movement was simply a stratagem to help block the expected nomination of the nationalist Henry Clay by the Whig convention. However, even after the Whigs nominated Harrison and the State Rights party endorsed him in June 1840, Stephens refused to commit himself to support of the General.[37] But Stephens eventually came to realize that he had to cast his lot with either the Democrats or the Whigs, or consign himself to political impotence. Unfortunately, there are no written traces of the personal ordeal (if any) Stephens' conversion to Whiggery entailed. It is known that in the waning weeks of the 1840 campaign, Stephens attended several Harrison meetings in Georgia with Toombs, who may have influenced his decision to back the candidate.[38] Stephens' panegyric on the death of Harrison indicates that the high-minded pronouncements of the deceased President may have strengthened his attachment to his new party. Whereas Stephens had feared that both major parties were corrupt and unprincipled, Harrison had demonstrated that the Whigs could nominate a statesman. "There was nothing sectional or partisan or offensive about his inaugural . . . No other man living could have wielded such influence over public opinion as he could, because he had the confidence of the people . . . I fear [his death] will give rise to feuds, dissensions, and divisions."[39]

Once he aligned himself with the Whigs, Stephens took action to prove his party fidelity. At a Georgia barbecue in September 1841 he offered resolutions supporting Clay in his dispute with Tyler. As if to atone for his earlier deprecation of the Kentucky Senator, Stephens served on the executive committee of a meeting of the Georgia state Whig committee which endorsed Clay for President in June 1842.[40] Perhaps the most striking evidence of Stephens' conversion to Whiggery is the report he wrote for the Whig minority in the Committee on the State of the Republic of Georgia's House of Representatives. The report was issued in defense of Senator John MacPherson Berrien's refusal to submit to instruction by the Georgia state legislature, which the Democrats dominated. Hence, much of it is devoted to a defense of Berrien's conduct in office. This would seem to have been a difficult task for someone with Stephens' background, for Berrien had supported the entirety of the Whigs' program: distribution, a national bank, and the tariff of 1842.[41] And Stephens' explanation of Whig policies, rather than resting on a vigorous assertion of nationalistic principles, tried to square those policies with states' rights arguments. Stephens thus claimed that the Whigs of Georgia would warm to the Whigs' national bank when they saw that the only alternative was the Democrats' corrupt and centralizing subtreasury plan. Similarly, Stephens claimed that Georgians would welcome the distribution of the surplus because it would prevent the use of federal funds as "a kind of reserved fund of speculation for the political gamblers of the Presidency." In conclusion, Stephens denied that Berrien wanted a protective tariff which would discriminate against the South. Berrien and the Whigs of Georgia only wanted a *revenue* tariff in the interest of the whole country. Such a tariff would have "incidentally" protective features designed to foster the United States' "infant industries" and retaliate against protectionist foreign countries.[42]

[II]

As an apologia for the Whig program, Stephens' minority report is pretty feeble stuff. It may be cited in support of two propositions: that in antebellum Georgia, it was difficult for a politician to avow unabashedly his support of nationalistic policies; and that such policies had little to do with Stephens' Whiggery. Yet Stephens was rarely insincere with the public, and never with himself. The more declarations of party orthodoxy he made, the more substantial his arguments became. When Stephens joined the Whigs, he not only donned a new party label; he acquired a new political role and an "audience" to which he had to orient his conduct. Previously the member of a state party which had made few demands of regularity of him, he now had to find his bearings within a national party which imposed discipline upon its members. But in becoming a Whig, Stephens also acquired a new political outlook, a frame of reference which made this task easier. And there were flesh-and-blood models of how the Whig statesman should conduct himself: Clay, Webster, and men of their sort. Only if his party loyalty conflicted with his preeminent concern, that of securing and protecting southern rights, would Stephens feel compelled to reconsider his partisan affiliation.

When Stephens was elected to his first term in the U.S. House of Representatives in 1843 he experienced no such conflict of loyalties. Speaking in defense of the Whigs' 1842 tariff, he declared that southerners "sold what they had dearer, and bought what they wanted cheaper, than they did before the passage of the law of 1842."[43] Stephens also lent his assent to the Whig doctrine of a national "harmony of interests." He contended that, so far from being "just and oppressive" to the South, the Whig tariff had affected the economy of his section "beneficently."[44]

Following the lead of Clay, whose "Raleigh letter" he read and approved in advance of publication, Stephens opposed the immediate annexation of Texas in 1844.[45] Although he publicly favored Texas' eventual admission into the Union, Stephens denounced the injection of the issue into the presidential campaign as a cheap political trick. He tried to counter the proannexationist Democrats' appeal to sectional feeling by appealing to the party loyalties and unionism of his fellow southern Whigs. The Texas commotion was "a miserable political humbug got up as a ruse to divide and distract the Whig party at the South." Worse yet, it might have been stirred up with "an ulterior view— that is, the dissolution of the present Confederacy."[46] Even after Texas annexation proved to be popular in the South, Stephens continued to repeat these arguments. But he also took pains to make clear that he did not oppose the acquisition of Texas per se. In June 1844 he spurred the Georgia state Whig convention to endorse annexation if it could be effected without damage to the national honor or the risk of war with Mexico. Stephens denied that Tyler's Texas treaty met these specifi-cations, and he suggested that northern congressmen actually favored it because it made no mention of the status of slavery in the proposed new state. He argued that northerners might vote to admit Texas into the Union under the terms of the Tyler plan, and then amend it to exclude slavery from Texas.[47]

Stephens' rhetoric about Texas was sectional and inflammatory. But the Georgian shared Clay's apprehensions about the potentially divisive effects of annexation and his concern for the preservation of inter-sectional concord. Stephens' heated oratory was a way he could retain credibility as a southern spokesman, while hoping to avert a clash between the North and the South over the status of slavery in Texas. In his private correspondence, Stephens expressed the fear that annexation might occur "upon terms that will herafter endanger the old Re-public."[48] Yet by imputing questionable motives to the northern supporters of annexation, Stephens contributed to the mutual suspicions dividing the sections, a problem which would long survive the resolution of the Texas problem. It is a sobering irony of Stephens' statesmanship that in the process of trying to save the Union, he felt compelled to exacerbate the feelings which would eventually help destroy it.

Stephens survived the Whig debacle of 1844, but the Democratic victory left him in a difficult position. As a Whig, he was pledged to oppose immediate and unilateral action on annexation. But he also believed that annexation could not be prevented, and he feared that northern congressmen might try to exclude slavery from any newly acquired territory. This prospect, of course, raised the possibility that the Whig party (and perhaps the Union as well) might split along sectional lines, something Stephens wanted to avoid without making concessions to the antislavery men. He resolved his quandary by supporting a compromise annexation plan introduced by Congressman Milton Brown, a Whig from Tennessee. Under the provisions of Brown's bill, Texas was to be admitted as a state, with the United States settling its borders but not assuming its debts. New states (whose number was fixed at four) could be carved out of Texas, and admitted into the Union with its consent; those situated south of the Missouri Compromise line could decide whether they would apply for admission as free or as slave states.

An amendment to the Brown bill prohibited slavery in any states that might be above the compromise line.[49]

The Brown scheme had several advantages for Stephens and its other advocates. It would bypass congressional authority on the slavery extension issue and thereby prevent antislavery congressmen from voting on the matter. The provision which allowed settlers south of the Missouri Compromise line to resolve the question themselves held out the promise of circumventing future controversy. Yet there were also problems with the Brown bill. Texas' veto power over the admission of new states in effect favored the interests of slavery. More important, the bill proposed to annex Texas by joint congressional resolution, not treaty. Since Texas was a separate nation, this procedure was highly irregular, if not unconstitutional. For this second reason, the Brown bill was first blocked in the Senate Foreign Relations Committee after it passed the House. Then, after lengthy wrangling, both houses of Congress passed a law giving the President the option of choosing the Brown plan or a rival scheme of Senator Thomas Hart Benton of Missouri, which would give the President the power to negotiate annexation terms with Texas. The law passed late in the congressional session preceding the inauguration of Polk, who it was expected would make the choice between the two plans. But Tyler seized the initiative in the last days of his presidency and decided in favor of Brown's.[50]

The Brown bill left unsettled the problems of Texas' boundaries and the debts owed Texans by the Mexican government. Polk pursued negotiations with Mexico over these issues, but he also prepared for the possibility of war. When he ordered troops into the area between the Nueces and Rio Grande rivers, which was in dispute between the two countries, a border clash ensued. This gave Polk the occasion he needed for requesting a congressional declaration of war, which declared that the hostilities had been caused by an act of Mexico. Stephens and other Whigs bristled at this claim, and charged that Polk had deliberately provoked the conflict. In league with other war critics, Stephens refused to vote for the war resolution and roundly condemned the administration's conduct of the fighting. Yet he also realized that the Whigs' criticisms of the war effort would have to be very temperate. Prowar Democrats were eager to seize upon every opportunity to allege that the antiwar Whigs were traitors to the country. What was the responsible, statesmanlike thing to do in this situation? In areas where the war was extremely unpopular, such as northern districts in which it was considered part of a conspiracy to extend slavery, Whig congressmen could oppose the war effort wholeheartedly. But Whigs from prowar districts, which were especially numerous in the South, could only retain their standing with their constituents by voting for war supplies. Otherwise, they would be charged with subverting the war, or even contributing to the death of American fighting men. How, then, could they attack the administration's prosecution of the conflict without compromising themselves politically, as had the Federalists during the War of 1812?[51]

Stephens was acutely aware of the quandary of antiwar Whigs. In two major addresses, he fashioned a critique of the administration's conduct of the Mexican War which his Whig colleagues could embrace with enthusiasm. At the time Stephens delivered his first war speech (June 16, 1846) the only official objectives of the war were the settlement of the Texas boundary question and the disposal of the debt claims of American citizens in Mexico. But there were already lurking fears that Polk's true aims included the acquisition of Mexican territory, an eventuality that might spark new controversy over slavery. In his initial assault on Polk's war policies, Stephens staked high moral ground and played upon apprehensions of the administration's expansionist designs without broaching the divisive subject of slavery. Deploring all wars as "great national calamities," to be avoided "when it can be done without a sacrifice of national rights or honor," he charged that the war was due to the "imprudence, indiscretion, and mismanagement of our own executive." "Young Hickory" had succeeded "Old Hickory," but there was still a "despot" in the White House. Although Texas had never established a legitimate claim to the territory between the Nueces and the Rio Grande, Polk had deliberately provoked war by sending troops into the region. Having done this without congressional authorization, he had then requested the legislature to declare that Mexico was responsible for the outbreak of fighting.[52]

Stephens professed shock at the administration's dishonorable course. But he disclaimed any desire to "check the ardor of our gallant army, which has already won such unfading laurels on the battle-field, or of the patriotic volunteers who have rushed to the rescue at the hour of their country's call." Like most of the war critics, he would vote for war supplies. But he also demanded that Polk define his war aims. Was he scheming to expand the national boundaries by force? Stephens confessed that he was "no enemy to the extension of our domain," but he hoped that the answer to this question was no. "Republics can never spread by arms. We can only properly enlarge by voluntary accessions, and should only attempt to act upon our neighbors by setting them a good example." The annexationists called themselves "the party of progress," but Stephens denied that they had legitimate title to this name. "Theirs, in my opinion, is a *downward progress*. It is a spirit of party—of excitement—of lust of power—a spirit of war—aggression—violence and licentiousness. It is a progress which, if indulged in, would sweep over all law—all order—and the constitution itself."[53]

Republics, Stephens asserted, could not achieve true progress by overstepping the bounds of civilized society. They had to discipline their base appetites for power, wealth, and territory, and reform themselves from within. Only then would other peoples want to join or emulate them. What, then, were the surest signs of a republic's progress? Stephens enumerated them:

> The improvement of mind: 'the increase and diffusion of knowledge amongst men'; the erection of schools, colleges, and temples of learning; the progress of intellect over matter; the triumph of the mind over the animal propensities; the advancement of kind feelings and good will amongst the nations of the earth; the cultivation of virtue and the pursuit of industry; the bringing into subjection and subserviency to the use of man of all the elements of nature about and around us; in a word, the progress of civilization and every thing that elevates, ennobles and dignifies man. This . . . is not done by war, whether foreign or domestic. Fields of blood and carnage can make men brave and heroic, but seldom tend to make nations either good, virtuous, or great.[54]

Stephens' first war speech skillfully interwove traditional Whig motifs. In Stephens' portrait, the prowar Democrats were the party of "executive usurpation," of lawlessness, and of unappeasable passions and appetites run wild. Through their bellicosity and licentiousness, they had given free rein to the baser elements of human nature. The Whigs, by implied contrast, had the attributes suited to a "civilized" republic—moderation, self-restraint, and obedience to the law. They had sublimated their lower urges into the pursuit of objectives which contributed to the construction of a more rational and harmonious society. Stephens' call for the internal reformation of the republic also struck a familiar Whig chord. Even the antislavery Whigs, whose reasons for opposing the war were quite different from Stephens', could agree with the sentiment that American institutions should be perfected before they were extended. What such men and Stephens did disagree about was whether slavery was capable of perfection. Yet Stephens' position of nonextensionism, if adopted as official policy, held out the hope that this disagreement would not have to enter into political debate.

The events which followed Stephens' maiden war address lent some credence to his apprehensions. In August 1846 David Wilmot's famous Proviso introduced the explosive subject of slavery into the debate on territorial acquisitions. In the summer and fall of 1846 American troops seized control of California and New Mexico, as if to confirm Stephens' charge that Polk had expansionist designs on Mexican territory. Yet, despite these victories on the battlefield, peace negotiations with Mexico bogged down. Angered by the Mexicans' recalcitrance, Polk spent the winter of 1846–47 considering ways in which he could break the deadlock.[55]

The immediate occasion of Stephens' second war speech (February 12, 1847) was Polk's request for $3 million, possibly for use as an indemnity to Mexico for any territory it might cede to the United States in a peace settlement. Ever alert to smell a rat, Stephens denounced the bill as a flagrant attempt to buy peace with Mexico. He professed to be appalled by those who were clamoring for the annexation of a part or the whole of Mexico. Stephens' condemnation of annexation invoked standard Whig principles. Above all, it rested upon the ideal of a Union which was based on the voluntary consent of its citizens, obedience to law, and a single, common culture. Stephens denied that acquisitions from Mexico would be a blessing; their inhabitants would have to be subdued by force, necessitating a large standing army, which would be a danger to the freedom of the republic. Moreover, "by this acquisition," the United States "would get nothing but the empty right of jurisdiction and government over an unwilling people, unused to the restraints of law, which will be the source of incalculable troubles and difficulties which no wisdom can now foresee." Stephens clearly implied that he believed the inhabitants of Mexico, because of their different culture, institutions, and racial composition, were ill suited for incorporation into a "civilized" republic. As he asked rhetorically of the advocates of Mexican annexation: "What will be done with the people themselves? Are they to be made into citizens? Spaniards, Indians, Mestizoes, Negroes, and all?"[56]

At the heart of Stephens' critique lay his concern for the preservation of the Union. The Wilmot Proviso, he pointed out, had already demonstrated that acquisitions from Mexico would open a Pandora's box of sectional hatreds. Although Stephens declared his willingness to defend slavery, his fondest wish was to restore the *status quo ante bellum*, and thereby prevent slavery from becoming the subject of further divisive debate. The existing Union, in which slavery was purely a concern of the states, was enough for him:

> May I not, with reverence, ask what we shall be profited as a nation, if we gain any part, or even the whole of Mexico, and lose the soul of our political existence? The Union is not only the life, but the soul of these States. It is this that gives them animation, vigor, power, prosperity, greatness, and renown; and from this alone springs our hopes of immortality as a common people.[57]

This speech had an electric effect. By linking nonexpansionism with the preservation of both the Union and states' rights, it helped popularize the "no territory" policy among Whigs throughout the country. Henry Clay, among others, recommended that the Whig national convention of 1848 officially adopt Stephens' position on the war and territorial annexation.[58] But the practical consequences of Stephens' speeches were negligible. When Polk sent Nicholas Trist's proposed peace treaty to the Senate in February 1848, most Whig senators felt compelled to support it for fear that prolongation of the war might result in the annexation of all of Mexico. As it was, the treaty brought a massive bloc of land into the Union, including the Mexican provinces of California and New Mexico. And as Stephens anticipated, the status of slavery in these new territories became a subject of heated debate in Congress.[59]

Many politicians staked their hopes for a resolution of the territorial controversy on the passage of the so-called "Clayton compromise." This "compromise" was in fact no compromise at all. Instead, it was a clever piece of political sidestepping, by which congressmen hoped to throw the territorial hot potato into the hands of the federal judiciary. As Thomas Corwin put it, the Clayton bill enacted a lawsuit, not a law. It would have prohibited the territorial legislatures of California and New Mexico from passing laws restricting slavery. But it also would have enabled slaves carried into those territories to sue in the federal courts to determine their status. The Clayton plan had almost solid southern support in Congress, largely because the Supreme Court was dominated by southerners, who would presumably rule in favor of the interests of slaveholders. But Stephens led 9 southern Whigs in the House who voted with 103 free state congressmen to table the measure, an action which effectively killed it.[60]

Stephens' argument against the Clayton compromise was characteristic in its legalism, though questionable in its scholarship. Stephens claimed that the federal courts would, in accordance with common law tradition, decide any questions pertaining to slavery in California and New Mexico in conformity with the laws in force at the time of their conquest. Turning to his southern colleagues, he pointed out that Mexico had abolished slavery in its provinces in 1829. Therefore, Stephens asserted, the Clayton bill would be a *"covert* surrender of the South's just rights . . . to an equal participation in the new acquisitions of territory."[61]

But what was the nature of the "South's just rights" in the territories, if they did not exist in law, and had to be legislated into existence by Congress? Stephens, of course, did not want to concede to the federal government the power to actively promote slavery; this might also imply that it had the power to suppress it. He knew that if he based his arguments for southern claims in the territories upon the alleged "right" of slaveholders to carry their slaves into the national domain, his position would be rejected outright by northerners. Stephens therefore asserted that the territorial question had nothing directly to do with slavery. Rather, it was a matter of equitable regard for the South and its honor. The South had sacrificed more than its share of "blood and treasure" in the Mexican War, and it was only just that its institutions be accorded equal treatment in the territories purchased at heavy cost in that conflict. The only alternative policy acceptable to Stephens, and one which he still favored in August 1848, was that the country renounce the Mexican Cession altogether. Since this policy was not likely to be implemented, Stephens urged one of "fair division" in the territories—i.e., that slavery be allowed in part of them. Failing equal provision for the South, the North would be guilty of sectional oppression:

I speak to the North, irrespective of parties. I recognize no party association in affiliation upon this subject. If the two parties at the North combine, and make a sectional issue, and by their numerical strength vote down the South, and deny us those equal rights to which I think we are in justice entitled, it will be for the people of the South then to adopt such a course as they may deem proper.[62]

Stephens injected an issue of principle into the debate over the Clayton plan, and helped confound the schemes of men more opportunistically inclined. He may also have helped block the settlement in the expectation of the election of the Whig presidential candidate, Zachary Taylor, under whom a more acceptable (and less ambiguous) compromise might emerge. Stephens was an early champion of the Taylor candidacy. In December 1846 he participated in the formation of a group of congressmen, the so-called Young Indians, who supported Taylor for the Whig nomination. During the congressional session of 1848 Stephens lived in the same boardinghouse as Toombs and Senator John J. Crittenden of Kentucky, and the three helped mastermind the successful movement to make Taylor the Whigs' choice. Taylor's candidacy had several advantages from Stephens' point of view. Taylor was a war hero, so his candidacy was an effective Whig rebuttal to Democratic charges of disloyalty. More, Taylor was a large slaveowner, leading Stephens to believe that he would respect the interests of slavery if he had to pass on legislation relating to the territorial issue.[63]

In the interim between Taylor's election and his inauguration, Stephens tried to keep open the possibility of compromise. In January 1849 Calhoun attempted to unite southern congressmen behind an address demanding equal treatment for the South in the territories. But Stephens and the overwhelming majority of southern Whigs refused to join the movement.[64] Stephens did support a bill submitted in the House by William Preston of Virginia, which would have admitted the Mexican Cession into the Union as a single state. This new state, it was widely assumed, would exclude slavery within its borders. But Stephens supported the Preston plan because the prohibition would be accomplished without conceding to the federal government the power to restrict slavery's expansion.[65]

The well-laid plans of Stephens exploded in his face. The Preston bill won the votes of absolutely no one when free state congressmen amended it to exclude slavery from the proposed new state.[66] And the newly elected President, on whom Stephens had staked so many hopes, proved a bitter disappointment. Taylor's close relationship with Seward, a southern bête noire, was understandably disturbing to the Georgian and his other southern supporters.[67] So, too, were hints by Taylor in August 1849 that he would sign the Wilmot Proviso if it passed Congress.[68] The most severe political embarassment for the southern Whigs was Taylor's proposal for the immediate admission of California as a free state. Like the Preston bill, this plan had the advantage of bypassing the territorial stage, and thus avoided the issue of positive exclusion. But it was anticipated that, with Taylor's approval, New Mexico would also apply for admission as a free state, worsening the South's minority position in the Senate. More, the southern Democrats made the Taylor plan a partisan issue in the South, condemning it as the Wilmot Proviso in all but name. The support of the administration scheme by Seward and other antislavery Whigs lent credibility to these charges.[69]

The southern reaction against the Taylor plan pushed Stephens into greater verbal militancy on the issue of southern rights. He did not oppose the admission of California with its antislavery constitution, for he thought that slavery stood no chance of taking root there. But he insisted that the rest of the Mexican Cession be organized as territories which would be open to slavery; that way, southern honor would have its due. At the same time, Stephens angrily denounced legislation which would have discriminated against slavery wherever the federal government had authority over it. He condemned not only the Wilmot Proviso but a bill introduced by Congressman William Gott of New York which would have abolished slavery in the District of Columbia.[70]

Stephens considered his position on southern rights moderate and statesmanlike. He hoped it would buttress his credibility as a spokesman for the South, and thus enable him to head off extremists who advocated secession if California were admitted as a free state. Believing that southern interests would be most secure within the Union, Stephens shuddered at the prospect of a secessionist "revolution." The advocates of such a radical resort were good at fire-eating rhetoric, but Stephens doubted that they could govern a republic. The fact that the militant southern righters tended to be Democrats also made Stephens suspicious of both their motives and their abilities. His concern with southern rights was principled; theirs, opportunistic:

Whether a separation of the union and the organization and establishment of a Southern Confederacy would give final and ultimate security to the form of society as it exists with us, I am not prepared to say. I have no doubt [that] if we had unity, virtue, intelligence, and patriotism in all our councils, such an experiment might succeed. But unfortunately for our country at this time, we have if I am not mistaken too much demagogism and too little statesmanship. Most of the *fighting resolves* of our Legislatures I fear are nothing but gascondade put forth by partisan leaders for partisan effect.[71]

The best hope of heading off the southern militants was, of course, some type of compromise. Such a settlement would require the support of northerners if it were to pass Congress, and Stephens naturally looked first for help from the northern Whigs. When the first session of the Thirty-first Congress convened, he and Toombs requested that the Whig caucus declare itself officially against the Wilmot Proviso and the Gott bill. If the northern majority complied with this request, it would mean that they were willing to make concessions to the South. But most of the northern Whig congressmen had campaigned as supporters of the Wilmot Proviso, and were not willing to risk their local political prospects (or sacrifice their antislavery principles) for the sake of national party unity. The test vote therefore failed. This reversal did not merely disappoint Stephens; it placed in question the very rationale for his adherence to the Whig party. Having seen the Whigs as the party of statesmanship, he now believed that the northern members of the party could not be counted on to uphold southern rights when to do so would be contrary to political expediency. Angered by their northern colleagues' "unsoundness" on the sectional issue, Stephens, along with Toombs and four other southern Whigs, stalked out of the meeting of the Whig caucus.[72]

Having failed to obtain satisfaction through partisan channels, Stephens and his sturdy band operated outside the major party framework, hoping to force concessions out of the leaders of the two parties. In the election for a Speaker of the House of Representatives, they refused to vote for either the Democratic (Howell Cobb) or Whig (Robert Winthrop) candidate, and thereby helped deadlock the voting for more than fifty ballots. But their obstructive tactics were thwarted on the sixty-third ballot, when, in line with a prior arrangement between the major parties, Cobb was elected Speaker by a plurality vote.[73]

The maverick Whigs also hoped to exert some influence upon the President, but were equally unsuccessful. Several deputations they dispatched to Taylor returned with news that he was obdurately insistent on his plan for the immediate admission of California. One visit was prompted by rumors that the President would send federal troops to coerce Texas if it invaded New Mexico because of a boundary dispute. Stephens and Toombs visited Taylor to remonstrate with him over such a policy, suggesting that it would lead to the secession of the southern states and civil war. The exchange apparently grew heated, as Taylor, indignant at this threat to federal authority, denounced the Georgians as traitors. Stephens and other southern Whigs despaired of swaying so stubborn an opponent.[74]

The crisis of 1850 dramatized the difficulty southerners such as Stephens had in harmonizing their devotion to southern rights with their dedication to the preservation of the Union. It also cast into sharp relief the differences between the sectional wings of the Whig party on the part the South should have in a consolidated Union. To the southern Whigs (for whom Stephens was one of the most eloquent spokesmen), the Union had to be pluralistic in nature. They demanded that, through equal treatment in the territories, the North acknowledge that the unique social system of the South was an intrinsic part of the national "harmony of interests." It was precisely this that the free soil Whigs of the North refused to concede. For them, Whig ideals led in the direction of greater national homogeneity, as material progress swept away the regressive institutions of the past. Slavery, of course, was such an institution, and it was therefore essential to the free soil Whigs that the South be excluded from an equal share in the spoils of territorial conquest. This in turn implied that the South occupied a subordinate place in the Union, something that a stern defender of southern honor like Stephens would not abide.

Ironically, it was Henry Clay who rescued the day for Stephens and the southern Whigs. They had rejected Clay as a presidential candidate in 1848 because they felt that he could not win the South and thought Taylor would be sounder on the slavery extension issue. But it was Clay's compromise proposals which provided them with a palatable alternative to the administration's plan. Like Taylor, Clay called for California's immediate admission as a free state. However, he proposed that New Mexico and Utah be organized as territories without stipulations concerning slavery, thus avoiding federal policies which the South would find discriminatory. The other elements in Clay's plan also held out the promise of settling the questions agitating the nation without sacrificing southern rights. The abolition of the slave trade in the nation's capital would do away with a traffic many Americans considered odious, but not concede to the federal government the power to eliminate slavery itself. The Fugitive Slave Law would strengthen federal enforcement of the constitutional requirement for the return of runaway slaves, something demanded by the South because of the widespread noncompliance in the North. And the settlement of the border dispute between New Mexico and Texas would avert a possible civil conflict on terms generous to the Lone Star State.[75]

[III]

When Stephens returned to Georgia as an advocate of the compromise, he was neither a Democrat nor a Whig. But no longer was he a man without a party. Pro- and anticompromise men had been located in the ranks of the Georgia Democrats and Whigs, and both state parties cracked under the ideological strain. Stephens and Toombs led the procompromise Whigs of Georgia into a new state organization, the Constitutional Union party, where they were joined by the procompromise Democrats. In turn, anticompromise Democrats and Whigs formed their own Southern Rights party. The Constitutional Unionists brought together nationalistic Whigs, conservative planters who feared that secession might result in anarchy, and Jacksonian small farmers who did not want to increase the political power of large slaveholders through territorial expansion.[76] The Southern Righters were also a motley group, internally divided on the measures of resistance they wanted to take against the admission of California as a free state. Some were outright secessionists, while others advocated commercial retaliation against the North.[77]

But no kind of resistance to the settlement of 1850 seemed justified to most Georgia voters. No catastrophe ensued upon its passage, President Fillmore signaled his resolve to enforce the Fugitive Slave Law, and cotton prices were high in Georgia.[78] The Constitutional Unionists overwhelmingly won the election of delegates to a special state convention called to consider Georgia's response to the compromise. This body, which met from December 10 to December 14, 1850, endorsed the intersectional bargain. But it also issued the so-called Georgia Platform, which made it clear that the state's adherence to the Union was contingent on the preservation of "southern rights." This declaration was an astute political stratagem, by which the Constitutional Unionists undercut their opponents' claim to be the sole proponents of those rights. But it also entailed a Unionism which later disunionists would find congenial. The Union of the Georgia Platform was not a mystical communion, bringing together Americans of all persuasions; it was a compact binding upon its members only so long as their mutual advantage was served by it. It was, as the Platform put it, of secondary importance "to the rights and principles it was designed to perpetuate." The authors of the Platform (who may have included Stephens) made it clear that they did not think that these "rights and principles" inhered in the compact itself. Any congressional restriction of slavery in the territories, they announced, would justify "the disruption of every tie which binds [Georgia] to the Union." The Platform added that "upon the faithful execution of the Fugitive Slave Bill by the proper authorities depends the preservation of the Union."[79]

The unionism of the Georgia Platform was a far cry from the exultant sentiment of Stephens' second speech on the Mexican War. But Stephens could at least take comfort in the fact that he and likeminded men had effected the rhetorical switch. He also realized, however, that the "finality" of the compromise measures rested upon the firm political resolve of its adherents throughout the country. A mere "acquiescence" in the settlement, motivated by expediency, would not prevent the reopening of the controversies which had necessitated compromise in the first place. Indeed, with the northern states outstripping the South in population and political power, such an eventuality was almost guaranteed so long as politicians exploited issues for partisan gain. Those in the North would continue to press for new "aggressions" upon southern rights, while those in the South would demand new protections for slavery. Many Constitutional Unionists hoped for the emergence of a new national party of sound, conservative men committed *in principle* to the preservation of the settlement of 1850. Stephens had hoped that the Whig party would be such an organization, but the antislavery stance of most of the northern Whigs had disabused him of that notion. The

Democrats, who had first mastered the art of political opportunism, seemed hopelessly corrupt to Stephens. In his view, neither major party could resist the temptation to agitate sectional issues, for they were interested in power, not the public good. Only a party of truly disinterested statesmen could redeem the republic from the degeneration of public morals caused by the two-party system.[80]

But the party of Stephens' hopes never materialized. The crisis prompted the realignment of the parties only in Alabama, Georgia, and Mississippi. In the rest of the states, traditional partisan loyalties persisted, and the Democrats and Whigs embraced both advocates and opponents of the compromise. Furthermore, the crisis parties in Georgia (and in Alabama and Mississippi as well) themselves succumbed to pressures to align with the national parties. In Georgia, the Southern Righters, who had lost disastrously in 1850, were the first to realize the hopelessness of sustaining themselves without patronage or ties to a national party, and joined the Democrats. The Union Democrats, whose leader, Howell Cobb, had ambitions for national office, followed suit.[81] But the Union Whigs—which meant the overwhelming majority of former Whigs—split over rejoining their old party.[82] Some, led by Senator William Dawson, endorsed the Whigs's national ticket in 1852. But a sizable number refused to consummate an alliance with either of the national parties that year. Stephens, who had already been burned by his affiliation with the Whigs, was the leading spokesman of this faction. He denounced the Democrats because they had accepted into their ranks both Free Soilers and Southern Righters, even while they endorsed the compromise in their platform. The Whigs were hardly better. Their presidential choice, Winfield Scott, refused to give his unequivocal endorsement to the 1850 settlement for fear of alienating its opponents within the party. Worse still, Scott, like Taylor before him, was a protégé of Seward.[83]

Stephens bolted the convention of the remnant of the Georgia Constitutional Union party after it endorsed Scott for President. Soon afterward, he embarked upon the most quixotic political crusade of his life, that of running Daniel Webster as an independent presidential candidate. Futility was the hallmark of the Webster campaign; the Secretary of State was on the state ballot only in Georgia, and he died shortly before the voting. Even fate seemed to mock Stephens' vision of a party of principled "conservatives."[84]

[IV]

With the ill-starred Webster campaign, Stephens broke his last, largely sentimental ties to the national Whig party. The rest of his career hence lies outside the scope of this essay. But in a synoptic statement, it is fair to say that the preconceptions of Stephens in his Whig phase remained with him for the rest of his life. When he joined the Democrats in 1855, he vigorously embraced Stephen Douglas' "popular sovereignty" doctrine, believing that it was the best way for the South to preserve its rights within the Union. He even supported Douglas and his doctrine in 1860, when to do so consigned him to a tiny political minority in Georgia.[85] In the secession crisis, Stephens opposed the immediate severing of Georgia's ties to the Union, arguing that only overt aggressions upon the rights of the southern states could justify so radical a step. But when his home state voted to secede, Stephens yielded to its judgment.[86] Elected Vice President of the Confederacy, Stephens quickly assumed the role of an oppositionist. He had usually played such a role as a Whig, and, because he had almost always been in the minority, he was not accustomed to accepting the limitations and responsibilities that come with power. The official ideology of the Confederacy also lent legitimacy to the position of the independent, for it frowned upon parties.[87] Thus, when the Davis administration pursued policies of which he disapproved, Stephens protested vocally. Having fought throughout his career to preserve local liberties against consolidated power, he was appalled when Davis called for the suspension of habeas corpus, military conscription, and a declaration of martial law. Stephens even pursued his position to the perverse extreme of considering Georgia's secession from the Confederacy.[88] But with the defeat of the Confederacy, he quickly became a symbol of the Lost Cause, almost as if his personal infirmity had become a metaphor for the prostration of the South. For the remainder of his life, until his death in 1882, Stephens was revered as a southern statesman whom the world had passed by, a provincial antique embalmed in the "principles" he cherished to the grave.

CHAPTER 9

Conclusion

THE FEDERAL GOVERNMENT, as James Sterling Young has written, was "at a distance and out of sight" for most Americans at the end of James Monroe's presidency. John Quincy Adams wanted to remedy this state of affairs by creating an activistic federal regime, but his plans collided against a rising tide of sectionalism and particularism.[1] Instead, it was the Jacksonian Democrats who revived popular interest in affairs at the center of government. But to many Americans, they did so at too great a cost, by creating a centralized party apparatus that required the blind loyalty of its votaries and promoted factionalism in the electorate. It was this reaction against the Jacksonian system of party politics which provided the impetus for the formation of the Whig party.

The revulsion against Jacksonian party government transcended conventional political distinctions, uniting men whose affinities were as much instinctive as conscious. Only a shared disenchantment could have brought together the motley collection of Antimasons, National Republicans, and disaffected Jacksonians who comprised the Whig party. The heterogeneity of the Whig party in its early stages was no better revealed than in the 1836 presidential election, in which there were three party aspirants. One of these candidates (Daniel Webster) was a fervent nationalist, another (Hugh Lawson White) was an unreconstructed Jeffersonian Republican, while the third (William Henry Harrison) occupied no distinct political position at all.

The diversity of the Whig party did not mean that its members had no principles. In the very act of repudiating the political style and methods of the Democrats, the Whigs signified their adherence to a contrary set of ideals, beliefs, and assumptions. While the Democrats saw fundamental divisions in the polity, the Whigs saw an underlying harmony. While the

Democrats believed politics should be an instrument of the aggrieved against exploitation by special privileged interests, Whigs argued that it should help cement unity and consensus. And while the Democrats asserted that party organization and discipline were necessary to concert opposition to subverters of the republic, the Whigs condemned party politics as itself a danger to republican government. Model citizens and statesmen, they asserted, were disinterestedly devoted to the common good because the shackles of partisanship had not deprived them of free judgment or political independence. The baleful effects the Whigs saw flowing from Jacksonian party politics were summarized well by a Mississippi newspaper editor:

> Politics, the fruitful theme for knavish demagogues and unscrupulous aspirants, has lost all its charm and influence in directing, protecting, supporting, and advancing the great principles of a good and salutary government. The boldest villain in striking at the foundation of well regulated political society, is now esteemed the greatest hero, and he will have his partisans shouting at his heels and ready to do his commands, even to firing the temple of liberty. There is no doctrine so foul, so blasting to our republican institutions, which would not have its advocates under a bold, unscrupulous, and daring leader. . . . When an effort is made by the patriotic and order-loving community to preserve just laws from hasty and inconsiderate innovations, they are generally owned down by reckless partisans as the *frowning down* class of the community. They are ever ready to arouse the feelings and prejudices of one class of the community against another, although all intelligent men know that the protection and prosperity of each particular class is necessary to the advancement of the whole and to the preservation of a sound and healthy action of government. Calmness and moderation in thought and action are indispensable to well regulated society. However each particular interest may differ, a general harmony, in all the component parts, is requisite to complete the order of the whole.[2]

By itself, the emergence of Jacksonian party politics was disturbing enough to the Whigs. But many of them feared that it was symptomatic of more profound problems. If men followed factious demagogues and politicians who attacked established institutions and spread pernicious doctrines of class conflict, it must be because they felt they had no stake in the common good. Indeed, the Jacksonians' preoccupation with securing personal "liberty"—which the Whigs interpreted to mean license—seemed to appeal to men who wanted to cast off the bonds of community. Furthermore, the Whigs feared that social change had eroded the traditional foundations of personal discipline and collective order. In the more fluid society produced by industrialization and the national marketplace, mobility and opportunity were put at a premium. Because men no longer felt they had a fixed "place" in the social structure, the traditional restraints of community, custom, and deference seemed like onerous limits on their freedom.[3]

Yet for all their misgivings about the centrifugal effects of change, the Whigs were no reactionaries. They believed that a return to a simpler, less trying time was neither possible nor desirable; if anything, they were fervent believers in the nineteenth-century gospel of progress. Furthermore, as faithful republicans, they were not prepared to see severe restrictions imposed upon individual liberty and opportunity. The man striving to lift himself out of poverty was only seeking to establish himself as a solid, property-owning citizen.

The Whigs, then, saw their basic task as the creation of stronger communal bonds among the American people without the sacrifice of the benefits of modernity. One way they hoped to meet this challenge was through dedication to the ideal and practice of statesmanship. The arts of the Whig statesman, above all, were directed at creating a sense of shared destiny among a people with seemingly disparate goals and ambitions. Clay, Webster, and other Whig orators invested great faith in the unifying power of patriotic rhetoric: Americans might be brought together by devotion to principles which were grandly stated and elucidated. The Whigs' attacks on executive and party "influence" were an integral part of their crusade to reestablish the ascendancy of statesmanship. For if men were liberated from partisan fetters and irrational party loyalties, they might be more receptive to the statesman's appeals to subordinate their private concerns to the national interest. The converse, of course, was also true: by following Whig statesmen, Americans could feel that they had not sacrificed their public virtue through blind submission to a party.

The Whigs believed that there were tangible ways of supplementing the patriotic appeals of the statesman. Through the public promotion of economic growth, they hoped to provide a material foundation for the maintenance of public virtue. If men felt they owed their prosperity to the collective will of the community, expressed through the state, they would be more likely to identify their personal well-being with the common good. In addition, national systems of finance and transport might strengthen national unity by creating bonds of mutual reliance between individuals and regions. The Whigs also attached great value to institutions which promoted individual self-discipline and social order without the sacrifice of personal liberty. They hoped that the churches, schools, and legal system would inculcate in the people the capacity for self-government—the ability to subject the passions and appetites to the control of the rational faculties. They wanted such educative agencies to teach Americans to revere established institutions for their services to the general welfare, and not see them as simply encumbrances to be changed when they did not suit their personal needs.

The Whigs, in short, wanted to foster economic development within a corporate social framework which would ensure that it did not undermine public order, national unity, or individual self-discipline. Ironically, the Whigs' promotional programs had their greatest popularity in periods when the American economic system was in the worst operating condition. It was at such times, after all, that the economy seemed most in need of the helping hand of government. Thus, the economic recovery after the failure of the Whigs to implement much of their program in 1841 harmed the party's political prospects. It also left Henry Clay less partisan ammunition with which to counter the sectionally divisive effects of the Texas annexation question. Similarly, the failure of economic disaster to follow upon the reestablishment of the subtreasury and the lowering of the tariff in 1846 deprived the Whigs of vital issues, and provided the rationale for running the nonpartisan Zachary Taylor on no platform in 1848.[4]

There were also events below the national level which undermined the appeal of the Whigs' economic policies. In the 1840s many states established systems of "free banking," which opened banking privileges to all associations which could meet certain specified conditions. These systems blurred partisan differences on the bank question by satisfying the Whigs' demands for public recognition of private enterprize and softening the Democrats' objections to exclusive privilege. Likewise, the infusion of gold and silver into the economy from California in the late 1840s made meaningless the Whigs' contention that the country lacked enough specie to have a national metallic currency. The increasing use of railroads in the 1840s and '50s took much of the impact out of another issue which had traditionally divided the Whigs from the Democrats, the public financing of canal construction.[5]

While economic change deprived the Whigs of lively issues, the slavery question divided the party along sectional lines. Slavery symbolized incompatible perspectives among the Whigs on how the pursuit of material progress could be reconciled with the maintenance of communal unity. The different outlooks of the Whigs in the North and South were, in turn, rooted in the different social conditions of the two sections. For the northern Whigs, the basis of class harmony was the provision of abundant opportunity within a system of formally free labor. To them, slavery was abhorrent because it repressed energy and ambition, and created an aristocratic class which lived off the labor of other members of society. But for most southern Whigs, slavery was one of the major foundations for the harmony of their social system. By consigning dependency and manual labor to the members of a supposedly inferior race, it affirmed the unity of all white men. As a consequence, most southern Whigs considered any threat to slavery a danger to the racial basis of interclass solidarity in their section.

This disparity in the outlooks and objectives of the sectional wings of the Whig party was not always apparent. Reasoning from within their own limited frames of reference, Whigs in one section often mistook their own views for those of their colleagues in the other section. A northern Whig could thus argue earnestly that *all* Whigs disliked slavery, while a southern Whig could assert that the northern Whigs were "sounder" on the slavery issue than the northern Democrats.[6] But this illusion of agreement was only sustainable so long as slavery was purely a local matter. While this condition pertained, the latent antislavery propensities of the northern Whigs were held in check by their regard for the constitutional prerogatives of the states and the property rights of the slaveholders. By the same token, southern Whigs could hail their northern counterparts as more reliable allies of the South than the unprincipled demagogues and radical majoritarians of the northern Democracy. It was another matter whenever slavery became a national concern. On such issues as the reception of abolitionist petitions, the abolition of slavery in the District of Columbia, and the status of slavery in the territories, Whig congressmen tended to polarize along sectional lines.[7]

The Democrats, to be sure, were wracked by some of the same intersectional stresses. But they were never as badly divided over matters of slavery and race, and were far more adept at managing intraparty conflict. This was partly because the Democrats did not assign to government the primary responsibility for securing the public good; to them, the proper sphere of the federal government did not extend far beyond the protection of the rights of white male citizens. More, to the Democrats, moral questions were almost exclusively private matters, best left to the consciences of individuals.[8] The Whigs, by contrast, did see the government as a positive agency for the promotion of social progress. Furthermore, many northern members of the party believed that it should help instill the standards of belief and conduct required by a capitalistic economy based on free labor. Thus, when the territorial issue pitted the respective social systems of the North and South against each other, the Whigs found themselves in a quandary. Each sectional wing adhered to its own position rather than appear to betray the ideals it had claimed were essential to the good society. Further, since each side considered its stance the only right one to assume, it could only conclude that its opponent had the lowest of motives. Rather than concede an honest difference of opinion, each accused the other of pursuing immediate political advantage. Statesmanship, in short, had given way to politics.

Many Whigs, of course, tried to respond to the territorial question in a manner consistent with the party's ideal of consensus. The pacifying influence of such men (who were led by Clay) was evident in the substantial Whig support for the "no territory" policy during the Mexican War. But that policy was thwarted, and in 1848, the northern and southern Whigs had diametrically opposed positions on the Wilmot Proviso.[9] Any hope that the Whigs might reach an agreement on the territorial question was quickly dispelled by the crisis of 1850. To be certain, the "Union-saving" Whigs led by Clay and Webster claimed that their compromise was consistent with the Whigs's corporate ideal of the national interest. But the piecemeal passage of the compromise bills belied the pretension that they expressed a bisectional Whig consensus. More, free soil Whigs, led by Seward, remained unreconciled to the compromise's concessions to the South, and vigorously asserted the right to press for their repeal. This, in turn, prompted demands from procompromise Whigs that Seward and his followers declare their willingness to abide by the settlement. Perhaps most significantly, even the Whig supporters of compromise felt obliged to couch their arguments in sectional terms. When Webster declared that it was unnecessary to enact legislation to exclude slavery from New Mexico because nature would accomplish the same end, he was reflecting the antislavery sentiment of northern Whigs of every ideological hue. Contrariwise, Webster's counterparts in the South, such as Alexander Stephens, defended the compromise on terms which were attuned to the special sensibilities of *their* section. They asserted that the primary virtue of the settlement was that it acknowledged the "rights" and "honor" of the South, particularly with regard to the territorial and fugitive slave issues.

The crisis of 1850 thus played a substantial role in revealing the internal strains which would eventually lead to the disintegration of the Whig party. The truth of this observation has been obscured somewhat by the fact that the Whigs managed to maintain a semblance of unity even after the ordeal of 1850. But while the Whig party may have survived the controversies of that fateful year, it never fully recovered from them. In the four years following the enactment of the compromise measures, the Whigs suffered a continuous erosion of support at the local level, losing governorships and seats in Congress and state legislatures.[10] Part of the Whigs' problem, it must be granted, had nothing to do with the politics of sectionalism. The influx of three million immigrants into the country between 1846 and 1854 hurt the Whigs by giving the Democrats enlarged constituencies in the northern states. The overwhelming majority of the newcomers were Germans and Irish Catholics who looked to the Democrats as protectors of their distinctive subcultures against nativist Whig "meddling." Furthermore, many Whigs joined local nativist, reform, and temperance parties in reaction against the new immigrants. These political organizations rejected the traditional position of most Whigs, that the immigrant could be assimilated into American society through education and moral suasion. Their spokesmen claimed that because Germans and Irish Catholics lived outside the cultural mainstream, the values of the dominant society would have to be imposed upon them.[11]

But many of those alienated from the Whig party in the early 1850s felt no attraction to the anti-immigrant movement, and a large proportion were from the South, where there were few immigrants to react against.

Furthermore, there is considerable evidence that the Whigs continued to be plagued by intraparty conflict after the passage of the compromise bills in 1850. The issue of the "finality" of the compromise both exposed and aggravated their differences. To the procompromise Whigs, acceptance of "finality" was the test of the party's devotion to principle. As they saw it, "finality" involved the question of whether the Whigs would continue to be a party of national statesmanship, in which each section moderated its demands in pursuit of the transcendent national interest. The alternative was that it would fall under the sway of demagogues without fixed principles, who would continue to "agitate" divisive sectional issues without concern for the turmoil they might create.[12]

However, to the free soil Whigs of the North, what the advocates of "finality" were demanding was a *sacrifice* of principle. In effect, they were calling upon free men to relinquish their freedoms of conscience and action, and to treat ordinary legislative enactments like sacred pronouncements. Free soil Whigs took particular umbrage at the proposal that the Fugitive Slave Law should not be subject to amendment or repeal. This was the one compromise measure that directly impinged upon the North, and many northern consciences were offended by its provisions. Among its objectionable features were the denial of the right to a jury trial to accused fugitives and the requirement that northern civilians assist in the capture of alleged runaways. As one northern Whig complained, no law had done more to "nationalize" the institution of slavery.[13]

"Finality" first became an important national issue in December 1850, only a few months after the last compromise measure was passed. Henry Clay circulated a petition in Congress which pledged its signees not to support candidates for President and Vice President who did not proclaim their adherence to the compromise. Although it was presented as a bipartisan effort, this "Round Robin" was almost exclusively a Whig affair. The Democrats, perhaps already scenting victory in 1852, evinced little interest in cooperating. They wanted to claim as much credit for the compromise as possible rather than have to share it with their opponents. Thus, of the 44 signatures on the Round Robin, only 6 were those of Democrats. More significant for the Whigs was the fact that of the 38 signatures they provided, 28 were by southerners, and 10 by northerners associated with the Fillmore administration. Free-soil Whigs were conspicuously absent among the signers of the Round Robin.[14]

Finality resurfaced as a national issue when the first session of the Thirty-second Congress convened in December 1851. In the Whig caucus, an attempt was made to commit the party officially to upholding the compromise of 1850. A finality resolution was passed, but the caucus was so poorly attended that its decision provided the Democrats with cause for ridicule.[15] Later in the session, finality resolutions were submitted on the floor of the House, and the Democrats and southern Whigs supported them by substantial majorities. But the bulk of northern Whigs voted against them.[16]

The split among the congressional Whigs was paralleled at the state level. In the South, Whigs rallied behind the Fillmore administration and the cause of finality. But in the North, the forces of free soil Whiggery tended to prevail against the supporters of the compromise. In 1850 and 1851 Whig conventions met in the three most populous states of the North, New York, Ohio, and Pennsylvania. At all three conclaves, resolutions praising the administration and the compromise were introduced by supporters of President Fillmore, only to be voted down overwhelmingly. The three conventions also nominated for governor men who favored modification or repeal of the Fugitive Slave Law.[17]

The tensions the Whigs experienced over the finality question came to a peak during the preconvention maneuvering for the party's presidential nomination in 1852. The procompromise forces rallied behind President Fillmore and Secretary of State Webster, while their opponents backed Winfield Scott. The southern proponents of finality noted ominously that Scott was a confidant of "that dangerous and designing man," William Seward, and that the state conventions which nominated Scott delegations remained silent on the compromise.[18] When the Whig congressional caucus met on April 20, 1852, to set a date for the national convention, yet another finality resolution was introduced. But it was tabled because of overwhelming northern opposition, prompting eleven southerners to bolt the meeting.[19] When the national convention met at Baltimore, it passed a platform with a plank affirming the Whigs' "acquiescence" in the compromise laws. However, one-half of the delegates who supported Scott on the first ballot voted against this plank. Despite some of the delegates' misgivings about his stand on the compromise, Scott was nominated on the fifty-third ballot after the Fillmore and Webster forces failed to combine behind a single candidate. He then proceeded to compound his problems with his opponents within the party by failing to mention the compromise in his letter of acceptance. This tactic reflected his desire not to alienate the free soil Whigs, but it led such prominent southerners as Alexander Stephens to refuse to endorse his candidacy. In addition, some of the procompromise Whigs of the North, especially those with business ties to the South, defected from the party to back Pierce.[20]

In retrospect, Scott's defeat in 1852 does not seem to have been of calamitous proportions. Although he carried only four states, Scott did receive more than 45 percent of the major party vote, and the presidential contest in most states was rather close. But statistics cannot capture moods and emotions, and after the 1852 elections, many Whigs were in a demoralized, defeatist state of mind. The symbolic leaders of the party, Clay and Webster, both died in 1852, as if to indicate the passing of an old order.[21] What is more, the issues which had previously galvanized the party—"executive usurpation," banking, the tariff, and distribution—were no longer prominent topics of discussion.[22] Even more important, substantial factions among the Whigs felt that the party had abandoned principle in the pursuit of partisan advantage. Procompromise Whigs believed that the northern wing of the party had been captured by demagogues and extremists, led by William Seward, who used antislavery appeals to win the support of abolitionists and free soilers. Contrariwise, antislavery Whigs had found themselves saddled with an obnoxious national platform and an administration which strictly enforced the morally objectionable Fugitive Slave Law. Nativist Whigs, too, had reason for unhappiness because of Scott's clumsy overtures to the new immigrant voters.[23]

With all these groups feeling disaffected, the malaise which overtook the Whigs after Scott's defeat may seem comprehensible. The party, it appeared, had lost all sense of direction. Principle had been sacrificed to politics, and constructive statesmanship had been abandoned in favor of expediency. The local and state elections of 1853 furnished additional evidence of the party's degeneration. In several southern states, the Whigs virtually collapsed as an effective opposition to the Democrats, while in Georgia, they gave up the "Whig" name to avoid being identified with the free soil Whigs of the North. Contrastingly, the Whigs lost substantial support to the Free Democratic party in Connecticut,

Ohio, and Michigan. The affinity of northern Whiggery for free-soilism was most evident in Wisconsin, where there was a coalition between the Whigs and the Free Democrats.[24]

The Kansas-Nebraska controversy of 1854 precipitated the dissolution of the Whigs as a national party. The Kansas-Nebraska Act caused an uproar in the North because it nullified the exclusion of slavery from the section of the Louisiana Purchase above the Missouri Compromise line. Nevertheless, the majority of southern Whig congressmen supported the measure. In doing so, they arrayed themselves on the opposite side of the issue from every northern Whig who cast a vote on Stephen Douglas' bill.[25] The southern Whig supporters of Kansas-Nebraska declared that they were only being true to the principles of the 1850 compromise. That settlement, they pointed out, had left to the citizens of New Mexico and Utah the decision as to whether they would allow slavery into their territories. The Kansas-Nebraska Act simply extended this policy of federal "nonintervention" to the newly organized territories which gave the law its name. In the process, it removed an odious discrimination against the rights of slaveholders, and established the equality of all white men in the national domain. What was vital in the principle of nonintervention was not that it permitted the extension of slavery. Indeed, some southern Whigs said publicly that they did not believe that slavery would take root in either Kansas or Nebraska. Rather, nonintervention accorded equal treatment and legitimacy to the "peculiar institution" of the South. It thereby vindicated the southern belief that slavery and freedom were thoroughly compatible. As Senator Robert Toombs of Georgia intoned: "The friends of the measure place their support of it upon conformity to the Constitution, to the great American principle of popular sovereignty, and upon the absolute requirements of political justice and equality." "It is not demanded," Toombs avowed, "as a measure of justice to the South, though such is its effects; but it is demanded as an act of obedience to these sound catholic national principles."[26]

Of course, it was precisely what Toombs found commendable in the Kansas-Nebraska Act that appalled free soil Whigs. A thirty-four-year-old policy that preferred freedom over slavery was to be abandoned in favor of one of professed neutrality toward the iniquitous institution. Surely this was a sign of the degeneracy of the republic from the example set by the Founding Fathers in the Northwest Territory; ground consecrated to freedom was to be opened to slavery. To accept Douglas' measure would be to betray a lack of devotion to liberty. Considered in this light, the question of whether slavery would actually enter Kansas or Nebraska was of secondary importance. The main point was the United States' professed devotion to the ideals of republicanism. Even if the question of repealing the Missouri Compromise line was an "abstraction," declared Seward, "yet even that abstraction would involve the testing of the United States on the expediency, wisdom, morality, and justice of the system of human bondage, with which this and other parties of the world have been so long afflicted." Seward added that it would be a "melancholy day for the Republic and for mankind, when her decision on even such an abstraction shall command no respect, and inspire no hope into the hearts of the oppressed."[27]

Free soil Whigs also complained that Kansas-Nebraska violated a "solemn compact" between the sections. Although it was only an ordinary legislative enactment (or rather a series of them), the Missouri Compromise had acquired the prescriptive force of public acceptance for more than a third of a century. But now the South, with the assistance of some corrupt northern "dough-faces," proposed to repeal it. Kansas-Nebraska was no simple piece of legislation. Rather, it was a flagrant "aggression" upon the North, an illegitimate attempt to extend slavery where there was no demand for it. Nothing else could give greater credence to the notion that the South, in its eagerness to spread slavery, would not abide by compacts with the North. From this many northern Whigs drew a conclusion: if Kansas-Nebraska established nonintervention as national policy, then the tradition of intersectional concession would be hopelessly discredited. Lincoln, a moderate Whig who had supported the compromise of 1850, stated this point very forcibly:

> Slavery may or may not be established in Nebraska. But whether it be or not, we shall have repudiated—discarded from the councils of the Nation—the SPIRIT OF COMPROMISE; for who after this will ever trust in a national compromise? The spirit of mutual concession—that spirit which first gave us the constitution, and which has thrice saved the Union—we shall have strangled and cast from us forever. And what shall we have in lieu of it? The South flushed with triumph and tempted to excesses; the North, betrayed, as they believe, brooding on wrong and burning for revenge. One side will provoke; the other resent. The one will taunt, the other defy; one [aggresses], the other retaliates.[28]

Lincoln's sentiments were shared by many northern Whigs who had previously championed compromise with the South. A goodly number of these men had risked—and in some cases, sacrificed—their public careers by supporting the agreement of 1850.[29] But now, the Clay-Webster legacy of intersectional consensus seemed to have been destroyed. A leading Union-saving Senator, James Cooper of Pennsylvania, predicted that those in the North most likely to feel resentment at the passage of the Kansas-Nebraska "are the same who have been heretofore reproached at home as enemies of freedom, and allies of an institution repugnant to humanity and the spirit of enlightened civilization." Cooper explained: "Heretofore, these reproaches to the criminal indifference to the wrongs of slavery, and concession to what is denominated the aggressive spirit of the South, were easily turned aside by showing that the South acted in good faith, and asked for nothing which the Constitution, and laws did not secure to her." "But this shield," Cooper observed, "is no longer available for that purpose." The compromise agreements has been "violated and set at naught by the South itself." More, "the effect of the settlement of 1850" had been "abrogated and broken up along with others older and consented by a longer observance." Cooper concluded his philippic against Kansas-Nebraska with a warning to the South: "Breed contempt for compromises in the minds of the people, and those of the Constitution, by which slavery is recognized, and the reclamation of fugitive slaves secured, will lose their sacredness and be broken up—as the Missouri Compromise is now proposed to be broken up."[30]

Senator Truman Smith of Connecticut foresaw the consequence the passage of Kansas-Nebraska would have for the national Whig party. By destroying the tradition of bisectional statesmanship, it would make impossible future cooperation between northern and southern Whigs. Speaking directly to the Whigs of the South who backed the Kansas-Nebraska Act, Smith prophesied:

> Sir, the very moment you pass this measure, you explode, not only the Missouri compromise, but the adjustment of 1850, and the Baltimore Whig platform of 1852. You blow the Whig party into ten thousand atoms. Another Whig national convention will be impossible. Nothing can induce me to become, on the contingency named, a party to such a convention. It will be idle to attempt any understanding with southern Whigs on the subject of slavery. Did we not go at Baltimore [for] the finality

of the compromise of 1850? Did we not agree to stand by even the fugitive slave law, so distasteful to many of our people? . . . Do you now tell us in effect that all such covenants are binding on us *in perpetuo*, but not binding on you any longer than you choose to be bound?[31]

In their complaints against the Kansas-Nebraska Act, northern Union-saving Whigs were joined by some of their southern counterparts. Senator John Bell of Tennessee, while conceding his support of the principle of nonintervention, condemned Douglas' bill as a needless provocation. He perceived the danger that because of the measure, "sober-minded and reflecting citizens" of the North who rejected abolition but opposed the expansion of slavery would begin to follow "professional agitators" such as Salmon Chase and Charles Sumner. The act was therefore imprudent because it disregarded the deeply ingrained prejudice of the northern public against slavery. It was the duty of the statesman to work within the limits set by prevailing public opinion; to do otherwise was to endanger the peace and stability of the republic. Bell compared the advocates of Kansas-Nebraska to a British politician who, according to one of his colleagues, would urge any measure which suited his predilections "though it might excite the opposition and inflame the passions of the whole country."[32]

Kansas-Nebraska virtually destroyed the Whigs as a national party,[33] but it did not shatter the dreams which had originally brought the Whigs together. Indeed, there were many who hoped to organize a new national party among those northern Whigs who refused to join the Republicans and those southern Whigs who would not defect to the Democrats. Its promoters hoped that, purged of extremists in both sections, such a party might restore the tradition of moderate statesmanship which had been championed by Clay and Webster in 1850. Its leaders would be pure men of principle, who would abjure agitation and restore virtue and reason to the republic. Many Whigs with such a vision hoped that the American ("Know-Nothing") party would provide a congenial political host. Know-Nothingism was, of course, based on nativist feeling, which had always been a powerful force within the Whig party. Anti-Catholicism, to which the Know-Nothings ap-pealed, was on the rise in the early 1850s, partly because of a perceived increase in the self-assertiveness of the Church of Rome in the United States.[34] The Know-Nothings also attacked an old Whig target, political corruption. They wanted to disenfranchise unnaturalized immigrants, whom they claimed were manipulated by demagogues and put their votes up for sale to unscrupulous politicians.[35] Perhaps the key element in the appeal of Know-Nothingism to former Whigs was its nationalism. The Know-Nothings identified themselves with America's republican heritage, which they proposed to regenerate by purging the country of alien political influence. Many Know-Nothings thus hoped that their party would bring about a revival of national feeling, which would quell sectional sentiment on both sides of the Mason-Dixon line. A crusade to restore pure government might indeed provide Americans throughout the nation with a common, unifying cause.[36]

Unfortunately for the nationalist Whigs, the Know-Nothings were not exempt from the sectional tensions which had split the Whig party apart. Many Know-Nothings of the North abhorred slavery as much as the Catholic Church, considering both institutions backward, oppressive, and antirepublican.[37] Most southern Know-Nothings were as devoted to the protection of slavery as their Democratic opponents.[38] Hence, the Know-Nothings made their best electoral showings in 1854 and 1855, when their sectional wings were not burdened by a national party line on slavery. But the Know-Nothings could not escape entanglement in the politics of sectionalism in 1856, a presidential election year. When the national convention of the party rejected demands that the platform call for the restoration of the Missouri Compromise line, many northern Know-Nothings defected to the Republicans. In the ensuing elections, the Know-Nothing presidential candidate, former President Fillmore, received almost 44 percent of the vote in the slave states. But he won only slightly more than 13 percent in the free states. The Know-Nothing party disintegrated rapidly after its disappointing performance in 1856, the victim of failed expectations and unmet promise.[39]

The Whigs, in the end, were the victims of their own aspirations. Although enthusiastic proponents of economic progress, they wanted to contain it within a corporate social and political framework. But by the 1850s, it had become increasingly difficult to define, let alone implement, the Whig ideal of a homogeneous national interest. The Whigs wanted a more economically interdependent country, but most Americans had lost interest in a national banking system and federal financing of internal improvements. The Whigs wanted a more culturally uniform nation, but seemingly unassimilable new immigrants had flooded into the United States from Germany and Ireland. The Whigs wanted to promote sectional unity, but the sectional controversies of the 1850s left northerners and southerners at daggers drawn.

Of course, the Whigs were not the only ones affected by the forces dividing the country in the 1850s. The other national parties—the Democrats as well as the Know-Nothings—would also disintegrate over sectional differences. Indeed, only in the trials of war would many Americans rediscover the sense of unity and common purpose which the Whigs had tried to foster by peaceable means.

NOTES

1. Introduction

1. Henry Adams, *Life of Albert Gallatin* (Philadelphia, 1879), p. 635.

2. U.S. Congress, Senate, *Congressional Globe,* 39th Cong., 1st sess., January 22, 1866, p. 341, quoted in William R. Brock, *An American Crisis: Congress and Reconstruction, 1865–1867* (New York: Harper and Row, 1966), p. 65.

3. Andrew Lane, quoted in Francis Weisenburger, *The Passing of the Frontier* (Columbus, Ohio: Ohio State Historical and Archaeological Society, 1941), p. 294.

4. See Vernon Parrington, *Main Currents in American Thought,* 3 vols. (New York: Harcourt, Brace, and World, 1954), 2:289; Arthur Schlesinger, Jr., *The Age of Jackson,* p. 279. Although so-called "consensus history" is often sharply counterposed to "progressive history," the "consensus" historian Louis Hartz had a view of the Whigs similar to that of such "progressives" as Parrington and Schlesinger. What distinguished Hartz from the "progressives," of course, was his evaluation of the "reality" of the social conflict between the Democrats and Whigs. Hartz thought that the Democrats were as afflicted with capitalistic drives as the Whigs; Parrington and Schlesinger did not. See Louis Hartz, *The Liberal Tradition in America: An Interpretation of American Political Thought Since the Revolution* (New York: Harcourt, Brace, and World, 1955), pp. 89–113.

5. See Glyndon G. Van Deusen, "Some Aspects of Whig Thought and Theory in the Jacksonian Period," *American Historical Review* (January 1958), 58:305–22. See also Van Deusen, *The Life of Henry Clay; Thurlow Weed; Horace Greeley, Nineteenth Century Crusader* (Philadelphia: Lippincott, 1953); *The Jacksonian Era,* pp. 96–98; *William Henry Seward.* The quotation is from Van Deusen, "Some Aspects," p. 306.

6. Lynn L. Marshall, "The Strange Stillbirth of the Whig Party."

7. See Lee Benson, *The Concept of Jacksonian Democracy;* Ronald P. Formisano, *The Birth of Mass Political Parties;* Donald B. Cole, *Jacksonian Democracy in New Hampshire;* Michael F. Holt, *Forging a Majority;* William G. Shade, *Banks or No Banks.* The findings of some of these studies are summarized in Robert Kelley, *The Cultural Pattern in American Politics: The First Century* (New York: Knopf, 1979),

pp. 164–76. In all fairness to Kelley and Shade, it should be pointed out that they do try to relate the cultural differences between the two parties to their positions on the banking issue. But their explanations remain, for the most part, "cultural" in a narrow sense; for them, culture means simply a combination of religion and ethnicity. For perceptive critiques of the methodology of quantitative studies of nineteenth-century voting behavior, see Richard L. McCormick, "Ethno-Cultural Interpretations of Nineteenth Century Voting Behavior"; James E. Wright, "The Ethnocultural Model of Voting: A Behavioral and Historical Critique," *American Behavioral Scientist* (May–June 1973), 16:658–74.

8. Daniel Walker Howe, *The Political Culture of the American Whigs.*

9. Thus, most interpretations of the Whigs fall apart when they try to account for the southern Whigs. For a lengthy critique of the historical literature on the Whigs, see Thomas Brown, "Politics and Statesmanship: A Study of the American Whig Party" (Ph.D. diss., Columbia University, 1981), pp. 3–15.

10. Richard P. McCormick, *The Second American Party System*, p. 354. For evidence of how much partisan politics pervaded American society in the Jacksonian era, see William E. Gienapp, "'Politics Seem to Enter into Everything'" and Thomas B. Alexander, "The Dimensions of Voter Partisan Consistency."

11. Marvin Meyers, *The Jacksonian Persuasion*, p. ix.

12. Wilson Carey McWilliams, *The Idea of Fraternity in America*, p. 71. Richard L. McCormick has perceptively suggested that the party politics of the period from the 1830s to the early 1900s may be considered a transition between the deferential politics which preceded it and the interest group politics which followed it. Building upon this observation, I might suggest that party politics combined the corporate objectives of deferential politics with the methods of interest group politics. To put this point more clearly, the nineteenth-century parties addressed themselves to Americans' broad visions of the public good, but tried to further them through the politics of material "influence." See Richard L. McCormick, "The Party Period and Public Policy: An Exploratory Hypothesis," *Journal of American History* (September 1979), 66:279–98.

13. Bernard Bailyn, *The Ideological Origins of the American Revolution*, pp. 55–65; Gordon S. Wood, *The Creation of the American Republic*, pp. 18–28. The discussion of republicanism here will deal only with those of its aspects which survived into the Jacksonian era, while ignoring those (such as the theory of "mixed government") which were discarded. For the persistence of classical republican assumptions in nineteenth-century American politics, see Lance Banning, *The Jeffersonian Persuasion: Evolution of a Party Ideology* (Ithaca, N.Y.: Cornell University Press, 1978); Perry M. Goldman, "The Republic of Virtue"; Linda K. Kerber, *Federalists in Dissent*; Drew R. McCoy, *The Elusive Republic*; Rowland Berthoff, "Independence and Attachment, Virtue and Interest: From Republican Citizen to Free Enterpriser, 1787–1837," in Richard L. Bushman, et al., eds., *Uprooted Americans: Essays to Honor Oscar Handlin* (Boston: Little, Brown, 1979), pp. 97–124; J. G. A. Pocock, *The Machiavellian Moment*, ch. 15.

14. Bailyn, *Ideological Origins*, p. 160; Wood, *Creation*, pp. 46–69, 118–24.

15. Richard L. Bushman, "'This New Man': Dependence and Independence, 1776," in Bushman, et al., *Uprooted Americans*, pp. 77–96.

16. Wood, *Creation*, p. 58.

17. *Ibid.*, pp. 58–59.

18. *Ibid.*, pp. 34–35, 53–65, ch. 3; Bailyn, *Ideological Origins*, pp. 160, 308–9; Kerber, *Federalists*, pp. 121–26; Banning, *Jeffersonian Persuasion*, p. 198.

19. Bailyn, *Ideological Origins*, pp. 273–301; Wood, *Creation*, pp. 70–75. Of course, it was possible to emphasize different aspects of American republicanism. Thus, New Englanders tended to stress its communitarian elements, while Southerners placed a higher value on its libertarian elements. Such a sectional distinction does seem to have existed between the northern and southern Whigs. For some evidence of the early development of such a distinction, see H. James Henderson, *Party Politics in the Continental Congress* (New York: McGraw-Hill, 1974), pp. 178–82, 350–51, 369, 438–40.

20. Bailyn, *Ideological Origins*, p. 160; Wood, *Creation*, pp. 114–18; Rowland Berthoff and John M. Murrin, "Feudalism, Communalism, and the Yeoman Freeholder: The American Revolution Considered as a Social Accident," in James H. Hutson and Stephen G. Kurtz, eds., *Essays on the American Revolution* (Chapel Hill: University of North Carolina Press, 1973), pp. 256–88.

21. For the economic changes in the Jacksonian era, see Douglas T. Miller, *The Birth of Modern America* (Indianapolis: Pegasus Books, 1970); Douglass C. North, *The Economic Growth of the United States;* George R. Taylor, *The Transporation Revolution.* For the misgivings about prosperity, see Fred Somkin, *Unquiet Eagle.*

22. See Richard Hofstadter, *The Idea of a Party System*, chs. 5–6.

23. McCormick, *Second American Party System*, ch. 2.

24. See Ronald P. Formisano, "Political Character, Antipartyism, and the Second Party System"; Michael L. Wallace, "Ideologies of Party in the Ante-Bellum Republic," ch. 5.

25. Alexis de Tocqueville coined the term "individualism" to describe the prevalent pattern of behavior he found in the United States in the early 1830s. Tocqueville used the word to denote the tendency of Americans to become largely indifferent to public concerns, and to psychologically withdraw into a realm of mostly private concerns. However, Tocqueville himself recognized that Americans did not entirely repudiate the public realm. He devised the phrase "self-interest rightly understood" (*intérêt bien entendu*) to describe the prevalent American attitude that the pursuit of self-interest could be harmonized with the public good, so long as citizens took into account how their actions impinged upon the general welfare. See Alexis de Tocqueville, *Democracy in America*, tr. by Phillips Bradley, 2 vols. (New York: Random House, 1945), 2:104–5; Melvin Richter, "The Uses of Theory: Tocqueville's Adaptation of Montesquieu," in Richter, ed., *Essays in Theory and History* (Cambridge, Mass.: Harvard University Press, 1970), pp. 96–97; James T. Schleifer, *The Making of Tocqueville's Democracy in America* (Chapel Hill: University of North Carolina Press, 1980), pp. 235–37. But the rhetoric of the parties indicates that, so far as *politics* was concerned, Jacksonian-era Americans did not completely assume that the individual pursuit

of self-interest could be harmonized easily with the general betterment.

26. Meyers, *Jacksonian Persuasion*, pp. 12, 14. With the possible exception of some "agrarian" and Old Republican ideologues, the Democrats did not actually propose to reverse the course of social "progress." But by thwarting the Whigs' schemes to stimulate economic development, they did hope to ensure that it would proceed at an unforced, "natural" pace, and thus be assimilated to traditional republican ideals.

27. See Congressman Howell Cobb of Georgia, *Congressional Globe*, 30th Cong., 1st sess., July 1, 1848, p. 775; Martin Van Buren, *An Inquiry into the Origin and Course of the Political Parties in the United States* (New York, 1867); Michael L. Wallace, "Changing Concepts of Party."

28. This, of course, is a major theme of the chapters below. But see "Political Parties," *New England Magazine* (October 1834), 7:265–76; *The Political Mirror; or, Review of Jacksonism*; C. M. Thompson, "Attitude of the Western Whigs Toward the Convention System," *Proceedings of the Mississippi Valley Historical Association* (1911–12), 5:167–89; Formisano, "Political Character, Antipartyism, and the Second Party System"; Edward L. Mayo, "The *National Intelligencer* and Jacksonian Democracy."

29. See *The Whig Textbook, or Democracy Unmasked to the People of the United States*, pp. 29–30; "Political Parties," p. 270; "The Position of the Parties," *American Whig Review* (January 1845), 1:59–61; Mayo, "*National Intelligencer*," passim.

30. "Political Education—Statesmanship," *American Whig Review* (April 1846), 3:355.

31. [Joseph Story], "Statesmen: Their Rareness and Importance," *New England Magazine* (August 1834), 7:93.

32. *Ibid.*, p. 94. For a formulation of the nature of statesmanship similar to that of the Whigs, see Paul Eidelberg, *A Discourse on Statesmanship: The Design and Transformation of the American Polity* (Urbana: University of Illinois Press, 1974), pp. 10–11.

33. [Story], "Statesmen," p. 94.

34. R. McKinley Ormsby, *A History of the Whig Party . . . to the Present Time, etc. etc.*, p. 176.

35. "Calhoun's Speech Against the Conquest of Mexico," *American Whig Review* (April 1848), 7:225. Howe, *Political Culture*, p. 31, makes the connection between the statesman ideal and the "rational" faculties, but mistakenly, I believe, claims that the Whigs adhered to the ideal of a deferential society. As the text quotation should make clear, the Whigs did not call upon men to "defer" to statesmen because they were members of a class possessing certain easily recognizable attributes which specially qualified them for the public service. Rather, they urged voters to cast their ballots for statesmen who exhibited qualities of *character* considered desirable in all republican citizens. Cf. the sentiments expressed in the quotation with the ideas outlined in J. G. A. Pocock, "The Classical Theory of Deference," *American Historical Review* (April 1975), 80:516–23.

36. See Mayo, *"National Intelligencer,"* pp. 141–52; Ormsby, *History of Whig Party*, p. 370; Clement Eaton, "Southern Senators and the Right of Instruction." The quotation is from the *National Intelligencer*, December 27, 1828. In practice, however, the Whigs sometimes employed the power of instruction to bind Democratic senators; but since they considered Democratic politicians mere party men, unmotivated by considerations of principle, they felt that such use of the instruction power implied no sacrifice of statesmanlike ideals. At the state as well as the national level, the Whigs tried to curtail executive power over the legislative branch. See Shade, *Banks or No Banks*, p. 121; Rush Welter, *The Mind of America*, p. 202.

37. See Mayo, *"National Intelligencer,"* pp. 6, 71–73; Congressman Robert C. Winthrop of Massachusetts, *Congressional Globe*, 29th Cong., 1st sess., March 12, 1846, app., p. 487; "Party Discontents," *American Whig Review* (April 1848), 7:340. See also Eidelberg, *Discourse on Statesmanship*, pp. 17, 155–57. The Whigs' ideal of congressional leadership bore close similarities to that projected in the *Federalist Papers*. See Gary Wills, *Explaining America: The Federalist* (Garden City, N.Y.: Doubleday, 1981), pp. 223–59.

2. The Whig Party in the North: The Rhetoric of Party Formation

1. Richard L. McCormick, "Ethno-Cultural Interpretations of Nineteenth Century American Voting Behavior," pp. 351–77, points to this implication of ethnocultural interpretations of Jacksonian era northern politics. Such interpretations are suggested in Benson, *Concept of Jacksonian Democracy*; Formisano, *Birth of Parties*; Holt, *Forging Majority*; Roger Dewey Peterson, "The Reaction to a Heterogeneous Society: A Behavioral and Quantitative Analysis of Northern Voting Behavior, 1845–1870: Pennsylvania as a Test Case" (Ph.D. diss., University of Pittsburgh, 1970). Formisano and Holt seem to have recanted their views somewhat, in favor of interpretations that take into account the ideologies advanced by Democratic and Whig spokesmen. See Formisano, *The Transformation of Political Culture*; Holt, *The Political Crisis of the 1850s*.

2. For evidence of high voter turnout and low levels of split-ticket voting from the mid-1830s to the early 1850s, see Walter Dean Burnham, "The Changing Shape of the American Political Universe," *American Political Science Review* (March 1965), 59:7–28; William G. Shade, "Political Pluralism and Party Development: The Creation of a Modern Party System, 1815–1852," in Paul Kleppner, et al., *The Evolution of American Electoral Systems* (Westport, Conn.: Greenwood Press, 1981), pp. 82, 84, 92–93.

3. See, for example, Formisano, *Birth of Parties*, pp. 11–12.

4. For the functions of political rhetoric, see Paul F. Lazarsfeld, Bernard Berelson, and Hazel Gaudet, *The People's Choice: How the Voter Makes Up His Mind in a Presidential Campaign*, 2d ed. (New York: Columbia University Press, 1948), pp. 73–104. For the concept of the perspective and the functions of party

identification, see Tamotsu Shibutani, "Reference Groups as Perspectives," *American Journal of Sociology* (May 1955), 60:562–69; Benjamin Page and Raymond Wolfinger, "Party Identification," in Wolfinger, ed., *Readings in American Political Behavior*, 2d ed. (Englewood Cliffs, N.J.: Prentice-Hall, 1970), pp. 289–99.

5. See George Dangerfield, *The Awakening of American Nationalism*, ch. 8; Richard P. McCormick, "New Perspectives on Jacksonian Politics," *American Historical Review* (January 1960), 65:288–301; Paul C. Nagel, "The Election of 1824: A Reconsideration Based on Newspaper Opinion," *Journal of Southern History* (August 1960), 26:315–29.

6. John Quincy Adams, "Inaugural Address," March 4, 1825, in James D. Richardson, comp., *The Messages and Papers of the Presidents*, 3:294.

7. See John Quincy Adams, *Memoirs of John Quincy Adams, Comprising Portions of His Diary from 1795 to 1848*, 7:163–64, 343, 349, 364; Samuel Flagg Bemis, *John Quincy Adams and the Union*, pp. 56, 59. For complaints that Adams failed to use the patronage effectively, see Daniel Webster to Henry Clay, March 25, 1827, in Charles Wiltse, ed., *The Papers of Daniel Webster*, 2:175–77; Henry Clay to Daniel Webster, April 14, 1827, *ibid.*, 2:191.

8. John Quincy Adams, "First Annual Message," December 6, 1825, in Richardson, comp., *Messages and Papers*, 2:296–97. For fuller discussions of Adams' ideology of economic development, see George A. Lipsky, *John Quincy Adams;* Dan Martin, "John Quincy Adams and the Whig Ideology" (Ph.D. diss., Yale University, 1968).

9. See Richard Rush, *A Letter from the Secretary of the Treasury Enclosing the Annual Report on the State of the Finances* (Washington, 1825); U.S. Congress, *Report on the State of the Finances, Dec. 8, 1827*, Cong. Doc. 786, 20th Cong., 1st sess., 1827. Adams privately praised Rush's views on the land issue. See Adams, *Memoirs*, 7:36.

10. Adams, "First Annual Message," Richardson, comp., *Messages and Papers*, 2:316; "Fourth Annual Message," December 2, 1828, *ibid.*, 2:413. See also Major P. Wilson, *Space, Time, and Freedom*, pp. 55–57.

11. See Dangerfield, *American Nationalism*, pp. 295–96, 299; Robert V. Remini, *The Election of Andrew Jackson*, pp. 24–25; Norman Risjord, *The Old Republicans*, pp. 258, 263–70.

12. For Jackson's public image, see John William Ward, *Andrew Jackson*.

13. See Remini, *Election of Jackson*, pp. 73–80, 83–95. Jackson's only clearly defined position was on a nationally financed system of internal improvements, which he opposed.

14. See Charles Hammond, *A View of General Jackson's Domestic Relations* (Cincinnati, 1828); Bemis, *Adams and the Union*, pp. 140–42.

15. *Proceedings and Address of the Republican Young Men of the State of New-York, Assembled at Utica, on the Twelfth Day of August, 1828*, pp. 12, 14. See also *Address of the Central Committee . . . friendly to the Election of John Q. Adams as President . . . to their Fellow Citizens*, pp. 18–19, 22; *Report of the Proceedings of the Town Meeting in . . . Philadelphia, July 7th, 1828*, pp. 8, 11, 16, 18.

16. The quotation is from *Address of the Great State Convention . . . Assembled*

. . . *in Concord* [New Hampshire] *June 12, 1828* . . . , p. 8. See also *Address of the Central Committee*, pp. 13–18, 24; *Proceedings and Address of the Convention of Delegates that met at Columbus, Ohio, December 28, 1827* . . . , pp. 8–10; *Report of the State Convention Held at the Capitol in Albany, to Select Suitable Candidates for President and Vice-President of the United States*, pp. 4–5, 6–7; *Report of Philadelphia Town Meeting*, p. 6; Walter R. Fee, *The Transition from Aristocracy to Democracy in New Jersey*, p. 266.

17. *Address of the Central Committee*, p. 4. See also Donald B. Cole, *Jacksonian Democracy in New Hampshire*, p. 266; *Proceedings and Address of Republican Young Men*, p. 12.

18. The elitist approach of the Adamsites is evident in *Address of the Central Committee*, pp. 5–6. On the Adams organization, see Remini, *Election of Jackson*, pp. 183–91.

19. The ideological outlook of Clay and his followers is discussed below in the chapter, "Henry Clay and the Politics of Consensus." See also L. B. Hamlin, ed., "Selections from the Follet Papers," *Quarterly Publications of the Historical and Philosophical Society of Ohio* (April–June 1918), 18:42–78; Robert J. Rayback, *Millard Fillmore: Biography of a President* (Buffalo: Buffalo Historical Society, 1959), pp. 30–31, 60–61; Van Deusen, *Jacksonian Era*, pp. 28–29, 55, 56–57.

20. See Ronald P. Formisano and Kathleen Smith Kutolowski, "Antimasonry and Masonry: The Genesis of Protest," *American Quarterly* (Summer 1977), 29:139–65; William Preston Vaughn, *The Antimasonic Party in the United States*, ch. 1.

21. See *An Abstract of the Proceedings of the Anti-Masonic State Convention of Massachusetts, Held . . . Dec. 30 and 31, 1829 and Jan. 1, 1830*, pp. 10–16; *The Proceedings of the United States Antimasonic Convention, Held at Philadelphia, September 11, 1830 . . . and the Address to the People*, pp. 43–64; *Proceedings of the Second United States Anti-Masonic Convention . . . and the Address to the People*, pp. 69, 80.

22. See Vaughn, *Antimasonic Party*, pp. 129–30, 149.

23. For the links between northern evangelical Protestantism, antimasonry, and antiparty attitudes, see Formisano, "Political Character, Antipartyism." On evangelical antimasonry, see also William Brackney, "Religious Antimasonry: The Genesis of a Political Party" (Ph.D. diss., Temple University, 1976); Whitney R. Cross, *The Burned-Over District*, ch. 6; Formisano, *Birth of Parties*, pp. 60–71; Dorothy Ann Lipson, *Freemasonry in Federalist Connecticut*, ch. 8; Charles McCarthy, "The Antimasonic Party: A Study of Political Antimasonry in the United States, 1827–1840," American Historical Association *Annual Report for 1901* (Washington: Government Printing Office, 1902), 1:537, 544–46. In Massachusetts, the Antimasonic movement seems to have gained most of its adherents among orthodox Congregationalists who opposed the state's rationalistic Unitarian establishment. See Formisano, *Transformation of Political Culture*, ch. 9.

24. See *Abstract of Antimasonic Convention of Massachusetts*, p. 14; *Proceedings of Second United States Convention*, pp. 77, 80–81; "Myron Holley's Address," Rochester (N.Y.) *Anti-Masonic Enquirer*, October 6, 1829.

25. See *Abstract of Antimasonic Convention of Massachusetts*, pp. 13, 15–16;

"Address" of Antimasonic Meeting in Waterbury, Vermont, Hartford (Conn.) *Anti-Masonic Intelligencer*, December 8, 1829; *Proceedings of United States Convention*, pp. 43–64, 118; *Proceedings of Second United States Convention*, pp. 62, 69, 80; Elizabeth V. Haigh, "New York Antimasons" (Ph.D. diss., University of Rochester, 1980), pp. 344–45.

26. See *Abstract of Anti-Masonic Convention of Massachusetts*, pp. 14–15; "Address and Resolutions of the Anti-Masonic Convention at Utica," August 11, 1830, Rochester *Anti-Masonic Enquirer*, August 24, 1830; *Proceedings of United States Convention*, pp. 37, 82, 105–6, 110; *Proceedings of Second United States Convention*, p. 77; Solomon Southwick, *A Solemn Warning Against Free-Masonry. Addressed to the Young Men of the United States . . .* , pp. 23–25, 32.

27. The "hack politicians" quotation is in Oran Follett to Henry D. Chipman, August 6, 1832, Hamlin, ed., "Follet Papers," p. 65. For more evidence of friction between the Antimasons and National Republicans, see Rochester (N.Y.) *Anti-Masonic Enquirer*, September 15, 1829, November 16, 1830, November 23, 1830, November 30, 1830.

28. See Vaughn, *Antimasonic Party*, pp. 41–43, 54–69, 95–96, 156–58.

29. See Eric McKinley Erikkson, "The Federal Civil Service Under President Jackson," *Mississippi Valley Historical Review* (March 1927), 13:517–40; Leonard D. White, *The Jacksonians*, p. 379; Carl Fish, "Removal of Officials by Presidents of the United States," American Historical Association, *Annual Report for 1889* (Washington: Government Printing Office, 1890), 1:70–72.

30. See "Address of the New York State Antimasonic Convention," Albany (N.Y.) *Evening Journal*, June 28, 1832; "Address" of the Vermont Antimasonic State Convention, Montpelier (Vt.) *State Journal*, July 2, 1832; *An Address to the Freemen of Vermont, By their Delegation to the National Republican Convention, Holden at Baltimore, Maryland, in December, 1831*, pp. 10–11; Horace Binney, *Speech . . . At the Anti-Jackson Meeting, Held in the State House Yard, Philadelphia, October 20, 1832*, pp. 1–3; *Journal of the National Republican Convention, . . . in the City of Baltimore, December 12, 1831 for the Nominations of Candidates to Fill the Offices of President and Vice President . . .* , pp. 20, 22; Vaughn, *Antimasonic Party*, pp. 41–43, 77–78.

31. See "Address of the New York State Antimasonic Convention"; "Address" of the Vermont Antimasonic Convention; *Address to Freemen of Vermont*, p. 7; Binney, *Speech at Meeting*, p. 5; *Journal of National Republican Convention*, pp. 26–27; *Proceedings of the State Convention of National Republican Young Men, Holden at Hartford, . . . October 17, 1832* (Hartford [Conn.], 1832), p. 10. On Jacksonian Indian policy, see Grant Foreman, *Indian Removal* (Norman: Oklahoma University Press, 1932); Francis Paul Prucha, *American Indian Policy in the Formative Years: The Indian Trade and Intercourse Acts, 1790–1834* (Cambridge, Mass.: Harvard University Press, 1962).

32. *Proceedings of State Convention at Hartford*, pp. 9–10. See also "Address of the New York State Antimasonic Convention"; Binney, *Speech at Meeting*, p. 6. Clay's complaint is in Calvin Colton, ed., *The Works of Henry Clay*, 7:528.

33. See "Address of the New York State Antimasonic Convention"; "Address"

of the Vermont Antimasonic Convention; *Address to Freemen of Vermont*, pp. 4–7; *Journal of National Republican Convention*, pp. 24–25; *Proceedings of State Convention at Hartford*, pp. 8–9; *Proceedings of the National Republican Convention of Young Men, . . . in the City of Washington, May 7, 1832*, pp. 24–25.

34. Jackson, "Bank Veto," July 10, 1832, Richardson, comp., *Messages and Papers*, 2:576–77, 578–80, 591 (quotation).

35. See *ibid.*, 2:576. For evidence of support for a national bank among Jackson's supporters, see John M. McFaul, *The Politics of Jacksonian Finance*, pp. 44–45; Jean A. Wilburn, *Biddle's Bank*, pp. 11–12, 121–22, 134. Wilburn points out, too, that many state banks petitioned in favor of recharter of the bank, but McFaul (pp. 27–28) suggests—I think correctly—that recharter was opposed by state banks, such as those in New York and Virginia, which did not care for the national bank's restraints on credit. In any case, the "real" motives behind the bank veto are irrelevant here; my main concern is with its ideological significance. See also Bray Hammond, *Banks and Politics in America*, pp. 326–405; Ralph C. Catteral, *The Second Bank of the United States*, ch. 8–9; Robert V. Remini, *Andrew Jackson and the Bank War*. The discussion which perhaps captures best the complex appeal of the bank veto message is Meyers, *Jacksonian Persuasion*, pp. 24–28.

36. See Robert V. Remini, "Election of 1832," in Arthur Schlesinger, Jr., and Fred Israel, eds., *History of American Presidential Elections*, 1:516.

37. For the votes on the compromise tariff, see U.S. Congress, *Register of Debates*, 22d Cong., 2d sess., March 1, 1833, pp. 808–9; *ibid.*, February 26, 1833, pp. 1810–11.

38. On Webster's efforts for a coalition with Jackson and their ultimate collapse, see ch. 3 of this book, "Daniel Webster: Conservative Whig."

39. See U.S. Congress, House, *Removal Public Deposites. Report of the Minority of the Committee of Ways and Means. Submitted by Mr. Binney, March 4, 1834.* H.R. 313, 23d Cong., 1st sess., 1834; Tristam Burges, "Speech on the Removal of the Public Deposites, March 18, 1834," in Henry L. Bowen, *Memoir of Tristam Burges; with Selections from His Speeches and Occasional Writings*, pp. 324, 340–96; Thomas Corwin, "Speech on the Removal of the Deposits," April 4, 1834, in Josiah Morrow, ed., *Life and Speeches of Thomas Corwin*, pp. 100–1; Charles W. Cutter, *An Oration Delivered Before the Whigs of Portsmouth* [N.H.] *on the Fourth of July, A.D. 1834*, pp. 15–24, 30–31; Oliver Spencer Halsted, *Address Delivered Before the Whigs of Newark* [N.J.], *4 July 1834* (Newark, 1834); Thomas Larraine McKenney [Aristides], *Essays on the Spirit of Jacksonism, as Exemplified in its Deadly Hostility to the Bank of the United States, and in the Odious Calumnies Employed for Its Destruction*, pp. 68–135; William Morris Meredith, *An Oration Delivered by Request Before the Whigs of Philadelphia. on the Fourth of July, 1834*, pp. 15–17, 21. For the pro-Jackson bias of the "pets," see Frank Otto Gatell, "Spoils of the Bank War."

40. For the actions of the Senate, see U.S. Congress, Senate, *Register of Debates*, 23d Cong., 1st sess., February 11, 1833, pp. 30–37; *ibid.*, December 26, 1835, pp. 58–59, *ibid.*, March 28, 1834, p. 1187. The test of Jackson's "Protest" is in

Richardson, comp., *Messages and Papers*, 3:69. The resolutions of censure were expunged from the *Senate Journal* on January 16, 1837 (*Register of Debates*, 24th Cong., 2d sess., p. 504).

41. Clay, "Removal of the Deposits," December 26, 1833, in Colton, ed., *Works of Clay*, 7:577, 588, 597, 609, 576–77, 619–20. Webster's criticisms of removal were similar in substance, though more muted in tone. Webster, *Writings and Speeches*, 14:181–83, 213–21.

42. See Catterall, *Second Bank*, ch. 13; Thomas Payne Govan, *Nicholas Biddle*, pp. 245–47; Jacob Meerman, "The Climax of the Bank War: Biddle's Contraction, 1833–1834," *Journal of Political Economy* (August 1963), 71:378–88; Remini, *Jackson and Bank War*, pp. 126–29.

43. On the New York city mayoralty campaign, see Leo Hershkowitz, "New York City, 1834–1840: A Study in Local Politics" (Ph.D. diss., New York University, 1960), pp. 28–29, 36, 48; John David Morris, "The New York State Whigs," pp. 61–62, 74–75. The Whigs lost the mayoralty by 213 votes. Philip Hone, a prominent ex-merchant and man of letters, suggested to an anti-administration meeting that it follow the advice of the New York Morning *Courier and Enquirer*, edited by James Watson Webb, and adopt the "Whig" name. The idea spread quickly thereafter.

44. See Bailyn, *Ideological Origins*, pp. 33–54, 132–33 Wood, *Creation*, chs. 1–3. The Whigs of 1834, in accordance with their use of Revolutionary rhetoric, tried to brand the Jacksonians as "Tories," but the name never stuck.

45. See Wood, *Creation*, pp. 600–8.

46. Chandler Starr, *An Address Delivered at the Whig Convention Held at Utica, the Tenth of September, 1834*, p. 15. See also Burges, "Speech on Removal," in Bowen, *Memoir of Burges*, pp. 345–46, 393–96; Corwin, "Speech on Removal," in Morrow, ed., *Life and Speeches of Corwin*, p. 100; Cutter, *Oration*, pp. 15, 30; Meredith, *Oration*, p. 21; *Political Mirror*, pp. 244–302; Columbus (Ohio) *State Journal*, June 14, 1834; Newark (N.J.) *Sentinel*, February 4, 1834.

47. For Clay's embrace of the Whig name, see "On the State of the Country," in Colton, ed., *Works of Clay*, 7:628–29. The fusion of Antimasons, disaffected Democrats, and National Republicans in the Whig party did not occur instantaneously in the spring of 1834. In some states, such as Massachusetts, New York, and Ohio, the fusion process was largely completed in 1834–35. But in others, such as Pennsylvania and Vermont, the fusion process took more time; in Pennsylvania, the process was not completed until 1840. The important point here, however, is that when the anti-Jackson elements did unite, they did so under the "Whig" name, and justified fusion with charges of "executive usurpation." See Robert J. Haws, "Massachusetts Whigs," pp. 46–48; John J. Reed, "The Emergence of the Whig Party in the North" (Ph.D. diss., University of Pennsylvania, 1953); Vaughn, *Antimasonic Party*, pp. 48–50, 80–81, 83–84, 99–112, 124–30, 159–60, 163–67.

48. On the end of the contraction, see Catterall, *Second Bank*, ch. 13. For the House and Senate committee reports, see U.S. Congress, House, *Committee*

Reports, Serial 261, H. Rept. 312, 23d Cong., 1st sess., 1834; *ibid.*, Serial 262, H.
Rept. 481, 23d Cong., 1st sess., 1834; U.S. Congress, Senate, *Senate Documents*,
Serial 234, Doc. 72, 23d Cong., 1st sess., 1834. In the congressional elections, the
Democrats captured 145 seats in the House to the Whigs' 98. In the Senate, the
Democrats gained a majority of seats over the opposition, 27–25, as a result of
the elections. In the preceding Congress, the opposition had held 113 seats in the
House (to the Democrats' 147) and 28 seats (to the Democrats' 20) in the Senate.
Van Deusen, *Jacksonian Era*, p. 86, n. 36 and p. 90.

49. See Clay, "On the Appointing and Removing Power," February 18, 1835,
Works of Clay, 8:11–26; Webster, "Speech in the Senate," February 10, 1835,
Writings and Speeches, 7:179–99; U.S. Congress, Senate, *Register of Debates*, 23d
Cong., 2d sess., February 16, 1835, pp. 446–47, 479. For the abandonment of the
recharter issue, see Clay, "On the Appointing and Removing Power," p. 12;
Webster, "The Regulation of the Deposits," *Writings and Speeches*, 7:200.

50. See U.S. Congress, Senate, S. Doc. 86, 23d Cong., 2d sess., January 27,
1835; White, *The Jacksonians*, pp. 251–67. Ewing described the results of the post
office inquiry in *Speech . . . Delivered at a Public Festival, Given Him by the Whigs of Ross
County, Ohio, June 10, 1837* (Chillicothe, 1837).

51. See Henry R. Mueller, *The Whig Party in Pennsylvania*, p. 29; *Proceedings of a
State Convention of Delegates . . . assembled at the Capitol* [Albany, N.Y.] *February 3,
1836* (Albany, 1836), pp. 9–10; *Proceedings of a General Convention of the People of
Ohio; Held in the City of Columbus, February 22 and 23, A.D. 1836 . . .* , p. 10.

52. For the major themes of the Webster and White campaigns, which were
much the same as those of the Harrison campaign, see "Resolutions Passed by
the Illinois Senate," *Niles' National Register* (January 30, 1836), 49:384; Charles
Manfred Thompson, *The Illinois Whigs Before 1846*, pp. 55–56; Sydney Nathans,
Daniel Webster and Jacksonian Democracy, pp. 90–99; Webster, *Writings and Speeches*,
2:164–65, 13:57–60.

53. See William Henry Harrison to Sherrod Williams, May 1, 1836, in
Schlesinger and Israel, comp., *History of Presidential Elections*, 1:608–13; Dorothy
Burne Goebel, *William Henry Harrison*, pp. 307–10, 316–17.

54. *Proceedings of Convention of Ohio*, p. 10. See also *A Biographical Sketch of the Life
and Services of Gen. William Henry Harrison, together with his Letter to Simon Bolivar*
(Montpelier, Vt., 1836); James Hall, *A Memoir of the Public Services of William Henry
Harrison* (Philadephia, 1836); Adam A. Leonard, "Personal Politics in Indiana,
1816–1840," *Indiana Magazine of History* (June 1923), 19:155; Mueller, *Whig Party
in Pennsylvania*, pp. 32–33; Newark (N.J.) *Sentinel*, September 20, 1836.

55. *Proceedings of State Convention at Capitol* [Albany, N.Y.], pp. 10, 15–16. See
also Columbus (Ohio) *State Journal*, August 2, 1836; Leonard, "Personal Politics,"
p. 155; *Proceedings of Convention of Ohio*, p. 10. An interesting and important
denunciation of Van Buren and his political system by an Antimason (soon to
turn Whig) is William Slade, *To the Public* [Washington, D.C., 1835]. This
pamphlet is a vigorous restatement of Antimasonic antiparty attitudes.

56. Joel Silbey, "Election of 1836," in Schlesinger and Israel, comp., *History of*

Presidential Elections, 1:577–600. The other states Harrison carried were Delaware, Kentucky, and Maryland. Weed is quoted in Robert Gray Gunderson, *The Log Cabin Campaign,* p. 41.

57. See Reginald C. McGrane, *The Panic of 1837,* pp. 1–42; Samuel Reznick, "Social History of an American Depression, 1837–1843"; Van Deusen, *Jacksonian Era,* pp. 116–17. Peter Temin, *The Jacksonian Economy,* pp. 11, 16–23, 148 emphasizes the roots of the crisis in international economic factors beyond Jackson's control.

58. See McFaul, *Politics of Finance,* ch. 6; Arthur M. Schlesinger, Jr., *The Age of Jackson,* pp. 128–30.

59. Van Buren, "Special Session Message," September 4, 1837, in Richardson, comp., *Messages and Papers,* 3:324–28. For the fate of the subtreasury in Congress, see James C. Curtis, *The Fox at Bay,* pp. 100–4, 147–48; McFaul, *Politics of Finance,* pp. 199–202.

60. Van Buren, "Special Session Message," pp. 325–27; Schlesinger, *Age of Jackson,* chs. 19, 21; Congressman C. C. Cambreleng of New York, *Register of Debates,* 25th Cong., 1st sess., October 13, 1837, p. 1629; Senator Thomas Hart Benton of Missouri, *Congressional Globe,* 25th Cong., 2d sess., March 14, 1838, app., pp. 217–18; Hammond, *Banks and Politics,* ch. 15.

61. See James Roger Sharp, *The Jacksonians Versus the Banks;* Shade, *Banks or No Banks,* chs. 2–4.

62. Van Buren, "Special Session Message," p. 344.

63. See "National Democratic Convention," *Niles' National Register* (May 23, 1840), 58:183, 186; *The Rough-Hewer* (Albany, N.Y.), February 27, 1840, p. 12; John Ashworth, "The Jacksonian as Leveller," pp. 416–17; McFaul, *Politics of Finance,* pp. 208–9. For the Democrats' faith in a "natural" social order, see "Democracy," *United States Magazine and Democratic Review* (March 1840), 7:219–21.

64. For the outlook of the northern Conservative Democrats, see John C. Clark, *To the Republican Electors of Chenago County* (N.p., n.d.); "Conservative Convention of New York. Address to the Democratic Republican Electors of the State of New York," *Niles' National Register* (November 16, 1839), 57:187–89; Curtis, *Fox at Bay,* pp. 102–3; Jean E. Friedman, *The Revolt of the Conservative Democrats;* McFaul, *Politics of Finance,* pp. 179, 182, 189–91. On the Democratic radicals, see Fitzwilliam Byrdsall, *The History of the Loco-Foco or Equal Rights Party* (New York, 1842); Walter Hugins, *Jacksonian Democracy and the Working Class;* Schlesinger, *Age of Jackson,* pp. 132–43, 177–209.

65. See Lee Benson, Joel H. Silbey and Phyllis Field, "Toward a Theory of Stability and Change in American Voting Patterns: New York State, 1792–1970," in Joel H. Silbey, Allan G. Bogue, and William Flanigan, eds., *The History of American Voting Patterns: Electoral Behavior: Quantitative Studies* (Princeton: Princeton University Press, 1978), pp. 88–89; Herbert Ershkowitz and William G. Shade, "Consensus or Conflict?"; Holt, *Political Crisis,* pp. 26–27, 115–16; Shade, "Political Pluralism and Party Development," pp. 64, 94, 96–97.

66. See Francis Baylies, *Speech . . . Before the Whigs of Taunton, on the 13th of Sept., 1837*, pp. 6–7; Calvin Colton [Junius], *The Crisis of the Country*, pp. 7, 10–11; Abraham Lincoln, "Speech on the Sub-Treasury," December [26], 1839, in Roy P. Basler, ed., *The Collected Works of Abraham Lincoln*, 1:161–62; [Massachusetts State Whig Central Committee], *To the People of Massachusetts*, p. 10; *Proceedings of the Democratic Whig County Convention Held . . . in the City of Troy* [New York] *. . . October 3, 1837*, pp. 2, 5–6; *Proceedings of the Democratic Whig Convention, which Assembled at Harrisburg, Pennsylvania, on the Fourth of December, 1839 . . .* (Harrisburg, 1839); Edgar Allan Holt, *Party Politics in Ohio*, pp. 26–27; Mueller, *Whigs of Pennsylvania*, pp. 46–47; Thompson, *Illinois Whigs*, p. 65.

67. See Baylies, *Speech Before the Whigs of Taunton*, pp. 5–6; Concivis [pseud.], *Letters to the People of the United States*, pp. 29–30; Lincoln, "Speech on the Sub-Treasury," 1:160–63; *Proceedings of Convention in Troy*, p. 4.

68. Colton, *Crisis of Country*, p. 2. See also Daniel D. Barnard, "Speech on Banking, Currency, and Credit, Delivered upon the Passage of the General Banking Law," March 29, 1838, *Speeches and Reports in the Assembly of New-York, At the Annual Session of 1838*, p. 156; Concivis, *Letters to People*, p. 82; Corwin, "Inaugural Address as Governor of Ohio," December 16, 1840, in Morrow, ed., *Life and Speeches of Corwin*, p. 105; *Proceedings of a State Convention of the Whig Young Men of Connecticut, Assembled at Hartford, Connecticut, February 26, 1840*, pp. 4, 6; "Tucker's Theory of Money and Banks," *New York Review* (October 1839), 5:335. The Whigs articulated here what J.G.A. Pocock has called "a civic morality of investment and exhange." See Pocock, *Machiavellian Moment*, pp. 440–59. See also Ralph Lerner, "Commerce and Character."

69. See Baylies, *Speech Before Whigs of Taunton*, p. 4; Colton, *Crisis of Country*, pp. 7–8; Concivis, *Letters to People*, pp. 29–30; Edward Everett, "Accumulation, Property, Capital, Credit," September 13, 1838, in Everett, *Orations and Speeches on Various Occasions*, 2:301–2; *Proceedings of a Convention of Democratic Young Men, Delegates from the Citizens of Pennsylvania . . . Opposed to Martin Van Buren and the Sub-Treasury. Assembled at Reading, June 4th, 1838*, pp. 18–19. The Whigs seems to have derived their notions of a commerical, "civilized" republic from Montesquieu and the Scottish social philosophers of the Enlightenment. See Gladys Bryson, *Man and Society*, pp. 87–95, 209–10, 212–14; Albert O. Hirschman, *The Passions and the Interests*, pp. 51–73, 87–110; David Kettler, *The Social and Political Thought of Adam Ferguson*, pp. 234, 279–80; Jane Rendall, *The Origins of the Scottish Enlightenment*, pp. 176–80. For evidence of the Scots' influence on Whig thought, especially on the historical development of a "civilized" society, see John Quincy Adams, "Society and Civilization," *American Whig Review* (July 1845), 2:80–89; Concivis, *Letters to People*, pp. 68–70; Edward Everett, *Orations and Speeches*, 1:289–93, 613; Willard Phillips, *Manual of Political Economy*, pp. 9–10, 34, 163–65. On American "commercial republicanism," see Lerner, "Commerce and Character."

70. "Address to the People" of New York Whig Convention, 1838, *New York Courier and Enquirer*, October 2, 1838. See also Baylies, *Speech Before the Whigs of*

Taunton, pp. 4–5; Colton, *Crisis of Country*, pp. 1–3; (Albany, N.Y.) *Jeffersonian*, May 12, May 15, 1838; *Proceedings of Whig Convention of Connecticut*, p. 6.

71. See Curtis, *Fox at Bay*, pp. 150–51.

72. For the convention maneuvering which led up to Harrison's nomination, see Gunderson, *Log Cabin Campaign*, ch. 5.

73. See [Caleb Cushing], *Outline of the Life and Public Services, Civil and Military, of William Henry Harrison, of Ohio*, pp. 20–21; Richard Hildreth, *The People's Presidential Candidate; or the Life of William Henry Harrison of Ohio*, pp. 118–19; [Isaac Rand Jackson], *The Life of William Henry Harrison . . . With a History of the Wars with the British and Indians on our Northwestern Frontier; Life in a Log Cabin, with Hard Cider*, pp. 2–4; Jacob B. Moore [An Old Democrat], *The Contrast: or, Plain Reasons why William Henry Harrison should be Elected President of the United States, and why Martin Van Buren Should Not Be Re-Elected*, pp. 2–9.

74. See Concivis, *Letters to People*, pp. 90–96, 109–11, 113–24; *Life in Log Cabin*, pp. 5–6; Charles Ogle, *Speech . . . on the Regal Splendor of the President's Palace; Pictures of the Times; or, A Contrast Between the Effects of the True Democratic System, . . . and the Effects of the Aristocratic Sub-Treasury System, as Displayed in Martin Van Buren's Time*; Moore, *Plain Reasons*, pp. 10–16. See also Gunderson, *Log Cabin Campaign*, pp. 94–95, 101–3, 113–15.

75. *Proceedings of Whig Convention of Connecticut*, p. 5. See also [Cushing], *Harrison*, pp. 20–21; Hildreth, *People's Candidate*, pp. 118–26; [Jackson], *Life of Harrison*, pp. 58–60; *Life in Log Cabin*, pp. 2–5; *Pictures of Times*, pp. 4, 8, 12; Moore, *The Contrast*, pp. 2–9. For useful collections of Whig propaganda in 1840 (whose sheer volume was immense), see Arthur Banning Norton, *The Great Revolution of 1840. Reminiscences of the Log Cabin and Hard Cider Campaign* (Mount Vernon, Ohio, and Dallas, Tex., 1888); Norton, *Tippecanoe Songs of the Log Cabin Boys and Girls of 1840* (Mount Vernon, Ohio, and Dallas, Tex., 1888). George Julian later attested to the effectiveness of the Whigs' campaign: "So far as ideas entered into my support of the Whig candidate, I simply ʳegarded him as a poor man, whose home was in a log cabin, and who would in some way help the people . . . while I was fully persuaded that Van Buren was not only a graceless aristocrat and a dandy, but a cunning conspirator, seeking the overthrow of this country's liberties." Julian, *Political Recollections: 1840 to 1872* (Chicago, 1883), pp. 11–12.

76. Harrison, "Inaugural Address," [March 4, 1841], in Richardson, comp., *Messages and Papers*, 5:5–21.

77. For the circular, see U.S. Congress, Senate, S. Doc. 26, 27th Cong., 1st sess., March 20, 1841.

78. These events are described in greater detail below in the chapters "Daniel Webster: Conservative Whig" and "Henry Clay and the Politics of Consensus." For the congressional Whigs' unity behind the party platform in the special and regular sessions, see Joel H. Silbey, *The Shrine of Party*, ch. 4.

79. For the proceedings of the caucus, see (Washington, D.C.) *National Intelligencer*, September 16, 1841.

80. For evidence of the northern Whigs' rally behind Clay and his program,

see "Clay Meeting in Lancaster, July 29, 1843," *Niles' National Register* (August 19, 1843), 64:395; Abraham Lincoln, "Campaign Circular from Whig Committee," in Roy P. Basler, ed., *Works of Lincoln*, 1:309–18; Floyd Benjamin Streeter, *Political Parties in Michigan* pp. 77–79; Calvin Colton, *The Junius Tracts*; William R. Watson [Hamilton], *The Whig Party*; . . . *An Address to the People of Rhode-Island, published in the Providence Journal . . . 1844*, pp. 6, 11–12, 17–18, 20–21, 30–34; [Whig Congressional Committee], *Tariff Doctrine* (Washington, D.C., 1844).

81. See Calvin Colton, "The Tariff," *Junius Tracts* (July 1843), pp. 10, 15; Nathan Appleton, *Labor, Its Relations in Europe and the United States Compared* (Boston, 1844), pp. 12–13; Everett, *Orations and Speeches*, 1:260–61; Robert C. Winthrop, *Addresses and Speeches on Varius Occasions*, 2:64.

82. See Rufus Choate, "Speech on the Subject of Protecting American Labor by Duties on Imports," Samuel Gilman Brown, ed., *The Works of Rufus Choate with a Memoir of His Life*, 2:212–13; "Nature and Effects of a Protective Tariff," *American Whig Review* (July 1851), 14:85; Daniel Webster, "Lecture Before the Society for the Diffusion of Useful Knowledge, " *Writings and Speeches*, 13:63–78.

83. D. Francis Bacon, *Progressive Democracy: A Discourse . . . Delivered . . . Before a Large Mass Meeting of Whigs and Young Men*, p. 18. See also New York *Tribune*, November 16, December 21, 1844; Watson, *Whig Party*, pp. 4–5. Personal reminiscences and autobiographies indicate that northern Whigs perceived themselves as they were depicted in Whig rhetoric. Typically, they prided themselves on their industry, sobriety, social respectability, and devotion to economic and moral "improvement." By contrast, they saw the Democrats as a party of social marginals and n'er-do-wells who were manipulated by self-seeking demagogues and officeholders. See Jeremiah Church, *Journal of Travels, Adventures, and Remarks of Jerry Church* (Harrisburg, Pa.: Privately Printed by the Aurand Press, 1933), pp. 44–47; Neal Dow, *The Reminiscences of Neal Dow* (Portland, Maine, 1898), pp. 120–41; Richard S. Elliott, *Notes Taken in Sixty Years* (Boston, 1884), pp. 52–55, 89–90, 120–26, 131; Horace Greeley, *Recollections of a Busy Life* (New York, 1868), pp. 108, 136; Hone, *Diary*, 1:120, 139, 141–42, 189–90, 197, 230–31, 284, 352–53, 427–31; William C. Howells, *Recollections of Life in Ohio from 1813–1840* (Cincinnati, 1895), pp. 194–95; E. D. Mansfield, *Personal Memories . . . 1803–1843* (Cincinnati, 1879), pp. 284–85, 294–95, 312; Ole Munch Raeder, *America in the Forties* ed. by Gunnar J. Malmin (Minneapolis: University of Minnesota Press, 1929), pp. 22–23, 25–27.

84. See Daniel D. Barnard, "Report on the Subject of Religious Exercises, and the Use of the Bible, in Schools," January 23, 1838, Barnard, *Speeches and Reports*, pp. 56–57, 60–61; Brown, ed., *Works of Choate*, 1:397–400; Everett, *Orations and Speeches*, 2:315–21; Lincoln, "Address Before the Young Men's Lyceum of Springfield, Illinois," January 27, 1838, in Basler, ed., *Works of Lincoln*, 1:108–11; Horace Mann, "The Necessity of Education in a Republican Government" [1838], in Mary Mann, ed., *The Life and Works of Horace Mann* (Cambridge, Mass., 1867), 2:143–58; Watson, *Whig Party*, p. 35; Webster, "Whig Principles and Purposes," September 10, 1840, *Writings and Speeches*, 3:42.

85. The best discussion of the Democrats' "personal liberty" ideology is in Formisano, *Birth of Parties*, pp. 418–19; Ershkowitz and Shade, "Consensus or Conflict," pp. 616–17.

86. For the southern Whigs' rejection of moral legislation, see Ershkowitz and Shade, "Consensus or Conflict," pp. 616–17. When there was an attempt to organize a temperance campaign in Georgia, the leaders of both major parties united to suppress it. See Donald A. Debats, "Elites and Masses," pp. 241–48. To a great degree, the northern Whigs' support of morally coercive reform to instill "virtue" reflected the influence of the Arminian evangelical Protestants in the party, who were brought into the Whig coalition via the Antimasonic Party. See Formisano, *Birth of Parties*, chs. 4–5; John L. Hammond, *The Politics of Benevolence*; Paul E. Johnson, *A Shopkeeper's Millennium*; Linda K. Pritchard, "Religious Change in a Developing Region." The Whigs' commercial republicanism, with its emphasis on internalized self-restraint and personal responsibility, had a natural appeal for the northern evangelicals. For the northern evangelicals' response to the slavery extension issue, see the chapters, "Daniel Webster: Conservative Whig" and "William Seward and the Politics of Progress."

87. Thus, Whigs in Illinois and Ohio expressly rejected changes in the naturalization laws which might discourage immigration to the United States. See Abraham Lincoln, "Speech and Resolutions Concerning Philadelphia Riots," June 12, 1844, in Basler, ed., *Works of Lincoln*, 1:337–38; "Ohio State Convention at Columbus," March 4, 1846, *Niles' National Register* (March 14, 1846), 70:20.

88. For northern Whigs' view of German and Irish immigrants, see Nicholas B. Wainwright, ed., *A Philadelphia Perspective: The Diary of Sidney George Fisher Covering the Years, 1834–1871*, p. 177; Allan Nevins, ed., *The Diary of Philip Hone, 1828–1851*, 1:190; New York *Evening Star*, April 3, 14, 21, 1835; New York Morning *Courier and Enquirer*, April 7, 8, 1844; New York *Tribune*, November 16, December 21, 1844; Streeter, *Parties in Michigan*, pp. 27–29, 164; Thompson, *Illinois Whigs*, pp. 78–80.

89. For the position of non-nativist Whigs, see chapter 4, "William Seward and the Politics of Progress"; Congressman Washington Hunt of New York, *Congressional Globe*, 29th Cong., 1st sess., December 29, 1845, app., pp. 64–66; Abraham Lincoln, "Speech and Resolutions Concerning Philadelphia Riots," in Basler, ed., *Works of Lincoln*, 1:337–38. For evidence of some Whigs' sympathy with nativism, see Holt, *Forging Majority*, pp. 77–78, 135–36; Mueller, *Whigs of Pennsylvania*, pp. 131–33; L. D. Scisco, *Political Nativism in New York State* (New York: Columbia University Press, 1901), pp. 19–20; New York *Commercial Advertiser*, February 27, 1840; Streeter, *Parties in Michigan*, pp. 27–29, 164–65; Sister M. Evangeline Thomas, *Nativism in the Old Northwest*, pp. 60, 99; Thompson, *Illinois Whigs*, pp. 78–80. On the public school controversy in New York, see Vincent P. Lannie, *Public Money and Parochial Education: Bishop Hughes, Governor Seward, and the New York School Controversy* (Cleveland: Case Western Reserve University Press, 1968). Although Webster was not closely identified with the nativist movement, he did endorse the reform of the naturalization laws after

the election of 1844. See "Speech at Faneuil Hall, Boston," November 8, 1844, *Writings and Speeches*, 13:304–5.

90. The northern Whigs' distaste for slavery (and dislike of discrimination against free blacks) is suggested by the almost uniformly antislavery voting records of northern Whig congressmen. See Silbey, *Shrine of Party*, pp. 59–60, 90–91, 93, 96, 110–14. For a small sampling of the northern Whigs' antislavery views, see Thomas Corwin, "On the Clayton Compromise Bill," July 24, 1848, in Morrow, ed., *Life and Speeches of Corwin*, pp. 352–57; Joshua Giddings, "Speech upon Resolutions Annexing Texas. Delivered . . . Jan 22, 1845," Giddings, *Speeches in Congress* (New York, 1853), pp. 134–37; Wainwright, ed., *Fisher Diary*, pp. 175 (July 28, 1844), 189 (May 13, 1846), 211 (June 11, 1848); Congressman Harvey Putnam of New York, *Congressional Globe*, 31st Cong., 1st sess., June 30, 1850, pp. 1029–32; New York *Tribune*, March 19, 1844, July 3, 1848; Watson, *Whig Party*, pp. 13, 40; Streeter, *Parties in Michigan*, pp. 37–38, 66–67.

3. Daniel Webster: Conservative Whig

1. See Irving Bartlett, "Daniel Webster as a Symbolic Hero," *New England Quarterly* (December 1972), 45:485–86; George W. Bungay, *Crayon Sketches and Off-Hand Takings* (Boston, 1852), p. 82.

2. Nathan Sargent, *Public Men and Events*, 2 vols. (Philadelphia, 1875), 1:172, Benjamin Perley Poore, *Perley's Reminiscences of Sixty Years in the National Metropolis*, 2 vols. (Philadelphia, 1886), 1:79, 118; Thomas Carlyle to Ralph Waldo Emerson, June 24, 1839, in Joseph Slater, ed., *The Correspondence of Emerson and Carlyle* (New York: Columbia University Press, 1964), p. 240.

3. Henry W. Hilliard, *Politics and Pen Pictures* (New York, 1892), p. 2.

4. Poore, *Reminiscences*, 1:118; Henry Cabot Lodge, *Daniel Webster* (Boston, 1883), p. 187.

5. William A. Stearns, *The Great Lamentation: A Sermon in Commemoration of Daniel Webster, Delivered in Cambridge . . . November 21, 1852 . . .* (Boston and Cambridge, 1852), pp. 9–10.

6. Webster's presidential candidacies will be discussed later in this chapter.

7. Francis Grund, *Aristocracy in America* (New York, 1859), p. 170.

8. Francis Lieber, *The Life and Letters of Francis Lieber*, ed. by Thomas Sergeant Perry (Boston, 1882), p. 256.

9. Nathaniel Hawthorne, "The Great Stone Face," *The Complete Writings of Nathaniel Hawthorne*, 22 vols. (Boston: Houghton, Mifflin, 1900), 3:51.

10. Edward A. Lawrence, *A Discourse on the Death of Hon. Daniel Webster, Delivered October 31, 1852 . . .* (Boston, 1852), p. 13. See also Edward N. Kirk, *Great Men are God's Gift: A Discourse on the Death of the Hon. Daniel Webster, Delivered . . . October 31, 1852* (Boston, 1852), p. 21; [Joseph Story], "Statesmen: Their Rareness and Importance. Daniel Webster," *New England Magazine* (August 1834), 7:96–104.

11. Ira Perley, *Eulogy . . . on the Late Daniel Webster, Pronounced Before the Executive and Legislative Departments of New Hampshire, December 22, 1852* (Concord, 1852),

pp. 28–29 (first quotation); S. K. Lothrop, *"The Divine Presence a Support to Human Frailty"; A Sermon Preached in the Brattle Square Church, on the Sunday Succeeding the Death of Hon. Daniel Webster* (Boston, 1852), p. 11.

12. Ralph Waldo Emerson to Thomas Carlyle, August 8, 1839, in Slater, ed., *Correspondence of Emerson and Carlyle*, p. 245; Emerson, *Journals and Miscellaneous Notebooks*, ed. by William H. Gilman, 14 vols. (Cambridge: Belknap Press of Harvard University, 1960–78), 10:393, 398.

13. Webster, [Autobiography], in Charles M. Wiltse, ed., *The Papers of Daniel Webster*, 1:4–5.

14. *Ibid.*, 1:7–22; Irving Bartlett, *Daniel Webster*, pp. 66–71; Richard N. Current, *Daniel Webster and the Rise of National Conservatism*, pp. 9–14, 24.

15. Bartlett, *Webster*, pp. 66, 70–71; Current, *Webster and Conservatism*, p. 24.

16. Bartlett, *Webster*, pp. 70–74. On the Boston elite, see Paul Goodman, "Ethics and Enterprize"; Thomas H. O'Connor, *Lords of the Loom*, ch. 2.

17. Bartlett, *Webster*, pp. 58–64. For Webster's praise of the Hartford Convention, see Daniel Webster to [William F. Rowland], January 11, 1815, in Wiltse, ed., *Papers of Webster*, 1:181. For his later attempts to disassociate himself from the convention, see Daniel Webster to Jeremiah Mason, March 2, 1825, *ibid.*, 3:21; Daniel Webster to James Hervey Bingham, August 24, 1835, *ibid.*, 4:49–50; Daniel Webster to [Joseph Lawrence?], [c. December 10, 1835], *ibid.*, 4:73.

18. Daniel Webster, *The Writings and Speeches of Daniel Webster*, 14:44–45.

19. David Hackett Fischer, *The Revolution of American Conservatism*, pp. 238–39.

20. On Federalist ideology, see James Banner, *To the Hartford Convention: The Federalists and the Origins of Party Politics in Massachusetts, 1789–1815*, passim; Fischer, *Revolution of Conservatism*, pp. 3–5, 29–30; Linda K. Kerber, *Federalists in Dissent: Imagery and Ideology in Jeffersonian America*, passim.

21. Daniel Webster to James Hervey Bingham, May 18, 1802, in Wiltse, ed., *Papers of Webster*, 1:41; Daniel Webster to Thomas Albert Merrill, March 8, 1807, *ibid.*, 1:92; Webster, *Writings and Speeches*, 15:7–8. For the Federalists' tendency toward the apocalyptic, see Kerber, *Federalists in Dissent*, pp. 122–23, 173–78, 201–7.

22. Webster, *Writings and Speeches*, 3:14, 14:35–36. See also Pocock, "Classical Theory of Deference."

23. On the spread of universal white manhood suffrage, see Chilton Williamson, *American Suffrage from Property to Democracy, 1760–1860* (Princeton: Princeton University Press, 1960). On the changes in the American economy, see Current, *Webster and Conservatism*, chs. 2, 3; O'Connor, *Lords of the Loom*, ch. 1; George Rogers Taylor, *The Transportation Revolution*.

24. See Current, *Webster and Conservatism*, pp. 28–34; Bartlett, *Webster*, pp. 76–80. For Webster's career as a constitutional lawyer, which will not be discussed extensively here, see Maurice Baxter, *Daniel Webster and the Supreme Court* (Amherst: University of Massachusetts Press, 1966).

25. See Fischer, *Revolution of Conservatism*, pp. 3–7; Kerber, *Federalists in Dissent*, ch. 6.

26. See Webster, *Writings and Speeches*, 8:170–76, 9:227, 13:76–78.

27. See *Ibid.*, 3:175–77; 4:116; 8:170–76; 13:226–27. For more detailed expositions of the ideas outlined here, see Thomas Brown, "Politics and Statesmanship: A Study of the American Whig Party" (Ph.D. diss., Columbia University, 1981), ch. 3; Melvyn Dubofsky, "Daniel Webster and the Whig Theory of Economic Growth."

28. Webster, *Writings and Speeches*, 2:134, 3:174–77, 5:226, 9:231, 13:264–65.

29. *Ibid.*, 6:127–28, 152, 273, 7:92–93, 8:170.

30. *Ibid.*, 6:127–28, 152, 265–67, 273, 7:92–95.

31. *Ibid.*, 13:73–74.

32. *Ibid.*, 2:102–3, 199–201, 7:250–51, 15:143.

33. *Ibid.*, 2:253, 3:107–8, 4:91, 301, 13:469.

34. For the clearest exposition of Webster's view of the Union, see "The Constitution Not a Compact Between Sovereign States," February 16, 1833, *Writings and Speeches*, 6:182–238.

35. Webster, *Writings and Speeches*, 8:235, 6:193, 211, 13:389, 12:242, 10:32.

36. "Reception at Bangor," August 28, 1835, *ibid.*, 2:163.

37. Bartlett, *Webster*, pp. 31–32; Current, *Webster and Conservatism*, pp. 59–60.

38. Webster, *Writings and Speeches*, 5:248–69.

39. Robert Y. Hayne and Daniel Webster, *The Several Speeches Made During the Debate in the Senate of the United States, on Mr. Foot's Resolution . . .* (Charleston, 1830), pp. 17–36.

40. Webster, "Second Speech on Foot's Resolution," *Writings and Speeches*, 6:10, 15–16.

41. *Ibid.*, 6:23. Webster generally favored prowestern land and improvements measures. In this respect, he was unlike most of the conservative Whigs of New England, who feared that such measures would accelerate the drain of population from their region, and who looked upon the West as wild, barbaric, and "uncivilized." See Peter J. Parish, "Daniel Webster, New England, and the West," *Journal of American History* (December 1967), 54:524–49.

42. "Second Speech on Foot's Resolution," *Writings and Speeches*, 6:75.

43. For favorable responses to the speech, see Wiltse, ed., *Papers of Webster*, 3:17, 20–21, 27, 30, 32–33, 35, 37, 43, 49–50, 52, 56–57, 62.

44. Webster, *Writings and Speeches*, 15:5–8, 44; Bartlett, *Webster*, p. 80; Daniel Webster to Jeremiah Mason, November 20, 1820, in Wiltse, ed., *Papers of Webster*, 1:278–79.

45. For Webster's pre-election advice to fellow Federalists, see Daniel Webster to Jeremiah Mason, February 15, 1824, in Wiltse, ed., *Papers of Webster*, 1:353; Daniel Webster to William Gaston, Sep. 8, 1824, *ibid.*, 1:363. For his role in Adams' election, see Henry R. Warfield to Daniel Webster, February 3, 1825, *ibid.*, 2:18; Daniel Webster to Daniel R. Warfield, February 5, 1825, *ibid.*, 2:21–22; Charles Francis Adams, ed., *Memoirs of John Quincy Adams*, 6:493.

46. For evidence of Webster's disenchantment with Jackson's political conduct, see Daniel Webster to Ezekiel Webster, February 5, 1829, *Writings and Speeches*, 16:186 (quotation); Daniel Webster to Joseph Hopkinson, [January 15, 1830], in Wiltse, ed., *Papers of Webster*, 3:8–9; Sydney Nathans, *Daniel Webster and Jacksonian Democracy*, pp. 29–30, 35. For Webster's efforts to promote himself as a presidential candidate, see Daniel Webster to [Charles Miner], August 28, 1831, in Wiltse, ed., *Papers of Webster*, 3:119; Charles Miner to Daniel Webster, September 8, 1831, *ibid.*, 3:122; Bartlett, *Webster*, p. 127.

47. Webster, "The Nomination of Mr. Van Buren as Minister to England," January 24, 1832, *Writings and Speeches*, 6:92; "The Presidential Veto of the United States Bank Bill," July 11, 1832, *ibid.*, 6:180; Daniel Webster to Nicholas Biddle, December 18, 1831, in Wiltse, ed., *Papers of Webster*, 3:139; Daniel Webster to Nicholas Biddle, September 24, 1832, *Writings and Speeches*, 6:190.

48. Webster, *Writings and Speeches*, 13:40–42; 6:182–238; Wiltse, ed., *Papers of Webster*, 3:203, 204–5, 206–8, 211, 213–16, 219–20; Nathans, *Webster and Democracy*, pp. 50–59; Norman D. Brown, *Daniel Webster and the Politics of Availability*, ch. 2.

49. Daniel Webster to Benjamin Franklin Perry, April 27, 1833, in Wiltse, ed., *Papers of Webster*, 3:246–47; Daniel Webster to Joel Roberts Poinsett, May 7, 1833, *ibid.*, 3:248–49; Brown, *Webster and Politics*, pp. 29–67; Nathans, *Webster and Democracy*, pp. 60–67.

50. See Wiltse, ed., *Papers of Webster*, 3:234, 236–37, 237–38, 244, 273.

51. See Martin Van Buren, *The Autobiography of Martin Van Buren*, ed. by J. C. Fitzpatrick (Washington: American Historical Association, 1920), p. 676–79, 707, 710–11; Brown, *Webster and Politics*, pp. 58–61; Nathans, *Webster and Democracy*, pp. 69–71.

52. For Webster's efforts to win the endorsement of the Pennsylvania Antimasons, see Wiltse, ed., *Papers of Webster*, 4:58–70, 73; Brown, *Webster and Politics*, chs. 6–7.

53. For Webster's efforts to win the 1840 nomination and his withdrawal, see Wiltse, ed., *Papers of Webster*, 4:268–69, 275, 277, 290–91, 331, 341, 355, 370. On his friends' role in Harrison's nomination, see Bartlett, *Webster*, p. 156; Nathans, *Webster and Democracy*, pp. 122–29.

54. Nathans, *Webster and Democracy*, pp. 152–54.

55. See his editorials of June 15, 16, and 17, 1841, reprinted in *Writings and Speeches*, 15:124–26, 126–29, 129–33; and his letters to Hiram Ketchum, July 16, 17, 1841, *ibid.*, 16:344–48, 348–51.

56. "Memorandum Regarding the Bank Bill & the Vetoes" [1841], Webster Papers, Reel 16, Frame 21025.

57. *Ibid.*, Frames 21028–34; Thomas Ewing, "The Diary of Thomas Ewing, August and September, 1841," pp. 101–3; Webster, "To Messrs. Bates and Choate," *Writings and Speeches*, 16:355–56.

58. Daniel Webster to Hiram Ketchum, September 11, 1841, *Writings and Speeches*, 16:351; Lyon Gardiner Tyler, *Letters and Times of the Tylers*, 2:121–22.

59. Robert C. Winthrop to Daniel Webster, September 13, 1841, Webster Papers, Reel 16, Frame 20222.

60. "The Message" [December 1841], in Claude H. Van Tyne, ed., *The Letters of Daniel Webster, from Documents Owned Principally by the New Hampshire Historical Society*, p. 243.

61. For the details of the exchequer plan, see U.S. Congress, House, *House Documents*, 27th Cong., 2d sess., 1841, Doc. 20, pp. 1–2. For Webster's defense of the plan, see Webster, *Writings and Speeches*, 15:144–47.

62. See Current, *Webster and Conservatism*, pp. 119–24; Nathans, *Webster and Democracy*, pp. 190–91, 194; Frederick Merk and Lois Banner Merk, *Fruits of Propaganda in the Tyler Administration* (Cambridge: Harvard University Press, 1971), pp. 62–64, 73–87, 150–53, 156–57, 174–77, 179–80, 201–2, 204–5.

63. Current, *Webster and Conservatism*, pp. 126, 138–39; Merk and Merk, *Fruits of Propaganda*, pp. 12, 14, 180–98, 210–14.

64. Daniel Webster to Edward Everett, November 28, 1842, Webster Papers, Reel 18, Frame 23787.

65. Daniel Webster to Edward Everett, August 25, 1842, Webster Papers, Reel 17, Fame 23295; [John Tyler to L. W. Tazewell], October 24, 1842, Tyler Papers; H. Shaw to Daniel Webster, February 28, 1843, Webster Papers, Reel 18, Frames 24450–51; Daniel Webster to John Tyler, May 8, 1843, *ibid.*, Frame 25057; John Tyler to Daniel Webster, May 8, 1843, *ibid.*, Frame 25063.

66. Nathans, *Webster and Democracy*, pp. 210–13, 216–18.

67. Webster, "Convention at Andover," November 9, 1843, *Writings and Speeches*, 3:159–85; Bartlett, *Webster*, p. 187.

68. "For the Repertory" [October 2, 1804], in Wiltse, ed., *Papers of Webster*, 1:59–60. For Webster's positions on the slave trade and the Missouri Compromise, see *Writings and Speeches*, 1:221, 15:56–61.

69. Webster, *Writings and Speeches*, 6:11, 12, 14.

70. "Slavery and the Slave Trade in the District of Columbia," March 16, 1836, *Writings and Speeches*, 7:231–33. See also Daniel Webster to [Luther Christopher] Peck, January 11, 1838, in Wiltse, ed., *Papers of Webster*, 4:261.

71. Daniel Webster to Douglas Silliman, January 29, 1838, in Wiltse, ed., *Papers of Webster*, 4:265.

72. Webster, "Reception at New York," March 15, 1837, *Writings and Speeches*, 2:206–7; John Tyler to Daniel Webster, October 11, 1841, Tyler Papers; Daniel Webster to Waddy Thompson, June 27, 1842, in Van Tyne, ed., *Letters of Webster*, pp. 269–70; George Ticknor Curtis, *The Life of Daniel Webster*, 2:230–35; Daniel Webster to Edward Everett, April 1, 1844, Webster Papers, Reel 19, Frames 25764–65; Robert Dalzell, *Daniel Webster and the Trial of American Nationalism*, pp. 82–90; Nathans, *Webster and Democracy*, p. 219.

73. Nathans, *Webster and Democracy*, pp. 220–21. For Webster's speeches in the 1844 campaign, see Webster, *Writings and Speeches*, 3:217–48, 249–74, 275–94; 13:196–202, 203–11, 212–15, 216–37, 238–42, 243–45, 254–69, 270–75, 276–300.

74. Webster, "Address on the Annexation of Texas," January 29, 1845, *Writings and Speeches*, 15:192–203; "The Admission of Texas," December 22, 1845, *ibid.*, 9:56–57.

75. The clearest exposition of the Young Whigs' outlook is John Gorham Palfrey, *Papers on the Slave Power* (Boston, 1846). See also John Mayfield, *Rehearsal for Republicanism: Free Soil and the Politics of Antislavery* (Port Washington, N.Y.: Kennikat Press, 1980), ch. 2.

76. Webster in fact had congenial personal relations with many southerners. When he visited the South in 1847, he was greeted warmly and found the region quite to his liking. He was alleged to have said, after visiting Wade Hampton's plantation in South Carolina, that "no change could be made which would benefit the slave." See Webster, *Writings and Speeches*, 18:242–43, 249; Benjamin F. Perry, *Reminiscences of Public Men* (Philadelphia, 1883), p. 65.

77. Charles Francis Adams, Diary, September 23, 1846, Adams Family Papers; Webster, *Writings and Speeches*, 13:327–29; Dalzell, *Webster and Nationalism*, pp. 114–20.

78. Webster, "The Mexican War," March 1, 1847, *Writings and Speeches*, 9:253–61; "Objects of the Mexican War," March 23, 1848, *ibid.*, 10:3–33. See also Dalzell, *Webster and Nationalism*, pp. 123–31.

79. Webster, *Writings and Speeches*, 4:123–24; Dalzell, *Webster and Nationalism*, pp. 147–52.

80. Webster, *Writings and Speeches*, 16:505–6, 516–18, 519–20; 18:302, 352–53; Peter Harvey, *Reminiscences and Anecdotes of Daniel Webster* (Boston, 1882), pp. 176–78; Dalzell, *Webster and Nationalism*, pp. 159–61.

81. This point is made in David M. Potter, *The Impending Crisis*, pp. 48–49.

82. See Daniel Webster to Peter Harvey, May 29, 1850, *Writings and Speeches*, 16:541–42; Daniel Webster to Franklin Haven [August 9, 1850], *ibid.*, 16:557; Daniel Webster to Peter Harvey, September 13, 1850, *ibid.*, 18:388; Daniel Webster to Thomas B. Curtis, March 21, 1850, Webster Papers, Reel 22, Frame 30056.

83. Daniel Webster to the Rev. Mr. Furness, February 15, 1850, *Writings and Speeches*, 16:354.

84. Curtis, *Life of Webster*, 2:397–98.

85. Webster, *Writings and Speeches*, 16:532–33.

86. Herbert Darling Foster, "Webster's Seventh of March Speech and the Secession Movement"; Daniel Webster to Fletcher Webster, February 24, 1850, *Writings and Speeches*, 16:533–34; Daniel Webster to Charles Henry Warren, March 1, 1850, *ibid.*, 16:534–35.

87. "The Constitution and the Union," *Writings and Speeches*, 10:61–64. Cf. the original version in U.S. Congress, Senate, *Congressional Globe*, 31st Cong., 1st sess., March 7, 1850, p. 477.

88. "The Constitution and the Union," pp. 65–70. Cf. the original version in *Congressional Globe*, 31st Cong., 1st sess., 1850, pp. 478–79.

89. "The Constitution and the Union," pp. 82–85. Cf. the original in

Congressional Globe, 31st Cong., 1st sess., 1850, pp. 480–81. Interestingly, Webster inquired into the suitability of New Mexico for plantation slavery *after* the March 7 speech. The response to his inquiry confirmed his views. See Daniel Webster to Hugh W. Smith, April 8, 1850, Webster Papers, Reel 22, Frames 30194–95; Hugh W. Smith to Daniel Webster, April 9, 1850, *ibid.*, Frames 31021–23. This exchange would tend to substantiate the thesis that Webster adapted his perceptions to his preconceptions. Having concluded that it would be expedient to argue that the Mexican Cession was ill suited for slavery, he then sought out evidence in support of that argument. Webster's arguments to the contrary, the opponents of compromise, both in the North and South, claimed that the Mexican Cession was indeed suited to slavery—if not on plantations, than in mines. See Charles Desmond Hart, "The Natural Limits to Slavery Expansion': The Mexican Territories as a Test Case," *Mid-America* (April 1970), 52:119–31.

90. "The Constitution and the Union," pp. 90–92. Cf. the original in *Congressional Globe*, 31st Cong., 1st sess., 1850, pp. 481–82.

91. "The Constitution and the Union," pp. 93–98. Cf. the original version in *Congressional Globe*, 31st Cong., 1st sess., pp. 483–84.

92. Daniel Webster to Fletcher Webster, March 21, 1850, *Writings and Speeches*, 16:535; Edward Curtis to Peter Harvey, March 28, 1850, in Van Tyne, ed., *Letters of Webster*, p. 407. For the favorable responses of northern conservatives, see H.A.S. Dearborn to Daniel Webster, March 11, 1850, Webster Papers, Reel 22, Frame 29944; Daniel Dewey Barnard to Daniel Webster, April 10, 1850, *ibid.*, Frames 30228–31; Parker Noyes to Daniel Webster, June 5, 1850, *ibid.*, Frames 30526–27; Henry W. Warner to Daniel Webster, June 5, 1850, *ibid.*, Frame 30529.

93. See T. H. Perkins, et al. to Daniel Webster, March 25, 1850, Webster Papers, Reel 22, Frames 30083–30106; Charles L. Vose, et al. to Daniel Webster, March 28, 1850, *Writings and Speeches*, 18:361; David Van Tassel, "Gentlemen of Property and Standing: Compromise Sentiment in Boston, 1850," *New England Quarterly* (September 1950), 23:312–13.

94. For favorable southern responses to the March 7 speech, see Branch Archer Sanders to Daniel Webster, March 15, 1850, Webster Papers, Reel 22, Frames 30007–8; William B. Inge to Daniel Webster, March 22, 1850, *ibid.*, Frame 30020; James W. Allen to Daniel Webster, March 26, 1850, *ibid.*, Frame 30108; H. J. Anderson to Daniel Webster, April 8, 1850, *ibid.*, Frames 30202–4; John Tyler to Daniel Webster, April 17, 1850, Tyler Papers. For Webster's possible role in squelching the secessionist movement, see Foster, "Webster's Seventh of March Speech"; Allan Nevins, *The Ordeal of the Union*, 2 vols. (New York: Scribner's, 1947), 1:297–98.

95. The most important exposition of the conservative clergy's point of view is Moses Stuart, *Conscience and the Constitution, with Remarks on the Recent Speech of the Hon. Daniel Webster . . .* (Boston, 1850), esp. pp. 23–29, 43–61. Webster read this book and praised it effusively. See Daniel Webster to Peter Harvey, June 2, 1850, *Writings and Speeches*, 16:542; Daniel Webster to Moses Stuart, June 3, 1850, *ibid.*,

18:371. For views similar to Stuart's, see [Caleb Sprague Henry], *Politics and the Pulpit: A Series of Articles which Appeared in the Journal of Commerce and in the Independent, during the Year 1850* . . . (New York, 1851), pp. 7–9, 15, 41, 44; John C. Lord, *"The Higher Law" in its Application to the Fugitive Slave Bill. A Sermon on the Duties Men owe to God and to Governments. Delivered at the Central Presbyterian Church, Buffalo, on Thanksgiving Day* (New York, 1851); Ichabod Smith Spencer, *The Fugitive Slave Law. The Religious Duty of Obedience to Law: A Sermon Preached in the Second Presbyterian Church in Brooklyn, November 24, 1850* (New York, 1850).

96. Sumner is quoted in John Bach McMaster, *Daniel Webster* (New York: Century, 1902), pp. 317–18. Whittier's "Ichabod" is quoted in Nevins, *Ordeal of the Union*, 1:292. The Emerson quotation is from *The Complete Works of Ralph Waldo Emerson*, Centenary ed. (Boston and New York: Houghton, Mifflin, 1911), p. 202.

97. See [Henry], *Politics and Pulpit*, pp. 28–30, 33, 49–50; [Horace T. Love], *Slavery in its Relation to God: A Review of the Rev. Dr. Lord's Thanksgiving Sermon, in Favor of Domestic Slavery* . . . (Buffalo, 1851), pp. 28–37; Theodore Parker, *The Function and Place of Conscience in Relation to the Laws of Man; A Sermon for the Times; Preached at the Melodeon* . . . *September 22, 1850* (Boston, 1850); G. W. Perkins, *Prof. Stuart and Slave Catching: Remarks on Mr. Stuart's Book "Conscience and the Constitution," at* . . . *Guilford* [Connecticut], *August 1, 1850* . . . (West Meriden, Conn., 1850), pp. 2–6.

98. [Henry], *Politics and Pulpit*, p. 51. See also Parker, *Function and Place of Conscience*, pp. 34–55.

99. Perkins, *Stuart and Slave Catching*, pp. 19–20. See also [Love], *Slavery in Relation to God*, pp. 21–22; Parker, *Function and Place of Conscience*, pp. 14–15, 24–25. A related issue was whether those who resisted the law could use violence. Love said no (*Slavery in Relation to God*, p. 56), while Parker said yes, if it was necessary to prevent the seizure of fugitives (*Function and Place of Conscience*, pp. 25–26).

100. See Edward Everett to Daniel Webster, March 22, April 3, 1850, Webster Papers, Reel 22, Frames 30062 and 30163. The original version of Webster's speech (*Congressional Globe*, 31st Cong., 1st sess., 1850, p. 481) has the following comment on Mason's fugitive slave bill: "my friend at the head of the Judiciary Committee has a bill on the subject, with some amendments to it, which I propose to support, with all its provisions, to the fullest extent." The revised pamphlet version of this passage ("The Constitution and the Union," *Writings and Speeches*, 10:86–87) reads as follows: "a bill, which, with some amendments to it, I propose to support, with all its provisions, to the fullest extent." For Webster's proposed amendment, see *Writings and Speeches*, 10:103–4; for its eventual fate, see Brock, *Parties*, p. 298, n. 32.

101. See Daniel Webster to President Fillmore, July 30, 1850, *Writings and Speeches*, 16:554–55; Daniel Webster to President Fillmore, August 6, 1850, *ibid.*, 16:555; Daniel Webster to Franklin Haven, August 10, 1850, *ibid.*, 16:558–59. For the Texas message, dated August 6, 1850, see Richardson, comp., *Messages and Papers*, 5:67–73.

102. See Webster, *Writings and Speeches*, 16:582–83; Van Tyne, ed., *Letters of Webster*, pp. 427–28, 430–31.

103. See Daniel Webster to Millard Fillmore, October 29, 1850, Webster Papers, Reel 22, Frame 31563.

104. Harold Schwartz, "Fugitive Slave Days in Boston," *New England Quarterly* (June 1954), 27:191–92.

105. See Webster, *Writings and Speeches*, 2:256–60, 16:576–77, 604, 611; Van Tyne, ed., *Letters of Webster*, p. 434; Schwartz, "Fugitive Slave Days," pp. 193–201.

106. Daniel Webster to Edward Everett, September 26, 1850, Webster Papers, Reel 22, Frame 31224; Dalzell, *Webster and Nationalism*, p. 218.

107. See Daniel Webster to Edward Everett, September 26, 1850, Webster Papers, Reel 22, Frame 31222; Daniel Webster to Millard Fillmore, September 19, 1850, in Van Tyne, ed., *Letters of Webster*, p. 432; Daniel Webster to Peter Harvey, October 2, 1850, *ibid.*, pp. 433–34; Daniel Webster to Millard Fillmore, October 24, 1850, *ibid.*, pp. 437–38.

108. Webster, *Writings and Speeches*, 12:251–60; 16:629–30; 18:399, 400, 406; Daniel Webster to Thomas B. Curtis, January 24, 1851, Webster Papers, Reel 23, Frame 32245; Curtis, *Life of Webster*, 2:579–81; Dalzell, *Webster and Nationalism*, pp. 235–36.

109. Daniel Webster to Franklin Haven, November 30, 1851, *Writings and Speeches*, 16:629–30; Curtis, *Life of Webster*, 2:578–82.

110. Dalzell, *Webster and Nationalism*, pp. 233–34, 239.

111. Daniel Webster to Edward Everett, March 13, 1852, Webster Papers, Reel 23, Frame 36215; Dalzell, *Webster and Nationalism*, pp. 255–57; Daniel Webster to Fletcher Webster [May 1852], *Writings and Speeches*, 16:643.

112. Dalzell, *Webster and Nationalism*, pp. 243–46, 266–67; Robert J. Rayback, *Millard Fillmore: Biography of a President* (Buffalo: Buffalo Historical Society, 1959), pp. 333–49; Bartlett, *Webster*, pp. 232–33.

113. See Van Tyne, ed., *Letters of Webster*, pp. 517, 519, 525, 529; Dalzell, *Webster and Nationalism*, p. 267.

114. Dalzell, *Webster and Nationalism*, pp. 269–70. For the vote on all 53 ballots, see Curtis, *Life of Webster*, 2:621.

115. Dalzell, *Webster and Nationalism*, pp. 275–76.

116. Webster, *Writings and Speeches*, 16:657.

117. Harvey, *Reminiscences and Anecdotes*, pp. 201–3; Curtis, *Life of Webster*, 2:651–52; Daniel Webster to Fletcher Webster, August 26, 1852, Webster Papers, Reel 27, Frame 37702; Daniel Webster to M. H. Grinnell et al., October 12, 1852, *Writings and Speeches*, 16:667; Dalzell, *Webster and Nationalism*, pp. 282–302.

118. Harvey, *Reminiscences and Anecdotes*, pp. 198–200.

119. Hofstadter, *Idea of Party System*, p. 216; Gideon Welles, *The Diary of Gideon Welles, Secretary of the Navy under Lincoln and Johnson*, ed. by John T. Morse, 3 vols. (Boston: Houghton, Mifflin, 1911), 1:507.

120. Emerson, *Journals and Miscellaneous Notebooks*, 13:111.

4. William Seward and the Politics of Progress

1. For various assessments of Seward, see Frederic Bancroft, *The Life of William H. Seward*, 1:263; Henry S. Foote, *Casket of Reminiscences* (Washington, 1874), pp. 123–25; Henry Cabot Lodge, "William Henry Seward," *Historical and Political Essays* (New York, 1892), pp. 1–41; William V. Miller, "The Emergence of William H. Seward as a National Political Leader, 1847–1859" (Ph.D. diss., University of Southern California, 1957), pp. 285–86; Allan Nevins, *The Emergence of Lincoln*, 2 vols. (New York: Scribner's, 1950), 2:300; Glyndon G. Van Deusen, *William Henry Seward*, pp. 198–210.

2. Seward to his wife [Frances Miller Seward], late 1833, quoted in Bancroft, *Life of Seward*, 1:51–52.

3. William Seward to Richard Blatchford, February 13, 1858, Greeley Papers.

4. One of Seward's law students recalled the following comments from a lecture by Seward: "But I have sacrificed, as a lawyer, all that I have gained as a statesman. The pursuit of office is a thorny path. If you value domestic happiness, the pleasures of home, and a life of ease and quiet, keep out of that path by all means, for you will probably never succeed in attaining your ideal; and meanwhile, you must part with much that renders life most pleasant and most useful." Quoted in Frederick W. Seward, *William H. Seward: An Autobiography . . . with a Memoir of His Life and Selections from His Letters*, p. 708.

5. William Seward to Theodore Parker, December 1855, quoted in Frederick W. Seward, *Seward at Washington . . . A Memoir of His Life, with Selections from His Letters, 1846–1861*, p. 263.

6. F. W. Seward, *Autobiography*, p. 57. For Seward's role in the Freeman case, see Bancroft, *Life of Seward*, 1:174–79; Van Deusen, *Seward*, pp. 95–97. Seward complained of considerable public pressure not to take the case. See William Seward to Thurlow Weed, May 29, 1846, Weed Papers.

7. The basic source for the details of Seward's early life is F. W. Seward, *Autobiography*, pp. 19–28. See also Van Deusen, *Seward*, pp. 3–7.

8. F. W. Seward, *Autobiography*, pp. 29–55; Van Deusen, *Seward*, p. 5–7.

9. Van Deusen, *Seward*, pp. 10–11. The Bucktail Republicans, who were led by Martin Van Buren, had a more orthodox Jeffersonian view of such issues as internal improvements than the other major Republican faction in New York, the followers of DeWitt Clinton. The Bucktails eventually became the Democratic party of New York State.

10. F. W. Seward, *Autobiography*, pp. 56–68; Van Deusen, *Seward*, pp. 7–12.

11. See Glyndon G. Van Deusen, *Thurlow Weed*, pp. 80–81; Van Deusen, *Seward*, pp. 17–18, 25.

12. George E. Baker, ed., *The Works of William H. Seward*, 3:18–20; 4:177. See also William Seward, *The Elements of Empire in America* (New York, 1844), p. 13–16.

13. Seward, *Works*, 4:302.

14. *Ibid.*, 3:166.

15. *Ibid.*, 3:213.

16. *Ibid.*, 3:176–90, 4:154–55; Seward, *Elements of Empire*, pp. 25–28.

17. See William G. Sharrow, "William Henry Seward," pp. 17–18; Seward, *Elements of Empire*, pp. 28–29.

18. Sharrow, "Seward," pp. 10, 19; Seward, *Elements of Empire*, pp. 18–19.

19. Seward, *Works*, 4:284.

20. *Ibid.*, 3:209–10; Seward, *Elements of Empire*, p. 25.

21. Seward, *Works*, 3:139.

22. *Ibid.*, 3:23.

23. *Ibid.*, 2:240–41.

24. *Ibid.*, 2:90.

25. *Ibid.*, 4:181. It should be noted that Seward was a close student of the works of Edmund Burke.

26. F. W. Seward, *Autobiography*, pp. 268–71, 806; Seward, *Elements of Empire*, pp. 20–22.

27. Seward, *Works*, 4:268. See also *ibid.*, 1:197–98, 2:80, 3:407–9, 4:190–91.

28. Sharrow, "Seward," p. 27.

29. Seward, *Works*, 3:260–74, 295–96; F. W. Seward, *Autobiography*, pp. 54, 57–60, 74.

30. See Ernest N. Paolino, *The Foundations of the American Empire: William Henry Seward and U.S. Foreign Policy* (Ithaca: Cornell University Press, 1973), pp. 8–14; Seward, *Elements of Empire*, pp. 7–12.

31. Seward, *Works*, 3:295–96.

32. *Ibid.*, 3:238.

33. *Ibid.*, 3:77, 281; F. W. Seward, *Autobiography*, p. 89. Adams' antislavery views had a clear influence on Seward. See John Quincy Adams to William Seward, May 10, 1844, Adams Family Papers.

34. Seward, *Works*, 3:261, 288–89, 294–95, 304–5; F. W. Seward, *Autobiography*, p. 707. For physical descriptions of Seward, see George W. Bungay, *Crayon Sketches and Off-Hand Takings* (Boston, 1852), p. 81; Henry S. Foote, *Casket of Reminiscences* (Washington, 1824), pp. 125–26; John W. Forney, *Anecdotes of Public Men*, 2 vols. (New York, 1873–81), 2:164.

35. Seward, *Works*, 3:294; Seward, *Elements of Empire*, p. 19.

36. See David M. Ellis, *Landlords and Farmers in the Hudson-Mohawk Region, 1790–1850* (Ithaca: Cornell University Press, 1946), ch. 7; Vincent P. Lannie, *Public Money and Parochial Education: Bishop Hughes, Governor Seward, and the New York School Controversy* (Cleveland: Case Western Reserve University Press, 1968), pp. 15–27, 66–67, 119–26, 142, 170–71, 181, 191, 205–7; Van Deusen, *Seward*, pp. 61–63, 65–75, 80–83.

37. Seward, *Works*, 2:240–41, 244–46. After the Democrats won a majority of seats in the state legislature in 1841, they suspended work on internal improvements and levied a property tax to finance further construction. Van Deusen, *Seward*, p. 82.

38. Seward, *Works*, 2:215, 278–81, 306–9; Van Deusen, *Seward*, pp. 67–68. The school controversy was finally resolved by a law passed in 1842 which prohibited

state support to religious schools in New York City, and put the city's schools under the supervision of elected school commissioners. This law effectively brought to an end the monopoly control the Protestant-dominated Public School Society had over public school money in New York City, thus giving Catholics equal rights in the public schools.

39. Seward, *Works*, 2:220–21. In response to the disturbances, Seward called out some of the state militia and issued a proclamation requesting the rioters to obey the law. He also promised to bring their complaints before the legislature. These acts ended violent resistance to the enforcement of the manorial tenures, but the antirenters' problems were not resolved satisfactorily until the 1850s.

40. Seward, *Works*, 2:221–22; Van Deusen, *Seward*, pp. 65–66.

41. William Seward to Christopher Morgan, June 10, 1841, Seward Papers.

42. Bancroft, *Life of Seward*, 1:105–7; F. W. Seward, *Seward at Washington*, p. 161; Van Deusen, *Seward*, pp. 65–67.

43. William Seward to Thurlow Weed, April 11, 1847, Weed Papers; Seward to his wife, February 29, 1847, in F. W. Seward, *Seward at Washington*, p. 37; Van Deusen, *Seward*, pp. 97, 103, 105.

44. Seward, *Works*, 3:295.

45. *Ibid.*, 3:299–300. Seward was not enthusiastic about Taylor's candidacy, and was reluctant to campaign for the Whigs' national ticket in 1848. See William Seward to Thurlow Weed, June 23, 24, 1848, Weed Papers. Despite his efforts, Cass carried Ohio.

46. Seward, *Works*, 3:301.

47. *Ibid.*, 3:301–2.

48. Van Deusen, *Seward*, pp. 114, 118–20.

49. Seward to Judge [Alfred] Conkling, late December, 1849, quoted in F. W. Seward, *Seward at Washington*, p. 116.

50. William Seward to Thurlow Weed, December 27, November 30, 1849, Weed Papers.

51. U.S. Congress, Senate, *Congressional Globe*, 31st Cong., 1st sess., March 5, 1850, p. 461.

52. William Seward to Thurlow Weed, January 25, 1850, Weed Papers.

53. *Congressional Globe*, 31st Cong., 1st sess., March 11, 1850, app., pp. 261–63. Seward wrote to Weed that Webster's speech had prepared the North to hear his own position, "but has rendered of little value the little of moderation I can practice in regard to the other portion of the Union." William Seward to Thurlow Weed, March 11, 1850, Weed Papers.

54. *Congressional Globe*, 31st Cong., 1st sess., March 11, 1850, app., p. 263.

55. *Ibid.*, pp. 262–65.

56. *Ibid.*, p. 266.

57. *Ibid.*, p. 268.

58. *Ibid.*, For an intelligent discussion of the meaning and significance of the "higher law" speech, see Brock, *Parties*, pp. 300–4.

59. See, for example, the angry rejoinder to Seward by the normally moderate

Senator George E. Badger of North Carolina, *Congressional Globe*, 31st Cong., 1st sess., March 18, 1850, app., p. 387.

60. *Congressional Globe*, 31st Cong., 1st sess., May 13, 1850, app., p. 572. For an extended discussion of reactions to the "higher law" speech, see John P. Lynch, "The Higher Law Argument in American History, 1850–1860" (M.A. thesis, Columbia University, 1947), pp. 28–31, 32–35, 90–93.

61. John L. Schoolcraft to Thurlow Weed, March 15, 1850, Weed Papers.

62. Thurlow Weed to William Seward, March 14, 17, 24, 26, 1850, Seward Papers.

63. See Simeon Draper to William Seward, March 12, 1850; J. Van Vechten to William Seward, March 16, 1850; Lewis Tappan to William Seward, March 12, 1850; Lyman Spaulding to William Seward, March 16, 1850; Ethan Warden to William Seward, March 17, 1850; Cassius Clay to William Seward, April 6, 1850; Henry Ward Beecher to William Seward, May 27, 1850, all in Seward Papers.

64. William Seward to Thurlow Weed, March 15, 1850, Weed Papers.

65. *Congressional Globe*, 31st Cong., 1st sess., July 2, 1850, app., pp. 1444–45.

66. See the "Dedication" of William Hosmer, *The Higher Law in Its Relations to Civil Government with Particular Reference to Slavery and the Fugitive Slave Law* (Auburn, N.Y., 1852). Seward also approved the manuscript of this book before its publication. See Van Deusen, *Seward*, p. 584, n. 14. On the use of the "higher law" by antislavery men who were critical of Webster's March 7 speech, see chapter 3, "Daniel Webster: Conservative Whig."

67. *Congressional Globe*, 31st Cong., 1st sess., July 2, 1850, app., p. 1023.

68. See Seward, *Works*, 1:111–31, 348–57. On the hostility between Fillmore and Seward, see Harry J. Carman and Reinhard H. Luthin, "The Seward-Fillmore Feud and the Crisis of 1850," *New York History* (April 1943), 24:163–84; Carman and Luthin, "The Seward-Fillmore Feud and the Disruption of the Whig Party," *ibid.* (July 1943), 24:335–57.

69. See Lee H. Warner, "The Silver Grays: New York State Conservative Whigs, 1846–1856" (Ph.D. diss., University of Wisconsin at Madison, 1971), chs. 3, 5.

70. See Bancroft, *Life of Seward*, 1:301–2; Holt, *Political Crisis*, pp. 123–26; Potter, *Impending Crisis*, pp. 232–34; Van Deusen, *Weed*, p. 91.

71. See Bancroft, *Life of Seward*, 1:310–11; F. W. Seward, *Seward at Washington*, p. 196; Van Deusen, *Weed*, pp. 192–93. Seward described the Whigs' 1852 platform as "wretched," and wrote that he voted for Scott "with a protest." William Seward to Thurlow Weed, June 25, 1852, in F. W. Seward, *Seward at Washington*, p. 188; Van Deusen, *Seward*, p. 142.

72. This was the sentiment Lincoln probably alluded to when he claimed that until the Kansas-Nebraska Act (1854), most Americans were secure in the belief that slavery was on the road to extinction. See his "Speech at Peoria," October 16, 1854, in Basler, ed., *Works of Lincoln*, 2:274–76.

73. For Seward's remarks on the Kansas-Nebraska Act, see *Congressional Globe*, 33d Cong., 1st sess., May 25, 1854, app., pp. 768–71. Seward later claimed that

he had encouraged Senator Archibald Dixon, a Kentucky Whig, to force Stephen Douglas to include in the act the explicit repeal of the Missouri Compromise as a condition for obtaining southern support. Seward claimed that his motive in doing so was to turn northern opinion against the Democratic party. However, Dixon denied the claim, and there is no third-party evidence to support Seward's story. See Mrs. Archibald Dixon, *The True History of the Missouri Compromise and Its' Repeal* (Cincinnati, 1899), pp. 437, 444; F. W. Seward, *Seward at Washington*, p. 213; Van Deusen, *Seward*, pp. 150, 586–87, n. 3.

74. For the text of the "Irrepressible Conflict" speech, see Seward, *Works*, 4:289–302. The speech was delivered at Rochester, New York, on October 25, 1858.

75. *Congressional Globe*, 35th Cong., 1st sess., March 3, 1858, pp. 943–45.

76. On the reasons for Seward's rejection as the Republican presidential choice in 1860, see Don E. Fehrenbacher, *Prelude to Greatness: Lincoln in the 1850's* (Stanford, Cal.: Stanford University Press, 1962), pp. 153, 157–59; Eric Foner, *Free Soil, Free Labor, Free Men: The Ideology of the Republican Party Before the Civil War*, pp. 181–82, 211–15; Sharrow, "Seward," pp. 271–73, 284.

5. Henry Clay and the Politics of Consensus

1. James Parton, *Famous Americans of Recent Times* (Boston, 1867), p. 4; Nathan Sargent, *Public Men and Events*, 2 vols. (Philadelphia, 1875), 2:250; William S. Robinson, *"Warrington" Pen Portraits: A Collection of Personal and Political Reminiscences* (Boston, 1877), p. 187.

2. Robert C. Winthrop, "Henry Clay: A Memoir," *Addresses and Speeches*, 4:60. See also Joseph G. Baldwin, *Party Leaders: Sketches of Thomas Jefferson, Alexander Hamilton, Andrew Jackson, Henry Clay, John Randolph . . .* (New York, 1855), pp. 357, 359–60; Parton, *Famous Americans*, p. 43; Benjamin Perley Poore, *Perley's Reminiscences of Sixty Years in the National Metropolis*, 2 vols. (Philadelphia, 1886), 1:35, 144–45.

3. Claude Bowers, *Party Battles of the Jackson Period* (Boston: Houghton, Mifflin, 1922), pp. 173–74 (Calhoun quotation); J. W. Watson, "Interviews with Clay, William H. Thackeray and Others," *North American Review* (November 1888), 147:588–89 (Weed quotation); T. C. Grattan, *Civilized America* (London, 1859), 1:395.

4. Grattan, *Civilized America*, 1:396; Adolph de Bacourt, *Souvenirs d'un Diplomate* (Paris, 1882), p. 69. See also Baldwin, *Party Leaders*, p. 209; Perley, *Reminiscences*, 1:34.

5. Parton, *Famous Americans*, p. 10; Winthrop, "Clay Memoir," p. 61. On Clay's abilities as an orator, see E. G. Parks, "Henry Clay as an Orator," *Putnams* (May 1854), 3:493–502; Perley, *Reminiscences*, 1:143; Sargent, *Public Men*, 2:34.

6. See Samuel Gilman Brown, *A Eulogy on the Life and Character of Henry Clay, Delivered Before the Students of Dartmouth College, October 15, 1852* (Boston, 1852), pp. 36–37; U.S. Congress, *Obituary Addresses on the Occasion of the Death of the Hon. Henry*

Clay . . . (Washington, 1852), pp. 10–11, 55, 72; [Alexander Hill Everett], "Life of Henry Clay," *North American Review* (October 1831), 33:351–53, 395; Henry W. Hilliard, *Politics and Pen Pictures* (New York, 1892), p. 216; Abraham Lincoln, "Eulogy on Henry Clay," July 6, 1852, in Basler, ed., *Works of Lincoln*, 2:125–26.

7. Parton, *Famous Americans*, p. 6.

8. See Baldwin, *Party Leaders*, p. 289; U.S. Congress, *Obituary Addresses*, pp. 6–7, 24–25, 37; *Life of Henry Clay, the Statesman and the Patriot; Containing Numerous Anecdotes* (Philadelphia, 1852), pp. 16–17.

9. Clement Eaton, *Henry Clay and the Art of American Politics*, pp. 5–6; George R. Poage, *Henry Clay and the Whig Party*, p. 2; Carl Schurz, *The Life of Henry Clay*, 1:2–4; Glyndon G. Van Deusen, *The Life of Henry Clay*, pp. 3–9.

10. Eaton, *Clay and Politics*, pp. 6–7; Schurz, *Clay*, 1:5–8; Van Deusen, *Life of Clay*, pp. 8–14. For the "Mill Boy of the Slashes" myth, see [Calvin Colton], "Life of Henry Clay," *The Junius Tracts* (September 1843), no. 4, p. 2; *Life of Henry Clay*, pp. iii–iv, 16–17; R. McKinley Ormsby, *History of Whig Party*, pp. 118–19. "The Slashes" was the part of Virginia where Clay lived.

11. Eaton, *Clay and Politics*, pp. 10–24; Schurz, *Clay*, 1:14–67; Van Deusen, *Life of Clay*, pp. 21–54.

12. See E. Merton Coulter, "The Genesis of Henry Clay's American System," pp. 46–51; Robert W. Binkley, Jr., "The American System," pp. 58–90. On the split within the Republican party over promotional economics, see Richard E. Ellis, *The Jeffersonian Crisis*, pp. 281–84.

13. Coulter, "Genesis," pp. 51–53; Binkley, "American System," pp. 121–48.

14. "On Renewing the Charter of the Bank of the United States," 1811, Calvin Colton, ed., *The Works of Henry Clay*, 6:25–27, 30.

15. "On Domestic Manufactures," April 6, 1810, *Works of Clay*, 6:8–21.

16. For Clay's role in the War of 1812, see Roger A. Brown, *The Republic in Peril: 1812* (New York: Columbia University Press, 1964), pp. 49–51, 54, 59–60, 65, 70–71, 86–87. On Clay's concern with exports, and its consonance with republican ideology, see Clay, *Annals of Congress*, 12th Cong., 1st sess., December 31, 1811, p. 601; McCoy, *Elusive Republic*, p. 238.

17. Binkley, "American System," pp. 172–80.

18. "On the Bank of the United States," June 3, 1816, *Works of Clay*, 6:75–80; "On Internal Improvements," March 13, 1818, *ibid.*, 6:116–35. On the vetoes, see George Dangerfield, *The Awakening of American Nationalism*, pp. 18–19, 199.

19. See Margaret Ruth Morley, "The Edge of Empire: Henry Clay's American System and the Formation of American Foreign Policy, 1810–1833" (Ph.D. diss., University of Wisconsin, 1972), ch. 2.

20. "On Protection of Home Industry," April 26, 1820," *Works of Clay*, 6:219–22, 227–33; "On American Industry," March 30, 31, 1824, *ibid.*, 6:255–70.

21. "On the American System," February 2, 3, 6, 1832, *Works of Clay*, 7:474. See also "On American Industry," March 30–31, 1824, *ibid.*, 6:263–64, 278–79, 292; "Nullification and Other Topics," August 3, 1830, *ibid.*, 7:396–99.

22. See Arndt M. Stickles, *The Critical Court Struggle in Kentucky* (Bloomington, Ind.: The Graduate Council, Indiana University, 1929); Dangerfield, *American Nationalism*, pp. 208–10; Frank Furlong Mathias, "The Turbulent Years of Kentucky Politics, 1820–1850" (Ph.D. diss., University of Kentucky, 1966), ch. 2

23. See Lynn L. Marshall, "The Genesis of Grass-Roots Democracy in Kentucky," *Mid-America* (October 1965), 47:269–87; Mathias, "Kentucky Politics," pp. 75–85; Jasper B. Shannon and Ruth McQuowm, *Presidential Politics in Kentucky, 1824–1948: A Compilation of Election Statistics and an Analysis of Political Behavior* (Lexington, Ky.: Bureau of Government Research, College of Arts and Sciences, University of Kentucky, 1950), pp. 3–17, 20.

24. William W. Freehling, *Prelude to Civil War*, ch. 4.

25. "Reduction of Duties on Imports," January 11, 1832, *Works of Clay*, 7:417–28. For Clay's view of the "tariff of abominations," see Henry Clay to John J. Crittenden, February 14, 1828, cited in Robert V. Remini, *Martin Van Buren and the Making of the Democratic Party*, pp. 170–71. Remini (*ibid.*) concludes, however, that Clay's conspiracy theory was unfounded.

26. Freehling, *Nullification*, pp. 247–49; Merrill D. Peterson, *Olive Branch and Sword*, pp. 22–38.

27. Andrew Jackson, "Fourth Annual Message," December 4, 1832, in James D. Richardson, comp., *Messages and Papers*, 5:591–95; Freehling, *Nullification*, pp. 254–91; Peterson, *Compromise*, pp. 40–49.

28. Peterson, *Compromise*, pp. 40–46, 51; Van Deusen, *Life of Clay*, p. 267.

29. "The Compromise Tariff," January 12, 1833, *Works of Clay*, 7:537–50; U.S. Congress, Senate, *Register of Debates*, 22d Cong., 2d sess., February 12–13, 1833, pp. 462–86; *ibid.*, February 23–25, 1833, pp. 717–42; Freehling, *Nullification*, pp. 292–93; Frederick L. Nussbaum, "The Compromise of 1833: A Study in Practical Politics," *South Atlantic Quarterly* (October 1912), 11:339; Peterson, *Compromise*, pp. 52–55.

30. "The Compromise Tariff," February 12, 1833, *Works of Clay*, 7:537–39, 543–46.

31. *Ibid.*, pp. 556–59, 561.

32. Freehling, *Nullification*, pp. 292–93; Nussbaum, "Compromise of 1833," pp. 341–49; Peterson, *Compromise*, pp. 52–82.

33. "On the Public Lands," June 20, 1832, *Works of Clay*, 7:488–515; Peterson, *Compromise*, pp. 10–11.

34. See Peterson, *Compromise*, p. 83; Roy M. Robbins, *Our Landed Heritage*, pp. 55–57. On the ideological basis of the differences over land policy and distribution, see Mary E. Young, "Congress Looks West: Liberal Ideology and Public Land Policy in the Nineteenth Century," in David M. Ellis, et al., eds., *The Frontier in American Development: Essays in Honor of Paul Wallace Gates* (Ithaca, N.Y.: Cornell University Press, 1969), pp. 74–112.

35. See Edward G. Bourne, *The History of the Surplus Revenue of 1837* (New York, 1885); Van Deusen, *Life of Clay*, pp. 286–87.

36. Robbins, *Landed Heritage*, pp. 86–89; Van Deusen, *Life of Clay*, pp. 160–62; Raynor G. Wellington, *The Political and Sectional Influence of the Public Lands, 1828–1842*, pp. 96–103.

37. William R. Brock, *Parties and Political Conscience*, pp. 101–5; Robbins, *Landed Heritage*, p. 89. For the text of Tyler's veto messages, see Richardson, comp., *Messages and Papers*, 4:180–89. For the congressional voting on the tariff, see *Congressional Globe*, 27th Cong., 2d sess., August 16, 1842, p. 912; *ibid.*, August 22, 1842, pp. 923–26; *ibid*, August 27, 1842, p. 960; *ibid*, August 29, 1842, p. 963. For the text of the tariff in its final form, see U.S. Congress, House, *House Documents*, 61st Cong., 2d sess., H. Rept. 671, pp. 120–39.

38. See Henry Clay to Francis Brooke, June 29, 1832, *Works of Clay*, 4:340; "On the State of the Country," March 14, 1834, *ibid.*, 7:625–27; Eaton, *Clay and Politics*, pp. 99–100; Van Deusen, *Life of Clay*, pp. 255–57; Sydney Nathans, *Daniel Webster and Jacksonian Democracy*, pp. 76–77.

39. See Henry A. Wise, *Seven Decades of the Union* (Philadelphia, 1872), pp. 167–69; "State of the Country under Mr. Van Buren," June 27, 1840, *Works of Clay*, 8:210.

40. Henry Clay to William Henry Harrison, March 13, 1841; William Henry Harrison to Henry Clay, March 13, 1841; Henry Clay to William Henry Harrison, March 15, 1841, Clay Papers. Sydney Nathans, *Webster and Democracy*, p. 160.

41. Clay to Francis Brooke, May 14, 1841, *Works of Clay*, 5:454; Richardson, comp., *Messages and Papers*, 4:36–39, 42–47; *Congressional Globe*, 27th Cong., 1st sess., May 7, 1841, p. 22.

42. For the texts of Tyler's veto messages, see Richardson, comp., *Messages and Papers*, 4:63–68 (August 16, 1841), 68–72 (September 9, 1841). The roles of Ewing and Webster are discussed in the chapter "Daniel Webster: Conservative Whig."

43. Clay, "On Mr. Tyler's Veto of the Bank Bill," August 19, 1841, *Works of Clay*, 8:292–94; Brock, *Parties*, pp. 81–101; David W. Krueger, "The Clay-Tyler Feud, 1841–1842," *Filson Club Historical Quarterly* (April 1968), 42:162–77; Poage, *Clay and Whig Party*, pp. 37–100.

44. Clay, "Valedictory to Senate," March 31, 1842, *Works of Clay*, 9:353–58. See also Eaton, *Clay and Politics*, p. 147; Schurz, *Clay*, 2:208.

45. For Clay's response to some of the Whigs' legislative record, see Henry Clay to John MacPherson Berrien, August 15, 1842; Clay to Berrien, September 4, 1842, Berrien Papers.

46. Clay, "To the Electors of Fayette County," April 16, 1798, in James F. Hopkins and Mary Hargreaves, eds., *The Papers of Henry Clay*, 1:5.

47. "To the Electors of Fayette," [February 1799], *ibid.*, p. 14.

48. J. Winston Coleman, Jr., "Henry Clay, Kentucky, and Liberia," *Register of the Kentucky Historical Society* (October 1947), 45:310–11; *African Repository* (January 1837), 13:38.

49. See "African Colonization," January 20, 1827, *Works of Clay*, 6:329–40;

"Remarks at the Colonization Meeting Held at Lexington, Kentucky, August 26, 1836," *African Repository* (October 1836), 12:297–99. My analysis owes much to George M. Fredrickson, *The Black Image in the White Mind*, pp. 16–17.

50. See "Remarks at Colonization Meeting at Lexington," p. 299; *African Repository* (January 1838), 14:17–18.

51. See Fredrickson, *Black Image*, pp. 11, 41, 61–62, 67–68. An essay which helps place colonization within the framework of republican ideology is David M. Streifford, "The American Colonization Society: An Application of Republican Ideology to Early Antebellum Reform," *Journal of Southern History* (May 1979), 45:201–20.

52. See *African Repository* (January 1838), 14:17; "Speech at the Fourteenth Annual Meeting," *ibid.* (April 1851), 27:108–13. For the pitiful performance of the colonizationists, see P. J. Staudenraus, *The African Colonization Movement*; Coleman, "Clay, Kentucky, and Liberia," pp. 316–20. Clay at times appealed for colonization as a way to make slaves more docile. See Clay, "Remarks at Colonization Meeting at Lexington," p. 299.

53. Eaton, *Clay and Politics*, pp. 76, 120–21; Van Deusen, *Works of Clay*, pp. 311–12. Part of Clay's will is reprinted in *Works of Clay*, 3:153–54. There are some interesting parallels to Clay's attitudes toward blacks in his attitudes toward Indians. Although he opposed the forceful removal of Indian tribes under Jackson, he favored a policy of "voluntary" removal as Adams' Secretary of State. Clay believed that the Indians' cultures were clearly inferior to the culture of the white majority, and that the Indians must either be absorbed into the mainstream or be allowed to disappear. His only positive provision for the Indians was a policy of moral "uplift," which would extinguish any distinctive Indian culture: "Let us confer upon them, if we can, the inestimable blessings of Christianity, and civilization, and then, if they must sink beneath the progressive wave of civilized population, we are free from all reproach, and stand acquitted in the sight of God and man." Quoted from "On Our Relations with the Cherokee Indians," February 4, 1835, *Works of Clay*, 8:655. Of course, Clay's attitudes toward Indians may have been less crassly ethnocentric than his opinion of blacks. He *was* willing to accept *some* absorption of the Indians into the white culture; perhaps because the Indians were indigenously "American," he did not suggest their total removal. But he supported assimilation so long as it was entirely on the terms of the dominant white culture. Here, too, the limits of Clay's "benevolent" conservatism and reform were evident. See Ronald N. Satz, *American Indian Policy in the Jacksonian Era* (Lincoln, Neb.: University of Nebraska Press, 1975), pp. 40, 52.

54. Clay, "Speech on the Admission of Maine," December 30, 1819, in Hopkins and Hargreaves, eds., *Clay Papers*, 1:740–47; Glover Moore, *The Missouri Controversy, 1819–1821*, pp. 46, 87.

55. Dangerfield, *Nationalism*, pp. 134–37; Moore, *Missouri Controversy*, pp.102–3, 148–59.

56. See Dangerfield, *Nationalism*, pp. 124, 135–36; Moore, *Missouri Controversy*, p. 111.

57. This discussion owes much to Fredrickson, *Black Image*, pp. 25–42, 61–64.

58. See U.S. Congress, *Register of Debates*, 24th Cong., 1st sess., June 6, 1836, pp. 1721–29; Russel B. Nye, *Fettered Freedom: Civil Liberties and the Slavery Controversy, 1830–1860* (East Lansing: Michigan State University Press, 1963), p. 84.

59. See U.S. Congress, *Register of Debates*, 24th Cong., 1st sess., March 9, 1836, pp. 779–81; William Van Deburg, "Henry Clay, the Right of Petition, and Slavery in the Nation's Capital," *Register of the Kentucky Historical Society* (April 1970), 68:132–45.

60. U.S. Congress, Senate, *Senate Journal*, 24th Cong., 1st sess., pp. 82–85 (December 27, 1837), 106–7 (January 3, 1838), 116–17 (January 6, 1838), 122–26 (January 10, 1838), 130–32 (January 12, 1838), 136–37 (January 15, 1838).

61. Clay, "On Abolition," February 7, 1839, *Works of Clay*, 8:140–59; Gunderson, *Log-Cabin Campaign*, pp. 44–46, 53–54, 58–60.

62. "To the Editors of the National Intelligencer," April 17, 1844, *Works of Clay*, 3:25–31.

63. Clay to Stephen F. Miller, July 1, 1844, *Works of Clay*, 5:490–91; Henry Clay to Thomas M. Peters and John M. Jackson, *Niles' National Register* (August 31, 1844), 66:439.

64. See Brock, *Parties*, p. 154, for a sage discussion of the results. For Clay's cool response to political nativism, see Henry Clay to John S. Littell, November 17, 1846, *Works of Clay*, 5:536–37; Henry Clay to John J. Crittenden, Nov. 28, 1844, in Mrs. Chapman Coleman, ed., *The Life of John J. Crittenden . . .* , 2:223–25.

65. Henry Clay to Epes Sargent, February 15, 1847, quoted in Brock, *Parties*, p. 185. Correspondents who wrote letters of condolence to Clay mostly blamed his loss on illegal immigrant voting, while some also ascribed an important role to the abolitionist Liberty party in New York. See the letters reprinted in *Works of Clay*, 5:492–513, 515–20, 523, 526, 526–27. See also J. D. Mighels to Henry Clay, November 11, 1844; Samuel Boyd Tobey to Henry Clay, November 18, 1844; Ambrose Spencer to Henry Clay, November 21, 1844; Thomas Nevill to Henry Clay, November 26, 1844, all in Clay Papers. There is some reason to doubt Clay's explanation of his defeat in New York. Actually, he ran *ahead* of the Whig gubernatorial candidate, Millard Fillmore, in New York City and other cites in the state where naturalized voters were most numerous. By contrast, he ran *behind* Fillmore in western New York, where antislavery sentiment was strongest. Of course, Clay may have done even better in New York City if there had been no fusion between the Whigs and nativists there. See Robert J. Rayback, *Millard Fillmore: Biography of a President* (Buffalo: Buffalo Historical Society, 1959), p. 158.

66. "Speech at Lexington," November 13, 1847, *Works of Clay*, 3:61–69.

67. *Ibid.*, 3:68–69.

68. Holman Hamilton, *Zachary Taylor: Soldier in the White House* (Indianapolis: Bobbs-Merrill, 1951), pp. 66–67, 74; Poage, *Clay and Whig Party*, pp. 168–69.

69. Henry Clay to Thomas B. Stevenson, September 4, 1848, *Works of Clay*,

3:483; Henry Clay to Thomas B. Stevenson, October 9, 1848, *ibid.*, 3:485; Henry Clay to James Harlan, June 22, 1848, *ibid.*, 5:565–66; Henry Clay to a Committee of Louisville, June 28, 1848, *ibid.*, 5:566–68; Henry Clay to Nicholas Dean, August 24, 1848, *ibid.*, 5:572–73; Henry Clay to Henry White, September 9, 1848, *ibid.*, 5:573–74; Henry Clay to Daniel Ullmann, September 16, 1848, *ibid.*, 5:574–75; Henry Clay to James Lynch, et al., September 20, 1848, *ibid.*, 5:575–77; Van Deusen, *Life of Clay*, pp. 392–93.

70. Henry Clay to Richard Pindell, February 17, 1849, *Works of Clay*, 3:346–52.

71. Brock, *Parties*, p. 273; Jeffrey Brooke Allen, "Did Southern Colonizationists Oppose Slavery? Kentucky as a Test Case," *Register of the Kentucky Historical Society* (April 1977), 75:92–111; James P. Gregory, "The Question of Slavery in the Kentucky Constitutional Convention of 1849," *Filson Club History Quarterly* (April 1949), 23:89–100; Asa Earl Martin, *The Anti-Slavery Movement in Kentucky Before 1850* (Louisville: Standard Printing, 1918), pp. 130–31.

72. "Speech of Mr. Clay on the Foregoing Resolutions," February 5, 6, 1850, *Works of Clay*, 3:305–13.

73. *Ibid.*, 3:314–36.

74. "On the Compromise Resolutions," January 29, 1850, *Works of Clay*, 3:122–23.

75. See "On Mr. Foote's Motion," April 8, 1850, *Works of Clay*, 9:418; "General Review of the Debate on the Compromise Bills," July 22, 1850, *ibid.*, 9:563–64. My argument here owes much to Paul Nagel, *One Nation Indivisible: The Union in American Thought* (New York: Oxford University Press, 1964), pp. 96–97, 267; Paul Nagel, *This Sacred Trust: American Nationality, 1798–1898* (New York: Oxford University Press, 1971), pp. 131, 158, 161.

76. See "On the Admission of California," February 14, 1850, *Works of Clay*, 9:394–409; "On Mr. Foote's Motion," April 8, 1850, *ibid.*, 9:410–18; "On the Report of the Committee of Thirteen," May 13, 1850, *ibid.*, 9:426–51; "On the Admission of California," July 15, 19, 1850, *ibid.*, 9:516–28; Holman Hamilton, *Prologue to Conflict*, pp. 53–59, 92–96; Potter, *Impending Crisis*, pp. 99–100, 103–04.

77. See "Who Occasioned the Loss of the Bill," August 1, 1850, *Works of Clay*, 9:569–75; Hamilton, *Crisis and Compromise*, pp. 102–65; Potter, *Impending Crisis*, pp. 107–12.

78. The extent to which the settlement of 1850 was not actually a compromise is best discussed in Potter, *Impending Crisis*, pp. 113–20.

79. Hamilton, *Crisis and Compromise*, pp. 99–100.

80. "On Violations of the Fugitive Slave Law," Feb. 21, 24, 1851, *Works of Clay*, 9:609–28; Van Deusen, *Life of Clay*, pp. 418–19.

81. Schurz, *Clay*, 3:406; Van Deusen, *Life of Clay*, pp. 423–24; Thomas Clay to James Clay, June 29, 1852, Clay Papers.

6. Southern Whigs and the Politics of Statesmanship

1. Charles S. Sydnor, *The Development of Southern Sectionalism, 1819–1848* (Baton Rouge: Louisiana State University Press, 1948), p. 316.

2. For some indications of the ideological distinctions between the parties in the South with respect to national issues, see Alexander, *Sectional Stress and Party Strength*; Silbey, *Shrine of Party*.

3. Sellers, "Who Were the Southern Whigs?" Let me add that I am by no means satisifed with the "explanation" of the southern Democracy suggested in this paragraph.

4. *Ibid.*, p. 341.

5. There is a large number of works on the social composition of political elites in the antebellum South. Almost all of them stress the great similarity between the leaders of the Democratic and Whig parties. See, among other works, Donald A. Debats, "Elites and Masses," pp. 217–20; Burton W. Folsom II, "The Politics of Elites: Prominence and Party in Davidson County, Tennessee, 1835–1861," *Journal of Southern History* (August 1973), 39:359–78; Milton Henry, "Summary of Tennessee Representation in Congress from 1845 to 1861," *Tennessee Historical Quarterly* (June 1951), 10:140–44; Grady McWhiney, "Were the Whigs a Class Party in Alabama?" *Journal of Southern History* (November 1957), 23:510–22; Ralph A. Wooster, *The People in Power: Courthouse and Statehouse in the Lower South, 1850–1860* (Knoxville: University of Tennessee Press, 1969), pp. 43–46; Wooster, *Politicians, Planters, and Plain Folk: Courthouse and Statehouse in the Upper South, 1850–1860* (Knoxville: University of Tennessee Press, 1975), pp. 45–54, 120–21.

6. Several studies indicate that southern Whigs tended to live in communities with great commercial activity, while southern Democrats tended to live in areas with little involvement in the marketplace. The argument that Whiggery flourished in a certain social milieu is quite different from Sellers' thesis that it expressed the economic interests of specific occupational groups. See Thomas B. Alexander, Kit C. Carter, et al., "Who Were the Alabama Whigs?"; Thomas B. Alexander, Peggy Duckworth Elmore, et al., "The Basis of Alabama's Ante-Bellum Two-Party System"; Frank Mitchell Lowrey, "Tennessee Voters During the Second Two-Party System"; Harry L. Watson, *Jacksonian Politics and Community Conflict*.

7. See Charles Henry Ambler, *Sectionalism in Virginia from 1776 to 1861*, pp. 46–49, 99–101; William J. Cooper, Jr., *The South and the Politics of Slavery*, pp. 3–8; William J. Evitts, *A Matter of Allegiances*, pp. 19–20; William S. Hoffmann *Andrew Jackson and North Carolina Politics* chs. 1–2; Joseph G. Tregle, "Louisiana and the Tariff, 1816–1846," *Louisiana Historical Quarterly* (January 1942), 25:47–52.

8. See *Address of the Administration Convention, Held in the Capitol at Raleigh, Dec. 20, 1827* [Raleigh, N.C., 1827]; *Address of the Young Men of the National Republican Party, of the Fifth Congressional District, To the Young Men of the State of Maryland* (N.p. [1832]); *An Address to the People of Maryland, from their Delegates in the Late National Republican Convention: Made in Obedience to a Resolution of that Body* (Baltimore, 1832); [Administration Convention, Virginia], *The Virginia Address* (N.p., 1828); *Proceedings of the Delegates of the Friends of the Administration of John Quincy Adams, Assembled in Convention at Baton Rouge* (New Orleans, 1827).

9. Both Adams and Clay received less than one-third of the vote in the slave states. In the future Confederate states that were then in the Union, Jackson

received 81.4 percent of the vote in 1828 and 88 percent of the vote in 1832. See Arthur M. Schlesinger, Jr., and Fred L. Israel, eds., *History of American Presidential Elections*, 1:492, 574. The one act of Jackson which did disappoint many southerners was his choice of Martin Van Buren as his running mate (and heir apparent) in 1832. This disappointment was expressed in several southern states by the running of election tickets which listed Jackson for President and Philip B. Barbour of Virginia for Vice President. The Jackson-Barbour ticket received 14 percent of the vote in Alabama, 27 percent in Mississippi, 13 percent in North Carolina, less than 1 percent in Virginia, and almost 33 percent of the vote in Georgia. See Cooper *South and Politics*, pp. 19–22.

10. For the background and probable intent of the Force Bill, see Freehling, *Nullification*, pp. 265–67, 284–86. While congressmen from the slave states voted 85–1 for the compromise tariff, they voted 46–38 in favor of the Revenue Collection ("Force") Bill. Many of the southern congressmen who voted for the compromise tariff but against the "Force" bill would become Whigs. See the analysis of the congressional votes in *Niles' National Register* (March 16, 1833), 44:44.

11. For the impact of the removal and instruction controversies upon politics in the southern states, see William H. Adams, *The Whig Party of Louisiana*, pp. 53–61; Cooper, *South and Politics*, pp. 44–58; Clement Eaton, "Southern Senators and the Right of Instruction"; William S. Hoffmann, *Andrew Jackson and North Carolina Politics*, pp. 70–73; Paul Murray, *The Whig Party in Georgia*, pp. 57–61; Henry H. Simms, *The Rise of the Whigs in Virginia*, pp. 80–82; John Tyler to L. Tazewell, December 25, 1833, June 23, 1834, Tyler Papers; Senator Alexander Porter of Louisiana to James Gowen et al., June 24, 1834, *Niles' National Register* (May 10, 1834), 46:178–79; "Answer of Mr. Poindexter to an Invitation to a Public Dinner at Louisville, Kentucky," *ibid.* (August 16, 1834), 46:415; Senator Gabriel Moore of Alabama, *ibid.* (September 6, 1834), 47:12; William Alexander Graham, "Speech on Instruction," December 1834, J. G. deRoulhac Hamilton and Max R. Williams, eds., *The Papers of William Alexander Graham*, 1:341–56; Senator William Preston of South Carolina, U.S. Congress, Senate, *Register of Debates*, 22d Cong. 1st sess., March 13, 1834, pp. 950–55; Senator Benjamin Watkins Leigh of Virginia, *ibid.*, March 18, 1834, pp. 1002–3; Congressman William S. Archer of Virginia, U.S. Congress, House, *Register of Debates*, 22d Cong., 1st sess., February 5, 6, 1834, pp. 2641–46; Congressman Augustin Clayton of Georgia, *ibid.*, March 6, 1834, pp. 2916–18; Congressman Samuel McDowell Moore of Virginia, *ibid.*, March 10, 1834, pp. 2949–50; Raleigh (N.C.) *Register*, October 1, 1833, January 7, February 11, 18, March 5, 18, 25, April 15, June 10, 1834; Richmond *Whig*, quoted in Milledgeville (Ga.) *Recorder*, February 12, 1834; Vicksburg (Miss.) *Register*, March 5, 19, 26, June 5, July 3, 1834.

The opponents of removal were not necessarily supporters of the recharter of the Bank of the United States. The House voted 134–82 against a resolution for recharter, but only 118–103 against a resolution in favor of the restoration of the deposits. Of the 20 House members who voted against recharter but in favor of restoring the deposits, 18 were from slave states. Most of these men became

Whigs. See U.S. Congress, House, *Register of Debates*, 22d Cong., 2d sess., April 4, 1834, p. 3473–76.

12. On the weaknesses of the presidency before Jackson's accession, see James S. Young, *The Washington Community*, pp. 229–49. For Jackson's definition of his role as President, see C. Perry Patterson, *Presidential Government in the United States*, pp. 50–53.

13. Henry T. Clark to Willie P. Mangum, March 12, 1834, in Henry T. Shanks, ed., *The Papers of Willie Person Mangum*, 2:120–21. See also *ibid.*, 2:29–30, 147–48, 265; Charles H. Ambler, ed., *The Life and Diary of John Floyd*, pp. 175–76, 203–04, 232; Milledgeville (Ga.), *Recorder*, March 19, 1833; "Resolutions of a Meeting of Citizens of Taliaferro County, Georgia," May 23, 1833, *Niles' National Register* (May 25, 1833), 44:202; Edwin A. Miles, *Jacksonian Democracy in Mississippi*, pp. 68–69; Simms, *Whigs in Virginia*, pp. 70–71; John Tyler to L. Tazewell, February 2, 1833; [John Hampden Pleasants to John Tyler], January 1, 1833, Tyler Papers.

14. See Graham, "Speech on Instructions," *Graham Papers*, 1:358–63; Willie Person Mangum, "National Defense," Speech in the Senate, February 2, 1836, *Mangum Papers*, 5:597–98; Senator William C. Preston of South Carolina, U.S. Congress, Senate, *Register of Debates*, 23d Cong., 2d sess., January 13, 1837, pp. 397–98; "Protest in the Legislature of Virginia," February 11, 1836, *Niles' National Register* (March 19, 1836), 50:43; John Tyler to L. W. Tazewell, June 23, 1834; Benjamin Watkins Leigh to John Tyler, July 5, 1835; James Barbour to John Tyler, January 14, 1836, Tyler Papers; Raleigh *Register*, November 25, 1834, December 2, 23, 1834; "Speech of William Outlaw," *ibid.*, February 10, 1835.

15. For incipient southern Whigs' admiration of Clay's role in the nullification crisis, see *Southern Patriot*, March 4, 1833, *Niles' National Register* (March 16, 1833), 44:44; William H. Crawford, et al. to Henry Clay, March 6, 1833, *ibid.* (April 27, 1833), 44:137; W. R. Chaplain to Clay, February 25, 1833, *ibid.*; Hoffman, *North Carolina Politics*, pp. 65–67; Milledgeville (Ga.), *Recorder*, February 27, 1833; Richmond *Whig*, quoted in Raleigh *Register*, April 9, 1833. Joseph G. Baldwin, a Mississippi Whig, later wrote of Clay's role in the nullification crisis: "It presented him before the whole nation in an aspect at once of power and of goodness; as a magnanimous man and a public benefactor; and it prepared the way for a co-operation with those, who were to be, afterwards, his most efficient allies." Baldwin, *Party Leaders*, p. 341.

16. See Graham, "Speech on Instructions," *Graham Papers*, 1:358–59; Mangum, "National Defense," *Mangum Papers*, 5:600–1; Congressman Samuel McDowell Moore of Virginia, U.S. Congress, House, *Register of Debates*, 22d Cong., 2d sess., March 10, 1834, p. 2949; Congressman Henry A. Wise of Virginia, *ibid.*, June 20, 1834, pp. 4626–27; Richmond *Whig*, January 9, February 6, 11, 1835, April 28, 1836; Vicksburg *Whig*, July 8, 1834; George Tucker to Henry Clay, February 8, 1834, Clay Papers.

17. For evidence of incipient southern Whigs rallying behind Clay, see Ambler, ed., *Life and Diary of Floyd*, pp. 212, 221–27, 232; Shanks, ed., *Mangum Papers*, 2:36–38, 98–101, 312–14; 5:585; George Poindexter to Felix Huston,

March 9, 1834, Mississippi Historical Society *Publications* (1901), 4:331–33; Lyon G. Tyler, ed., *The Letters and Times of the Tylers*, 1:451–52, 587.

18. White and the other Whig presidential candidates were nominated by Whig caucuses in the state legislatures. White was first nominated by the Whigs in the Alabama and Tennessee legislatures. See Mary R. Bartus, "The Presidential Election of 1836" (Ph.D. diss., Fordham University, 1967), ch. 5.

19. See Cooper, *South and Politics*, pp. 93–94; William S. Hoffmann, "The Election of 1836 in North Carolina," *North Carolina Historical Review* (January 1955), 32:49–50.

20. On the convention issue, see Cooper, *South and Politics*, p. 80; Jonathan Mills Thornton III, *Politics and Power in a Slave Society: Alabama, 1800–1860*, p. 32. For White's political persona, see Nancy N. Scott, *A Memoir of Hugh Lawson White . . .* , pp. 336–45. White's supporters were at first careful not to criticize Jackson directly. But after Jackson began to attack White for his independent candidacy, they asserted that the chief issue of 1836 was whether the people would submit to Jackson's "dictation" of his successor to the presidency. See "Mr. Bell's Speech, Delivered at Vauxhall, Nashville," *Niles' National Register* (July 11, 1835), 48:333–35; Balie Peyton to Gen. S. D. Jacobs, et al., August 18, 1836, *ibid.* (October 15, 1836), 51:104; Benjamin Watkins Leigh to Cadwallader Jones, et al., September 10, 1836, *ibid.* (October 8, 1836), 51:89; Mangum, "National Defense," *Mangum Papers*, 5:586–90, 597–98; Raleigh *Register*, December 29, 1835; Richmond *Whig*, August 26, 1836; *The People, Against Official Dictation. Republican Whig Ticket. For President, Hugh Lawson White of Tennessee . . . for Vice-President, that tried Republican Statesman and Patriot, John Tyler . . .* [Richmond, 1836].

21. The quotations are from White's letter accepting the presidential nomination of members of the Tennessee legislature (October 23, 1835) and his Senate speech attacking the partisan use of the patronage (February 16, 1835), in Scott, *Memoir of White*, pp. 333–34, 173–74; first two quotations on p. 334, third and fourth on p. 173.

22. *Ibid.*, p. 174.

23. *Ibid.*, 178, 347–50; quotation on p. 350.

24. "Report and Resolutions, Orange County Whig Meeting, February 24, 1836" and "Political Circular: The Liberty of the People Against the Caucus System. To the Freemen of Orange," *Graham Papers*, 1:412–16 and 442–48; quotation on p. 447. See also Cooper, *South and Politics*, pp. 81–84; Hoffmann, *North Carolina Politics*, pp. 108–9; Simms, *Whigs in Virginia*, pp. 108–10, 113–14; Memphis (Tenn.) *Enquirer*, May 4, 18, 1836; Milledgeville (Ga.) *Southern Recorder*, March 3, 1835, September 13, 1836; Raleigh *Register*, April 17, 1835; Vicksburg (Miss.) *Register*, September 15, 29, October 27, 1836; "Address of the Whig Central Committee to the People of Virginia," Richmond *Whig*, August 23, 1836; "Letter of John Tyler to the Editor of the Whig," September 4, 1836, *ibid.*, September 13, 1836; Mangum, "National Defense," *Mangum Papers*, 5:607.

25. "Report and Resolutions, Orange County Whig Meeting," *Graham Papers*, 1:412–15 (first and second quotations on p. 414, third on p. 415); "Political

Circular," *ibid.*, 1:447. See also Hoffmann, *North Carolina Politics*, p. 103; Simms, *Whigs in Virginia*, pp. 108–11, 113–14; Henry A. Wise to S. D. Jacobs, et al., August 29, 1836, *Niles' National Register* (October 15, 1836), 51:104; *Memphis Enquirer*, March 21, April 5, 19, May 11, June 22, September 30, 1836; *Raleigh Register*, April 17, December 29, 1835; *Richmond Whig*, December 14, 1835, January 22, 1836. Another issue in the 1836 campaign (though not one of relevance here) was the intimate personal relationship between a mulatto woman and the Democratic Vice Presidential candidate, Richard Johnson. Whig propaganda did not dwell on the issue (perhaps because of considerations of taste), but vaguely alluded to Johnson's "domestic relations."

26. On the massive Whig gains in the South in 1836 (when compared to the National Republicans' performance in the South in 1832), see Joel H. Silbey, "Election of 1836," in Schlesinger and Israel, eds., *History of American Presidential Elections*, 1:597. Although White carried only Georgia and Tennessee, he made a respectable showing in the other southern states in which he was a candidate.

27. For the Conservative Democrats' response to the subtreasury, see Jean E. Friedman, *The Revolt of the Conservative Democrats*; Harold D. Moser, "Subtreasury Politics and the Virginia Conservative Democrats"; Hugh S. Legare, "Spirit of the Sub-Treasury," in Mary S. Legare, ed., *Writings of Hugh Swinton Legare . . .*, 2 vols. (Charleston, 1845–46), 1:280–321; *Letter of James Garland to His Constituents* (Washington, 1840), pp. 10–11. The Whig view that the scheme would benefit officeholders is presented in "A Communication from Ephraim Foster, a Senator . . . from the State of Tennessee, to the General Assembly of that State, Touching Certain Instructing Resolutions Passed on the 14th Nov., 1839," *Niles' National Register* (December 14, 1839), 57:253; Hugh Lawson White, "Speech on the Sub-Treasury," in Scott, *Memoir of White*, p. 229; Henry Hilliard, "The Sub-Treasury System. A Speech Delivered in the House of Representatives of Alabama, Jan. 1839," *Speeches and Addresses*, p. 33.

28. See Calhoun, "Speech on His Amendment to Separate the Government and the Banks" [October 3, 1837], in Clyde N. Wilson, ed., *The Papers of John C. Calhoun*, 13:592–615; John C. Calhoun to J[ohn] Bauskett and others, November 3, 1837, *ibid.*, 13:636–40; Charles M. Wiltse, *John C. Calhoun: Nullifier, 1829–1839* (Indianapolis: Bobbs-Merrill, 1949), pp. 347–48, 351–53, 356–60. Those Calhounites who followed their hero back into the Democratic party repeated Calhoun's arguments for the subtreasury. See Congressman Francis W. Pickens of South Carolina, U.S. Congress, House, *Register of Debates*, 25th Cong., 1st sess., October 10, 1837, pp. 1393–95. Typically, the southern Whig press ridiculed Calhoun for his inconsistencies on the bank issue and ascribed his decision to rejoin the Democrats to ambition. See *Richmond Whig*, June 16, 1838; *Lynchburg Virginian*, September 15, 1838; "A Nullifier," *Raleigh Register*, January 17, 1840.

29. Thompson, U.S. Congress, House, *Congressional Globe*, 26th Cong., 1st sess., December 30, 1839, p. 222. See also Hilliard, "The Sub-Treasury System," *Speeches and Addresses*, pp. 44–46; White, "Speech on Sub-Treasury," in Scott, *Memoir of White*, pp. 228, 233–34; "A Communication from Ephraim Foster,"

Niles' National Register (December 14, 1839), 57:252–53; J. A. Crockett to A. M. Hamtramck, et al., July 20, 1838, *ibid.* (September 1, 1838), 55:15; "Public Meeting of the Opponents of the Present Administration, Held in the City of Washington, . . . Feb. 15, 1840," *ibid.* (March 14, 1840), 58:19; "Louisiana State Whig Convention," *ibid.* (October 17, 1840), 59:101; Sargeant S. Prentiss, "Letter to the Whigs of Madison County," August 10, 1839, in George L. Prentiss, *A Memoir of S. S. Prentiss,* 2:132–33; *Whig Committee Address to the People of Arkansas* [Little Rock, 1838].

30. For the views of southern Whigs who favored a new national bank, see Congressman John Pendleton Kennedy of Maryland, U.S. Congress, House, *Congressional Globe,* 25th Cong., 2d sess., June 22, 1838, p. 593; Sargeant S. Prentiss, "Address to the People of Mississippi," in G. L. Prentiss, *Memoir of Prentiss,* 1:228–29; "Letter to the Whigs of Madison County," *ibid.,* 2:131–32.

31. Henry Hilliard, for example, proposed a special bank to service the South, while Waddy Thompson suggested that the federal deposits be lodged in banks owned by the states. See Hilliard, "The Sub-Treasury System," *Speeches and Addresses,* pp. 47–48; "Letter from Waddy Thompson, Jr.," *Niles' National Register* (October 30, 1838), 54:576.

32. In addition to the sources cited above, see "Address of William C. Dawson, Richard W. Habersham, Thomas Butler King, E. A. Nisbet and Lott Warren . . . to their Constituents . . . May 27, 1840," Milledgeville *Southern Recorder,* June 23, 1840; Camillus [pseud.], *The Essays of Camillus, Addressed to the Hon. Joel Holloman . . . ,* pp. 67–69; "Brunswick County Whig Meeting," Raleigh *Register,* March 27, 1840.

33. For the northern Whigs' view of the subtreasury, see chapter 2 above, "The Whig Party in the North: The Rhetoric of Party Formation."

34. Harrison stated these positions before a convention at Dayton, Ohio, and Tyler endorsed them. See *Niles' National Register* (October 3, 1840), 59:71 (both quotations); Oliver P. Chitwood, *John Tyler: Champion of the Old South* (New York: Appleton-Century, 1939), p. 190. Harrison's statements on the bank issue were cited by southern Whigs who tried to refute Democratic charges that their presidential candidate was committed to support a new national bank. See Camillus *Essays,* pp. 63–64; Address of George E. Badger, Raleigh *Register,* April 17, 1840.

35. For the convention maneuvering that led to Clay being denied the nomination, see Gunderson, *Log Cabin Campaign,* ch. 5.

36. See Camillus *Essays,* pp. 81–90; "Public Meeting of the Opponents of the Administration," *Niles' National Register* (March 14, 1840), 58:20; "Louisiana State Whig Convention," *ibid.* (October 17, 1840), 59:101; "The Unanimous Declaration of the Whigs of North Carolina, in Convention Assembled, October 5, 1840," *ibid.* (October 24, 1840), 59:118; "Address of Dawson, Habersham, King, Nisbet, and Warren," Milledgeville *Southern Recorder,* June 23, 1840; "Address of the Whig Convention, for the Nomination of Electors, to the People of Virginia," Richmond *Whig,* March 6, 1840; Charlottesville (Va.) *Jeffersonian Republican,* quoted in Washington, D.C., *Madisonian,* March 2, 1840; Georgia *Republican,*

ibid., March 14, 1840; Harrison meeting in Florida, *ibid.*, May 30, 1840; Speech of Kenneth Rayner of North Carolina, *ibid.*, September 22, 1840; "Address to the People of Maryland," *ibid.*, September 25, 1840; Memphis *Enquirer*, December 12, 22, 28, 1839, February 11, 21, 1840. See also the platforms of the local Whig conventions reprinted in Raleigh *Register*, February 25, March 3, 10, 20, 27, April 2, 17, 24, May 1, 5, 15, July 31, August 28, 1840; Cooper, *South and Politics*, pp. 133–38.

37. See Camillus *Essays*, p. 21–30, 58, 63–64, 81–90; Republican Committee of Seventy-Six, *The Northern Man with Southern Principles and the Southern Man with American Principles* . . . (Washington, 1840); "Address of the Whig Convention to the People of Virginia," Richmond *Whig*, March 6, 1840; Washington, D.C., *Madisonian*, January 23, March 26, April 2, 1840; "To the Democratic Portion of the Van Buren Party," *ibid.*, June 30, 1840; Raleigh *Register*, March 10, June 26, 1840; Cooper, *South and Politics*, pp. 134–35, 146.

38. Camillus, *Essays*, p. 90. For more on the major themes of the Whigs' 1840 campaign in the South, see (in addition to the works cited above) *Address of the Committee of the Whig Convention to the People of Alabama* [Tuscaloosa, 1840?]; *Address to the People of Tennessee, by the Whig Convention, which Assembled at Knoxville, Tennessee* (N.p., 1840); *Democratic Whig Convention, Monday, March 16, 1840* [Little Rock, 1840].

39. "Inaugural Address," March 4, 1841, in Richardson, comp., *Messages and Papers*, 4:10. Harrison also promised in his inaugural to use the veto against legislation which discriminated in favor of the interests of a majority in the Union to the detriment of one of the sections (*ibid.*, 4:10–11). This promise was aimed at the South.

40. It is not clear whether Tyler explicitly approved the second bank bill before it passed Congress, but it was widely believed that he had. See the discussion in chapter 3, "Daniel Webster: Conservative Whig." See also Nathans, *Webster and Democracy*, pp. 161–80; Poage, *Clay and Whig Party*, pp. 33–91.

41. The quotations from the address are taken from *Niles' National Register* (September 18, 1841), 61:35.

42. [Kennedy], *Defence of the Whigs, by a Member of the Twenty-Seventh Congress*, pp. 101–6. For evidence of the southern Whigs' repudiation of Tyler, see *Address of [Congressman] Joseph L. Williams [of Tennessee] to His Constituents* (N.p., 1841); "Resolutions, as Adopted at the North Carolina Whig Convention, Held at Raleigh, the 4th and 8th Inst.," *Niles' National Register* (April 23, 1842), 62:117; "Harrisburg Convention. To the Whigs of Maryland, September 10, 1842," *ibid.* (October 1, 1842), 63:79; Fayette (Va.) Clay Club to Henry Clay, September 8, 1843, *ibid.* (October 28, 1843), 65:142; Raleigh *Register*, September 14, 17, 21, December 10, 1841; Richmond *Whig*, September 14, 17, 1841; Vicksburg (Miss.) *Tri-Weekly Whig*, September 25, October 7, 1841.

43. After the Tyler trauma, the Whigs exalted the virtues of party loyalty and the two-party system, and ridiculed the Tylerite's proposal of a new third party. See Cooper, *South and Politics*, pp. 153–54; Raleigh *Register*, September 24, 1841; Richmond *Whig*, September 8, 10, 1841; the exchange between the Richmond

Enquirer, Richmond *Whig*, and Washington *Globe* in *Niles' National Register* (July 22, 1843), 64:332. For Clay's embrace of the two-party system, see his speech at Milledgeville, Ga., March 19, 1844, *Niles' National Register* (April 20, 1844), 66:119.

44. *Letter of Hon. William C. Rives, Giving His Reasons for Preferring Mr. Clay to Mr. Van Buren for Next President*, p. 4. For evidence of the southern Whigs' rally behind Clay, see Cooper, *South and Politics*, pp. 154–55, 162–63; Raleigh *Register*, September 24, November 2, December 10, 1841, April 1, 5, 8, 12, 26, 1842; "Address of the Whig Convention of Georgia," *ibid.*, July 1, 1842; Richmond *Whig*, September 24, 1841; "Resolutions at North Carolina Whig Convention," *Niles' National Register* (April 23, 1842), 62:117; "Harrisburg Convention. To the Whigs of Maryland, Sep. 10, 1842," *ibid* (October 1, 1842), 63:79; "Address of the Whig Convention. To the People of Virginia," *ibid*. (March 2, 1844), 66:9.

7. The Southern Whigs and Economic Development

1. See Cooper, *South and Politics*, pp. 153–66, 206–17.

2. This is the title of chapter 5 of Cooper, *South and Politics*.

3. See Congressman Roger L. Gamble of Georgia, U.S. Congress, House, *Congressional Globe*, 27th Cong., 2d sess., July 7, 1842, app., p. 832; Congressman Daniel M. Barringer of North Carolina, *ibid.*, 29th Cong., 1st sess., July 1, 1846, app., p. 1052; Raleigh (N.C.) *Register*, June 23, 1844; Richmond (Va.) *Whig*, March 10, June 27, 1843. Clay himself pitched his arguments for tariff legislation to the special concerns of southerners. While on a tour of the South in 1844, he declared that he favored a "moderate" and "reasonable" tariff, but opposed one with "prohibitory" duties. See "Mr. Clay in Savannah. His Reception," *Niles' National Register* (April 13, 1844), 66:100; "Mr. Clay at Charleston," *ibid.*, 66:105–6; "Speech at Milledgeville, Georgia, March 19, 1844," *ibid.*, 66:120.

4. Distribution was popular with the southern Whigs because it would result in the southern states receiving benefits which would balance off those which the tariff would yield for the more industrialized North. Moreover, some southern Whigs hoped that, by separating the land revenue (which tended to fluctuate) from tariff receipts, distribution would eliminate the rationale for future increases in tariff levels. But Tyler feared that the flow of federal revenue to the states would be used to justify increases in import duties, and therefore insisted that a distribution provision be separated from the Whig tariff of 1842. Confronted with a choice between distribution or a higher tariff (at a time when the federal government was strapped for revenue), the Whigs' congressional leadership chose the latter, but at the expense of some southern votes. See Brock, *Parties*, p. 104; Robert J. Rayback, *Millard Fillmore: Biography of a President* (Buffalo: Buffalo Historical Society, 1959), pp. 129–32; William G. Brownlow, *A Political Register, . . . with the Life and Public Services of Henry Clay*, pp. 127–31; Raleigh (N.C.), *Register*, August 30, 1842, August 23, 1844; "Whig Address to the People of Virginia," Richmond (Va.) *Whig*, March 10, 1843; "Address of the Whig

Convention. To the People of Virginia," *Niles' National Register* (March 2, 1844), 66:8–9. Once the 1842 tariff was enacted, however, the southern Whigs supported it as a party measure. In 1844 only one southern Whig (Chappell of Georgia) voted against tabling a bill introduced in the House which would have lowered the levels of 1842 to a revenue standard. See "The American Tariff," *Niles' National Register* (May 18, 1844), 66:177. Only one southern Whig in the House of Representatives voted for the Walker tariff of 1846, while three Whig congressmen (one each from Georgia, Illinois, and Maryland) were absent for the vote. Twenty-one slave state Whigs in the House voted against the measure. See the analysis of the vote in *Niles' National Register* (July 11, 1846), 70:290.

5. For expressions of the Whigs' social organicism, see Senator Willie P. Mangum of North Carolina, *Congressional Globe*, 26th Cong., 3d sess., January 11, 1841, app., pp. 51, 59; Abraham Poindexter Maury, *Address on the Choice of a Profession, Delivered Before the Amasgassian and Philomathian Societies of Cumberland University, Lebanon, Tennessee, on the 28th of July, 1847* (Lebanon, 1847), pp. 9–10, 22–24; George A. Prentiss, *A Memoir of S. S. Prentiss*, 2:251, 304–6, 351–52; Jackson (Miss.) *Southron*, April 26, 1843; Raleigh (N.C.) *Register*, December 19, 1845.

6. For the southern Whigs' "Antipartyism," see chapter 6, "Southern Whigs and the Politics of Statesmanship." See also Formisano, "Political Character, Antipartyism"; Wallace, "Ideologies of Party."

7. The southern Whigs' nostalgia grew stronger in the declining phases of their party, as, in their point of view, agitators and demagogues gained the ascendancy in American politics. See William L. Barney, *The Road to Secession: A New Perspective on the Old South* (New York: Pantheon Books, 1972), pp. 137–39.

8. See Camillus, *Essays*, pp. 65–67, 69–70, 73–74; "A Communication from Ephraim Foster," *Niles' National Register* (December 14, 1839), 57:253; Hilliard, "The Sub-Treasury," *Speeches and Addresses*, pp. 35–41; Prentiss, "Letter to Whigs of Madison County," in G. L. Prentiss, *Memoir of Prentiss*, 2:130; Senator William C. Preston of South Carolina, *Register of Debates*, 25th Cong., 1st sess., September 29, 1837, pp. 384–89; Hugh Lawson White, "Speech on the Sub-Treasury," in Scott, *Memoir of White*, pp. 227–28; *Proceedings of the Whig Convention of the State of Alabama, Held at Tuskaloosa, on the 7th, 8th, 9th, and 10th of January, 1839. With an Address to the People of Alabama* (Tuskaloosa, 1839), pp. 10–11; George E. Badger, quoted in Raleigh *Register*, April 17, 1840; "The Address of Richard Davison, Esq., at a Whig Meeting Held in Warrenton on the 14th ult.," *ibid.*, May 22, 1840; Sharp, *Jacksonians Versus Banks*, pp. 55–122, 215–84.

9. See Camillus *Essays*, pp. 69–77; Hilliard, "The Sub-Treasury System," *Addresses and Speeches*, pp. 38–41; Congressman William Cost Johnson, "Speech on the Sub-Treasury," *Niles' National Register* (January 6, 1838), 53:301–3; "Address and Proceedings, Virginia Whig State Convention," *ibid.* (October 19, 1839), 57:126–27; White, "Speech on the Sub-Treasury," in Scott, *Memoir of White*, pp. 227–28.

10. Camillus *Essays*, p. 77 (first quotation), 73 (second quotation). See also Congressman William Cost Johnson of Maryland, *Register of Debates*, 25th Cong.,

1st sess., October 12, 1837, p. 1520; Representative Henry A. Wise of Virginia, *ibid.*, 25th Cong., 1st sess., October 13, 1837, pp. 1677–78.

11. Representative Roger L. Gamble of Georgia, *Congressional Globe*, 27th Cong., 1st sess., August 4, 1841, Appendix, pp. xv–xvi; Senator John MacPherson Berrien of Georgia, *ibid.*, September 1, 1841, app., p. 337; Congressman Alexander H.H. Stuart of Virginia, *ibid.*, August 2, 1841, pp. 376–77.

12. "Mr. Clay in Savannah. His Reception," *Niles' National Register* (April 13, 1844), 66:100; "Mr. Clay at Charleston," *ibid.*, 66:105–6. See also Congressman John Pendleton Kennedy of Maryland, *Congressional Globe*, 25th Cong., 2d sess., June 22, 1838, app., pp. 593–97; Congressman Alexander H. H. Stuart of Virginia, *ibid.*, 27th Cong., 1st sess., August 2, 1841, p. 377.

13. *Niles' National Register* (May 18, 1844), 66:188 (Toombs quotation); *ibid.* (June 27, 1844), 66:348 (Berrien quotation).

14. Speech on the Tariff, July 7, 1842, quoted in Alexander F. Robertson, *Alexander Hugh Holmes Stuart: A Biography*, pp. 37–39.

15. Bell, *Congressional Globe*, 26th Cong., 2d sess., January 20, 1841, app., p. 242; Prentiss, *Memoir of Prentiss*, 2:346–47; William G. Brownlow, *A Political Register . . .* , pp. 66–68; Clingman, "On the Causes of Mr. Clay's Defeat," *Selections from the Speeches and Writings of Hon. Thomas L. Clingman . . .* , pp. 185–86.

16. See Alexander H. H. Stuart, *Congressional Globe*, 27th Cong., 3d sess., July 7, 1842, app., p. 256; Prentiss, *Memoir of Prentiss*, 2:353; Savannah *Georgian*, quoted in *Niles' National Register* (March 12, 1842), 62:18; Richmond *Whig, ibid.* (June 11, 1842), 62:231; Arthur C. Cole, *The Whig Party in the South*, pp. 96–97.

17. "Manifest of Seventy-Nine Cotton Planters of Adams County, Mississippi, in Favor of Protection to American Manufacturers," *The Plough, the Loom, and the Anvil* (November 1848), 1:288–89. Dated October 24, 1844, this "Manifest" was obviously inspired by the then-current presidential campaign, and was reprinted in several southern Whig newspapers. See also Jackson (Miss.) *Southron*, April 19, 26, 1844; Milledgeville (Ga.) *Southern Recorder*, August 27, 1841, September 3, 1844; Prentiss, *Memoir of Prentiss*, 2:350.

18. Augusta *Chronicle*, March 9, 1849. For similar predictions, see Congressman Everett H. Ewing of Tennessee, *Congressional Globe*, 29th Cong., 1st sess., June 27, 1846, p. 991; Senator William Jarnagin of Tennessee, *ibid.*, July 27, 1846, app., p. 1152.

19. See Congressman Robert Toombs of Georgia, *Congressional Globe*, 29th Cong., 1st sess., July 1, 1846, app., pp. 1032–33; Jackson (Miss.) *Southron*, March 7, 28, 1844; "Address of the Whig Convention to the People of Virginia," *Niles' National Register* (March 2, 1844), 66:8; Haller Nutt to Dr. C. B. W. New, et al., September 26, 1844, *ibid.* (November 9, 1844), 67:150.

20. Barringer, *Congressional Globe*, 29th Cong., 1st sess., July 1, 1846, app., pp. 1051–53; Berrien, *ibid.*, 28th Cong., 1st sess., April 9, 1844, p. 493.

21. *Niles' National Register* (May 18, 1844), 66:188.

22. See Carl N. Degler, *The Other South*, ch. 3 (esp. pp. 95–96); J. Stephen

Knight, Jr., "Discontent, Disunity, and Dissent in the Antebellum South: Virginia as a Test Case, 1844–1846," *Virginia Magazine of History and Biography* (October 1973), 81:445–47. The limitations of the colonization movement are discussed in chapter 5, "Henry Clay and the Politics of Consensus."

23. See, for example, "The General Aspect of Politics in Missouri and Kentucky" and "Manufactures in South Carolina and Georgia," *American Whig Review* (August 1849), 20:214, 216; Henry Carey, "The Slave Question," *The Plough, the Loom, and the Anvil* (January 1849), 1:404–11.

24. Augusta *Chronicle*, May 17, 1849.

25. See Jackson (Miss.) *Southron*, April 19, 1844; Nashville (Tenn.) *Whig* quoted in Richmond (Va.) *Whig*, June 28, 1845; Louisville (Ky.) *Weekly Journal*, quoted in *Scientific American* (October 3, 1846), 2:13; Milledgeville (Ga.) *Southern Recorder*, quoted in *Niles' National Register* (April 2, 1842), 62:71; *Address of Representative* [Felix] *Zollicoffer, of Tennessee, to His Constituents*, quoted in *The Plough, the Loom, and the Anvil* (September 1849), 2:140–42; Prentiss, *Memoir of Prentiss*, 2:347–49; "N," "The State of Georgia—Its Duties and Destiny," *Southern Quarterly Review* (October 1845), 8:445–46; Robert R. Russel, *Economic Aspects of Southern Sectionalism*, p. 87.

26. See A[lonzo] Church, *A Discourse Delivered Before the Georgia Historical Society . . . 12th February, 1845* (Savannah, 1845), p. 8; Cole, *Whig Party in South*, pp. 69–75; Richard H. Shryock, *Georgia and the Union in 1850*, pp. 34–35; Richmond *Whig*, quoted in *Niles' National Register* (November 16, 1844), 67:169–70. The "federal basis" of representation, which counted slaves as three-fifths of a human being when apportioning legislative districts, favored the large slaveholding regions of the Deep South, which tended to be Whig. In a defense of the system, the Daily (Montgomery) *Alabama Journal*, February 19, 1850, declared: "If the institutions of the South are, or will ever be in peril, the cause will be from within, not without; and it is therefore the policy of the slaveholding interests and sections to retain in their own hands, as far as possible, political power, at least that conceded and given them in the original organization and formation of our institutions."

27. Randall M. Miller, "Daniel Pratt's Industrial Urbanism: The Cotton Mill Town in Antebellum Alabama," *Alabama Historical Quarterly* (Spring 1972), 24:22–24. On another Whig industrialist who copied some of the paternalistic practices of northern mill owners, see John H. Napier III, "Judge Edward McGhee: Cotton Planter, Pioneer Manufacturer and Mississippi Philanthropist," *Textile History Review* (January 1960), 1:27. For southern Whigs' praise of industrial paternalism in the South, see Raleigh *Register*, June 14, 1842; Richmond *Whig*, August 6, 1845; Tuscaloosa (Ala.) *Monitor*, quoted in *Niles' National Register* (June 23, 1838), 54:258; B[enjamin] F[aneuil] P[orter], "Characteristics of Alabama," *Southern Quarterly Review* (October 1849), 16:190; Richard W. Griffin and Diffie W. Standard, "The Cotton Textile Industry in Ante-Bellum North Carolina—Part II: An Era of Boom and Consolidation, 1830–1860," *North Carolina Historical Review* (April 1957), 34:155.

28. On the nature and sources of this problem, see Stanley Elkins and Eric L.

McKitrick, "A Meaning for Turner's Frontier, Part II," pp. 568–69; J. C. Bonner, "Profile of a Late Ante-Bellum Community," pp. 663–80. The southern Whigs' concern with the population drain to the West was one of the reasons for their opposition to territorial expansion. See "English Supremacy," Richmond *Whig*, June 6, 1843.

29. See Daily (Montgomery) *Alabama Journal*, October 21, 1850; "N," "The State of Georgia," pp. 447–48; Richard W. Griffin, "North Carolina: The Origin and Rise of the Cotton Textile Industry, 1830–1880" (Ph.D. diss., Ohio State University, 1954), p. 206.

30. See Congressman Kenneth R. Rayner of North Carolina, *Congressional Globe*, 27th Cong., 1st sess., July 6, 1841, app., p. 442; Congressman Meredith Gentry of Tennessee, *ibid.*, 27th Cong., 2d sess., July 11, 1842, app., p. 801; William Alexander Graham, "Inaugural Address as Governor, January 1, 1845," in Hamilton and Williams, eds., *Papers of Graham*, 3:12.

31. On the "Old Republican" gospel and its origins, see Norman K. Risjord, *The Old Republicans*; Robert E. Shalhope, "Thomas Jefferson's Republicanism and Antebellum Southern Thought."

32. See Norris W. Preyer, "Why Did Industrialization Lag in the Old South?" *Georgia Historical Quarterly* (Fall 1971), 55:378–96; Sharp, *Jacksonians Versus Banks*, pp. 266–67.

33. *Congressional Globe*, 29th Cong., 1st sess., June 27, 1846, app., p. 991.

34. The southern Whigs, like their northern counterparts, may have derived the idea that the restraints of a "civilized" society with a complex division of labor may help keep men "virtuous" from the thinkers of the Scottish Enlightenment. See Bryson, *Man and Society*, pp. 41–42, 87–95, 212–15; Chitnis, *Scottish Enlightenment*, pp. 100–1, 114–15; Rendall, *Origins of Scottish Enlightenment*, pp. 176–80.

35. Johnson, *Congressional Globe*, 29th Cong., 1st sess., July 18, 1846, app., p. 1124. See also "Address of John P. Kennedy . . . to His Constituents," *Niles' National Register* (September 27, 1845), 69:58; "N," "The State of Georgia," p. 468.

36. Richmond *Whig*, June 20, 1843. For similar comparisons, see Brownlow, *Political Register*, pp. 9–12; Haller Nutt to Dr. C. B. New, et al., September 26, 1844, *Niles' National Register* (November 9, 1844), 67:149; "Letter from J. P. Kennedy to Robert G. Campbell . . . November 21, 1844," *ibid.* (December 7, 1844), 67:217–18; S. S. Prentiss, "Speech on the Tariff," in G. L. Prentiss, *Memoir of Prentiss*, 2:342–43; Vicksburg (Miss.) *Weekly Whig*, October 28, November 28, 1844. Like their northern counterparts, the southern Whigs had nativistic tendencies; they believed that the "new immigrants" (Irish Catholics and Germans) lacked the "virtuous" self-restraint required of good citizens. See Brownlow, *Political Register*, pp. 75–119; "Letter from J. P. Kennedy to Robert G. Campbell," p. 218; Vicksburg *Weekly Whig*, November 20, 28, 1844.

37. Johnson, *Congressional Globe*, 25th Cong., 2d sess., February 1838, app., pp. 549–50; Clingman, "On the Principles of the Whig and Democratic Parties . . . ," *Selections from Speeches and Writings*, p. 152; B[enjamin] F[aneul] Porter, *The Past and*

the Present: A Discourse Delivered Before the Erosophic Society of the University of Alabama (Tuscaloosa, 1845), p. 35. See also "Common Schools," Raleigh *Register*, August 3, 1841.

38. Rayner, *Congressional Globe*, 27th Cong., 1st sess., July 6, 1842, app. 442. See also Church, *Discourse*, pp. 33–34; "N," "The State of Georgia," p. 468; Porter, *Past and Present*, p. 31.

39. Raleigh *Register*, November 2, 1850. See also New Orleans *Picayune*, June 26, 1844; Carolina *Gazette*, quoted in Raleigh *Register*, January 1, 1848.

40. Augusta *Chronicle*, July 21, 1849, quoted in Shryock, *Georgia in 1850*, p. 111; Raleigh *Register*, November 6, 1852. See also Rutherford (N.C.) *Republican*, quoted in Raleigh *Register*, November 20, 1847.

41. See Glyndon G. Van Deusen, *The Jacksonian Era*, p. 166; Russel, *Economic Aspects*, p. 33; Robert S. Starobin, *Industrial Slavery in the Old South*, p. 205.

42. On the subtreasury, distribution, and the repeal of the Whig tariff, see chapter 5 above, "Henry Clay and the Politics of Consensus"; Van Deusen, *Jacksonian Era*, pp. 160–64, 200–4. On the southern Whigs' abandonment of economic nationalism, see Cole, *Whig Party in South*, chs. 7 and 8. Writing in the aftermath of the crisis of 1850, Daniel Webster reported to a friend: "There is a clear majority in the House of Representatives in favor of a reform in the tariff of duties, although some Southern Whigs feel very angry. Three of the North Carolina members, for instance, good men and good Whigs, were found hanging off. I was asked to speak to them, or cause them to be spoken to. They said that the Northern members, Whigs and all, had done little else for six months, than assail their rights, their property, and their feelings, as Southern men, and now those Northern men might take care of their own interests." Daniel Webster to Mr. Haven, September 27, 1850, *The Writings and Speeches of Daniel Webster*, 18:391. These comments indicate the great degree to which the southern Whigs' support of high tariffs was dependent upon an atmosphere of intersectional cooperation; the North Carolinians quoted by Webster clearly believed that their northern colleagues stood more to gain from protectionism than their own wing of the party.

43. See Cole, *Whig Party in South*, pp. 207–11.

44. See Raleigh *Register*, November 9, December 11, 1850. On the efforts of the North Carolina Whig Calvin Wiley to give a sectional southern bias to educational practices in his state, see Kathryn A. Pippin, "The Common School Movement in the South, 1840–1860" (Ph.D. diss., University of North Carolina at Chapel Hill, 1977), pp. 136–37. There were, of course, parallel movements in other southern states (which were often led by Whigs).

45. See, for example, Congressman Edward P. Stanly of North Carolina, *Congressional Globe*, 32d Cong., 1st sess., June 12, 1850, app., p. 696.

46. See F. A. P. Barnard, *An Oration Delivered before the Citizens of Tuscaloosa, Alabama, July 4th, 1851* . . . (Tuscaloosa, 1851), pp. 26–27, 32; Cole, *Whig Party in South*, pp. 209–11.

47. On the Democrats' appropriation of Whiggish economic programs at the state level, see Holt, *Political Crisis*, pp. 113–19; Marc Wayne Kruman, "Parties

and Politics in North Carolina," pp. 104–7; Russel, *Economic Aspects*, p. 173. For the arguments of southern rights' Democrats in favor of the South's economic development (which closely paralleled those also used by the southern Whigs), see Eugene D. Genovese, *The Political Economy of Slavery*, pp. 227–30; Starobin, *Industrial Slavery*, pp. 207–8; Ronald T. Takaki, *A Proslavery Crusade*, pp. 40–42.

48. For material which suggests the appeal to former southern Whigs of Know-Nothingism and Constitutional Unionism, see William A. Graham, "Speech at Whig National Convention, September 17, 1856," *Papers of Graham*, 4:654–57; Burton Alva Konkle, *John Motley Morehead and the Development of North Carolina*, pp. 326–37, 366–69; Robertson, *Alexander H. H. Stuart*, pp. 59–162; Michael Marrius Carriere, Jr., "The Know Nothing Movement in Louisiana" (Ph.D. diss., Louisiana State Univesity, 1977); Degler, *Other South*, pp. 115–16, 160–61; W. Darrell Overdyke, *The Know-Nothing Party in the South*. Like the Whigs before them, the Constitutional Unionists (often praised by historians for their nationalism and moderation) presented themselves in the South as reliable protectors of slavery, while they denounced their opponents as untrustworthy on the issue. See John V. Mering, "The Slave-State Constitutional Unionists and the Politics of Consensus," *Journal of Southern History* (August 1977), 43:395–410; Mering, "The Constitutional Unionists of 1860: An Example of the Paranoid Style," *Mid-America* (April–July 1978), 60:95–106.

8. Alexander Stephens: States' Rights Whig

1. On the "ethic of responsibility," see H. H. Gerth and C. Wright Mills, eds., *From Max Webster: Essays in Sociology* (New York: Oxford University Press, 1946), pp. 120–28.

2. *Speech of Mr.* [Kenneth] *Rayner, of North Carolina, on the Sub-Treasury Bill, Made in the House of Representatives, June 22, 1840* (Washington, 1840), pp. 13–14.

3. *Ibid.*, pp. 13–14.

4. Of course, there was an older generation of southern and border-state politicians—best represented by Clay—who, influenced by the republicanism of the American Revolution, never embraced slavery as a "positive good." But, as statesmen, they would do nothing which might derange social relations in the South. It is worth noting, however, that Clay's ambivalent attitudes toward slavery allowed him to retain much moral and political capital with the antislavery Whigs of the North. This was not true, however, of the younger generation of southern politicians, including Stephens.

5. I have tried to suggest some of the problems the northern Whigs' nationalistic economic policies created for the southern Whigs in chapter 7, "The Southern Whigs and Economic Development."

6. Kinley J. Brauer, *Cotton Versus Conscience*.

7. See the passages from Stephens' speeches reprinted in Henry Cleveland, *Alexander H. Stephens, in Public and Private*, pp. 285–86, 337, 349, 414–15, 421–22, 555–56, 642–43, 647, 692–93.

8. See *ibid.*, pp. 421–22, 427–28, 555–56, 575.

9. *Ibid.*, p. 575.

10. On the code of southern "honor," see Eugene D. Genovese, *Roll, Jordan, Roll*, pp. 89–96; Bertram Wyatt-Brown, *Southern Honor: Ethics and Behavior in the Old South* (New York: Oxford University Press, 1982).

11. When he was a young man, Stephens adopted the middle name "Hamilton" as a tribute to one of his patrons, Alexander Hamilton Webster.

12. James Z. Rabun, ed., "Alexander H. Stephens' Diary, 1834–37," *Georgia Historical Quarterly* (March 1952), 36:73–74; Rabun, "Alexander H. Stephens," pp. 16–17.

13. Rabun, "Stephens," ch. 1.

14. As Rabun, "Stephens," pp. 68–69, points out, the Georgia judicial system did not permit appeals to the superior court of verdicts in criminal cases. Hence, the ability to win jury verdicts in the lower courts was a highly valued talent, and oratory was crucial to winning jury verdicts.

15. It has often been noted that the robust and mercurial Toombs was the perfect physical and emotional complement to the sickly and cerebral Stephens. Perhaps it is significant that Stephens once wrote of Toombs: "His true greatness did not consist in statesmanship; he was governed too much by passion and impulse." Quoted in Myrta L. Avery, ed., *Recollections of Alexander H. Stephens* (New York: Harper, 1910), p. 427.

16. Although farming was an avocation for Stephens, he owned 13 slaves by 1850 and 34 by 1860. Rabun, "Stephens," pp. 166–67. On Stephens' duel challenges (none of which were taken up), see Rabun, "Stephens," pp. 186–88.

17. Hamilton, *Crisis and Compromise*, p. 38 (first quotation); Varina Howell Davis, *Jefferson Davis, Ex-President of the Confederate States of America*, 2 vols. (New York, 1890), 1:411. Stephens' shrill voice and physique (he was five feet seven inches tall and usually weighed about a hundred pounds) often prompted comparisons between himself and John Randolph. For more descriptions of Stephens, see Forney, *Anecdotes of Public Men*, 2:165; Hilliard, *Politics and Pen Pictures*, pp. 118–19; Rabun, "Stephens," p. 111.

18. See Cleveland, *Stephens*, pp. 50–51, 54–55, 62–63; Rudolph Von Abele, *Alexander Stephens*, pp. 76, 83, 134–35; Rabun, ed., "Diary," pp. 78–80.

19. Alexander Stephens to Linton Stephens, February 3, 1851, quoted in Richard Malcolm Johnston and William Hand Browne, *Life of Alexander H. Stephens*, p. 263.

20. Some of the sources of Stephens' popularity with his constituents may be gathered from C. Vann Woodward, *Tom Watson: Agrarian Rebel* (New York: Oxford University Press, 1938), pp. 39–40.

21. Alexander Stephens to Linton Stephens, June 2, 1842, quoted in James D. Waddell, *Biographical Sketch of Linton Stephens*, p. 38.

22. For Stephens' observations of Crawfordville life, see Rabun, ed., "Diary," p. 93 (June 25, 1834); Rabun, ed., "Alexander Stephens' Diary, Part II," *Georgia Historical Quarterly* (June 1952), 36:165–66 (September 7, 1834), 177 (February 26,

1835). Of course, Stephens' religion was distinctively southern in nature. To him, religion was almost purely a *private* matter, pertaining to the salvation of the individual; it had no implications for the reconstruction of society, or for politics. Like southern politicians of both parties, Stephens had no truck for the "perfectionism" of the northern evangelicals who bulked large in the following of the Whig party above the Mason-Dixon line. See Anne C. Loveland, *Southern Evangelicals and the Social Order, 1800–1860* (Baton Rouge: Louisiana State University Press, 1980); Donald S. Mathews, *Religion in the Old South* (Chicago: University of Chicago Press, 1977), pp. 65, 77–78. Needless to say, the strict separation between private faith and public conduct was a necessary feature of religious faith in a slaveholding society. Stephens claimed that the Bible, when read literally, upheld the morality of slavery. See U.S. Congress, House, *Congressional Globe*, 29th Cong., 2d sess., February 12, 1847, app., p. 354.

23. Alexander Stephens to Linton Stephens, April 19, 1850, quoted in Waddell, *Linton Stephens*, pp. 103–5.

24. Alexander Stephens to Linton Stephens, February 2, 1840, *ibid.*, p. 19.

25. *Ibid.*

26. Stephens "reprinted" the 1834 speech in 1864, but the "reprinted" version probably reveals more about his attitudes in 1864 than thirty years earlier. See Rabun, "Stephens," pp. 51–52.

27. Rabun, ed., "Diary, Part II," p. 174 (July 4, 1835).

28. See Paul Murray, *The Whigs of Georgia*, chs. 3 and 4.

29. See Rabun, ed., "Diary," pp. 81–82 (May 8, 1834). Stephens was "upon the whole . . . favorably impressed" when he met Jackson in the Executive Mansion. Rabun, ed., "Diary, Part II," p. 187 (January 8, 1837).

30. See Von Abele, *Stephens Biography*, pp. 62–63. On the abolitionists' propaganda offensive, see Leonard Richards, *"Gentlemen of Property and Standing": Anti-Abolition Mobs in Jacksonian America* (New York: Oxford University Press, 1970), pp. 51–52.

31. Stephens was returned to the state legislature in 1837, 1839, and 1840. Von Abele, *Stephens Biography*, pp. 66–68.

32. Stephens, like other members of the State Rights party, was especially critical of Georgia's Central Bank. This institution, which was financed and run by the state, provided Georgians with credit when they could not obtain it from commercial banks. Stephens charged it with fueling inflation and selling political influence. See Rabun, "Stephens," pp. 92–93; Milton Heath, *Constructive Liberalism: The Role of the State in Economic Development in Georgia to 1860* (Cambridge, Mass.: Harvard University Press, 1954), pp. 211–15.

33. See Rabun, "Stephens," pp. 88–91.

34. See Forrest David Matthews, "The Politics of Education in the Deep South: Alabama and Georgia, 1830–1860" (Ph.D. diss., Columbia University, 1965), pp. 109–12.

35. Stephens' proslavery views and states' rightism were evidenced by his conduct during a controversy over several Maine residents accused of stealing

slaves from Georgia. Stephens introduced a bill in the state legislature under whose provisions all Maine residents who entered Georgia would be treated as if they were slave-stealers. See Rabun, "Stephens," pp. 98–99. For Stephens' involvement in the movement for direct southern trade with Europe, see Von Abele, *Stephens Biography*, pp. 71–73.

36. Quoted in Johnston and Browne, *Life of Stephens*, pp. 134–37.

37. Rabun, "Stephens," pp. 104–5. The anti-Clay theory is suggested by the fact that Stephens condemned Clay by name in the July 4, 1839 speech.

38. Rabun, "Stephens," pp. 104–5. In an 1868 letter (Johnston and Browne, *Lilfe of Stephens*, p. 140), Stephens lamented his having joined the Whigs.

39. Alexander Stephens to Linton Stephens, April 4, 1841, Stephens Papers (Purchase).

40. Rabun, "Stephens," pp. 136–37. Stephens had concluded his July 4, 1839 speech with the following peroration: "Henry Clay and Martin Van Buren: candidates for the next Presidency. When the strife is between Caesar and Pompey, the patriot shall rally to the standard of neither." Quoted in Johnston and Browne, *Life of Stephens*, p. 137.

41. "Report of the Minority of the Committee on the State of the Repubic," Cleveland, *Stephens*, pp. 246–49. For Stephens' claim to authorship of the minority report, see Alexander Stephens to John M. Berrien, December 8, 1842, Berrien Papers.

42. "Report of the Minority," Cleveland, *Stephens*, pp. 249–50, 255, 257–58.

43. U.S. Congress, House, *Congressional Globe*, 28th Cong., 1st sess., May 7, 1844, p. 582. Stephens was first elected to Congress on a statewide ticket. In later contests, he represented the Eighth Congressional District of Georgia.

44. *Ibid.*, pp. 582–83. On the land issue, Stephens opposed graduation, unless it took account of the quality of land. He also insisted on the distribution of the proceeds of the sale of the public lands, so the older states (including Georgia) would receive benefits in return for ceding territory to the Union. See *Congressional Globe*, 29th Cong., 1st sess., July 7, 1846, app., pp. 1103–7.

45. Stephens pronounced Clay's "Raleigh letter," which opposed the immediate annexation of Texas, "full, clear, and satisfactory." Alexander Stephens to Linton Stephens, April 22, 1844, Stephens Papers (Purchase).

46. Alexander Stephens to James Thomas, May 5, 1844, in Ulrich B. Phillips, ed., "The Correspondence of Robert Toombs, Alexander Stephens, and Howell Cobb," 2:57–58. Hereinafter referred to as "TSC Corr."

47. Rabun, "Stephens," p. 145.

48. Alexander Stephens to George W. Crawford, December 23, 1844, quoted in Rabun, "Stephens," p. 150.

49. See the discussion of Texas annexation in Brock, *Parties*, pp. 158–59.

50. *Ibid.*, pp. 160–61. Stephens' role in Texas' annexation created unhappiness among some of the Whigs of Georgia, especially the faction of Senator Berrien, which disliked the bypassing of the treaty-making power of the Senate. Stephens, however, reportedly said that it would be politically "fatal" for the

Georgia Whigs to oppose the immediate acquisition of Texas. See Charles J. Jenkins to John MacPherson Berrien, February 3, April 22, May 3, 1845, Berrien Papers.

51. The Whigs' delicate situation during the Mexican War is best discussed in John H. Schroeder, *Mr. Polk's War*, chs. 2, 3, 5, 8.

52. "Speech on the Subject of the Mexican War," in Cleveland, *Stephens*, pp. 313–14. Cf. the slightly different version in *Congressional Globe*, 29th Cong., 1st sess., June 16, 1846, app., p. 946.

53. "Speech on Mexican War," in Cleveland, *Stephens*, p. 319. Cf. *Congressional Globe*, 29th Cong., 1st sess., June 16, 1846, app., pp. 949–50.

54. "Speech on Mexican War," Cleveland, *Stephens*, pp. 160–61. Cf. *Congressional Globe*, 29th Cong., 1st sess., June 16, 1846, app., p. 950.

55. Schroeder, *Mr. Polk's War*, pp. 51–52, 62.

56. "Speech on the Mexican Appropriation, '3 Million Bill,'" in Cleveland, *Stephens*, p. 330. Cf. the version in *Congressional Globe*, 29th Cong., 2d sess., February 12, 1847, App., pp. 353–54.

57. "Speech on Mexican Appropriation," Cleveland, *Stephens*, p. 334. Cf. the version in *Congressional Globe*, 29th Cong., 2d sess., February 12, 1847, app., p. 354. Stephens' position on the Mexican War typified that of most of the southern Whigs. See Congressman M. P. Gentry of Tennessee, *Congressional Globe*, 29th Cong., 2d sess., December 16, 1846, app., pp. 56–61; Congressman E. H. Ewing of Tennessee, *ibid.*, 29th Cong., 2d sess., January 28, 1847, app., pp. 268–72; Senator John MacPherson Berrien of Georgia, *ibid.*, 29th Cong., 2d sess., February 5, 1847, app., pp. 296–302; Congressman Milton Brown of Tennessee, *ibid.*, 29th Cong., 2d sess., February 12, 1847, app., pp. 354–58; Senator George E. Badger of North Carolina, *ibid.*, 30th Cong., 1st sess., January 18, 1848, app., pp. 116–22; Senator John Bell of Tennessee, *ibid.*, 30th Cong., 1st sess., February 2, 3, 1848, app., pp. 189–201.

58. Rabun, "Stephens," pp. 191–92, 197–98. On the popularity of the "no territory" position among the Whigs, see Schroeder, *Mr. Polk's War*, pp. 86–87.

59. See Potter, *Impending Crisis*, pp. 1–6, 67–70.

60. *Ibid.*, p. 75. In the House, all 73 northern Whigs voted against the Clayton bill. They were joined by 9 southern Whigs and 30 northern Democrats. The Clayton bill was favored by 71 Democrats and 26 southern Whigs. Here, "southern" refers to all the states with slavery, "northern" to the nonslave states.

61. "Speech on the Territorial Bill, Delivered August 8, 1848," in Cleveland, *Stephens*, pp. 336–38. Cf. the slightly different version in *Congressional Globe*, 30th Cong., 1st sess., August 8, 1848, app., p. 1104.

62. "Speech on the Territorial Bill," in Cleveland, *Stephens*, p. 349. Cf. the slightly different version in *Congressional Globe*, 30th Cong., 1st sess., August 8, 1848, app., p. 1106. According to one observer, Stephens' position on the Clayton compromise was not popular in Georgia. By his estimate, two-thirds of the Whigs in the state favored the Clayton plan. Here, as in the controversy over Texas annexation, it is possible to see political motives behind Stephens' militant

defense of southern "rights." The Clayton bill was favored by Berrien, and Stephens' opposition may have been one way he demonstrated his independence of the Berrien faction by posing as a more faithful champion of southern interests. See Iverson Harris to John MacPherson Berrien, August 23, 1848, Berrien Papers. The relevant points here are that Stephens thought that there was a constituency for his position in Georgia, and that he considered it consistent with Whig principles.

63. Rabun, "Stephens," pp. 216–31; Cooper, *South and Politics*, pp. 245–46, 249.

64. See Toombs to Crittenden, January 3, 22, 1849, in Phillips, "TSC Corr.," pp. 139–42. Stephens dismissed the Calhoun movement as an effort of "the factionists of the South . . . to get up [excitement] about 'Niggers,' " in order to divide the Whigs. Stephens to G. W. Crawford, December 27, 1848, Stephens Papers (LC).

65. Rabun, "Stephens," pp. 235–36; Cooper, *South and Politics*, p. 272. The Dawson bill made provision for the possible partioning of the new state in the future.

66. Cooper, *South and Politics*, pp. 273, 377–78.

67. *Ibid.*, pp. 280–81.

68. Potter, *Impending Crisis*, p. 87.

69. *Ibid.*, pp. 88–89, 94; Cooper, *South and Politics*, pp. 277–78, 290, 292.

70. Rabun, "Stephens," pp. 255–60.

71. Alexander Stephens to James Thomas, February 13, 1850, in Phillips, ed., "TSC Corr.," p. 184.

72. Rabun, "Stephens," pp. 248–50.

73. *Ibid.*, p. 255.

74. Holman Hamilton, *Zachary Taylor: Soldier in the White House* (Indianapolis: Bobbs-Merrill, 1951), pp. 380–82; Harriet A. Weed, ed., *Life of Thurlow Weed, Including His Autobiography and a Memoir*, 2 vols. (Boston, 1883), 2:176–79. This was the encounter which prompted Webster's March 7 speech.

75. Potter, *Impending Crisis*, pp. 99–100.

76. During the 1850 and 1851 election campaigns in Georgia, the Constitutional Unionists exploited the resentments of the small farmers of northern Georgia (the "wool-hat boys") against the secessionist planters of the cotton belt. Stephens, for example, told one audience that if Georgia seceded, "you wool hat boys will have to do the fighting." Augusta *Constitutionalist*, August 13, 1851, quoted in Rabun, "Stephens," p. 310.

77. Some idea of the diverse constituencies of the crisis parties may be gathered from Horace Montgomery, *Cracker Parties*, pp. 26–32; Richard Shryock, *Georgia and the Union in 1850*, pp. 285–94, 308–13, 319–22.

78. Shryock, *Georgia and Union*, pp. 290–91, 313–14.

79. *Debates and Proceedings of the Georgia Convention, 1850* (Milledgeville, Ga., 1850), p. 9.

80. Stephens hoped for the emergence of a party of "Conservatives" or "Constitutional Union men" who would oppose the "Spoilsmen" agitating the

slavery issue. See Alexander Stephens to Linton Stephens, December 10, 1851, in Phillips, ed., "TSC Corr.," pp. 271–74. Toombs echoed this sentiment in his letter to A. H. Chappell, et al., in *Union Celebration in Macon, Georgia, February 22, 1851* (Macon, 1851), pp. 7–8. Significantly, Cobb and the Union Democrats never embraced the idea of a national third party.

81. Montgomery, *Cracker Parties*, pp. 44–45, 53–59. In 1852 Cobb's wing of the Democracy ran a separate ticket from that of the "regular" (Southern Rights) Democrats, but both Democratic factions backed the Pierce-King ticket.

82. The Milledgeville *Federal Union* estimated that in 1851 the Southern Rights party won the votes of 36,000 Democrats and 3,000 Whigs, while the Constitutional Unionists won those of 13,000 Democrats and 44,000 Whigs. Cited in Montgomery, *Cracker Parties*, p. 48, n. 41. While these numbers may not be precisely accurate, they probably do reflect the relative proportions of Democrats and Whigs in the "crisis parties."

83. Alexander Stephens to the editor of Augusta *Chronicle and Sentinel*, June 28, 1852, in Phillips, ed., "TSC Corr.," pp. 304–6; Montgomery, *Cracker Parties*, pp. 63–68.

84. Von Abele, *Stephens Biography*, pp. 139–40. Even though Webster was dead, his ticket received over 5,000 votes in Georgia, and it received a majority of the vote in Stephens' home county, Taliaferro.

85. In 1860 Breckinridge received 52,172 votes in Georgia; Bell, 43,069; and Douglas, 11,627.

86. Explaining his decision to yield to secession, Stephens wrote: "the wise man—the patriot and statesman in either section—will take the fact as it exists, and do the best he can under the circumstances as he finds them[,] for the good, peace, welfare, and happiness of his own country." Stephens to Samuel Glenn, February 8, 1861, Stephens Papers (LC).

87. For some of the consequences of the anti-party ideology of the Confederacy, see Eric L. McKitrick, "Party Politics and the Union and Confederate War Efforts," in W. N. Chambers and W. D. Burnham, eds., *The American Party Systems* (New York: Oxford University Press, 1967), pp. 117–51.

88. For the role of Stephens in the Confederacy, see Pendleton, *Alexander Stephens*, ch. 16; Von Abele, *Stephens Biography*, pp. 208–14, 220–27, 232–33.

9. Conclusion

1. Young, *Washington Community*, pp. 250–52. The phrase "at a distance and out of sight" was used by Hamilton in *The Federalist*, no. 27.

2. Jackson (Miss.) *Southron*, April 26, 1843.

3. For a perceptive discussion of this aspect of Whig thought, see Jean V. Matthews, *Rufus Choate*, pp. 81–103.

4. See Michael F. Holt, "Winding Roads to Recovery." Taylor himself realized the declining appeal of the Whigs' economic programs. See Zachary Taylor to Jefferson Davis, July 27, August 16, 1847, April 18, 1848, Taylor Papers. But a

mild recession in late 1848, which seems to have hit the industrialized northeast most severely, may have helped the Whigs by increasing popular support for a protective tariff. See Holt, "Winding Roads," p. 164.

5. See Holt, *Political Crisis*, pp. 109–21; Shade, *Banks or No Banks*, ch. 5; Sharp, *Jacksonians Versus Banks*, pp. 321–29. To be certain, there were controversies over government aid to railroads; but these tended to divide voters and politicians along geographical rather than partisan lines.

6. See Daniel D. Barnard, "The Whigs and Their Candidate," *American Whig Review* (September 1848), 8:234; J. A. Campbell to John C. Calhoun, November 20, 1847, in J. Franklin Jameson, ed., *Correspondence of John C. Calhoun* (Washington: Government Printing Office, 1900), p. 1141.

7. For the congressional Whigs' polarization on issues affecting slavery, see Alexander, *Sectional Stress and Party Strength*, p. 111; Richard Wallace Sadler, "The Impact of the Slavery Question on the Whig Party in Congress, 1843–1854" (Ph.D. diss, University of Utah, 1969); Silbey, *Shrine of Party*, ch. 8.

8. For some perceptive observations on the Democrats' largely indifferent response to the moral dimension of the slavery issue, see McFaul, "Expediency Versus Morality."

9. See Norman A. Graebner, "1848: Southern Politics at the Crossroads."

10. In the Thirty-first Congress (1849–1851), the Whigs held 105 of 233 seats in the House; in the Thirty-second (1851–1853), 88 of 233; in the Thirty-third, 72 of 234. In 1850 the Whigs held 10 of the 31 governorships; in 1852, 5; in 1853, 6; and in 1854, only 3. For these figures, and the Whigs' performance in state legislative elections, see *Whig Almanac and United States Register* (New York, 1848–53).

11. See John F. Coleman, *The Disruption of the Pennsylvania Democracy*, pp. 55, 58, 63–67; Arthur C. Cole, *The Era of the Civil War*, p. 112; Formisano, *Birth of Parties*, pp. 222–38; Clifford S. Griffin, *Their Brothers' Keepers*, pp. 116–51; Holt, *Forging Majority*, pp. 77–78, 81–83, 114–15, 135–36; Holt, *Political Crisis*, pp. 131–32; Potter, *Impending Crisis*, pp. 241–45.

12. See Congressman Christopher H. Williams of Tennessee, *Congressional Globe*, 32d Cong., 1st sess., March 31, 1852, app., pp. 371–73; Congressman Alexander H. Stephens of Georgia, *ibid.*, April 27, 1852, app., pp. 459–64; Congressman Ben Edwards Grey of Kentucky, *ibid.*, May 17, 1852, app., p. 622; Congressman Addison White of Kentucky, *ibid.*, May 26, 1852, app., pp. 629–36; Cooper, *South and Politics*, pp. 339–40; Holt, *Political Crisis*, pp. 90–91; Robert J. Rayback, *Millard Fillmore: Biography of a President* (Buffalo: Buffalo Historical Society, 1959), ch. 14.

13. Congressman Orin Fowler of Massachusetts, *Congressional Globe*, 32d Cong., 1st sess., March 31, 1852, app., p. 398. See also Senator John Davis of Massachusetts, *ibid.*, January 28, 1852, app., p. 133; Congressman Lewis D. Campbell of Ohio, *ibid.*, March 5, 1852, app., pp. 261–74; Congressman A. P. Hascall of New York, *ibid.*, May 17, 1852, app., pp. 585–98; Congressman Israel Washburn of Maine, *ibid.*, May 24, 1852, app., pp. 622–27. Northern Whigs in the House voted against the passage of the Fugitive Slave Law, 50–3,

while Democratic congressmen from the North favored it, 26–16. Potter, *Impending Crisis*, p. 236, n. 25.

14. For a list of those signing the Round Robin, see *Congressional Globe*, 32d Cong., 1st sess., March 31, 1852, app., p. 372. For an analysis of its signers, see Holt, *Political Crisis*, pp. 94–95.

15. *Congressional Globe*, 32d Cong., 1st sess., December 1, 1851, pp. 6–11.

16. For the votes on the "finality" resolutions, see *ibid.*, April 7, 1852, p. 983. According to Alexander Stephens, the "finality" resolution submitted by Congressman Julius Hillyer of Georgia was supported 36–20 by northern Democrats, 30–16 by southern Democrats, and 22–1 by southern Whigs. But the northern Whigs opposed the resolution, 27–10. See *Congressional Globe*, 32d Cong., 1st sess., April 27, 1851, app., p. 461.

17. The proceedings of these conventions were watched closely by southern Whig politicians. See, for example, Congressman C. J. Faulkner of Virginia, *Congressional Globe*, 32d Cong., 1st sess., August 2, 1852, p. 879. In Pennsylvania, the Democrats sought the repeal of a law which forbade the use of the state's jails for the incarceration of fugitive slaves. The Whig governor and state legislators opposed this effort. See Coleman, *Disruption of Pennsylvania Democracy*, pp. 45–46.

18. The quotation is from Augustine Shepperd to William Alexander Graham, April 26, 1852, Hamilton and Williams, eds., *Papers of Graham*, 4:295. See also Congressman Christopher H. Williams of Tennessee, *Congressional Globe*, 32d Cong., 1st sess., March 31, 1852, app., p. 373; Congressman David Outlaw of North Carolina, *ibid.*, June 10, 1852, app., p. 678; Cole, *Whig Party in South*, pp. 224–25, 230–32; Cooper, *South and Politics*, pp. 324–25.

19. For the vote declaring the finality resolutions out of order, see Congressman Ben Edwards Grey of Kentucky, *Congressional Globe*, 32d Cong., 1st sess., May 17, 1852, app., p. 622. The northern Whigs who were present voted 39–7 in favor of tabling, while the southern Whigs who were present voted 14–7 against. For descriptions of the caucus' proceedings, see Congressman David Outlaw of North Carolina, *ibid.*, June 10, 1852, app., pp. 675–76; Congressman C. J. Faulkner of Virginia, *ibid.*, August 2, 1852, app., pp. 880–81.

20. See Cole, *Whig Party in South*, pp. 258–59; Cooper, *South and Politics*, pp. 327, 335–37, 339–40; Lawrence Bruser, "Political Anti-Slavery in Connecticut," pp. 156–57; Philip S. Foner, *Business and Slavery*, pp. 82, 84–87.

21. See Kenneth B. Shover, "The Free State Whig and the Idea of a Conservative Strategy," pp. 261–62.

22. Some Whigs confessed this openly. See Congressman David Outlaw of North Carolina, *Congressional Globe*, 32d Cong., 1st sess., June 10, 1852, app., p. 676; Congressman C. J. Faulkner of Virginia, *ibid.*, August 2, 1852, app., p. 876; Stephen L. Hanson, *The Making of the Third Party System*, pp. 8–9. Fillmore's partisan use of the patronage, especially to favor the procompromise faction within the Whig party, undercut the Whigs' claims to being a party above such practices.

23. See Coleman, *Disruption of Pennsylvania Democracy*, pp.55–58; Holt, *Forging Majority*, p. 108; Holt, *Political Crisis*, pp. 125–26; Potter, *Impending Crisis*, p. 234.

24. See Bruser, "Anti-Slavery in Connecticut," pp. 158–59; Formisano, *Birth of Parties*, pp. 205–6; Holt, *Political Crisis*, p. 131; Eugene H. Roseboom, *The Civil War Era*, pp. 205–6. "Free Democratic" was the new name adopted by the Free Soil party. In Georgia, the Whigs referred to themselves as "the conservative men of Georgia." On the Whig decline in the South in 1853, see Cooper, *South and Politics*, pp. 341–44.

25. The northern Whigs voted 44–0 against the bill in the House and 6–0 against it in the Senate. The southern Whigs voted 12–7 for Kansas-Nebraska in the House and 9–1 in its favor in the Senate. These figures for the southern Whigs are subject to dispute, however, for some southerners counted as Whigs (such as Stephens and Toombs) had already disavowed their ties with the northern Whigs. See Arthur C. Cole, *The Whig Party in the South*, p. 287, n. 17; Potter, *Impending Crisis*, p. 167, n. 39. My purpose here will be to provide a broad survey of the reasons for the disintegration of the Whig party in the Kansas-Nebraska crisis. For more detailed studies of the Whigs' decline, and the consequent rise of the Know-Nothing and Republican parties, see Foner, *Free Soil*, passim; William E. Gienapp, "The Origins of the Republican Party" (Ph.D. diss., University of California at Berkeley, 1980); Paul Kleppner, *The Third Electoral System*, chs. 2–4.

26. *Congressional Globe*, 33d Cong., 1st sess., February 23, 1854, app., p. 346. See also Senator Archibald Dixon of Kentucky, *ibid.*, February 4, 1854, app., pp. 140–45; Senator George E. Badger of North Carolina, *ibid.*, February 16, 1854, app., pp. 145–50; Congressman Alexander H. Stephens of Georgia, *ibid.*, February 17, 1854, app., pp. 193–97; Congressman Felix Zollicoffer of Tennessee, *ibid.*, May 9, 1854, app., pp. 584–87; Senator Judah Benjamin of Louisiana, *ibid.*, May 25, 1854, app., pp. 766–68; Cooper, *South and Politics*, pp. 349–62.

27. *Congressional Globe*, 33d Cong., 1st sess., February 17, 1854, app., p. 151. In any case, the northern Whigs in Congress did argue that Kansas and Nebraska were suited to slavery. See Charles D. Hart, "The Natural Limits of Slavery Expansion: Kansas-Nebraska, 1854," *Kansas Historical Quarterly* (February 1968), 34:32–40.

28. "Speech at Peoria," October 16, 1854, in Basler, ed., *Works of Lincoln*, 2:274. See also Congressman Lewis D. Campbell of Ohio, *Congressional Globe*, 33d Cong., 1st sess., February 17, 1854, app., pp. 245–46; Senator Benjamin Wade of Ohio, *ibid.*, March 3, 1854, app., p. 300; Senator William P. Fessenden of Maine, *ibid.*, March 3, 1854, app., pp. 321–22; Congressman Thomas D. Eliot of Massachusetts, *ibid.*, May 10, 1854, app., p. 575; Congressman George A. Simmons of New York, *ibid.*, May 10, 1854, app., p. 592. For the similar responses of northern Whig politicians at the state level, see Cole, *Era of Civil War*, pp. 119–20; Coleman, *Disruption of Pennsylvania Democracy*, p. 69; Hanson, *Third Party System*, pp. 41–42; Roseboom, *Civil War Era*, pp. 279–80; Streeter, *Parties in*

Michigan, pp. 184–85; Emma Lou Thornbrough, *Indiana in the Civil War Era*, pp. 54–55.

29. The situation of these Whigs was well described by Congressman James Brooks of New York in *Congressional Globe*, 32d Cong., 1st sess., April 23, 1852, p. 1172.

30. *Congressional Globe*, 33d Cong., 1st sess., February 27, 1854, app., pp. 505, 508. See also Senator Edward Everett of Massachusetts, *ibid.*, February 8, 1854, app., pp. 158–63; Bruser, "Anti-Slavery in Connecticut," pp. 198–201; Foner, *Free Soil*, pp. 193–94; O'Connor, *Lords of Loom*, ch. 6; Roseboom, *Civil War Era*, p. 298; Warner, "Silver Grays," pp. 252–53.

31. *Congressional Globe*, 33d Cong., 1st sess., February 10, 11, 1854, app., p. 177. See also Edward Everett, *ibid.*, February 8, 1854, app., p. 163; Bruser, "Anti-Slavery in Connecticut," pp. 188–89; Warner, "Silver Grays," ch. 4.

32. *Congressional Globe*, 33d Cong., 1st sess., March 3, 1854, app., p. 414. See also Congressman William Preston of Kentucky, *ibid.*, April 6, 1854, app., pp. 478–82; Congressman Emerson Etheridge of Tennessee, *ibid.*, May 17, 1854, app., pp. 830–37; Congressman Theodore G. Hunt of Louisiana, *ibid.*, May 23, 1854, app., pp. 434–39.

33. To be sure, local remnants of the Whig party survived the Kansas-Nebraska crisis, and there were periodic attempts to revive the Whigs as a national party. A national Whig convention did meet in 1856, but it served largely as an adjunct to the Know-Nothing party, whose national ticket it endorsed. For the proceedings of this convention, see New York *Times*, September 18, 1856.

34. See Ray Allen Billington, *The Protestant Crusade*, chs. 7 and 8; Holt, *Political Crisis*, pp. 162–63. The nativists were particularly upset by the arrival in the United States of a papal nuncio sent to settle disputes over the control of ecclesiastical property. Anti-Catholicism was consistent with the Whigs' emphasis on freedom of conscience, as the "popish" church was condemned by nativists for being dictatorial in matters of faith and doctrine. However, some former Antimasons among the Whigs were repelled by the Know-Nothings' secrecy, which they saw as an unacceptable limitation on individual freedom of expression. See Holt, *Forging Majority*, pp. 150, 308–9.

35. See, for example, Anna Ella Carroll, *The Great American Battle . . .* (New York, 1856), pp. 108–9, 149, 176; Thomas R. Whitney, *A Defence of the American Policy* (New York, 1856).

36. See Carroll, *Great American Battle*, pp. 117, 120–23, 135–27; Jean H. Baker, *Ambivalent Americans: The Know-Nothing Party in Maryland* (Baltimore: Johns Hopkins University Press, 1977), ch. 2; Foner, *Free Soil*, pp. 195–97; W. Darrell Overdyke, *The Know-Nothing Party in the South*; Roseboom, *Civil War Era*, pp. 298–300; Shover, "Free State Whig," pp. 262–63; Streeter, *Parties in Michigan*, pp. 178–82. The Know-Nothing party arose out of the Order of the Star-Spangled Banner, a secret society dominated by conservative, fervently nationalistic Whigs. See Billington, *Protestant Crusade*, p. 380–407.

37. Southern Democrats were well aware of this fact, and used it to embarass the southern Know-Nothings. See James P. Hambleton, *A Biographical Sketch of Henry A. Wise* . . . (Richmond, 1855), pp. 106–7, 127, 212–13, 250–52, 304–8, 330, 335. See also William G. Bean, "An Aspect of Know-Nothingism: The Immigrant and Slavery," *South Atlantic Quarterly* (October 1924), 23:320–24; Potter, *Impending Crisis*, p. 252.

38. See Bean, "Immigrant and Slavery," pp. 324–25; Harry J. Carman and Reinhard H. Luthin, "Some Aspects of the Know-Nothing Movement Reconsidered," *South Atlantic Quarterly* (June 1940), 39:221–22; Overdyke, *Know-Nothing Party in South*, ch. 11.

39. Stephen E. Maizlish, "The Meaning of Nativism and the Crisis of the Union"; Potter, *Impending Crisis*, pp. 255–57; Rayback, *Fillmore*, p. 413. The Constitutional Union party, which emerged out of the wreckage of the Know-Nothing movement, was also dominated by its pro-slavery southern wing. See Mering, "Slave-State Constitutional Unionists"; Potter, *Impending Crisis*, p. 439.

SELECTED BIBLIOGRAPHY

MANUSCRIPT COLLECTIONS

Adams Family Papers. Microfilm edition. Massachusetts Historical Society, Boston, Massachusetts.

John MacPherson Berrien Papers. Southern Historical Collection, University of North Carolina at Chapel Hill.

Henry Clay Papers. Library of Congress, Washington, D.C.

Horace Greeley Papers. New York Public Library, New York, New York.

William H. Seward Papers. Rush Rhees Library, University of Rochester, Rochester, New York.

Alexander Stephens Papers. Library of Congress, Washington, D.C.

Alexander Stephens Papers. Manhattanville College of the Sacred Heart, Purchase, New York.

Zachary Taylor Papers. Library of Congress, Washington, D.C.

John Tyler Papers. Library of Congress, Washington, D.C.

Daniel Webster Papers. Microfilm edition. Edited by Charles M. Wiltse. Dartmouth College, Hanover, New Hampshire.

Thurlow Weed Papers. Rush Rhees Library, University of Rochester, Rochester, New York.

CONTEMPORARY BOOKS, MEMOIRS, AND OTHER WRITINGS

An Abstract of the Proceedings of the Anti-Masonic State Convention of Massachusetts, Held in Faneuil Hall, Boston, Dec. 30 and 31, 1829 and Jan. 1, 1830. Boston, 1830.

Adams, John Quincy. *Memoirs of John Quincy Adams, Comprising Portions of His Diary from 1795 to 1848*. Edited by Charles Francis Adams. 12 vols. Philadelphia, 1874–77.

Address of the Central Committee Appointed by a Convention of both Branches of the Legislature Friendly to the Election of John Q. Adams as President and Richard Rush as Vice-President of the U. States, Held at the State-House in Boston, June 10, 1828, to their Fellow Citizens. [Boston, 1828.]

An Address to the Freemen of Vermont, By Their Delegation to the National Republican Convention, Holden at Baltimore, Maryland, In December, 1831. Middlebury, Vt. [1832].

Address of the Great State Convention of Friends of the Administration, Assembled at the Capitol in Concord [New Hampshire], *June 12, 1828, with the Speech of Mr. Bartlett, in Reply to the Charges which Have Have Been Made Against Mr. Adams.* Concord, 1828.

Bacon, D. Francis. *Progressive Democracy: A Discourse on the History, Philosophy and Tendency of American Politics, Delivered in National Hall, New York City, Before a Large Mass Meeting of Whigs and Young Men.* New York, 1844.

Barnard, Daniel D. *Speeches and Reports in the Assembly of New York, At the Annual Session of 1838.* Albany, 1838.

Baylies, Francis. *Speech . . . Before the Whigs of Taunton* [Massachusetts], *on the 13th of Sept., 1837.* Taunton, 1837.

Binney, Horace. *Speech . . . At the Anti-Jackson Meeting, Held in the State House Yard, Philadelphia, October 20, 1832.* [Philadelphia, 1832.]

Bowen, Henry L. *Memoir of Tristam Burges; with Selections from His Speeches and Occasional Writings.* Providence, R.I., 1835.

A Brief Report of the Debates in the Antimasonic State Convention of the Commonwealth of Massachusetts, Held in Faneuil Hall, Boston, Dec. 30, 31, 1829 and Jan. 1, 1830. Boston, 1830.

Brownlow, William G. *A Political Register, Setting Forth the Principles of the Whig and Locofoco Parties in the United States, with the Life and Public Services of Henry Clay.* Jonesborough, Tenn., 1844.

Calhoun, John C. *The Papers of John C. Calhoun.* Edited by Robert C. Meriwether, W. Edwin Hemphill, and Clyde N. Wilson. 14 vols. to date. Columbia, S.C.: University of South Carolina Press, 1959–.

Camillus [pseud.]. *The Essays of Camillus, Addressed to the Hon. Joel Holleman, Originally Published in the Norfolk and Portsmouth Herald.* Norfolk, Va., 1841.

Chapman, Jonathan. *An Oration Delivered Before the Citizens of Boston, on the Sixty-First Anniversary of American Independence, July 4, 1837.* Boston, 1837.

Choate, Rufus. *The Works of Rufus Choate, with a Memoir of His Life.* Compiled by Samuel Gilman Brown. 2 vols. Boston, 1862.

Church, A[lonzo]. *A Discourse Delivered Before the Georgia Historical Society, on the Occasion of its Sixth Anniversary, on Wednesday, 12 February, 1845.* Savannah, Ga., 1845.

Clay, Henry. *The Papers of Henry Clay.* Edited by James F. Hopkins and Mary Hargreaves. 5 vols. to date. Lexington: University of Kentucky Press, 1959–.

―――― *The Works of Henry Clay.* National edition. Edited by Calvin Colton. 10 vols. New York: Putnam's, 1904.

Cleveland, Henry. *Alexander H. Stephens in Public and Private. With Letters and Speeches Before, During, and Since the War.* Philadelphia, 1866.

Clingman, Thomas L. *Selections from the Speeches and Writings of Hon. Thomas L. Clingman of North Carolina, with Additions and Explanatory Notes.* Raleigh, 1877.

Coleman, Mrs. Chapman. *The Life of John J. Crittenden, with Selections from His Correspondence and Speeches.* 2 vols. Philadelphia, 1871.

Colton, Calvin [Junius]. *The Crisis of the Country.* New York and Boston, 1840.

―――― *The Junius Tracts*, nos. 1–10 (March 1843–July 1844). New York, 1844.

Concivis [pseud.]. *Letters to the People of the United States.* New York, 1840.

Corwin, Thomas. *Life and Speeches of Thomas Corwin.* Edited by Josiah Morrow. Cincinnati, 1896.

Curtis, George Ticknor. *Life of Daniel Webster.* 2 vols. New York, 1872.

[Cushing, Caleb]. *Outline of the Life and Public Services, Civil and Military, of William Henry Harrison, of Ohio.* Washington, D.C., 1840.

Cutter, Charles W. *An Oration Delivered Before the Whigs of Portsmouth, on the Fourth of July, A.D. 1834.* Portsmouth, N.H., 1834.

Everett, Edward. *Orations and Speeches on Various Occasions.* 2d ed. 4 vols. Boston, 1850–68.

Ewing, Thomas. "The Diary of Thomas Ewing, August and September, 1841." *American Historical Review* (October 1912), 18:97–112.

Fisher, Sidney George. *A Philadelphia Perspective: The Diary of Sidney George Fisher Covering the Years, 1834–1871.* Edited by Nicholas B. Wainwright. Philadelphia: Historical Society of Pennsylvania, 1967.

Floyd, John. *The Life and Diary of John Floyd, Governor of Virginia, an Apostle of Secession, and the Father of the Oregon Country.* Edited by Charles H. Ambler. Richmond, Va.: Richmond Press, 1918.

Graham, William Alexander. *The Papers of William Alexander Graham.* Edited by Joseph Gregoire deRoulhac Hamilton and Max R.

Williams. 6 vols. Raleigh, N.C.: State Department of Archives and History, 1957–76.

Hildreth, Richard. *The People's Presidential Candidate; or the Life of William Henry Harrison.* Boston, 1840.

Hilliard, Henry W. *Speeches and Addresses.* New York, 1855.

Hone, Philip. *The Diary of Philip Hone, 1828–1851.* Edited by Allan Nevins. 2 vols. New York: Dodd, Mead, 1936.

[Jackson, Isaac Rand]. *The Life of William Henry Harrison, (of Ohio,) the People's Candidate for the Presidency. With a History of the Wars with the British and Indians on our Northwestern Frontier.* Philadelphia, 1840.

Johnston, Richard Malcolm and William Hande Browne. *Life of Alexander H. Stephens.* Philadelphia, 1883.

Journal of the National Republican Convention, which Assembled in the City of Baltimore, Dec. 12, 1831, for the Nominations of Candidates to Fill the Offices of President and Vice President. Published by Order of the Convention. Washington, D.C. [1832].

Journal of the Proceedings of the National Republican Convention, Held at Worcester [Massachusetts], *October 11, 1832. Published by order of the Convention.* Boston, 1832.

[Kennedy, John Pendleton]. *Defence of the Whigs. By a Member of the 27th Congress.* New York, 1844.

Legare, Hugh Swinton. *Writings of Hugh Swinton Legare.* Edited by Mary S. Legare. 2 vols. Charleston, S.C., 1846.

Life in a Log Cabin, with Hard Cider. Philadelphia, 1840.

Lincoln, Abraham. *The Collected Works of Abraham Lincoln.* Edited by Roy P. Basler. 9 vols. New Brunswick, N.J.: Rutgers University Press, 1953.

McKenney, Thomas Lorraine [Aristides]. *Essays on the Spirit of Jacksonism, as Exemplified in its Deadly Hostility to the Bank of the United States, and in the Odious Calumnies Employed for Its Destruction.* Philadelphia, 1835.

Mangum, Willie P. *The Papers of Willie P. Mangum.* Edited by Henry T. Shanks. 5 vols. Raleigh, N.C.: State Department of Archives and History, 1951–55.

[Massachusetts State Whig Central Committee]. *To the People of Massachusetts.* Boston, 1838.

Meredith, William Morris. *An Oration Delivered by Request Before the Whigs of Philadelphia, on the Fourth of July, 1834.* Philadelphia, 1834.

Moore, Jacob B. [An Old Democrat]. *The Contrast: or, Plain Reasons why William Henry Harrison should be Elected President of the United States, and why Martin Van Buren Should Not be Re-Elected.* New York, 1840.

Ogle, Charles. *Speech . . . on the Regal Splendor of the President's Palace.* Boston, 1840.

Ormsby, R. McKinley. *A History of the Whig Party, or Some of its Main Features; with . . . the Outlines of the History of the Principal Parties of the Country to the Present Time, etc., etc.* Boston, 1859.

Phillips, Ulrich B., ed. "The Correspondence of Robert Toombs, Alexander H. Stephens, and Howell Cobb." American Historical Association *Annual Report* (1911), vol. 2.

Phillips, Willard. *A Manual of Political Economy.* Boston, 1828.

Pictures of the Times; or, A Contrast Between the Effects of the True Democratic System, as Displayed under Jefferson, Madison and Jackson in Former Times, and the Effects of the Aristocratic Sub-Treasury System, as Displayed in Martin Van Buren's Time. Philadelphia, 1841.

The Political Mirror; or, Review of Jacksonism. New York, 1835.

Potter, A[lonzo]. *Political Economy: Its Objects, Uses and Principles: Considered with Reference to the Condition of the American People.* New York, 1840.

Prentice, George D. *Biography of Henry Clay.* Hartford, Conn., 1831.

[Prentiss, George L.]. *A Memoir of S. S. Prentiss, By His Brother.* 2 vols. New York, 1855.

Proceedings and Address of the Convention of Delegates, that met at Columbus, Ohio, Dec. 28, 1827, to Nominate a Ticket of Electors, Favorable to the Re-election of John Quincy Adams, . . . To be Supported at the Electoral Election of 1828. [N.p., 1827.]

Proceedings and Address of the Republican Young Men of the State of New York . . . August 12, 1828. New York, 1828.

Proceedings, at a Convention of Republican Antimasonic Delegates . . . Convened at the Court House at Ballston Spa, on the 8th Day of October, 1831 . . . To which is Added an Address Delivered . . . By the Hon. John W. Taylor. Ballston Spa, N.Y., 1831.

Proceedings of a Convention of Delegates from the Different Counties in the State of New York Opposed to Free-Masonry. Held . . . in the City of Albany, 19., 20., and 21. Days of February, 1829. Rochester, 1829.

Proceedings of a Convention of Democratic Young Men, Delegates from the Citizens of Pennsylvania, in Favor of the Re-Election of Joseph Ritner, and Opposed to Martin Van Buren and the Sub-Treasury. Assembled at Reading, June 4th, 1838. Reading [1838].

Proceedings of a General Convention of the People of Ohio; Held in the City of Columbus, February 22 and 23, A.D. 1836. For the Purpose of Nominating Candidates for President and Vice-President of the United States, and for Governor of the State of Ohio. Columbus, 1836.

Proceedings of a State Convention of the Whig Young Men of Connecticut, Assembled at Hartford, Connecticut, February 26, 1840. Hartford, 1840.

Proceedings of the Antimasonic Convention for the State of New York: Held at Utica, August 11, 1850. Utica, 1830.

Proceedings of the Democratic Whig County Convention, Held at the Court House, in the City of Troy [New York] . . . *October 3, 1837.* [N.p., n.d.]

Proceedings of the Democratic Whig National Convention, which Assembled at Harrisburg, Pennsylvania, on the Fourth of December, 1839. Harrisburg, 1839.

Proceedings of the Second United States Antimasonic Convention, Held at Baltimore, September, 1831: Journals and Reports, Nomination of Candidates for President and Vice President of the United States, Letters of Acceptance, Resolutions, and the Address to the People. Boston, 1832.

Proceedings of the State Convention of National Republican Young Men, Holden at Hartford [Connecticut], *on . . . October 17, 1832.* Hartford, 1832.

The Proceedings of the United States Anti-Masonic Convention, Held at Philadelphia, September 11, 1830. Embracing the Journal of Proceedings, the Reports, the Debates, and the Address to the People. New York, 1830.

Proceedings of the Whig State Convention, Held at Utica, on . . . the 12th and 13th of August, 1840, for the Purpose of Nominating Candidates for Governor, Lieutenant Governor, and Electors of President and Vice-President. Albany, N.Y. 1840.

Report of the Proceedings of the Town Meeting in the City of Philadelphia, July 7, 1828. [Philadelphia, 1828.]

Report of the State Convention Held at the Capitol in the City of Albany, to Select Suitable Candidates for President and Vice President of the United States of America. New York, 1828.

Richardson, James D., comp. *A Compilation of the Messages and Papers of the Presidents 1789–1907.* 11 vols. Washington, D.C.: Bureau of National Literature and Art, 1908.

Rives, William Cabell. *Letter from the Hon. William C. Rives, of Virginia.* Washington, 1840.

—— *Letter of Hon. William Cabell Rives, Giving His Reasons for Preferring Mr. Clay to Mr. Van Buren for Next President.* N.p., 1844.

—— *To the People of Virginia.* [N.p., 1839.]

Scott, Nancy N. *A Memoir of Hugh Lawson White, Judge of the Supreme Court of Tennessee, Member of the Senate of the United States, etc. With Selections from His Speeches and Correspondence.* Philadelphia, 1856.

Seward, Frederick W. *Seward at Washington, as Senator and Secretary of State.*

A Memoir of His Life, with Selections from His Letters, 1846–1861. New York, 1891.

_____ *William H. Seward; An Autobiography from 1801 to 1834. With a Memoir of His Life and Selections from His Letters.* New ed. New York, 1891.

Seward, William H. *The Works of William H. Seward.* Edited by George E. Baker. 5 vols. Boston and New York, 1884–89.

Skinner, A[aron] N. *An Oration Delivered at the Whig Celebration, New Haven [Connecticut], July 4, 1834.* New Haven, 1834.

Southwick, Solomon. *A Solemn Warning Against Free-Masonry. Addressed to the Young Men of the United States. With an Appendix, containing the Correspondence between Eliphalet Murdock . . . and the Author, Relating to the Supposed Murder of Mr. Murdock's Father, through Masonic Venegeance.* Albany, 1827.

Starr, Chandler. *An Address Delivered at the Whig Convention Held at Utica, the Tenth of September, 1834.* New York, 1834.

Summary of the Proceedings of a Convention of Republican Delegates . . . for the Purpose of Nominating Candidates for . . . President and Vice-President of the United States . . . With an Address, to the Republicans of the State of New York. Albany, 1832.

Tyler, Lyon Gardiner. *Letters and times of the Tylers.* 3 vols. Richmond, 1884–96.

U.S. Congress. *Congressional Globe.* 22d–33d Congresses, 1833–54.

_____ *Register of Debates in Congress.* 20th–24th Congresses, 1824–37.

Waddell, James D. *Biographical Sketch of Linton Stephens, (Late Associate Justice of the Supreme Court of Georgia,) containing a Selection of His Letters Speeches, State Papers, etc.* Atlanta, Ga., 1877.

Watson, William R. [Hamilton]. *The Whig Party; its Objects—its Principles—its Candidates—its Duties—and its Prospects. An Address to the People of Rhode Island, Published in the Providence Journal . . . 1844.* Providence, 1844.

Webster, Daniel. *The Letters of Daniel Webster, from Documents Owned Principally by the New Hampshire Historical Society.* Edited by Claude H. Van Tyne. New York: McClure, Phillips, 1902.

_____ *The Papers of Daniel Webster.* Edited by Charles M. Wiltse. Associate editors Harold D. Moser and David G. Allen. 4 vols. to date. Hanover, N.H.: University Press of New England, 1974–.

_____ *The Writings and Speeches of Daniel Webster.* National edition. 18 vols. Boston: Little, Brown, 1903.

Whig Congressional Committee. *To the Whigs and Conservatives of the United*

States. [Washington, D.C., 1840.]

The Whig Textbook, or Democracy Unmasked to the People of the United States. Washington, D.C., 1844.

Winthrop, Robert C. *Addresses and Speeches on Various Occasions*. 4 vols. Boston, 1852–86.

SECONDARY SOURCES

Adams, William H. *The Whig Party of Louisiana*. Lafayette, La.: University of Southwestern Louisiana Press, 1973.

Alexander, Thomas B. "The Dimensions of Voter Partisan Consistency in Presidential Elections from 1840 to 1860." In Stephen E. Maizlish and John J. Kushma, eds., *Essays on American Antebellum Politics*, pp. 70–121. College Station, Tex.: Texas A & M University Press, 1982.

_____ *Sectional Stress and Party Strength: A Study of Roll-Call Voting Patterns in the United States House of Representatives, 1836–1860*. Nashville: Vanderbilt University Press, 1967.

_____, Kit C. Carter, Jack R. Lister, Jerry C. Oldshue, and Winfred S. Sandlin. "Who Were the Alabama Whigs?" *Alabama Review* (January 1963), 16:5–19.

_____, Peggy Duckworth Elmore, Frank M. Lowrey, and Mary Jane Pickens Skinner. "The Basis of Alabama's Ante-Bellum Two-Party System." *Alabama Review* (October 1966), 19:243–76.

Ambler, Charles H. *Sectionalism in Virginia from 1776 to 1861*. Chicago: University of Chicago Press, 1910.

Ashworth, John. "The Jacksonian as Leveller." *Journal of American Studies* (December 1980), 16:407–22.

Bailyn, Bernard. *The Ideological Origins of the American Revolution*. Cambridge, Mass.: Belknap Press of Harvard University Press, 1967.

Bancroft, Frederic. *The Life of William H. Seward*. 2 vols. New York, 1899.

Bartlett, Irving. *Daniel Webster*. New York: Norton, 1978.

Bemis, Samuel Flagg. *John Quincy Adams and the Union*. New York: Knopf, 1956.

Benson, Lee. *The Concept of Jacksonian Democracy: New York as a Test Case*. Princeton: Princeton University Press, 1961.

Billington, Ray Allen. *The Protestant Crusade, 1800–1860: A Study of the Origins of American Nativism*. 1938. Reprint, Chicago: Quadrangle Books, 1964.

Binkley, Robert W., Jr. "The American System: An Example of Nineteenth-Century Economic Thinking. Its Definition by Its Author Henry Clay." Ph.D. dissertation, Columbia University, 1949.

Binkley, Wilfred E. *President and Congress.* 3d ed. New York: Knopf, 1959.

Bonner, J. C. "Profile of a Late Ante-Bellum Community." *American Historical Review* (January 1944), 49:663–80.

Brauer, Kinley J. *Cotton versus Conscience: Massachusetts Whig Politics and Southwestern Expansion, 1843–1848.* Lexington: University of Kentucky Press, 1967.

Brock, William R. *Parties and Political Conscience: American Dilemmas, 1840–1850.* Millwood, N.Y.: KTO Press, 1978.

Brown, Norman D. *Daniel Webster and the Politics of Availability.* Athens: University of Georgia Press, 1969.

Bruser, Lawrence. "Political Anti-Slavery in Connecticut, 1844–1858." Ph.D. dissertation, Columbia University, 1974.

Bryson, Gladys. *Man and Society: The Scottish Inquiry of the Eighteenth Century.* Princeton: Princeton University Press, 1945.

Carroll, E[ber] Malcolm. *Origins of the Whig Party.* Durham, N.C.: Duke University Press, 1925.

Catterall, Ralph C. *The Second Bank of the United States.* Chicago: University of Chicago Press, 1903.

Chitnis, Anand C. *The Scottish Enlightenment: A Social History.* Totawa, N.J.: Rowman and Littlefield, 1976.

Cole, Arthur C. *The Era of the Civil War, 1848–1870.* Springfield, Ill.: A. C. McClurg, 1919.

—— *The Whig Party in the South.* Washington, D.C.: American Historical Association, 1913.

Cole, Donald B. *Jacksonian Democracy in New Hampshire, 1800–1851.* Cambridge, Mass.: Harvard University Press, 1970.

Coleman, John F. *The Disruption of the Pennsylvania Democracy, 1848–1860.* Harrisburg: Pennsylvania Historical and Museum Commission, 1975.

Cooper, William J., Jr. *The South and the Politics of Slavery, 1828–1856.* Baton Rouge: Louisiana State University Press, 1978.

Corwin, Edward S. *The President: Office and Powers, 1787–1957.* 4th ed. New York: New York University Press, 1957.

Coulter, E. Merton. "The Genesis of Henry Clay's American System." *South Atlantic Quarterly* (January 1926), 26:45–54.

Cross, Whitney R. *The Burned-Over District: The Social and Intellectual History of Enthusiastic Religion in Western New York, 1800–1850*. New York: Harper and Row, 1850.

Current, Richard N. *Daniel Webster and the Rise of National Conservatism*. Boston: Little, Brown, 1955.

Curtis, James C. *The Fox at Bay: Martin Van Buren and the Presidency, 1837–1841*. Lexington: University of Kentucky Press, 1970.

Dalzell, Robert F., Jr. *Daniel Webster and the Trial of American Nationalism, 1843–1852*. Boston: Houghton Mifflin, 1973.

Dangerfield, George. *The Awakening of American Nationalism, 1815–1828*. New York: Harper and Row, 1965.

Davis, David Brion. *The Problem of Slavery in the Age of Revolution, 1770–1823*. Ithaca, N.Y.: Cornell University Press, 1975.

Debats, Donald Arthur. "Elites and Masses: Political Structure, Communication, and Behavior in Ante-Bellum Georgia." Ph.D. dissertation, University of Wisconsin at Madison, 1973.

Degler, Carl N. *The Other South: Southern Dissenters in the Nineteenth Century*. New York: Harper and Row, 1974.

Dubofsky, Melvyn. "Daniel Webster and the Whig Theory of Economic Growth, 1828–1848." *New England Quarterly* (December 1967), 42:551–72.

Eaton, Clement. *Henry Clay and the Art of American Politics*. Boston: Little, Brown, 1957.

——— "Southern Senators and the Right of Instruction." *Journal of Southern History* (August 1952), 18:303–19.

Elkins, Stanley and Eric L. McKitrick. "A Meaning for Turner's Frontier, Part II: The Southwest Frontier and New England." *Political Science Quarterly* (December 1954), 49:565–602.

Ellis, Richard E. *The Jeffersonian Crisis: Courts and Politics in the Young Republic*. New York: Oxford University Press, 1971.

Ershkowitz, Herbert and William G. Shade. "Consensus or Conflict? Political Behavior in the State Legislatures During the Jacksonian Era." *Journal of American History* (December 1971), 58:591–621.

Evitts, William J. *A Matter of Allegiances: Maryland from 1850 to 1861*. Baltimore: Johns Hopkins University Press, 1974.

Fee, Walter R. *The Transition from Aristocracy to Democracy in New Jersey, 1789–1829*. Somerville, N.J.: Somerset Press, 1933.

Fischer, David Hackett. *The Revolution of American Conservatism: The Federalist Party in the Era of Jeffersonian Democracy*. New York: Harper and Row, 1965.

Foner, Eric. "The Causes of the American Civil War: Recent Interpretations and New Directions." *Civil War History* (September 1974), 20:197–214.

_____ *Free Soil, Free Labor, Free Men: The Ideology of the Republican Party Before the Civil War.* New York: Oxford University Press, 1970.

Foner, Philip S. *Business and Slavery: The New York Merchants and the Irrepressible Conflict.* Chapel Hill: University of North Carolina Press, 1941.

Formisano, Ronald P. *The Birth of Mass Political Parties: Michigan, 1827–1861.* Princeton: Princeton University Press, 1971.

_____ "Political Character, Antipartyism, and the Second Party System." *American Quarterly* (Winter 1969), 21:683–709.

_____ *The Transformation of Political Culture: Massachusetts Parties, 1790s–1840s.* New York: Oxford University Press, 1983.

Foster, Herbert D. "Webster's Seventh of March Speech and the Secession Movement, 1850." *American Historical Review* (January 1922), 27:245–70.

Fredrickson, George M. *The Black Image in the White Mind: The Debate on Afro-American Character and Destiny, 1817–1914.* New York: Harper and Row, 1971.

Freehling, William W. *Prelude to Civil War: The Nullification Controversy in South Carolina, 1816–1836.* New York: Harper & Row, 1966.

Friedman, Jean E. *The Revolt of the Conservative Democrats: An Essay on American Political Culture and Political Development, 1837–1844.* Ann Arbor, Mich.: UMI Research Press, 1974.

Fuess, Claude Moore. *Life of Daniel Webster.* 2 vols. Boston: Little, Brown, 1930.

Gatell, Frank Otto. "Spoils of the Bank War: Political Bias in the Selection of Pet Banks." *American Historical Review* (October 1964), 70:35–58.

Genovese, Eugene D. *The Political Economy of Slavery: Studies in the Economy and Society of the Slave South.* New York: Vintage Books, 1965.

_____ *Roll, Jordan, Roll: The World The Slaves Made.* New York: Vintage, 1976.

Gienapp, William E. " 'Politics Seem to Enter into Everything': Political Culture in the North, 1840–1860." In Stephen E. Maizlish and John J. Kushma, eds., *Essays on American Antebellum Politics*, pp. 14–69. College Station: Texas A & M University Press, 1982.

Goebel, Dorothy Burne. *William Henry Harrison, A Political Biography.*

Indianapolis: Historical Bureau of the Indiana Library and Historical Department, 1926.

Goldman, Perry M. "The Republic of Virtue and Other Essays on the Politics of the Early National Period." Ph.D. dissertation, Columbia University, 1970.

Goodman, Paul. "Ethics and Enterprize: The Values of the Boston Elite, 1800–1860." *American Quarterly* (Fall 1966), 18:437–51.

Govan, Thomas Payne. *Nicholas Biddle: Nationalist and Public Banker, 1786–1844.* Chicago: University of Chicago Press, 1959.

Graebner, Norman A. "1848: Southern Politics at the Crossroads." *The Historian* (Winter 1962–63), 25:14–35.

Griffin, Clifford S. *Their Brothers' Keepers: Moral Stewardship in the United States, 1800–1865.* New Brunswick, N.J.: Rutgers University Press, 1960.

Gunderson, Robert Gray. *The Log Cabin Campaign.* Lexington: University of Kentucky Press, 1957.

Hamilton, Holman. *Prologue to Conflict: The Crisis and Compromise of 1850.* Lexington: University of Kentucky Press, 1963.

Hammond, Bray. *Banks and Politics in America: From the Revolution to the Civil War.* Princeton: Princeton University Press, 1957.

Hammond, John L. *The Politics of Benevolence: Revival Religion and American Voting Behavior.* Norwood, N.J.: Ablex, 1979.

Hanson, Stephen L. *The Making of the Third Party System: Voters and Parties in Illinois, 1850–1876.* Ann Arbor, Mich.: UMI Research Press, 1980.

Haws, Robert J. "Massachusetts Whigs, 1833–1854." Ph.D. dissertation, University of Nebraska, 1973.

Hirschman, Albert O. *The Passions and the Interests: Political Arguments for Capitalism Before Its Triumph.* Princeton: Princeton University Press, 1977.

Hoffmann, William S. *Andrew Jackson and North Carolina Politics.* Chapel Hill: University of North Carolina Press, 1958.

Hofstadter, Richard. *The Idea of a Party System: The Rise of Legitimate Opposition in the United States, 1780–1840.* Berkeley: University of California Press, 1969.

Holt, Edgar Allan. *Party Politics in Ohio, 1840–1850.* Columbus, Ohio: F. J. Heer, 1931.

Holt, Michael F. *Forging a Majority: The Formation of the Republican Party in Pittsburgh, 1848–1860.* New Haven: Yale University Press, 1969.

_____ *The Political Crisis of the 1850s.* New York: Wiley, 1978.

_____ "Winding Roads to Recovery: The Whig Party from 1844 to 1848." In Stephen E. Maizlish and John J. Kushma, eds., *Essays on American Antebellum Politics*, pp. 129–65. College Station: Texas A & M University Press, 1982.

Howe, Daniel Walker. *The Political Culture of the American Whigs.* Chicago: University of Chicago Press, 1979.

Hugins, Walter. *Jacksonian Democracy and the Working Class: A Study of the New York Workingmen's Movement, 1829–1837.* Stanford, Calif.: Stanford University Press, 1960.

Johnson, Paul E. *A Shopkeeper's Millennium: Society and Revivals in Rochester, New York, 1815–1837.* New York: Norton, 1978.

Kerber, Linda K. *Federalists in Dissent: Imagery and Ideology in Jeffersonian America.* Ithaca, N.Y.: Cornell University Press, 1970.

Kettler, David. *The Social and Political Thought of Adam Ferguson.* Columbus: Ohio State University Press, 1965.

Klein, Philip Shriver. *Pennsylvania Politics, 1817–1832: A Game Without Rules.* Philadelphia: Historical Society of Pennsylvania, 1940.

Kleppner, Paul. *The Third Electoral System, 1853–1892: Parties, Voters, and Political Cultures.* Chapel Hill: University of North Carolina Press, 1979.

Konkle, Burton Alva. *John Motley Morehead and the Development of North Carolina, 1796–1866.* Philadelphia: William J. Campbell, 1922.

Kruman, Marc W. "Parties and Politics in North Carolina, 1846–1865." Ph.D. dissertation, Yale University, 1978.

Lerner, Ralph. "Commerce and Character: The Anglo-American as New-Model Man." *William and Mary Quarterly* (January 1979), 36: 3–26.

Lipsky, George A. *John Quincy Adams: His Theory and Ideas.* New York: Thomas Y. Crowell, 1950.

Lipson, Dorothy Ann. *Freemasonry in Federalist Connecticut.* Princeton: Princeton University Press, 1977.

Livermore, Shaw, Jr. *The Twilight of Federalism: The Disintegration of the Federalist Party, 1815–1830.* Princeton: Princeton University Press, 1962.

Lowrey, Frank Mitchell. "Tennessee Voters During the Second Two-Party System, 1836–1860: A Study in Voter Continuity and in Socio-

Economic and Demographic Distinction." Ph.D. dissertation, University of Alabama, 1973.

Ludlum, David M. *Social Ferment in Vermont, 1791–1850.* New York: Columbia University Press, 1939.

McCormick, Richard L. "Ethno-Cultural Interpretations of Nineteenth Century Voting Behavior." *Political Science Quarterly* (June 1974), 89:359–77.

McCormick, Richard P. *The Second American Party System: Party Formation in the Jacksonian Era.* New York: Norton, 1966.

McCoy, Drew R. *The Elusive Republic: Political Economy in Jeffersonian America.* Chapel Hill: University of North Carolina Press, 1980.

McFaul, John M. "Expediency Versus Morality: Jacksonian Politics and Slavery." *Journal of American History* (June 1975), 42:24–39.

—— *The Politics of Jacksonian Finance.* Ithaca, N.Y.: Cornell University Press, 1972.

McGrane, Reginald C. *The Panic of 1837: Some Financial Problems of the Jacksonian Era.* 1924. Reprint, New York: Russell and Russell, 1965.

McWilliams, Wilson Carey. *The Idea of Fraternity in America.* Berkeley: University of California Press, 1974.

Maizlish, Stephen E. "The Meaning of Nativism and the Crisis of the Union: The Know-Nothing Movement in the Antebellum North." In Stephen E. Maizlish and John J. Kushma, eds., *Essays on American Antebellum Politics*, pp. 167–97. College Station: Texas A & M University Press, 1982.

Marshall, Lynn L. "The Strange Stillbirth of the Whig Party." *American Historical Review* (January 1967), 72:445–68.

Matthews, Jean V. *Rufus Choate: The Law and Civic Virtue.* Philadelphia: Temple University Press, 1980.

Mayo, Edward Lawrence. "The *National Intelligencer* and Jacksonian Democracy: A Whig Persuasion." Ph.D. dissertation, Claremont Graduate School, 1970.

Meyers, Marvin. *The Jacksonian Persuasion: Politics and Belief.* Stanford, Calif.: Stanford University Press, 1960.

Miles, Edwin A. *Jacksonian Democracy in Mississippi.* Chapel Hill: University of North Carolina Press, 1960.

—— "The Whig Party and the Menace of Caesar." *Tennessee Historical Quarterly* (Winter 1968), 27:361–79.

Montgomery, Horace. *Cracker Parties*. Baton Rouge: Louisiana State University Press, 1950.

Moore, Glover. *The Missouri Controversy, 1819–1821*. Lexington: University of Kentucky Press, 1953.

Morris, John David. "The New York State Whigs, 1834–1842: A Study of Political Organization." Ph.D. dissertation, University of Rochester, 1970.

Morse, Jarvis Means. *A Neglected Period of Connecticut's History, 1818–1850*. New Haven: Yale University Press, 1933.

Moser, Harold D. "Subtreasury Politics and the Virginia Conservative Democrats, 1835–1844." Ph.D. dissertation, University of Wisconsin at Madison, 1977.

Mueller, Henry R. *The Whig Party in Pennsylvania*. 1922. Reprint, New York: AMS Press, 1969.

Murray, Paul. *The Whig Party in Georgia*. Chapel Hill: University of North Carolina Press, 1948.

Nathans, Sydney. *Daniel Webster and Jacksonian Democracy*. Baltimore: Johns Hopkins University Press, 1973.

North, Douglas C. *The Economic Growth of the United States, 1790 to 1860*. New York: Norton, 1966.

O'Connor, Thomas H. *Lords of the Loom: The Cotton Whigs and the Coming of the Civil War*. New York: Scribner's, 1968.

Overdyke, William D. *The Know-Nothing Party in the South*. Baton Rouge: Louisiana State University Press, 1950.

Patterson, Caleb Perry. *Presidential Government in the United States: The Unwritten Constitution*. Chapel Hill: University of North Carolina Press, 1947.

Peterson, Merrill D. *Olive Branch and Sword—The Compromise of 1833*. Baton Rouge: Louisiana State University Press, 1982.

Poage, George R. *Henry Clay and the Whig Party*. Chapel Hill: University of North Carolina Press, 1936.

Pocock, J. G. A. *The Machiavellian Moment: Florentine Political Thought and the Atlantic Republican Tradition*. Princeton: Princeton University Press, 1975.

_____ *Politics, Language, and Time*. New York: Atheneum, 1971.

Potter, David. *The Impending Crisis, 1848–1861*. Completed and edited by Don E. Fehrenbacher. Harper Torchbooks. New York: Harper and Row, 1976.

Pritchard, Linda K. "Religious Change in a Developing Region: The Social Contexts of Evangelicalism in Western New York and the Upper Ohio Valley During the Mid Nineteenth Century." Ph.D. dissertation, University of Pittsburgh, 1980.

Rabun, James Z. "Alexander H. Stephens, 1812–1861." Ph.D. dissertation, University of Chicago, 1948.

Remini, Robert V. *Andrew Jackson and the Bank War: A Study in the Growth of Presidential Power.* New York: Norton, 1967.

———. *The Election of Andrew Jackson.* Philadelphia: Lippincott, 1963.

Rendall, Jane. *The Origins of the Scottish Enlightenment.* London: Macmillan, 1978.

Rezneck, Samuel. "Social History of an American Depression, 1837–1843." *American Historical Review* (July 1935), 40:662–87.

Risjord, Norman K. *The Old Republicans: Southern Conservatism in the Age of Jefferson.* New York: Columbia University Press, 1965.

Robbins, Roy M. *Our Landed Heritage: The Public Domain, 1776–1936.* Princeton: Princeton University Press, 1942.

Robertson, Alexander F. *Alexander Hugh Holmes Stuart.* Richmond, Va.: William Byrd Press, 1925.

Roseboom, Eugene H. *The Civil War Era, 1850–1873.* Columbus: Ohio Archaeological and Historical Society, 1944.

Russel, Robert R. *Economic Aspects of Southern Sectionalism, 1840–1861.* 1924. Reprint, New York: Russell and Russell, 1960.

Russo, David J. "The Major Political Issues of the Jacksonian Period and the Development of Party Loyalty in Congress, 1830–1840." *Transactions of the American Philosophical Society* (1972), n.s., no. 62.

Schlesinger, Arthur M., Jr. *The Age of Jackson.* Boston: Little, Brown, 1945.

——— and Fred I. Israel, eds. *The History of American Presidential Elections.* 4 vols. New York: Chelsea House, 1973.

——— and Fred I. Israel, eds. *History of U.S. Political Parties.* 4 vols. New York: Chelsea House, 1973.

Schroeder, John H. *Mr. Polk's War: American Opposition and Dissent, 1846–1848.* Madison: University of Wisconsin Press, 1973.

Schurz, Carl. *The Life of Henry Clay.* 2 vols. Boston, 1889.

Seager, Robert Jr. *And Tyler Too: A Biography of John and Julia Gardiner Tyler.* New York: McGraw-Hill, 1963.

Sellers, Charles Grier, Jr. "Who Were the Southern Whigs?" *American Historial Review* (January 1954), 59:335–46.

Shade, William G. *Banks or No Banks: The Money Issue in Western Politics, 1832–1865.* Detroit: Wayne State University Press, 1972.

Shalhope, Robert E. "Thomas Jefferson's Republicanism and Antebellum Thought." *Journal of Southern History* (November 1976), 42:529–56.

Sharp, James Roger. *The Jacksonians Versus the Banks: Politics in the States after the Panic of 1837.* New York: Columbia University Press, 1970.

Sharrow, Walter George. "William H. Seward: A Study in Nineteenth Century Politics and Nationalism, 1855–1861." Ph.D. dissertation, University of Rochester, 1965.

Shover, Kenneth B. "The Free State Whig and the Idea of a Conservative Strategy." *Mid-America* (October 1972), 54:251–66.

Shryock, Richard H. *Georgia and the Union in 1850.* Durham, N.C.: Duke University Press, 1926.

Silbey, Joel H. *The Shrine of Party: Congressional Voting Behavior, 1841–1852.* Pittsburgh: University of Pittsburgh Press, 1967.

Simms, Henry Harrison. *The Rise of the Whigs in Virginia.* Richmond, Va.: William Byrd Press, 1929.

Somkin, Fred. *Unquiet Eagle: Memory and Desire in the Idea of American Freedom, 1815–1860.* Ithaca, N.Y.: Cornell University Press, 1967.

Starobin, Robert S. *Industrial Slavery in the Old South.* New York: Oxford University Press, 1970.

Staudenraus, P. J. *The African Colonization Movement, 1816–1865.* New York: Columbia University Press, 1961.

Stephenson, George M. *The Political History of the Public Lands, from 1842–1862.* Boston: R. C. Badger, 1917.

Streeter, Floyd B. *Political Parties in Michigan, 1837–1860: An Historical Study of Political Issues and Parties in Michigan from the Admission of the State to the Civil War.* Lansing: Michigan Historical Commission, 1918.

Takaki, Ronald T. *A Pro-Slavery Crusade: The Agitation to Reopen the African Slave Trade.* New York: Free Press, 1971.

Taussig, F. W. *The Tariff History of the United States.* New York: Putnam's, 1931.

Taylor, George Rogers. *The Transportation Revolution, 1815–1860.* The

Economic History of the United States, vol. 4. New York: Harper and Row, 1951.

Temin, Peter. *The Jacksonian Economy*. New York: Norton, 1969.

Thomas, Sister M. Evangeline. *Nativism in the Old Northwest, 1850–1860*. Washington, D.C.: Catholic University Press, 1936.

Thompson, Charles Manfred. *The Illinois Whigs Before 1846*. Urbana: University of Illinois Press, 1915.

Thornbrough, Emma Lou. *Indiana in the Civil War Era, 1850–1880*. Indianapolis: Indiana Historical Bureau, 1965.

Thornton, Jonathan Mills III. *Politics and Power in a Slave Society: Alabama, 1806–1860*. Princeton: Princeton University Press, 1978.

Van Deusen, Glyndon G. *The Jacksonian Era, 1828–1848*. Harper Torchbooks. New York: Harper and Row, 1959.

—— *The Life of Henry Clay*. Boston: Little, Brown, 1937.

—— *Thurlow Weed: Wizard of the Lobby*. Boston: Little, Brown, 1947.

—— *William Henry Seward*. New York: Oxford University Press, 1967.

Vaughn, William Preston. *The Antimasonic Party in the United States, 1826–1843*. Lexington: University Press of Kentucky, 1983.

Von Abele, Rudolph. *Alexander Stephens: A Biography*. New York: Knopf, 1946.

Wallace, Michael L. "Changing Concepts of Party in the United States: New York: 1818–1828." *American Historical Review* (December 1968), 74:453–91.

—— "Ideologies of Party in the Ante-Bellum Republic." Ph.D. dissertation, Columbia University, 1973.

Ward, John William. *Andrew Jackson: Symbol for an Age*. New York: Oxford University Press, 1955.

Watson, Harry L. *Jacksonian Politics and Community Conflict: The Emergence of the Second American Party System in Cumberland County, North Carolina*. Baton Rouge: Louisiana State University Press, 1981.

Wellington, Raynor G. *The Political and Sectional Influence of the Public Lands, 1828–1842*. Cambridge Mass.: Harvard University Press, 1914.

Welter, Rush. *The Mind of America, 1820–1860*. New York: Columbia University Press, 1975.

White, Leonard D. *The Jacksonians: A Study in Administrative History, 1829–1861*. New York: Macmillan, 1954.

Wilburn, Jean A. *Biddle's Bank: The Crucial Years*. New York: Columbia University Press, 1967.

Wilson, Major P. *Space, Time, and Freedom: The Quest for Nationality and the Irrepressible Conflict, 1815–1861*. Westport, Conn.: Greenwood Press, 1974.

Wood, Gordon S. *The Creation of the American Republic, 1776–1787*. Chapel Hill: University of North Carolina Press, 1969.

Young, James Sterling. *The Washington Community, 1800–1828*. New York: Columbia University Press, 1966.

INDEX